HELEN OF TROY IN HOLLYWOOD

MARTIN CLASSICAL LECTURES

The Martin Classical Lectures are delivered annually at Oberlin College through a foundation established by his many friends in honor of Charles Beebe Martin, for forty-five years a teacher of classical literature and classical art at Oberlin.

John Peradotto, *Man in the Middle Voice: Name and Narration in the* Odyssey

Martha C. Nussbaum, *The Therapy of Desire: Theory and Practice in Hellenistic Ethics*

Josiah Ober, *Political Dissent in Democratic Athens: Intellectual Critics of Popular Rule*

Anne Carson, *Economy of the Unlost: (Reading Simonides of Keos with Paul Celan)*

Helene P. Foley, *Female Acts in Greek Tragedy*

Mark W. Edwards, *Sound, Sense, and Rhythm: Listening to Greek and Latin Poetry*

Michael C. J. Putnam, *Poetic Interplay: Catullus and Horace*

Julia Haig Gaisser, *The Fortunes of Apuleius and the* Golden Ass*: A Study in Transmission and Reception*

Kenneth J. Reckford, *Recognizing Persius*

Leslie Kurke, *Aesopic Conversations: Popular Tradition, Cultural Dialogue, and the Invention of Greek Prose*

Erich S. Gruen, *Rethinking the Other in Antiquity*

Simon Goldhill, *Victorian Culture and Classical Antiquity: Art, Opera, Fiction, and the Proclamation of Modernity*

Victoria Wohl, *Euripides and the Politics of Form*

David Frankfurter, *Christianizing Egypt: Syncretism and Local Worlds in Late Antiquity*

Robin Osborne, *The Transformation of Athens: Painted Pottery and the Creation of Classical Greece*

Joseph Farrell, *Juno's* Aeneid*: A Battle for Heroic Identity*

Ruby Blondell, *Helen of Troy in Hollywood*

Helen of Troy in Hollywood

RUBY BLONDELL

PRINCETON UNIVERSITY PRESS
PRINCETON & OXFORD

Published by Princeton University Press
41 William Street, Princeton, New Jersey 08540
99 Banbury Road, Oxford OX2 6JX

press.princeton.edu

Library of Congress Cataloging-in-Publication Data

Names: Blondell, Ruby, 1954– author.
Title: Helen of Troy in Hollywood / Ruby Blondell.
Description: Princeton : Princeton University Press, [2023] | Series: Martin classical lectures | Includes bibliographical references and index.
Identifiers: LCCN 2022030953 (print) | LCCN 2022030954 (ebook) | ISBN 9780691229621 (hardback ; acid-free paper) | ISBN 9780691229645 (ebook)
Subjects: LCSH: Helen, of Troy, Queen of Sparta—In motion pictures. | Helen, of Troy, Queen of Sparta—On television. | Mythology, Greek, in motion pictures. | Mythology, Greek, on television.
Classification: LCC PN1995.9.H416 B57 2023 (print) | LCC PN1995.9.H416 (ebook) | DDC 791.43/651—dc23/eng/20220714
LC record available at https://lccn.loc.gov/2022030953
LC ebook record available at https://lccn.loc.gov/2022030954British Library Cataloging-in-Publication Data is available

Editorial: Rob Tempio and Chloe Coy
Production Editorial: Sara Lerner
Jacket Design: Felix Summ
Production: Erin Suydam
Publicity: William Pagdatoon and Charlotte Coyne
Copyeditor: Lachlan Brooks

Jacket Credit: French postcard by Europe, no. 315. Photo: Mercure Film. Maria Corda as Helen of Troy in *The Private Life of Helen of Troy* (Alexander Korda, 1927).

Epigraph credit: **Till There Was You**
from Meredith Willson's THE MUSIC MAN
By Meredith Willson
© 1950, 1957 (Renewed) FRANK MUSIC CORP. and MEREDITH WILLSON MUSIC All Rights Reserved
Reprinted by Permission of Hal Leonard LLC

This book has been composed in Arno

Printed on acid-free paper. ∞

Printed in Canada

10 9 8 7 6 5 4 3 2 1

To Douglas

in memoriam

There was love all around
But I never heard it singing
No I never heard it at all
Till there was you

CONTENTS

PREFACE

> Along with the idea of romantic love, she was introduced to another—physical beauty. Probably the most destructive ideas in the history of human thought. Both originated in envy, thrived in insecurity, and ended in disillusion.
>
> —TONI MORRISON, *THE BLUEST EYE*

IN 2012 a basketball star named Tony Parker was injured in a brawl between fans of two rappers, Chris Brown and Drake, both of whom had been romantically involved with the singer Rihanna. When Parker sued the nightclub where the incident occurred, his attorney "compared Rihanna to 'Helen of Troy,' saying the club should have been well aware that she is known to 'cause trouble,' suggesting that it is their open ignorance of her romantic history that brought about this new Trojan War that—much like the scheming of Zeus—will eventually lead to the Earth being depopulated of its demigods, beginning with forcing Tony Parker to miss a game or two."[1]

As this casual example illustrates, ancient Greek mythology, and Helen of Troy in particular, remain a persistent presence in contemporary popular culture. Familiarity with the Trojan War story—often loosely identified with the *Iliad*—remains a cornerstone of middle-class American culture. As a result, Helen's story enjoys a "massive cultural permeation" comparable to that of Shakespeare; and as with Shakespeare, albeit at a linguistic remove, knowledge of these tales is unified across classes by "key phrases and key images."[2] One such phrase, Marlowe's "face that launched a thousand ships," crystalizes Helen's contemporary mythical identity far more durably than any evidence

1. O'Neal 2012.
2. Uricchio and Pearson 1996 [1990]: 226–27.

from antiquity.[3] (Unfortunately for her, it also provides a ready-made scale for judging her beauty and is, as such, a goldmine for jokes at her expense.)

This "massive cultural permeation" finds expression in the omnipresent "popular" renditions that have existed as long as the myths themselves, pervading society in ways that elite culture by definition does not. There are many ways of defining "popular" (as opposed to "high" or "elite") culture, but I take it to mean, crudely, any work intended to reach as large an audience as possible and to make money for its creators (even if it fails to do either).[4]

Though the ancient world has always provided such entertainments, the term "popular culture" is now commonly used to refer to the period since the industrial revolution, with its transformative technologies of mass production.[5] Popular culture embraces mass fiction, comic books, advertising, video games, and more; but commercial film and its cousin, television, have always been at its heart. It is often considered intrinsically "American," owing to its "invention" in "the great cities of the United States."[6] Geographic lines can be hard to draw, since many productions are multinational and globally distributed, but I deem "American" any work produced in the first instance for United States film or TV markets. The epicenter is Hollywood, "the motherland of popular entertainment," which is conceived of less as a geographic location than as a cultural institution with worldwide influence, or "the propaganda arm of the American Dream machine."[7]

Though popular media are still sometimes maligned as debasing the "legacy" of the classics,[8] antiquity would, as it were, be dead without them. It is through them that the ancient world remains a vital part of contemporary mainstream culture, a living, multiplying organism as opposed to an object of expert study or the exclusive domain of "high" culture. Yet this ubiquity

3. On this kind of allusion, see Paul 2013a: 60n.

4. For the history of "popular culture" as defined in contrast to elite or "high" culture (or "art"), see Gans 1975; Bourdieu 1984; Storey 2003; Storey 2006: ch. 1; Blanshard 2017: 429–31; Grig 2017. Cf. also R. Allen 1985: 11–18; Fiske 1991; Thumim 1992: ch. 1; Maltby 2003: 40–46. For the instability of the boundary between high and low culture, see Ferstl & Sarkhosh 2014: Introduction.

5. Storey 2006: 10. For a survey of both pre- and post-industrial "popular" classics, see Silk et al. 2013: §12 and cf. Hall & Stead 2020.

6. Maltby 1989: 11; cf. Strinati 2004: 19–33; Storey 2006: 7, 24–25.

7. Lovell & Sergi 2009: 5; Haskell 2016: 2.

8. Cf., e.g., Wyke 1997: 3–8; Paul 2008a: 304–5; Hall & Stead 2020: 39–42.

cannot be disentangled from the field's canonical status.[9] It is antiquity's canonicity that has ensured its persistence in education, both in and out of the classroom, which in turn makes it reverberate anew with each generation of adults. These pedagogical associations sometimes engender scorn for scholarly learning as dusty and tedious.[10] Yet in reclaiming the classics from Classics, popular culture continues to resanctify the ancient stories, reaffirming their "timeless" value. As we shall see, both producers and consumers of popular culture draw upon childhood memories to reconstruct, transform, and evaluate receptions of the ancient world. For a small number, those memories are grounded in study of the classical texts in the original languages; for the vast majority, they are mediated by earlier receptions aimed at the general public—translations, retellings, and adaptations.

This continuing vitality depends on the unavoidable fact that all classical receptions tell us more about ourselves than about the ancients—unavoidable both because it is we who are producing them (from a perspective that is inescapably ours) and because any effective popular retelling must appeal to a broad contemporary audience. Most claims about "timelessness" or "human nature" are, in fact, thinly veiled affirmations of our own centrality, as exemplars of the "universal" values we think we are discovering in antiquity.[11] Yet this does not undermine the "timelessness" of ancient stories. Rather it clarifies it, as consisting in their infinite adaptability to specific times and places, no matter how distant from ancient Greece. A corollary of presenting ancient people as "like us," moreover, is that we too are like them: the images of ourselves that we find in antiquity are reflections in a funhouse mirror. The resulting dialogue between ancient and modern is the interface at which all receptions are located.

The overriding goal of popular culture, as I have defined it, is entertainment. But this does not exclude other functions. Filmmakers may, for example, aspire to artistic self-expression, while audiences may use such works for purposes of self-improvement, self-discovery, social connection, and the

9. On adaptation and canonicity, see Sanders 2006: passim.

10. For the history of the tension between pop classics and the classroom, see Murnaghan 2011 and cf. S. Brown 2008.

11. This is true of period films generally (cf. Staiger 2000: 201) but is strongly reinforced for Greece by Victorian philhellenism's belief that "[t]he ancient Greeks are perfect; at the same time, because human nature is unchanging, they are so like us" (Jenkyns 1980: 316).

acquisition or display of cultural capital.[12] The last of these, especially, is inextricable from the entertainment potential of Helen's story. As Jonathan Burgess puts it, Homeric reception is "complicated tremendously" by the fact that "in our culture 'Homer' serves as a general signifier of epic, myth, grandiosity, etc."[13] Consequently, as Michael Wood remarked of Cecil B. DeMille's *Ten Commandments*, when you set out to film the story of the Trojan War "you are filming a classic not of literature, but of culture itself."[14]

This is a two-edged sword for filmmakers.[15] Such themes may lure mass audiences but may also alienate them if too closely allied with "high" cultural forms. Moreover, their prestige and pervasiveness give countless viewers a perceived stake in such films' "authenticity." This depends, to be sure, on the specific genre. Audiences for most "high" cultural receptions (e.g., opera) do not care if such works get the story "wrong." At the other end of the spectrum, viewers of a telefantasy show, like *Xena: Warrior Princess*, revel in the transformation of canonical traditions, and assess texts "not on the grounds of historical accuracy but on the basis of their characterization, emotional resonance, accessibility, and immediacy."[16] Viewers of an epic movie, on the other hand, tend to judge it not as an autonomous work but as a *version* whose first duty is a perceived "authenticity" to canonical sources—an expectation fostered by the discourse of "historical accuracy" so often used in promotion.

Such viewers enjoy exercising and displaying their own taste and discrimination, and thus participating in a process of collective legitimation and/or jousting for cultural capital. This means that those with preconceived views on the subject are more likely to be drawn to these films in the first place, leaving filmmakers with a Catch-22: the canonicity of the Trojan War story draws in viewers, but also gives them a sense of entitlement to judge the product for its inevitable "deviations" from a familiar—and often well-loved—tale. Nor is this impulse confined to scholars or the highly educated. As we shall

12. On the ways that people read and use popular (as opposed to elite) culture, see Fiske 1991.

13. Burgess 2008: 194n; cf. Grobéty 2014: 170–75.

14. Wood 1989: 177.

15. By "filmmakers" I mean in the first instance writers and directors, but without excluding the many other contributors to what is, without exception, a collectively produced medium. When I refer to a film as the director's it is primarily for convenience. Note, too, that in the case of TV series the showrunner is usually more important than an episode's director.

16. Willis 2017: 114.

see, those on the margins of scholarship can be the most stringent gatekeepers.

Central to most popular renditions of Greek myth and legend is the perception that these stories are full of "aspirational heroism and questing adventure."[17] In so far as heroism is a masculine concept, both historically and conceptually, it is relatively easy to translate the great male figures of legend to the screen.[18] To be sure, some of their rough edges must be sanded down, in order to fulfill the essential Hollywood requirement that a hero elicit a basic level of audience sympathy, in the form of moral approval or "liking." But this usually leaves adapters plenty of "questing adventure" to work with. Transforming Greek mythical females into Hollywood heroes is more difficult, given the persistent association of femininity with passivity and objectification.[19] One need only think of Penelope, heroine of the *Odyssey*, whose very virtue lies in her steadfast inaction—her refusal to act, whether by accepting a suitor or completing her weaving. She is admirable, to be sure, but she has very little to do.

Among female heroes Helen of Troy enjoys a special place. She is not only the sole daughter of Zeus, king of the gods, with a human mother, but by far the most prominent female cult hero of antiquity.[20] Since ancient times, "active" women have been considered "masculine," yet Helen, defined by her transgressive action, is the quintessential feminine. This is encoded in her signature trait, the supreme beauty bestowed on her by her divine father. All heroes have such traits (Odysseus is always crafty, Hercules always strong, Penelope always faithful). Other versions (slutty Penelope, cowardly Achilles), often comedic, are parasitic on these fundamentals. These key traits are always potentially problematic; but Helen's is uniquely so, thanks to the ancient and persistent association of female beauty with erotic transgression (by both men and women) and destruction (especially of men). Zeus conceived Helen specifically to generate the greatest war of all time. Like Pandora, the

17. Blanshard 2017: 440.

18. The masculinist history of heroism as such is well laid out by Silk et al. 2013: §21. On epic heroism, see Paul 2013a: 175–85 (she discusses no females). Heroes are now often perceived through the lens of "heroism" fashioned by Joseph Campbell (cf. Hunter 2007: 162; Rogers 2011).

19. On the specifically cinematic difficulty of "constructing female characters who can plausibly do, as well as be done to and looked at," see Brunsdon 1997: 70–73 and 61 (whence the quote).

20. On Helen and cult heroism, see Blondell 2013: 43–47.

"beautiful evil" that brought evil into an idyllic male world, she was literally created to make trouble.[21]

Ancient authors often scramble to defend Helen, as if the very creators of this "beautiful evil" were unable, ultimately, to deny that "what is beautiful is good."[22] But their arguments usually involve diminishing or eliminating her agency—no ancient author defends the elopement as such. Most modern pop-cultural defenses revolve, instead, around romantic self-assertion and female victimhood.[23] This allows filmmakers to present Helen as a victim of patriarchal oppression, trapped in a loveless marriage, who chooses to follow her heart; but it complicates her heroism by placing her in the role of love interest or romantic heroine—a term implying not active heroism but rather "a structural position in narratives in relation to a male protagonist—as the object of his quest or his love."[24]

As such, she must still, of course, be rendered sympathetically. This usually means altering certain awkward aspects of the Greek story in Helen's favor. Helen's daughter, Hermione, for instance, must be eliminated, since a Helen who abandoned her child would lose the sympathy of modern American popular culture, which values only parenthood above romantic coupledom.[25] Paris, too, must be rehabilitated. The romantic defense would be shattered if Helen declared, as she does in the *Iliad*, that Menelaus is a "better man" and that she should never have left him.[26]

21. On Helen in Greek myth and her treatment in various ancient Greek authors, see Blondell 2013.

22. This view is expounded most famously by Plato, but modern research shows that it points to a more worldly underlying truth (e.g., Dion et al. 1972).

23. The romantic treatment of the Paris/Helen plot has classical roots (cf. Solomon 2007b: 98) and became popular in the Middle Ages (Scherer 1967; Mac Sweeney 2018: 127–29). For the development of ideas about love and marriage, "from the acceptance of the Victorian notion of separate spheres to the companionate ideal to the validation of romance as a key to individual identity," and their expression in the movies, see Wexman 1993 (the quotation is from p. 13).

24. Dyer 1998: 159.

25. Cf. Winkler 2009: 222–23; Haskell 2016: 168–71. Unusually, Hermione does feature in the BBC miniseries *Troy: Fall of a City* (2018).

26. "The five premises of romantic 'love' are (1) love at first sight; (2) there is only one 'true love' for each person; (3) love conquers all; (4) true love is absolutely perfect; (5) we should choose a partner for love rather than for other (more practical) reasons" (Hendrick & Hendrick 1992: 61; cf. Mellencamp 1995: 219). For the rise of love as a kind of "transcendent alchemy" in the early twentieth century, see Haag 1992: 552–56).

The romantic paradigm culminates, ideally, in the kind of happy ending, beloved of Hollywood, in which the hero and heroine are finally united. Yet even Hollywood does not allow Paris and Helen to live happily ever after.[27] Wolfgang Petersen's *Troy* does flirt with the idea of romantic closure (as we shall see in chapter 4), but typically Paris dies and Helen is returned to Menelaus, as in antiquity.[28] This moves her story into the territory of melodrama, which focuses on (usually female) victims of oppressive social circumstances.[29] Melodrama provides an entirely different way of centering a woman's story—one that does not render her secondary to a male lover, but locates her suffering at the story's heart. Helen is a perfect fit for the model posited by the filmmaker Todd Haynes, in whose view "the most amazing melodramas are the ones where, when a person makes a tiny step toward fulfilling a desire that their social role is built to discourage, they end up hurting everybody else."[30]

It is scarcely necessary to observe that the issues Helen represents are still with us today. Contemporary culture is obsessively attentive to female beauty and its impact on both men and women. Young women's use of their sexuality as a form of empowerment is being both valorized and scrutinized as never before.[31] This makes Helen, willy-nilly, a vehicle for pop-cultural feminism.[32] All female heroes from ancient Greece (including the "good" ones) are problematic for feminism in one way or another, but Helen's function as a site for concerns about beauty and erotic agency locates her in a particular contemporary niche. As Carole Vance wrote decades ago, "For women to

27. Happy endings are central to Hollywood film style, though less mandatory than often assumed (cf. Lovell & Sergi 2009: 9–10, 14, 19). M. Smith 1995: 213–14 argues that "Hollywood morality" is more fundamental than happy endings per se.

28. Dell Movie Classic Comics, however, a series promising to eliminate all "objectionable" material, replaces the escape of Aeneas after the fall of Troy (as shown in Wise's movie; see below, ch. 3) with the escape of Paris and Helen, which receives Priam's blessing.

29. For this conception of melodrama, see Schatz 1981: ch. 8; Ang 1985: 61–68, 78–83, 88; L. Williams 2001: ch. 1; see further Byars 1991; Landy 1991; M. Smith 1995: 197, 205–12; Neale 2000: ch. 5. For the centrality of suffering and disappointment to "women's culture," cf. also Berlant 2008: 12.

30. Lahr 2019: 59.

31. The recuperation of agency for the objectified female has been a prominent theme in recent feminist studies of film, women, and beauty. See, e.g., Stacey 1994: esp. 217–23; Studlar 1996 [1991]; Hansen 1991; Banet-Weiser 1999; Barbas 2001; Bean & Negra 2002 (especially Bean's introduction); Conor 2004; Weinbaum et al. 2008.

32. On pop-cultural texts as vehicles for feminism, see Read 2000: 3–13 and cf. Projansky 2001: 236. For the social power of popular culture, see Rapping 1992: ch. 5, esp. 129–31.

experience autonomous desire and act in ways that give them sexual pleasure in a society that would nurture and protect their delights is our culture's worst nightmare and feminism's best fantasy."[33] In film and television these concerns intersect with issues of race and representation. Thanks to the racist philhellenic alchemy that transformed ancient Greeks into the progenitors of northern European beauty (and thus of "Western" beauty as such), Helen became the face of the blonde, blue-eyed whiteness that still constitutes the default model of beauty in American pop culture.[34] This makes her a vehicle for the affirmation (and occasionally the critique) of conventional, racialized beauty norms.

Anyone who decides to bring Helen to the popular screen must thus navigate a host of problematic issues surrounding gender, beauty, canonicity, and heroism, in an effort to produce a vision that will satisfy not only themselves but the largest possible audience. We may gain some sense of filmmakers' aims from publicity materials, such as press kits, advertisements, interviews, and magazine stories, which promise audiences fulfillment of the desires associated with the genre in question.[35] How effective a given text may have been in satisfying these expectations is, however, difficult to gauge, especially since response is not fixed at the moment of performance but develops and fluctuates with time and circumstances.[36] Published reviews can be helpful, but only up to a point.[37] Before the rise of the internet, nearly all film reviewers were professional critics (though they might comment on broader audience responses and cater to them in their remarks). Their judgments may diverge,

33. Vance 1992: xvi.

34. Such girls are "generic in the context of a popular culture, in which whiteness remains dominant and unspoken" (Projansky 2007: 51). On white—especially blonde—beauty, see Dyer 1997; Warner 1994: esp. 362–69, 371–86; Weitz 2004: 19–22; Church Gibson 2008. On blue eyes, see especially Dyer 1997: 43–44. For the whitening of the ancient Greeks, see below, p. 7.

35. On pressbooks ("the bona fide 'voice' of Hollywood") and other forms of publicity for ancient world films, see Llewellyn-Jones 2018: 65–80. "Publicity" is sometimes distinguished from "promotion" (Dyer 1998: 60–61), but for my purposes this blanket distinction is not necessary. Unless otherwise indicated, publicity materials are cited from the author's personal collection.

36. On the difficulties involved in audience reception studies (especially for older movies), see Staiger 1992; Staiger 2000; Stacey 1994: ch. 3; Studlar 1996 [1991]; Uricchio & Pearson 1996 [1990]; Stead 2011.

37. Early reviews, in particular, must be treated with caution, since the press and the movie business were hand in glove (Slide 2010: ch. 4; cf. also Maltby 2003: 495). Until recently, television was little reviewed.

often significantly, from audience approval as measured by box office or other criteria.[38] Yet all reviews affect the discourse of public response, recirculating to influence future reactions. By the end of the twentieth century, on the other hand, evidence for audience response had become mired in the great morass of online commentary, which poses problems of its own.

Audiences are, moreover, far from monolithic. Most commercial film and television is therefore aimed at multiple audience segments, in order to maximize viewership. Gender is fundamental here. Throughout film history it has been assumed—with some justification—that men will be drawn to action and bloodshed, and women to romance and personal relationships.[39] For this reason, Hollywood formula typically interweaves a main plot line of some kind (action, mystery, combat, adventure) with a heterosexual romance.[40] Real audiences are, however, far more diverse and complex than such generalizations might suggest.[41] Individual responses are shaped by many factors besides gender, including age, class, race, education, cultural background, national origin, and personal experience. Viewers' reasons for consuming such narratives vary, as do the desires they bring with them and consequently their responses. These depend not only on what is presented in the film itself (the text), and on personal factors, but on the cultural matrix in which it is produced and consumed (context and intertexts), with the associated generic, stylistic, and ideological frames, which may contradict or compete with each other.

The Trojan War's pervasiveness and canonicity give it different kinds of meaning for many different kinds of people. Those meanings are framed both by preconceptions about the Trojan War story and by any larger assumptions about Greek antiquity that viewers may have absorbed from other sources. Within these frameworks, viewers apply their own criteria and actively create

38. On this problem, see Thumim 1992: 169. On the review aggregator Rotten Tomatoes, ratings by the "critics" (especially "top critics") often diverge significantly from those of the audience. For the difference in film tastes between movie critics and mass audiences, see Lovell & Sergi 2009.

39. See, e.g., Handel 1950: esp. 121; Rapping 1992: 27; G. King 2002: 136–37; Maltby 2003: 21–22, 77–78.

40. Bordwell 1985: 157–58; Bordwell et al. 1985: 16; Maltby 2003: 21. This does not, of course, preclude frequent homoerotic subtexts.

41. On "audiences" and the problem of identifying them collectively (e.g., "women"), see Mayne 1993: ch. 8.

their own meanings.[42] Many viewers—notably women—prefer to read against the grain, resisting the "preferred" (or superficially obvious) reading in order to negotiate "resistant" meanings of their own.[43] There is therefore no such thing as a monolithic "audience response." We can judge a film's overall success by such factors as box office and aggregate viewer ratings, but must remain alert to the plurality of responses that may be masked by such numbers.

With sufficient ingenuity, just about any narrative of the past 3,000 years can be construed as a reception of ancient Greek mythology. If the field of classical reception studies is to mean anything at all, then, anyone so foolhardy as to engage in it must face the vexed question of defining its parameters. Much scholarship in the field examines works that echo ancient themes even though they make no explicit reference to antiquity.[44] Some films respond well to this treatment; others even invite it.[45] But the approach raises a host of methodological problems. How many evocations of antiquity does it take to mark a classical reception as such, and how explicit must they be, in order to avoid the all-too-tempting trap of "ghosting," or seeing classical connections everywhere one looks.[46]

I have severed this Gordian knot by selecting only receptions where Helen of Troy is a named character, thus drastically narrowing the field of available choices. This is not only for methodological convenience. Stories about female beauty bringing disaster are ten-a-penny worldwide, but the addition of Helen's well-known name raises associations that provide the audience with specific contexts, both ancient and modern, in which to evaluate her screen

42. For discussions of active spectatorship, especially by women, see Bordwell 1985: ch. 3; Rapping 1992: 89–90; Mayne 1993; Stacey 1994: 34–47; M. Smith 1995: ch. 2; Studlar 1996 [1991]; Staiger 2000: ch. 5.

43. On spectatorship as "negotiation," see Gledhill 1988. The preferred/resistant terminology derives from British cultural studies (see, e.g., Fiske 1992 and cf. Staiger 1992: 68–78). The "preferred" reading is more politely defined as "that understanding of a film's propositions which is inscribed in the narratives [sic] construction and its positioning of the audience" (Thumim 1992: 9). For examples of resistant female viewers, see Fiske 1991: 104–5, 107; Thumim 1992: 97–99. On TV's ability, in particular, to support both preferred and subcultural meanings, see Fiske 1986; H. Jenkins 2013: 82, 113–15.

44. These are suggestively dubbed "subterranean" receptions by Cyrino and Safran (2015: 5).

45. E.g., *O Brother Where Art Thou?* (on which, see Goldhill 2007; Paul 2008a: 309–10).

46. I borrow the term "ghosting" from Keen 2006. For more on this methodological difficulty, see Paul 2008a: 308–11; Paul 2010: 147–48; Paul 2013a: 85–92; Blondell 2016a.

representations. In other words, I am interested not only in the broader themes that Helen embodies, but in how she is viewed as a specific character from a specific tradition. As a named character in a canonical story, she serves as a vehicle for tracing two intertwined threads of cultural history, the reception of Greek myth and the history of beauty.

The following chapters will examine ways in which particular works address a range of interlocking questions about beauty, its representation, and the cinematic uses of myth, in a variety of generic, historical, and cultural contexts. I should make it clear at the outset that I have no interest in evaluating any of these works for its accuracy or "fidelity" to ancient sources, which I do not believe is a useful or even, ultimately, a coherent yardstick.[47] Nor am I concerned to assess them as works of art. I am interested, rather, in what filmmakers' choices and the responses of their audiences suggest about the available meanings of Helen at various pop-cultural moments. In some of them she is the central character (or "hero"); in others she is at the periphery of a masculine adventure; in episodic telefantasy, she typically embodies the problem of the week, placing her at the periphery of the series yet at the center of the episode. But in all of them she represents the threat of superhuman beauty as an inheritance from classical Greece.

The book is arranged in three parts. Part I, on early Hollywood, begins with an introduction outlining the importance of ideas about Greek beauty at the beginning of cinema, and highlighting some of the problems that continue to bedevil this topic, especially "realism" and the representation of superhuman beauty. I argue that the problematic of Helen is baked into Hollywood from the start. In chapter 2, I use this context to examine the sole Helenic feature film to emerge from Hollywood in this period, Alexander Korda's *Private Life of Helen of Troy* (1927). Part II moves to big screen epic, pairing one film from each of the two great waves of ancient world epic spanning the latter half of the twentieth century: Robert Wise's *Helen of Troy* (1956) and Wolfgang Petersen's more recent extravaganza, *Troy* (2004). In part III, I turn to television, with a chapter on episodic telefantasy followed by a study of the 2003 miniseries *Helen of Troy*. This arrangement, largely but not entirely chronological, is intended to challenge the too-easy assimilation of television to cinema.

47. Cf. Paul 2013a: 43–44, 51–53. On "fidelity," translation, and adaptation, see Marciniak 2007; Paul 2008b; Stam 2000; Sanders 2006; and below, ch. 6.

My professional training is that of a classicist, and like many of us I came to classical reception primarily out of a love of popular film. Though I have read fairly widely in film and television studies, I fear that my research betrays more breadth than depth. I have been aided invaluably, however, by experts in other fields, above all the wonderfully kind, helpful and impressive professional staff of the George Eastman House in Rochester, NY, and of the Roddenberry Collection at UCLA, the Warner Bros. Archives at USC, and the Margaret Herrick Library in Los Angeles. I owe special debts of gratitude, as well, to Karen Singson, for answering my questions about her students at the Assumption Antipolo school; James Porto, for generously waiving his copyright fee; Therese Bohn, for use of her collage and for help with *Star Trek* images; and Ronni Kern, screenwriter for the *Helen of Troy* miniseries, for allowing me to interview her, and giving me a delightful lunch at her home in Santa Monica.

Numerous friends and colleagues, at the University of Washington and around the world, have helped to make this a better book, including Jennifer Bean, Sarah Brucia Breitenfeld, Liz Conor, Ann Cumming, Pat Day, David Eldridge, Emily Hauser, Yurie Hong, Devin McDonald, Lindsay Morse, Mark Nugent, Kirk Ormand, Jen Sachs, Adriana Vasquez, the students in my undergraduate seminar (especially Yael Kochin), and participants in a number of conferences (especially "Xena: 20 Years On"). This book has been long in the making, and I apologize to anyone whose help I may have inadvertently failed to acknowledge. I apologize, too, to anyone whose recent work I have failed to consult. Although the manuscript was essentially completed in September 2020, publication has been delayed by factors outside my control, and I have been able to incorporate only a small amount of scholarship since that date.

I apologize, in addition, for the poor quality of some of the illustrations. Given the centrality of representation to my argument, it seemed important to provide as many of these as possible. The illustrations make specific and immediate the ways in which each of these stories is the product of a particular time and place: it is one thing to say a work is of the Jazz Age, but another to see what that era looked like to itself. They are drawn from a wide range of sources in different media, including movie and television frames, stills, promotional materials, fan art, and so on. The diversity in format and time period, and thus in the technology used to produce them, means that some of the material is not of the highest quality. I have decided to include them nonetheless due to their significance to the argument: Helen is always an image—an *eidolon*—and how she looks is central to her various appearances. Princeton

University Press is in no way responsible for any deficits in the quality of these illustrations. I am particularly grateful to Chloe Coy, at the Press, for helping to make them as good as they can be under the circumstances.

I would like to thank the Oberlin College Department of Classics for subsidizing the color plates, and the University of Washington's Simpson Center for the Humanities for research support. I am also, of course, most grateful to the faculty of Oberlin College for inviting me to present the Martin Lectures on which this book is based. They were generous, friendly and supportive hosts, undeterred by the fact that my topic was rather different from most entries in the Martin Lectures series. The week I spent there, especially the final celebratory evening, will linger long in my memory. I hope the resulting volume will be of interest to other classicists, especially as reception in popular culture becomes increasingly prominent in both scholarship and the classroom.

Finally, I am more thankful than I can say to all those who have supported me with their friendship over the past few years—years marked by personal and global crisis and loss. Besides the dear friends already included among my colleagues above, chief among them are Deb Kamen, Krissa and Marshall Lent, Sarah Levin-Richardson, my sister Emma Whitlock, and above all my spouse, Douglas Roach, not least of whose many extraordinary qualities was a sound appreciation of "bad" TV. During the last few weeks of his life, while suffering from two terminal cancers, Douglas made the effort to read through every part of my manuscript. Words cannot express how much he is missed.

PART I

Early Hollywood

1

Olympus Moves to Hollywood

The Pure Pleasure of Cinema Itself

SINCE THE birth of cinema, scholars have been eager to endow this distinctively modern medium with symbolic ancestors from ancient Greece. Plato's cave allegory, with its illusionistic images projected onto the wall of a dark chamber, is regularly invoked by film theorists, and the classicist Martin Winkler has declared Apollo film's patron deity.[1] I would like to propose adding Helen of Troy to this company. Unlike Plato or Apollo, she has been a staple of the large and small screen from their beginnings to the present day.[2] Unlike them, moreover, she gives the femininity of film its due. As the most beautiful woman in the world, she is a vehicle for questions about beauty, pleasure, desire, and power that lie at the heart both of cinema and of popular culture more broadly.

The Hollywood film industry emerged at a time when the intimate relationship between beauty and visuality, closely aligned since antiquity, had reached fever pitch.[3] The relative beauty of female stars was constantly evaluated, and contests were used to identify newcomers who might feed this obsession.[4] Such displays were aimed not only at the presumptively heterosexual male viewer, but also at the narcissistic female gaze. The latter has been signified

1. For the former, see especially Baudry 1999 [1970] and cf. Wyke 2003: 439; Conor 2004: 20–21. For the latter, see Winkler 2009.

2. Winkler 2009: ch. 2 surveys Apollo on screen, but the god rarely appears outside adaptations of Greek tragedy (plus a notable *Star Trek* episode discussed in ch. 5 below).

3. Conor 2004: 19–25 discusses modernism's inheritance of Greek ocularcentrism.

4. On beauty culture in the 1920s, see Banner 1983: ch. 12; Banet-Weiser 1999: ch. 1; Conor 2004; Carden-Coyne 2009: ch. 5.

since antiquity by the emblem of the mirror.[5] A mirror functions as a picture frame, which makes a woman "connive in treating herself as, first and foremost, a sight."[6] More than a frame, however, the mirror's ability to reflect "lifelike" moving images makes it a kind of proto-film.[7] The film screen, in turn, serves as a mirror to the world, showing the movie fan icons of feminine beauty to which she herself may aspire.[8] When she uses her own mirror to align her appearance with that of the stars,[9] what she sees is an echo of the filmic image, bridging the gap between viewer and viewed.

As a tool allowing women to construct their own appearance for their own purposes, the mirror betokens not only beauty and narcissism but feminine power. The garments, adornments and accessories that have served, from time immemorial, as a proxy for beauty, help to construct women as desirable objects for the male gaze. At the same time, however, they thwart that gaze, insisting on women's own power to reveal or withhold the mysteries that lie beneath.[10] The love of adornment that facilitates the pursuit of their erotic agenda thus becomes an encoding of women's own erotic desire. In the beauty culture of early Hollywood, as in antiquity, this was a source of considerable anxiety. In Liz Conor's words, "Women who actively sought a desiring gaze were associated with visual deceit, artifice, and the entrapment of men. They exhibited their desire to become sexual subjects by positioning themselves, rather duplicitously, as sexual objects."[11] This manipulative exercise of erotic agency was rendered still more dangerous by women's "peculiar susceptibility to the image—to the cinematic spectacle in general."[12] Young women flocked to the

5. For examples from Greek vase painting, showing Helen with a mirror, see Blondell 2013: 7, 50–51.

6. Berger 1972: 51. On the mirror as frame, see Hollander 1978: ch. 6; cf. also Banta 1987: 366–74.

7. Since ancient times, the mirror has betokened a deceptive "realism" (cf. Plato, *Republic* 596de).

8. For film as a mirror, cf., e.g., Bazin & Gray 1967: 97; Morin 2005: 121.

9. For the importance of the mirror to movie fans, see Blumer 1933: 35–37 and cf. Thumim 1992: 166–68; Stacey 1994: 67–68; Conor 2004: 150–51. On audience identification, see further below, p. 13 n. 36.

10. This effect is enhanced when the performer is a star (Haskell 2016: 324–25).

11. Conor 2004: 92. For ancient Greece, see Blondell 2013: ch. 1. In Victorian times, similarly, the "natural" female desire for fashionable clothing was "linked not only with weakness and fickleness but also somehow with godless and unaccountable female sexual power" (Hollander 1978: 361). On the lust for clothing as a placeholder for sex in the 1920s, cf. Ryan 1976: 373.

12. Doane 1987: 1.

cinema, and soon became the primary consumers of mass culture more generally, helping to "feminize" it as frivolous and disreputable.[13]

Helen of Troy is a fitting figurehead for this symbiosis of film and femininity. If the feminine is "an unattainable visual image of desirability,"[14] then she is its mythological quintessence: the object of all men's desire and all women's aspiration, whose uncanny beauty destroys men's wits and distorts their perception of reality.[15] This makes Helen a figure both for sensory pleasure—especially scopic pleasure—and for the dangers (real or imaginary) that it poses. As such, she is an early ancestor of Lulu, the seductive, destructive beauty played by Louise Brooks in G. W. Pabst's silent classic *Pandora's Box* (1929), who represents "the pure pleasure of cinema itself."[16]

This proto-cinematic role is vividly conveyed by a remarkable variant of Helen's story, in which it is not she who causes the Trojan War, but a double or *eidolon*, fabricated by the gods to be her exact visual counterpart.[17] Though nominally a "copy," as a reification of Helen's beauty the *eidolon* is not merely a deceptive image but also, in an important sense, the "real" Helen, since it fulfills her mythic function: it is divinely created to cause the Trojan War through its beauty. The story makes Helen a figure not only for visual enchantment, but for imitation, illusion, and the manufactured image.[18] Though quite

13. On the rise and gendering of the movie fan, and women as target audience, see J. Allen 1980: 486; Hansen 1991: 114–25; Stacey 1994: 85–86; Conor 2004: 100; Fuller 1996: ch. 6 & 7; Studlar 1996 [1991]: 263–64; Barbas 2001; Driscoll 2002: 224–26; Higashi 2002: 314–15. For the "femininity" of the popular, see L. Fischer 2003: ch. 2; Conor 2004: 225–27. For the contrast with "real" culture as masculine, see Huyssen 1986; Maltby 1989: 13; Modleski 1991: ch. 2. Even at the end of the twentieth century, when movies had long been targeted primarily at young males, mass culture was conceived of as a "bimbo" (Morris 1990: 23–24).

14. Stacey 1994: 66.

15. On the uncanniness of Helen's beauty, see E. Mansfield 2007: 29–35. Postrel argues that she is the mythic ancestor of the concept of glamor, which "allows us to imaginatively inhabit the ideal" (Postrel 2013: 41, 45; see further 147–50). On glamor, see also Massey 2000: 36–42; Moseley 2002; Shields 2013: ch. 2 and below, p. 000.

16. Doane apud L. Garcia 2013: 20.

17. The Greek word *eidolon* is one of a family of terms relating to vision, appearance, and beauty. On Helen's *eidolon*, see further Blondell 2013: 117–22 and ch. 10. For film's preoccupation with doubling, see Braudy 2002: 226–35.

18. Plato himself identifies Helen's *eidolon* with illusory visual pleasures like the images in his cave (*Republic* 586bc).

widespread in antiquity, this version has never to my knowledge been represented in popular cinema.[19] Yet every screen Helen is, in its way, an *eidolon*.

A Village near the Sea

Mediterranean antiquity offered cinema not only symbolic ancestors but an endless supply of varied and spectacular stories, whose permeation in European and American cultural traditions made them simultaneously exotic and familiar, prestigious and accessible. The Trojan War, in particular, offered a rich trove of cinematic possibilities for combat, adventure, camaraderie, and spectacle.[20] Thanks to Helen, this male-centered story can also be larded with heterosexual romance—a vital ingredient in the Hollywood formula. Antiquity also provided a way for Hollywood to assert its cultural legitimacy. Then as now, Hollywood was "criticized by the self-elected intelligentsia as glorifying the moron."[21] Eastern snobs looked down on this Western outpost as superficial, anti-intellectual, and unsophisticated. But the ancient world had long been "sacralized as the core of high culture and sanctified as the Eden of Western civilization."[22] The production of films about Greece and Rome thus allowed Hollywood to present itself as "the Athens of today," uplifting the masses by bringing education and culture to all.[23] Not coincidentally, such claims also helped to build audiences by attracting the middle class.[24]

One way classical Greece served this agenda was by giving the highest of high cultural endorsements to Hollywood's obsession with physical beauty. Assuming the mantle of antiquity allowed the movie business to lay claim to a "timeless" or "classical" ideal giving an intellectual, mythical, and transhistorical stamp to the idea of absolute beauty—a beauty that could be

19. It appears in high cultural forms such as opera, but very rarely in popular receptions of the classics. Wise's 1956 film alludes to it, however (below, ch. 3).

20. For a list of screen treatments of the Trojan War, see Winkler 2007b; cf. also Wieber 2005; Solomon 2015.

21. Waterbury 1928. Cf. Addison 2006: 6, 15.

22. Winterer 2002: 142.

23. The quote is from a 1929 letter to a fan magazine (M. Williams 2013a: 49). See further Hansen 1985: 326–30; Hansen 1991: 63–64; Olsson 2008: ch. 6; Slide 2010: 55; Christie 2013: 117–23; B. Dixon 2013: 32–34; M. Williams 2013a: 28.

24. For the influence of classicism on the middle class (especially women), see Winterer 2002: 144–47. For the cultural tie-ins used to attract middle class viewers to the movies in early Hollywood, see, e.g., Michelakis 2013: 149–50.

reincarnated, unchanged, in countless women, even thousands of years and thousands of miles from the culture that gave it birth. The beauty standards in question, based on ideas about symmetry and specific proportions, were enhanced for the screen by makeup and often surgery.[25] They were derived not from actual Greeks, but from the Aryanized ancient Greece devised by northern European philhellenists.[26] This was helped along by the ancients' own idealization of light skin for women (Helen, for example is described as "white-armed" in Homer), and "golden" hair for gods and heroes.[27] At a time when whiteness was being constructed to define "real" Americans, as opposed to Black people and immigrants, "Greek" beauty was one way to justify Anglo hegemony in the movies.[28]

As exemplars of unfading beauty, the Greek gods become an emblem for the supposed universality of film in a way that served the interests of Hollywood's increasing global reach. An article in *Photoplay*, the leading early fan magazine, explains: "The gods of Olympus ordained beauty of human face and figure the highest good," but "Greece fell before the barbarians. Over the ages its ideals were lost [until] the movies came with their demand for beauty, for youth, for health, for artistic productiveness," and in "a village near the sea . . . a community grew, made by beauty, urged by beauty, producing beauty" (figure 1.1).[29] The author, Ruth Waterbury, proves her point by comparing the measurements of male and female film stars with the Apollo Belvedere and Venus de Milo respectively. This leads to "the startling discovery that measurement for measurement movie gods and goddesses are beautiful as the ancient ones of Greece." Even movie stars grow old and die, of course; yet film

25. Cf. Annas 1987: 52–54; Morin 2005: 31–35; Addison 2006: 13. In nineteenth-century art the ideal was "regularity" of features, which "meant the straight, slender nose, the full yet controlled line of the lips, and the high 'pure' brow made familiar from endless plaster casts of Greek statuary" (Banta 1987: 115–16). As late as the 1970s, "contemporary" beauty could be said to be "derived from the classic Greeks . . . heroic yet serene in its dehumanized regularity" (Buchman 1973: 29).

26. On the "whitening" of ancient Greeks, see Bernal 1987: ch. 6–7; Dyer 1997: 20–22; Mohanram 2007: 49–52; Squire 2011: 18–23; McCoskey 2012: ch. 4; Inglis 2001: 81; Painter 2010: ch. 6.

27. As recent scholarship has emphasized, however, this does not mean the ancient Greeks conceived of "whiteness" as a racial category. Most recently, and comprehensively, see Derbew 2022.

28. Wexman 1993: 140.

29. Waterbury 1928b.

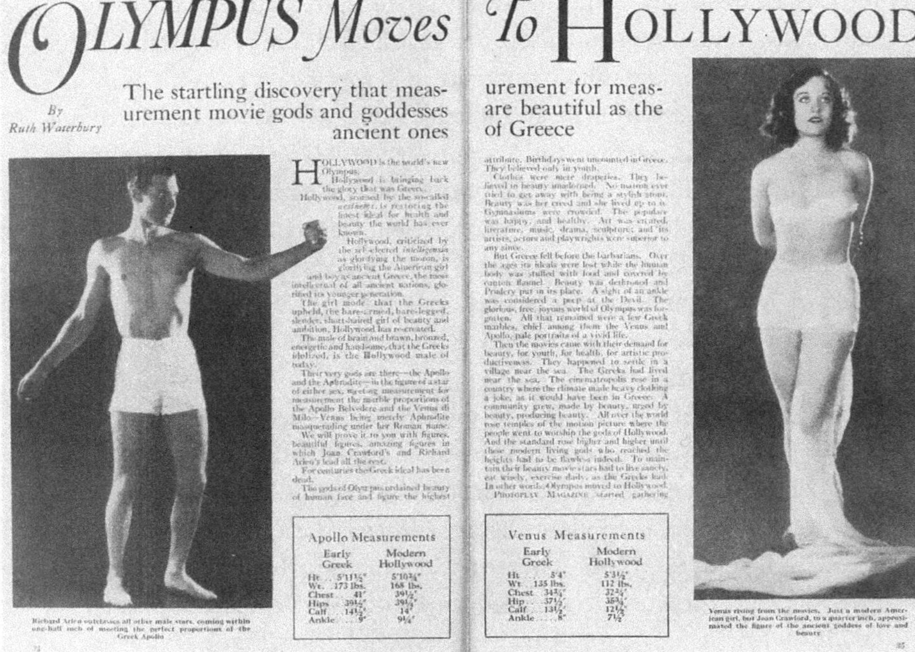

OLYMPUS Moves To HOLLYWOOD

By
Ruth Waterbury

The startling discovery that measurement for measurement movie gods and goddesses are beautiful as the ancient ones of Greece

HOLLYWOOD is the world's new Olympus.

Hollywood is bringing back the glory that was Greece.

Hollywood, scorned by the so-called *aesthetes*, is restoring the finest ideal for health and beauty the world has ever known.

Hollywood, criticized by the self-elected *intelligentsia* as glorifying the moron, is glorifying the American girl and boy as ancient Greece, the most intellectual of all ancient nations, glorified its younger generation.

The girl mode that the Greeks upheld, the bare-armed, bare-legged, slender, short-haired girl of beauty and ambition, Hollywood has re-created.

The male of brain and brawn, bronzed, energetic and handsome, that the Greeks idolized, is the Hollywood male of today.

Their very gods are there—the Apollo and the Aphrodite—in the figure of a star of either sex, meeting measurement for measurement the marble proportions of the Apollo Belvedere and the Venus di Milo—Venus being merely Aphrodite masquerading under her Roman name.

We will prove it to you with figures, beautiful figures, amazing figures in which Joan Crawford's and Richard Arlen's lead all the rest.

For centuries the Greek ideal has been dead.

The gods of Olympus ordained beauty of human face and figure the highest attribute. Birthdays went uncounted in Greece. They believed only in youth.

Clothes were mere draperies. They believed in beauty unadorned. No nation ever tried to get away with being a stylish stout. Beauty was her creed and she lived up to it. Gymnasiums were crowded. The populace was happy, and healthy. Art was created, literature, music, drama, sculpture; and its artists, actors and playwrights were superior to any since.

But Greece fell before the barbarians. Over the ages its ideals were lost while the human body was stuffed with food and covered by canton flannel. Beauty was dethroned and Prudery put in its place. A sight of an ankle was considered a peep at the Devil. The glorious, free, joyous world of Olympus was forgotten. All that remained were a few Greek marbles, chief among them the Venus and Apollo, pale portraits of a vivid life.

Then the movies came with their demand for beauty, for youth, for health, for artistic productiveness. They happened to settle in a village near the sea. The Greeks had lived near the sea. The cinematropolis rose in a country where the climate made heavy clothing a joke, as it would have been in Greece. A community grew, made by beauty, urged by beauty, producing beauty. All over the world rose temples of the motion picture where the people went to worship the gods of Hollywood. And the standard rose higher and higher until these modern living gods who reached the heights had to be flawless indeed. To maintain their beauty movie stars had to live sanely, eat wisely, exercise daily, as the Greeks had. In other words, Olympus moved to Hollywood.

PHOTOPLAY MAGAZINE started gathering

Apollo Measurements

	Early Greek	Modern Hollywood
Ht.	5'11½"	5'10¾"
Wt.	173 lbs.	168 lbs.
Chest	41"	39½"
Hips	39½"	39¼"
Calf	14½"	14"
Ankle	9"	9¼"

Venus Measurements

	Early Greek	Modern Hollywood
Ht.	5'4"	5'3½"
Wt.	135 lbs.	112 lbs.
Chest	34¾"	32¾"
Hip	37½"	35¾"
Calf	13½"	12½"
Ankle	8"	7½"

Richard Arlen outclasses all other male stars, coming within one-half inch of meeting the perfect proportions of the Greek Apollo

Venus rising from the movies. Just a modern American girl, but Joan Crawford, to a quarter inch, approximated the figure of the ancient goddess of love and beauty

FIGURE 1.1. Spread from *Photoplay*, April 1928. The caption at right reads, "Venus rising from the movies. Just a modern American girl, but Joan Crawford, to a quarter inch, approximated the figure of the ancient goddess of love and beauty."

immortalizes them as perpetually young and beautiful, allowing them to die—and live—"over and over," and thus be blessed with their classical forebears' immortality.[30]

The winners of Waterbury's involuntary beauty contest, shown posing as their ancient counterparts, are Richard Arlen (Most Like Apollo) and Joan Crawford (Most Like Venus). Waterbury was following in the footsteps of philhellenic art historians, archeologists, aesthetes, eugenicists, and anatomists, for whom the Venus de Milo in particular exemplified the ideal of female beauty. Crawford embraced the identity, even using the Venus on her

30. Tyler 1947: xviii. This kind of immortality may be assisted by an early death (Morin 2005: 107; Addison 2006: 10; Postrel 2013: 100–101). On the role of ancient Greek statuary in constructing the idea of the star as divinity, see M. Williams 2013a; M. Williams 2018. On stars' divinity, see also Braudy 2002: 212; Fowles 1992: 182–83; Stacey 1994: 67, 142–44, 235; and Morin 2005: 27–88.

personal bookplates, but many other stars were also compared measure-for-measure with the statue's imaginary vital statistics.[31] They often posed with it for photographs, making the Venus into an iconotext that "bathes [the star] in reflected glory, and imparts perceived European sophistication onto the American idol."[32] Venus also pervades the beauty discourse surrounding early Hollywood in other ways. Her name appeared in countless movie titles, such as *The American Venus* (1926), whose plot involved a beauty contest and featured the 1925 Miss America, Fay Lanphier. Miss America contestants were referred to as "Venuses," and beauty pageant connoisseurs found mythic precedent in the Judgment of Paris, which has been aptly labeled "the paradigmatic story of western male gazing."[33]

The use of statues, specifically, as evidence for "classical" ideals had a further advantage, since it authorized an otherwise potentially scandalous degree of skin exposure. This convenient alibi was likewise inherited from the Victorians, for whom "Greek art allowed one to contemplate the naked body with a good conscience, and at the same time to congratulate oneself on possessing a taste far removed from the common herd's."[34] In antiquity, Aphrodite is most definitely a goddess of carnal desire, and the legacy of Greece included the pre-Christian sensuality and primal emotions of the Nietzschean Dionysiac.[35] But the classical alibi depended on a desexualized aestheticism: Greek beauty was supposedly not erotic but innocent and wholesome.[36] Echoing the

31. E.g., Annette Kellerman (Conor 2004: 152) Thelma Todd (Donati 2012: 31); Greta Garbo (M. Williams 2013a: 15; M. Williams 2013b: 139); Gloria Swanson (M. Williams 2013b). On Crawford as Venus, see M. Williams 2013a: 64 and cf. M. Williams 2018: 7. On stars and statues, see also Carden-Coyne 2009: 241–47.

32. M. Williams 2013a: 55. The iconotext "comments on the star and her place within history as it is being constructed," so that "each icon reflects upon, and validates, the other" (M. Williams 2013a: 54). See further M. Williams 2013a: 164–65; M. Williams 2013b: 126–31.

33. Squire 2011: 80; cf. Deford 1971: 117; Conor 2004: 140–41.

34. Jenkyns 1980: 136. During the Greek revival, this alibi was used only for male nudity (Mosse 1988: ch. 5), but Hollywood had no difficulty applying the argument to both sexes. On the "double articulation" of the classical nude (i.e., the simultaneous provision and denial of eroticism), see Dyer 2004: 119 and cf. M. Williams 2013a: 2.

35. Cf. Ribeyrol 2013; Momigliano 2013; Banta 1987: 399–400. For Venus as the enemy of Christianity—even a satanic figure—see Ziolkowski 1977: 27, 44. For the double and intertwined "aesthetic and libidinal" artistic receptions of Venus, see Arscott & Scott 2000.

36. Carden-Coyne 2009: 228; Mosse 1988: 13–16, 48–53; Conor 2004: 164–66; cf. Jenkyns 1980: 133–35. Isadora Duncan used similar rhetoric to legitimize her "Greek" dancing as Culture (Daly 1995: ch. 3).

rhetoric of philhellenism, Waterbury explains that it is Hollywood's balmy climate that allows it to reproduce the "bare-legged" look that allegedly prevailed in ancient Greece, when "clothes were mere draperies," before "Beauty was dethroned and Prudery put in its place."

The double vision afforded by such high-minded rhetoric was assisted by the fact that the draperies of Greek antiquity, modest though they were in practice, are never more than one step away from lingerie, via the simple substitution of diaphanous fabrics (a technique already popular with ancient Greek artists). The looseness of such drapery—which tends to be only lightly attached—further assists the justification of sexiness via claims of "authenticity." Hollywood remained considerably more prudish than Greek statuary. Unlike the Venus de Milo, Joan Crawford appears in *Photoplay* wearing a bandeau top, and Richard Arlen wears shorts in place of Apollo's fig leaf (itself an addition to the ancient original). Yet the gloss imparted by such statuary's cultural associations enabled filmmakers to push propriety to the limit. As MGM's Irving Thalberg observed, "you could get away with anything in a movie, particularly sex, if you made it historical—and expensive."[37] Cecil B. DeMille, in particular, was notorious for "wallowing in sadistic sex but dodging recriminations with vast doses of historical nobility."[38]

The World's Greatest Vamp

Like her patron goddess, Helen of Troy represents, in Goethe's famous phrase, the "eternal feminine."[39] A newspaper article from 1916 informs us that an artist named Ray van Buren studied "the beauty of Helen as delineated in the finest Greek friezes and sculptures," before extolling the modern women who, in his view, have "the same classic, tantalizing, heart-storming beauty as the immortal Helen of Troy."[40] She also pervades the broader discourse of beauty culture. A tip for lustrous hair, for example (involving egg whites and carbolic acid), is

37. McConathy & Vreeland 1976: 27.

38. Card 1994: 219. On deviant sexuality in ancient world films, see Cyrino 2014.

39. On the "eternal feminine" as a status that "naturalizes the position of women as objects of the gaze," cf. Stacey 1994: 225.

40. Anon. 1916. Note that many such newspaper stories were syndicated, and thus read far more widely than their appearance in one local paper might suggest. Artists were often used as beauty contest judges, both for their "professional wisdom about female beauty" and as a way "to confer class on the spectacle" (Mifflin 2020: 29).

attributed to Helen's "beauty recipe books."[41] Her name appears less often than Venus's in movie titles, but advertisements for beauty products often invoke the goddess and her protégée in the same breath.[42] Sometimes they are even conflated, as if Helen had been the winner—not just a bribe—at the Judgment of Paris: "The Search for a New Helen of Troy Begins in France, [with] the Modern Judgment of Paris . . . to Determine Who Is Most Beautiful."[43]

As icons of female beauty, both Helen and her patron goddess were vehicles for contemporary ambivalence about the cultural legitimacy of modern America. Many sources opine that in Hollywood Helen would be nothing in comparison with the abundance of American beauties.[44] Despite Ray van Buren's enthusiasm for Helen, he contrasts her singularity in her own day with the alleged fact that "the measurements of fifteen hundred girls at Wellesley College average approximately the classic lines of Venus de Milo."[45] As a pagan goddess, however, Venus can enter modern life only in magical or symbolic ways. Like other such divinities, she is of interest primarily as a force that rules mortal lives or brings the human condition into focus through (often humorous) contrast. Helen, on the other hand, stands at the center of a narrative that can, if necessary, be stripped of the supernatural to become a strictly human love triangle.

With few exceptions, ancient reports of Helen's divinity are ignored. Opinions on her historicity diverged: though naysayers continued to consign her to legend, proof of her historicity was eagerly sought and often found. As one newspaper headline proclaims, "Helen of Troy Real—Not a Myth."[46] "Science" went "dredging for relics of the world's greatest vamp," and managed to unearth such artifacts as "Helen's safety pins."[47] There is endless speculation

41. Anon. 1926.

42. E.g., Anon. 1922a. On Venus in advertising, see M. Williams 2013b: 139–40.

43. Anon. 1920.

44. Even the Venus was sometimes criticized, usually for being too fat or "thick-waisted" (see, e.g., Conor 2004: 158; M. Williams 2013b: 139).

45. Anon. 1916. For Wellesley's rivalry with Swarthmore and other manifestations of Venus-mania in this period, see Morton 2016.

46. Anon. 1924a.

47. Anon. 1925; *El Paso Herald*, January 28, 1922. (Items like the latter with no byline or headline—such as gossip items, ads, and capsule reviews—are not cited in the bibliography.) Solomon 2015 argues that Schliemann's discoveries prompted the demythification of the Trojan War and a concomitant burst of interest in Helen.

as to what she "really" looked like, especially her hair color (was she a blonde or a redhead?), and her age at the time of her elopement, variously estimated at 40, 45, 46, 48, 60 or even 120 (as proven by German scientists).[48] This unfading beauty is presented as an aspirational model for modern women. Exercise guru Diana Watts, author of *The Renaissance of the Greek Ideal* (1914), touts her "Greek physical system" of exercises, which kept Helen young at 48, as the secret of beauty and "perpetual youth."[49]

The extraordinary popularity of Helen's name in this period gave her a different kind of link to the mortal world.[50] According to the widespread "What's in a name?" articles, it conjures "a dazzling figure of youth, beauty and cleverness."[51] The name's familiarity made it easy to attach mythical associations to real people, such as the beautiful Helen Norpoth (a.k.a. Helen of St. Louis), the tennis champion Helen Wills (a.k.a. Helen of California, Helen of Berkeley, or one of the Four Helens of Sport), and the political candidate Helen Pettigrew (a.k.a. Helen of Kansas). Her name was also used for non-Helens who are judged the most beautiful in a particular city, region, race, or class (St. Louis, "Gypsies," typists, athletes). It was especially resonant in Los Angeles because of the University of Southern California's Trojan theme, which included the selection of an annual "Helen of Troy" to represent the university. On the East Coast, the 1923 musical comedy *Helen of Troy, NY*, featuring a modern American Helen who works at a collar factory, was a smash hit on Broadway.

This pervasiveness makes Helen easily available for naturalization in modern terms—an availability reinforced by the paradigmatic character of her story, which taps into anxieties about female visibility, female movement, and especially female sexuality, with which cinema has always been, in its own way, as concerned as ancient Greece. In early Hollywood, that concern centered on the vamp, femme fatale, or siren—a seductive, sexually assertive woman who threatened men both by exposing herself to the male gaze and

48. Anon. 1911.

49. Watts 1919b; the article is illustrated with a woman archer mimicking the famous Trojan archer from the Temple of Aphaia on Aegina. For the importance of exercise in early twentieth-century beauty culture, see Banner 1983: ch. 10 and cf. below, pp. 70–71).

50. See Social Security, "Popular Baby Names by Decade," accessed April 9, 2020, http://www.ssa.gov/OACT/babynames/decades/. For the use of resonant names in film, cf. M. Smith 1995: 193.

51. Marshall 1921.

by actively pursuing them.[52] Helen's elopement made her a benchmark for such misbehavior. One newspaper explains that Homer gave the event "such widespread notoriety that wives even today are following the beauteous Helen's example."[53] Its consequences make her the go-to comparandum for any women fought over by men, whether the arena be warfare, politics, or the stage. All this renders Helen "the original vampire," "the world's greatest 'vamp,'" or one of the "vivid vamps of history."[54] She is a fitting emblem of the scandalously eroticized atmosphere of the film industry, a.k.a. "Los Angeles Love" (figure 1.2).[55] The author of the article illustrated here speculates that it was Helen's story—more specifically a certain painting of her story—that inspired a man named Edward Fawcett to abduct a woman named Elise Hilliger in his airplane.

Despite the lighthearted tone of such articles, the anxieties underlying them were quite real. With their supposedly innate susceptibility to the seductions of the moving image, women were expected to—and did—identify with film stars and strive to reproduce what they saw on screen.[56] Onscreen and off, the stars served as mannequins for the latest fashions and spokespersons for an endless procession of beauty products.[57] This influence extended beyond fashion as such, to the kind of "moral demise" associated with "excesses of finery."[58] One might think that shopping is one thing, adultery another, but the pleasures of conspicuous consumption and of sex, and thus the desires

52. The vamp evolved from the original movie "vampire," identified with Theda Bara. See further Walker 1967: 19–27; Higashi 1978: ch. 3; Card 1994: ch. 9; Staiger 1995: ch. 6; Negra 2001; Negra 2002a.

53. Anon. 1921a.

54. Currie 1925; Anon. 1925; Jordan 1922. Other oft cited vamps include Eve, Cleopatra, the Queen of Sheba, and Madame du Barry (cf. below, figure 2.4).

55. For the equation of scandalous sexual behavior with "Hollywood love," see Dyer 1998: 45–46.

56. Identification with stars is a complicated and theoretically contentious issue. See especially M. Smith 1995, who eschews psychologizing models to argue that we respond to characters as analogues of persons and distinguishes character "recognition" from both "alignment" (a shared point of view) and "allegiance" (which is moral). Cf. also Stacey 1991; Fowles 1992: ch. 7; Dyer 1998: passim; Hallam & Marshment 2000: ch. 5; Woodward 2003: ch. 3; Stacey 1994: ch. 5; Morin 2005: 78–81, 135–49.

57. On the symbiotic relationship between consumer marketing and early cinema, see J. Allen 1980; Eckert 1990; Higashi 2002; and cf. Wyke 1997: 97–100.

58. Conor 2004: 73.

And That's What They Call "Los Angeles Love"

How Speed, Thrills, Contempt of Conventions---the Hollywood Elements of Romance---Were Outdone in the Airplane Pursuit of the Flyer Carrying Off the Peeved Sweetheart

"Abduction of Helen of Troy," the Famous Painting by Rudolph von Deutsch That May Have Inspired Edward Fawcett to Carry Off Elise Hilliger in His Airplane.

Edward S. Fawcett and Miss Hilliger, Photographed in the Airplane in Which He Carried Her Back to Los Angeles—After Overhauling Her Chicago Train.

FIGURE 1.2. Article in *The Charleston Daily Mail,* December 11, 1921. The central panel is captioned, "'Abduction of Helen of Troy,' the Famous Painting by Rudolph von Deutsch that May Have Inspired Edward Fawcett to Carry Off Elise Hilliger in his Airplane."

unleashed by the movies, were not so easily distinguished.[59] A 1933 survey by the sociologist Herbert Blumer investigates in great detail the moral influence of the movies on young people.[60] Clothing, seduction, romance, and sexual behavior are prominent themes among both sexes, but especially among the female subjects, who claim to be learning not only fashion and beauty tips but

59. Cf. deCordova 1990: 138–39.

60. On Blumer and the Payne Fund studies, see Black 1994: 151–54; Jowett et al. 1996; Fuller 1996: ch. 9.

techniques for kissing and seduction. The glamor and independence of female stars were empowering in other ways too, allowing young women to fantasize about divorce as well as marriage, and fostering "resentment of parental control."[61]

In response to such threats, censors, critics, and censorious members of the public (even prior to the infamous Production Code) were alert for impropriety on screen, especially where female sexual behavior was concerned.[62] In order to evade censorship—formal or informal—the movie vamp or "fallen woman" had to receive her comeuppance.[63] At the end of *Flesh and the Devil* (1926), for example, the vamp (Greta Garbo) drowns in a freezing pond. Lulu (Louise Brooks), the hedonistic heroine of *Pandora's Box* (1929), ends up murdered by Jack the Ripper.[64] A "fallen" woman might be reformed, and even aspire to domestic bliss via love and marriage to the right man; but such affairs rarely work out; "motion picture morals dictated that infidelity lead to tragedy rather than divorce and remarriage."[65]

Among the many newspaper stories recounting her legend, vamp-Helen receives the appropriate comeuppance in a few more learned entries, by way of an obscure ancient tale about her death in Rhodes at the hands of vengeful women.[66] On screen, however, she always survives. As in antiquity, the beauty that makes her infinitely desirable saves her, in the end, from the fate merited by her scandalous ways. There is a marked contrast here with the other principal vamp from Mediterranean antiquity, the "dangerous but defeatable" Cleopatra, who is doomed in advance to the "inescapable closure" of death.[67]

61. Blumer 1933: 67, 157. The movies also spurred desires in girls for foreign travel and college, and inspired ambitions for careers ranging from professional musician to private secretary (Blumer 1933: 157–70). For the influence of Hollywood stars on fans in Britain, see S. Alexander 1989: 264–66; Stacey 1994: 158–59, 237–38. For Australia, see Conor 2004: ch. 3.

62. See further Schumach 1975; Everson 1978: 152–54; deCordova 1990: 129–36; L. Jacobs 1991; Card 1994: 6–7; Staiger 1995; Higashi 2002: 315–17; Olsson 2008: ch. 5.

63. On the "fallen woman" film, see Higashi 1978: 88–95; Fishbein 1989; L. Jacobs 1991. On the frustration or punishment of the female look in silent film, see L. Williams 1984.

64. For the US release, it was censored and the ending moralized to reform Lulu (Pratt 1973: 390; Card 1994: 207).

65. Higashi 1978: 93.

66. E.g., Anon. 1911; cf. Blondell 2013: 41–42.

67. Wyke 2002: 297; Wyke 1997: 89.

Though Helen is rarely granted a "happy" ending, her story never receives this particular kind of closure. The "world's greatest 'vamp'" is the one who gets away.

Beauty's Highest Form

Despite Helen's affinity for the Hollywood screen, there are complications in reconceptualizing this particular legendary figure in cinematic terms—complications arising directly from her mythic identity as the most beautiful woman in the world. The ancient Greeks seem to have thought of beauty—at least in principle—as an objective property.[68] Paris might appear to have based his famous Judgment on personal taste, but it is understood that any man would make the same choice, since Aphrodite just *is* erotic beauty. The same principle underpins the willingness of Paris—and indeed of all Helen's suitors—to choose her sight unseen.[69] Ideas about objectivity also underlie, in a slightly different way, the disturbingly popular notion that transcendent female beauty can be portrayed via an assemblage of body parts—a notion that can be traced back to a "portrait" of Helen by the famous fifth-century BCE Greek painter Zeuxis.[70]

Outside myth, however, the idea of absolute beauty runs aground on the undeniable fact that different people have different preferences, or to use the modern cliché, that beauty is in the eye of the beholder.[71] If beauty is, in its essence, a subjective response, then the notion of "*the* most beautiful woman in the world" simply makes no sense. We are *unable* to conceive of a Helen in the Greek sense, one who just *is* the most beautiful of all. To complicate things further, the romantic ideology of beauty values specificity and uniqueness, to the point where "flaws" may be deemed necessary to individuate even Helen from what would otherwise be a mere stereotype.[72]

68. Cf. Pollitt 1974: 12–23; Barasch 1985: 16–18, 20; Steiner 2001: 32–44; Blondell 2013: 2–3.

69. In Greek myth, Helen's suitors court her based solely on her renown (Blondell 2013: 30).

70. According to legend, Zeuxis combined the finest body parts from five young female models to produce his painting of Helen (Squire 2011: 81–84). His procedure was often imitated in the Renaissance (Barasch 1985: 125, 146). More recently, to create the truly perfect face, an "expert" named Julian De Silva "combined Amber Heard's nose, Kim Kardashian's eyebrows, Scarlett Johansson's eyes, Rihanna's face shape, Emily Ratajkowski's lips and Kate Moss' forehead" (Harrison 2017).

71. On the subjectivity of beauty, see Kirwan 1999 and cf. Maguire 2009: 74–78.

72. For the tradition of Helen's "flaw" (starting in the late sixteenth century), see Maguire 2009: 59–65, 69.

Yet the objectivity of beauty is not so easily dispatched. Its persistence in defiance of the beholder's eye creates a tension detectable throughout history. A famous poem about Helen by the Greek poet Sappho provides an early example.[73] In the competitive beauty culture of the early twentieth century the theme played a conspicuous role. One newspaper informs us that the choice of even twelve women as "most beautiful" has "aroused a storm of controversy," showing that beauty is "a matter of taste" and "as one sees it."[74] Yet if all personal judgments are equally legitimate, why should there be any controversy, let alone a "storm"? How, indeed, can we even hold such contests, since the very notion of competition implies some kind of objective criterion for judgment?[75]

In early Hollywood, the tension was mediated to some extent by classifying women into "types"—derived in part from the traditions of nineteenth-century art—which were coded by both appearance and behavior.[76] Some types were supplied by geography or nationalism (the American, and her subtypes, was a matter of special concern). Other notable types were the Vamp or Siren, the Madonna, the Flapper, and the Tomboy or Outdoor Girl. Several were derived from antiquity, including the Venus, the Diana, the Cleopatra, and the Helen.[77] All were in principle commensurable, but types could also be ranked as such. When two rival Australian beauties were designated a Venus and a Madonna respectively, the success of the latter pleased those who considered the Madonna type "beauty's highest form."[78] Thanks to the legacy of philhellenism, the "classic" beauty retained a certain normative status, associated with the timeless and universal.[79] This made her the preferred high-cultural choice. A woman known as "the American Beauty" may be the

73. See further Blondell 2013: 111–16. For this problem in treatments of Helen, see Maguire 2009: 74–78.

74. Anon. 1922b.

75. On the tension between subjective and "objective" criteria for judging the Miss America Pageant, see Deford 1971: 50–52, 101–2; Banet-Weiser 1999: 53–56.

76. The principal types are discussed in Conor 2004. On "typing" in nineteenth-century American art (especially the preoccupation with identifying an American type), see Banta 1987.

77. The latter two are variants of the Vamp or Siren (M. Williams 2013a: 50–51); the Venus embodied "female heterosexual maturity with sublime aesthetics and modern fashion," while the "modern Diana" was more boyish, slimmer, and sportier (Carden-Coyne 2009: 241).

78. Conor 2004: 287 n. 34; cf. figure 2.5 below.

79. In nineteenth-century art the "Grecian type . . . by tradition was the official Type, since Platonism rubbed off on all creatures in diaphanous draperies" (Banta 1987: 396).

FIGURE 1.3. Florence Colgate as shown on ABC News.

undisputed "champion of feminine loveliness" based on the "verdict of the masses," but an "expert" claims the title, instead, for a "perfect blonde" with "classic" and "distinctly Grecian features."[80] In the beauty culture of early Hollywood, however, even the "classic" is usually just another type.

Though typing allowed for some choice in these matters, it did not ultimately resolve the tension between objective and subjective judgment. In the twenty-first century, the popular commitment to the eye of the beholder remains stronger than ever, yet beauty contests persist, along with endless articles in the popular press implying that there are, in fact, objective criteria for judgment. In recent years such criteria have been given a "scientific" imprimatur by evolutionary psychologists. According to the *Daily Mail,* one Florence Colgate "is blessed with what is described as the perfect face. It matches an international blueprint for the optimum ratio between eyes, mouth, forehead and chin, endowing her with flawless proportions" (figure 1.3).[81] Another "expert," Julian De Silva, deems the actor Amber Heard's face the closest to perfection, based on both "scientific facial mapping software" and "ancient Greek" analysis of "the 12 key marker points of the face."[82]

80. Anon. 1921c.

81. P. Harris 2012.

82. Harrison 2017.

Not surprisingly, both these women accord with stereotypical white beauty norms, including blue or green eyes and long, blonde, straight or lightly waved hair: the enduring legacy of the nineteenth-century "fetishization of tall, pale, blond, beautiful Anglo-Saxons."[83] The same applies to the majority of those judged "beautiful" by the plethora of digital tools now available for evaluating beauty. One such app features a "'facial assessment tool': an AI-driven system that promises to look at images of your face to tell you how beautiful you are—or aren't—and then tell you what you can do about it."[84] Such "tools" give an imprimatur of "objectivity" to dominant racist preferences that are baked into the tools themselves, and further perpetuate these biases through their societal influence.[85] Such claims lead to the bizarre conclusion that the eye of the beholder may be mistaken. If you prefer, say, Angelina Jolie over Florence Colgate, you are simply wrong.

Ultimately, the only way to resolve this tension is for all eyes of all beholders to agree. It was, arguably, such agreement that caused the Trojan War.[86] But this solution only works in myth or fantasy. Thanks to the subjectivity of beauty, the closest we can get to "objectivity" in real life is via the democratic criterion of majority opinion. This means that if a majority (or even a plurality) of viewers *think* a particular rendition of Helen is (the most) beautiful then she *is* (the most) beautiful. If we follow this path, we can only conclude that the audience reception of a particular screen Helen tells us not only how effectively the film has impressed viewers with her beauty but how beautiful she actually is. In Yeats's phrase, her beauty is "the crowd's creation."[87] Until the day when the unanimous crowd consists of every viewer, however, the beauty in question will never have the authority of myth.

Mightier than Pen or Sword

Early Hollywood trumpeted the superiority of film over mere written text, bragging, for example, that "Universal Moving Pictures are Mightier than PEN or SWORD."[88] When it comes to transcendent beauty, however, the pen—if

83. Painter 2010: 200.

84. Ryan-Mosley 2021.

85. Levin 2016; Ryan-Mosley 2021.

86. "When men agree on the beauty of a woman war results" (Anon. 1921c).

87. Cf. Jeffares 1989: 9.

88. Everson 1978: 24.

not the sword—enjoys a distinct advantage. It is the verbal nature of epic poetry that allows Homer's Trojan elders, famously, to affirm Helen's godlike beauty without recourse to specifics.[89] Though Homeric epic is often described as "cinematic," a vast gulf remains between the quasi-divine power of the poetic narrator and the camera's inexorable eye.[90] A strictly narrative approach, with its verbal appeal to the imagination, is unavailable, by definition, to the visual artist.[91] Highly stylized genres may approximate such an approach, however, by using simple, easily legible tropes for beauty as such, leaving subtler details to the imagination. In Greek vase painting, for example, Helen's beauty is signified by the same short list of culturally accepted markers of desirability that we find in verbal texts (long hair, light skin, tall stature, fine clothing). Comic books, like Eric Shanower's *Age of Bronze*, work similarly. We are not asked to decide whether such images provide a convincing rendition of supreme beauty, let alone a plausible likeness of a "real" person. Their success depends, rather, on audience buy-in, which is earned by fulfilling certain cultural, generic, and narrative expectations.

Problems are bound to arise, however, if an artist makes any kind of claim to "realism." To be sure, all art is to some degree stylized: there is ultimately no such thing as realism (otherwise there would be no way of distinguishing representations from things). As Murray Smith puts it, "Praising something for its 'realism' depends implicitly on recognizing that it is not of the same order as the thing imitated."[92] Nevertheless, illusionistic realism has often been seen as the ultimate goal of the visual artist. Zeuxis—the same artist famed for his composite Helen—supposedly demonstrated his skill by making a painting of grapes so realistic that birds tried to peck at them.[93] Such anecdotes draw attention to the fact that a representation is just a representation, exposing the fantasy of illusionistic realism for what it is. Yet tradition is replete with the yearning to cross the line between image and living creature, especially where female beauty is concerned.[94]

89. See *Iliad* 3.156–58 and cf. Braudy 2002: 27. On the indescribability of (Helen's) beauty, and the hazards of supplying detail, see Maguire 2009: ch. 2.

90. For this aspect of Homer, see Clay 2011; Graziosi 2013: 24–33.

91. "The impossibility of rendering visible the ideal . . . is not simply an aesthetic predicament; it is an ontological one" (E. Mansfield 2007: xiii).

92. M. Smith 1995: 32–33.

93. See further E. Mansfield 2007.

94. This aspiration is conveyed by the many stories about agalmatophilia, of which the most famous concern the statue of Aphrodite known as the Cnidia (with which men allegedly tried

Photography took fantasies of illusionistic realism to a new level. The camera was thought of as a superior version of the eye, which captured reality in a more truthful and objective way than previous visual media.[95] A photograph gives the impression of an "invisible umbilicus joining image and referent, the link which commands, often beyond reason . . . a belief that the scene *did* exist."[96] This "indexical" realism is reinforced by the camera's ability to "reproduce" minute surface detail—the kind of specificity that says "*we are the real.*"[97] *Moving* pictures took these realisms still further by endowing "the changeless image" with "*the breath of life.*"[98] Echoing the Zeuxis anecdote, cinema's founding legend claims that spectators reacted to the first moving images—such as a speeding train—as if they were "real."[99] Synchronized sound rendered such images even more "realistic" by providing "PICTURES that TALK like LIVING PEOPLE!"[100]

This proud claim to the "realistic" presentation of "living people" gave the upstart new medium of film a way of asserting its superiority over traditional media. Despite their high-cultural halo, neither Venus de Milo nor Apollo Belvedere can walk, talk, breathe or sing. The difference is particularly clear when actors share the frame with artworks, producing a visual contrast between living people and static, monochrome objects. It is clarified more dramatically in the many films that set the latter in motion, using cinematic magic to bring artworks to life. In so doing, film seemed to realize, at last, the dreams of art and legend, which are replete with the yearning to animate static images.[101]

---

to have sex), and Pygmalion's passion for the sculpted Galatea (see Nead 2007: 58–68; cf. Konstan 2014: 21–24).

95. See McQuire 1998: part 1 and cf. Winkler 2009: 9–10.

96. McQuire 1998: 15.

97. Barthes 1986: 148. On indexical realism, see Bazin & Gray 1967: 12–14, 96–98; Barthes 1981: 4–6; Herwitz 2008: 71–77. On the plethora of film realisms, see further Comolli 1980 [1971]; Sontag 1982 [1963]: 350; Ang 1985: ch. 1; Carroll 1985; Fiske 1987: ch. 2; McQuire 1998; Hallam & Marshment 2000; C. Williams 2000; Braudy 2002: 20–33; Maltby 2003: 229–37; G. King 2005. For a good brief account, see Stam 2004: 7–15.

98. *Photoplay*, December 1918. On the equation of movement with life, cf. Nead 2007: 45–46.

99. See Gunning 1999 [1989]; and cf. Nead 2007: 26, 173.

100. *Photoplay* ad quoted in McQuire 1998: 85.

101. See K. Gross 1992. That yearning reached a peak in the late nineteenth century (Nead 2007: ch. 2). For ancient Greece, see Steiner 2001: ch. 3.

Not coincidentally, the fulfilment of such fantasies has been a perennial movie theme, ever since Méliès himself played Pygmalion.[102] Animating Greek statues, specifically, allowed Hollywood to appropriate the prestige of antiquity while implying that film is "more radiant, complete, modern, democratic and alive."[103] It is no coincidence that this trope so frequently concerns Venus, the divine exemplar of the desired and desiring female. The "realism" of even still photography was thought to make images of bodies more arousing, but *moving* pictures took "realistic" eroticism to a scandalous new level.[104]

The exaltation of photorealism has troubling implications for the representation of beauty. Close-ups, in particular, allow us to scrutinize and judge a subject's face and body in minute detail—and judge we will.[105] The camera's "fiendishly keen eye" makes even "a slight bump on the nose assume the proportions of Mount Everest."[106] From the earliest days of cinema, supposed imperfections were countered by makeup, surgery, and any other means available, in order to align newcomers with previously approved conventional types.[107] Yet despite the studios' preference for such types, they also wanted stars to be individual in appearance.[108] In live action cinema, moreover, no matter how generic a character may seem, the medium itself pulls away from typing and towards uniqueness. In Murray Smith's words, "The physical uniqueness of a real person (a performer) represents in an iconic and indexical fashion the physical uniqueness of a fictive person (the character)."[109] This is

102. Such films include *A Tinted Venus* (1921), *Night Life of the Gods* (1935), *One Touch of Venus* (1948, 1955), *Jupiter's Darling* (1955), *Love Goddess* (1988), *Purple Rose of Cairo* (1985), and the Disney *Hercules* (1997). On film as "pygmalionesque," see James 2011 (esp. ch. 4 on Venus) and cf. Nead 2007: ch. 2; Adriaensens 2013; M. Williams 2013a: ch. 2. For Méliès as Pygmalion, see Michelakis 2017: 26.

103. Michelakis & Wyke 2013: 19. A similar effect is produced by posing living stars with statues of Venus, which makes them seem "more vibrant, present and contemporary" than the goddess (M. Williams 2018: 138; cf. above, p. 9).

104. Nead 2007: 173. See further Nead 2007: ch. 5 and cf. Knippschild 2013: 320–21. In Ovid's account of Pygmalion, it is modesty that initially prevents the statue from *moving* (Ovid, *Metamorphoses* 10.250).

105. On the spectator's position of mastery, see Ellis 1992: 81–84.

106. H. Lang 1930; cf. Addison 2006: 10, 14. For the impact of the proximate gaze on the evaluation of beauty, see Conor 2004: 131–32.

107. Cf. Mellencamp 1995: 211–12.

108. Finler 2012: 39–40.

109. M. Smith 1995: 19.

especially true of the close-up, in so far as the face, as the site of human uniqueness, is "the portrait that reveals character."[110] The more "realistic" and individual the resulting image, the more strongly the viewer's subjective responses are activated, threatening the mythic power of stylized beauty. With its proximate gaze and ability to reach mass audiences, the camera invites disagreement among the multitude of beholding eyes.

One of the ways in which the studios touted film's unprecedented "realism" was by presenting the screen as a "window" through which we can look "directly at a 'real' world, present or past."[111] Better yet, film can "transport one to the very scene, defying time and distance."[112] As a magical mode of transportation, it enables the lucky viewer to "walk the streets of Paris; ride with the cowboy of the West; or delve in the depths of earth with swarthy miners."[113] As the same author explains, the traveler is also transported emotionally: "He feels . . . the thrill of human sympathy with some child of poverty or sorrow; perhaps with some dainty maid in silk attire." If we are cinematically transported to ancient Troy or Sparta, then, we may expect to "thrill" at the sight of the dainty Helen as if she "really is" the world's most beautiful woman.

The fact that such beauty is strictly mythical was no deterrent in itself. Indeed, one reason Hollywood was so enamored of Greek myth was precisely its provision of material that is not of this world—the supernatural, the monstrous, the unreal—as fodder for the new medium's illusionistic power. Even the most fantastical stories must be rendered "realistic" in the sense of transporting the spectator to a believable world.[114] Within such a world, film can "realistically" show us a Zeus hurling thunderbolts, the superhuman feats of a Hercules, or the size and monstrosity of a Polyphemus.[115] This is also the kind of world in which Helen's beauty is, after all, conceivable: only in myth can an

110. Bordwell et al. 1985: 54. This is why for facial close-ups, unlike longer shots or close-ups of a hand or foot, the actor cannot be replaced by a double.

111. Rosenstone 2001 [1995]: 54.

112. Hansen 1985: 331 (quoting Universal Pictures promotional copy). Theater architecture often presented the moviegoing experience as a window or entrance into the ancient world (Michelakis and Wyke 2013: 8).

113. Fitch 1910.

114. See Hallam & Marshment 2000: 82–84. On the importance of photographic "realism" in representing the *un*real, see Bazin 1997 [1946].

115. Portrayal of the Greek gods is a bone of contention among those concerned with "realism" in ancient world cinema. For various approaches, see F. Martin 2002: 90–93; Squire 2011: ch. 5; Winkler 2015d; Gordon 2017: 224–26. Arguably the gods should be excised because to

anthropomorphic god hurl thunder, a hero support the world on his shoulders, a cyclops dash men's brains out, or a woman's face cause the greatest war of all time. But beauty, as a subjective phenomenon, is crucially different from strength, size, one-eyed monstrosity, or even thunderbolt-hurling. We do not need to feel Hercules's fist in our faces to accept that he is strong; but we do need to feel the impact of Helen's beauty to believe that she is beautiful. If the viewer does not respond personally to a representation of beauty, its impact will be alienating (often comically so).

Fantasy genres can bypass at least some of these problems. They may simply stipulate, for example, that someone has superhuman powers, or that a love spell attracts all viewers (intradiegetically) to a person of even ordinary appearance. The viewer can accept such matters as "really" happening—in a world in which we do not live. But the effectiveness of such methods depends on the extradiegetic and intradiegetic framing of the phenomenon in question. When magic is used to denote the supernatural power of Helen's beauty, it is typically presented *not* as explaining an ordinary woman's extraordinary power, but as a true expression of her beauty. This originates in the *Odyssey*, where Helen's supernatural nature, as the daughter of Zeus, is symbolized by a magic drug that she uses to banish negative emotions.[116] The spell she casts does not defy the normal relations of cause and effect; it is inherent in the fact of her beauty.

A filmmaker who eschews blatant invocations of the supernatural must find other ways to suggest transcendence without sacrificing the relevant brand of realism.[117] Such methods include many cinematic techniques, from script to mise-en-scène, lighting, editing, soundtrack and so on.[118] A filmmaker can use the same conventions as stills artists, who "gilded their sitters" with "heavenly radiance" like the halo of a saint.[119] Cinematic tricks can also convey, for

---

modern eyes they appear to eliminate human agency (see, e.g., Purves 2014b). In practice, however, this is rarely an issue for viewers.

116. See further Blondell 2013: 79–81.

117. Victorian painters addressed the problem of Helen by using conventional signifiers (such as rich costume, sensuous luxury, and hair color) to suggest "timelessness" without erasing the sitter's individuality (Inglis 2001: 76–80). On ways to counteract the individuating power of faces, cf. M. Smith 1995: 135–37.

118. For examples of cinematically enhanced beauty, see Walker 1967: 124 (Jean Harlow); Dyer 1998: 64 (Marlene Dietrich); Barton 2010: 74 (Hedy Lamarr). Cf. also Mellencamp 1995: 28–31.

119. Shields 2013: 368.

example, Helen's extraordinary impact on the internal audience.[120] But they cannot bestow verisimilitude on that beauty as such. There is no special effect that can, by itself, make a specific image of a woman seem beautiful to all or even most viewers.[121] For this reason, cinematic effects can only take us so far in the quest to convey supernatural beauty in a "realistic" manner.

The Present Dressed in Funny Clothes

As if all this were not enough, classical Hollywood subscribes to yet another kind of realism, namely a storytelling style that stresses the importance of individual psychology and human agency in propelling choices and plot.[122] This requires movie characters to think and feel in ways that enable the audience to understand their motivations and "relate" to them as if they were "real people." Even characters from exotic cultures—including the past and future—must be represented as individualized characters with "personality," whose words and actions are "authentic" in terms that have been naturalized within the culture of viewing. This is often justified by invoking a "universal" human nature, which just happens to map onto the norms in question.[123]

Once again, the facial close-up is of special importance. By betraying all the subtleties of feeling and expression, such shots convey a sense of inner life that invites the audience to relate to the character as "real."[124] This is especially significant for the screen performance of romance, where the close-up

120. For a good example, see below, p. 233.

121. In films of the *Odyssey*, the song of the Sirens presents a comparable problem. As one critic of *Ulysses* (1954) observed, "To be convincingly enchanting, the music that Ulysses heard would have had to be of such surpassing beauty as to convince the audiences and enchant them as he was enchanted" (Hugh Gray 1956: 350). In *Ulysses*, the problem is solved by giving them Penelope's voice, which marks the effect as a subjective one (compare the incident in the *Odyssey* in which each man hears Helen's voice as his own wife's: Blondell 2013: 83–84).

122. The standard work on classical Hollywood style remains Bordwell et al. 1985. For the importance of emotional and psychological realism to consumers of popular culture, see Ang 1985: 28–34, 41–46; Jenkins 2013: 107–19.

123. On the tension between historical specificity and alleged "universality," see Staiger 2000: ch. 11.

124. On the emotional impact and "overpowering intimacy" of the close-up, see Card 1994: 21–23 and cf. Bordwell et al. 1985: 190–92; Stacey 1994: 210; Dyer 1998: 15, 118–21; Maltby 2003: 379. The performer's voice further fosters such involvement, in part by suggesting the existence of "the hidden self" (Braudy 2002: 217; cf. 189–90, 213–14).

"foreground[s] the star's position as an ideal of beauty and sexual desirability," especially by zeroing in on the kiss and accompanying facial expressions.[125] Facial close-ups not only raise the stakes regarding the representation of beauty, then, but invite identification with the woman behind the face as a particular "real" person, as opposed to a mere type.[126]

These realisms of character and psychology are typically reinforced, for people from the distant past, by locating them in an environment replete with "authentic" detail. Taking advantage of the contemporary enthusiasm for the *Realien* of archeology, Hollywood studios from the outset maintained research departments, whose remit was to dress the "window" into the past with appropriate concrete particulars—architecture, clothing, weaponry, and so on.[127] This in turn serves psychological realism, since "once a realist mise-en-scène is established, there is an impulse to read the characters and events within it according to realist expectations."[128] The result is, in most cases, a heavily stylized and historically arbitrary rendition of antiquity, whose ahistoricity is veiled by fetishizing the "authentic realism" of the mise-en-scène.[129] The antiquarianism to which most such films pay lip service thus functions, typically, as a way of distracting us from the *in*authenticity of emotions, thought-structures, and social interactions. The past turns out to be less, in L. P. Hartley's famous words, a "foreign country," than "the present dressed in funny clothes."[130]

The funny clothes are important, in so far as they are the primary signifier of historical difference.[131] Yet costume also supports psychological realism by assisting in the expression of character, especially by accumulating the kind of

125. Wexman 1993: 144. See also Wexman 1993: 17–19 and cf. Morin 2005: 145.

126. This is why, in Hirsch's view, characters in historical epic should be "observed as icons seen typically in long shot rather than close-up" (Hirsch 1978: 45). Cf. the way that the close-up "subverts melodramatic moral typage" (Affron 1991: 110).

127. On film's colonialist celebration of "its ethnographic and quasi-archaeological powers to resuscitate forgotten and distant civilizations," see Shohat 1991: 49–51 (the quotation is from p. 51).

128. Hallam & Marshment 2000: 82.

129. Custen 1992: 40 (quoting an MGM press book). On techniques for constructing "realism" in historical film, see Custen 1992: 34–45, 111–18; Sobchak 2003 [1990]; Lindner 2005; Pierson 2005; Stubbs 2013: ch. 2; Llewellyn-Jones 2018; M. Williams 2018: 204.

130. The latter phrase is from Braudy 2002: 91.

131. Wexman 1993: 138–39.

detail that promotes "identification and involvement."[132] This is particularly important for female characters. Clothing and accessories have always been integral to the construction of femininity: a woman "is what she wears."[133] Along with makeup, hairstyling, and other forms of decoration, costume is an extension of the body creating an (often ill-defined) transition between that body and the world.[134] This was already implicit in the Greek myth of Pandora, the first woman, who is literally constructed of clothing and adornments.[135] A women's magazine from 1923 makes the point more positively:

I love to watch women of commonplace molding
  Transformed by the wearing of exquisite things,
In garments of beauty their splendor unfolding
  As grubs into butterflies claiming their wings.[136]

As this poem suggests, the options open to a woman are often expressed through her available wardrobe, making her clothing preferences a means of revealing (or constructing) her appearance and, by extension, her character. The choices available to ancient Greek beauties, as conceived by Hollywood, are all variations on the theme of "mere draperies," ranging from the allure of modest virtue (subdued solid colors, matte textures, limited accessories),[137] to the vamp's outrageous eroticism (revealing, luminescent clothes and an abundance of gleaming jewelry).[138] Wherever they lie on this spectrum, however, all costume designs are informed not only by the designers' ideas about antiquity but by the period in which the film is made, helping contemporary viewers to respond to their wearers as people like themselves.[139]

132. Gaines 1990a: 19. On the use of costume to express character and advance narrative in classic Hollywood style, see Gaines 1990b.

133. Gaines 1990a: 1.

134. See further Steele 1985: ch. 7; Gaines & Herzog 1990.

135. See further Loraux 1993: ch. 2; Zeitlin 1996: ch. 2; Blondell 2013: 7–10, 15–22.

136. The poem, by Angela Morgan, is reprinted from *Red Book*, December 1923.

137. Unadorned, "classical" drapery traditionally conveys lofty nobility, virtue, truth and beauty (Hollander 1978: 2–3, 64–65, 81, 277). For "mere draperies," see above, p. 10.

138. For the ancient Greek equation of jewelry with the "shining" of erotic beauty, see Blondell 2013: 7–10. On sparkle and glamor, see Postrel 2013: 120–22 and cf. Hollander 1978: 342–44.

139. See further Hollander 1978: 295–307, and cf. Llewellyn-Jones's discussions of Cleopatra and Delilah (2002: 290–96; 2005). Hair and makeup, especially, are almost always modern (Annas 1987).

These various techniques for producing psychological realism can make the most stylized fantasy and absurdest narrative—not to mention the cheesiest special effects—seem "real."[140] But they create yet more problems for presenting the world's most beautiful woman on screen. If the dramatis personae must appear to have real, understandable feelings and motives for their behavior, then the woman brought before our eyes as Helen must seem beautiful enough to explain—if not justify—the willingness of two great armies to fight over her, for ten years, at enormous cost in slaughter on both sides. She must preempt the viewer's inclination toward skepticism, scorn, or amusement at the idea of fighting such a war over any woman, let alone this particular one. If the Helen in question seems subpar, we may decide that the Greek and/or Trojan men are making fools of themselves over a woman who does not match her reputation. While this is a linchpin of much comedy at Helen's expense, it is fatal to any attempt to convince us of a screen Helen's "real" beauty.

At this point the reader may reasonably object that even within the parameters of "realistic" cinema the audience is not foolish enough to confuse image with reality (the train anecdote notwithstanding).[141] The screen may pose as a window but is really a picture frame, which draws attention to the artfully constructed nature of what it presents to view. This is markedly true for historical films, as for myth and fantasy and other forms of exotica. Not only are their subjects and environments known to be dead or nonexistent, but viewers are constantly reminded of this fact by such distancing factors as exotic costume, extraordinary spectacle, and the familiar faces of modern stars—not to mention the fact that everyone typically speaks English.[142] Surely, then, we do not have to fall in love with the Helen on screen to accept her as a "realistic" representation of a woman with whom every man would fall in love.

140. NBC's head of programming was bowled over by the "reality" of the first pilot for the original *Star Trek*, despite its famously primitive special effects. He said that although he had seen many outer-space films, "I've never felt I was aboard a spacecraft. I never believed the crew was a real crew. But you guys gave me the feeling of total belief. I loved it" (Solow & Justman 1997: 59).

141. Cf. Maltby 2003: 380–84; Carroll 1985: 79–80. For the train anecdote, see above, p. 21.

142. This is exacerbated by the difficulty of finding an appropriate level of diction (cf. Llewellyn-Jones 2009: 574; Blanshard & Shahabudin 2011: 19). Hirsch argues that this makes silent film more suitable for ancient world epic (1978: 43–45).

Yet it is an inescapable fact that audiences have been "falling in love" with on-screen beauties since the beginning of cinema.[143] This is also the response to which we are predisposed as viewers. We are voluntarily trapped, "willingly undergoing a fixed term of imprisonment."[144] Just as we want to believe, however temporarily, in the "reality" of Zeus, Hercules and the monstrous cyclops, so we also want to believe (no more and no less) in a Helen beautiful enough to cause an epic war. Like Zeuxis's birds, we long to peck at those grapes. In subsequent chapters, we shall see this corroborated by the extent to which viewers disregard conventional wisdom—the eye of the beholder—and privilege their own responses to a Helen as a true measure of her beauty. This double vision, which subtends much of the pleasure of viewing, encourages us to judge that beauty by how it affects us personally—and condemn it if she fails.

The Choice Film Assignment of All Movie History

The pitfalls surrounding beauty, representation, and realism make bringing Helen to the screen a perilous enterprise. As the "essential" feminine, or the embodiment of physical perfection as such, she must transcend particularity; in so far as the goal is "realism," however, she must have a compelling visual and personal individuality, of a kind that makes her specific as well as extraordinary in the eyes of all beholders.

One approach, in theory, would be not to show Helen at all, but to use the reactions of the internal audience, combined with her concealed body, to provoke the imagination of the external audience and triangulate their desire. Indeed, if beauty is in its essence subjective, this is arguably the *only* effective approach. Many films have used this technique in the case of Jesus, for comparable reasons.[145] But Helen is not protected by piety. More to the point, in the context of popular cinema, her identity as the ultimate object of desire imposes an imperative to *show* her famous face. According to the trivia page for *Troy* on the Internet Movie Database (IMDb)—which I have not been

143. See, e.g., deCordova 1990: 90; Fowles 1992: 161–62; Babington 2001: 1–2; Barbas 2001: 16–17; Morin 2005: 60–67.

144. Elsaesser 1981: 271. On the complicitous spectator, see further Comolli 1980: 138–40; Neale 1990: 163–66; M. Smith 1995: 41–45, 54–58; Aaron 2005.

145. He is "a potent force for historical change yet also unrepresentable precisely because He also supposedly represents the timeless" (West 2015).

able to authenticate—"Wolfgang Petersen originally didn't want Helen to appear in the movie. He felt that an actress couldn't live up to the audience's expectations, but the producers insisted she appear." In the words of a medieval romance, "Nature had made her to be beheld and seen."[146] To put it in more contemporary terms, she is defined by her to-be-looked-at-ness.[147]

If beauty really is in the eye of the beholder, of course, it should not matter what Helen looks like (provided certain male characters respond appropriately in order to generate the story). The same applies to another narrative strategy that is often used to circumvent such problems, that is, declaring Helen merely an excuse for the Trojan War (as opposed to its cause). This means the war is not about her or her beauty, or even about men and their desire—at least not their desire for women; it is about their desire for wealth or power, for which Helen serves merely as a more or less plausible pretext. In such a scenario, she could, in theory, be portrayed as an average woman who just happens to appeal to certain men. Tellingly, however, directors have eschewed this approach. It is very clear in *Troy*, for example, that Helen is only a pretext for Greek aggression, but this did not prevent the director, Wolfgang Petersen, from declaring, "She has to be believable as the face that launched 1,000 ships."[148] As the inevitable Marlovian allusion reminds us, it is Helen's face and its consequences that give her myth its enduring power. No matter what turns her story may take, then, any representation must engage somehow with her identity as the most beautiful woman in the world.

In making Helen's beauty visible, most films begin with conventional signifiers, grounded in contemporary tastes and expectations, which are inflected to varying degrees by historicity. The foundation is always long hair (usually but not always blonde), a slender figure, and the "mere draperies" synonymous with antiquity, which range from voluminous to barely there. This kind of generic marker can be used to preempt questions of "realism," much as it does with Greek vase painting.[149] In *The Story of Mankind* (1957), for instance—an eccentric film about the afterlife featuring various historical events—Dani Crayne's hair, features, costume, and gestures, in her vignette as Helen, provide a cartoonlike sketch that makes its point without any

146. Scherer 1967: 371.

147. This influential term was coined in Mulvey 2009 [1975]; cf. also Squire 2011: 82.

148. Fleming 2003.

149. Cf. above, p. 20.

attempt at individuation.[150] The so-called peplum films present similarly stylized character types without apology—indeed, with relish.[151] Yet "types" are not intrinsically "unrealistic." Rather, they establish expectations, mediating between the viewer's experience and reality. Even the most generic live-action Helen is inhabited by an embodied performer and becomes "realistic" if we turn our attention to that performer's specificity.

This brings us to the all-important matter of casting. The movies' obsession with beauty would seem to make the role of Helen, as one 1950s Hollywood-watcher put it, "the choice film assignment of all movie history."[152] The selection of an actor for this assignment must begin with a "beautiful" face and figure, but it cannot end there.[153] Beauty and especially glamor are sometimes associated with impassivity or lack of movement, but if a woman looks her best in still photographs, her beauty is not "stageable."[154] In a *motion* picture, a static, expressionless face, however well proportioned, is alienating rather than alluring.[155] (It is no accident that "wooden" is a standard descriptor for poor acting.) The performance of beauty, in so far as it depends on the close-up, requires particular subtlety. As one beauty advisor warns us, a blank expression "will ruin the best of good looks."[156] An actor's voice is also important, especially considering voice's time-honored role in the expression of seductive femininity.

150. As the word "cartoon" implies, the use of typing is at its most extreme in animation, on which see Wells 2007: 201: "It is not an act of record, but of interpretation, and has the advantage of not having to be mediated through the available 'signs' of live actors, physical locations, material period costumes, etc." This means, ironically, that the characters are genuinely themselves (as opposed to being actors).

151. The term "peplum" refers to a wave of films about antiquity, often cheaply made and mostly Italian, that emerged in the post-WWII period alongside that period's historical epics. See further Lucanio 1994; Pomeroy 2008: ch. 3; Pomeroy 2013; Pomeroy 2017; Shahabudin 2009; O'Brien 2014; Rushing 2016; Blanshard 2017: 437–40.

152. Anon. 1954a.

153. The need to choose a single actor for the role is not absolute in principle, but multiple casting would prevent us from identifying (with) Helen as a specific real person (see M. Smith 1995: 24–29 and cf. 130–32).

154. Shields 2013: 44. Postrel argues that still photography conveys the glamor of the stars (2013: 177–78), as distinct from charisma, "which requires a live performance" (2013: 117).

155. That is the premise underlying, for example, the classic horror film *Eyes Without a Face* (1960). Even at rest, the beautiful face should convey "a sort of internal mobility like the mysteriously alive waters of a still fountain" (Tyler 1970 [1947]: 56).

156. Anon. 1923a.

The performer's effectiveness thus depends not only on her features but on her ability to employ the resources of gesture, demeanor, and voice—in other words, to act. As Hedy Lamarr put it (and she should know), "You can't just take some bosomy cutie and by giving her some sexy lines and tight costumes create a glamour girl. Sophia Loren would be a glamour girl even if she were in rags selling fish. She has the look, the movement, and the intellect."[157] A powerful performance can even trump supposedly "objective" appearances. Bette Davis, for example, is not conventionally beautiful. According to Molly Haskell, "She was universally considered unsexy" in Hollywood, "not to say unusable"; nevertheless, Haskell argues, she has a beauty and charm that are "willed into being"; she convinces us that she is beautiful and sexy "by the vividness of her own self-image."[158]

The next question is whether to cast an unknown or a star. Helen's mythic identity would seem to situate her at the apex of the star system, which was occupied, in Hollywood's golden age, by "that unique creature, the film goddess—one who provokes admiration, imitation and sometimes the most total and irrational devotion of a multitude of worshipers."[159] Such stars, often referred to as "love goddesses,"[160] become public signifiers, allowing audiences to draw on the collective desire that is produced and reproduced through circulation of their images.[161] This kind of iconic energy is concentrated in the sex symbols of collective fantasy—the Marilyn Monroes—whose burden of erotic signification far outstrips their identity as individuals.

Yet even the most brilliant star is at the same time a "real" person whose life extends beyond her screen presence, linking her many manifestations to provide a measure of coherence and continuity. There is a mutually reinforcing

157. Lamarr 1967: 85.

158. Haskell 2016: 217, 221. The first quotation refers to *Jezebel* (1938), the second to *Beyond the Forest* (1949).

159. Card 1994: 159. On stardom, see further deCordova 1990; Gledhill 1991; Ellis 1992: ch. 6; Allen & Gomery 1993: 172–85; Wexman 1993: 19–25; Mayne 1993: ch. 6; Stacey 1994; Geraghty 2000; Barbas 2001; Maltby 2003: 141–54; Dyer 1998; Dyer 2004; Morin 2005; Llewelyn-Jones 2018: ch. 4.

160. See further Wexman 1993: ch. 4 and cf. Haskell 2016: 102–17. For the analogy between Greek goddesses and Hollywood goddesses, see also Maurice 2019: 94–95.

161. For the "complicated game of desires that plays out around the figure of the star," see Ellis 1992: 98. For beauty and (heterosexual) love as the essence of stardom, see Morin 2005 with Dyer 1998: 45–46.

synergy between this "real" identity and a star's onscreen performances.[162] The effect is further enhanced by the nature of star acting. In so far as the essence of stardom is "to be recognized within and beyond any role," stars are not expected to act in a way that conceals their identity.[163] Rather, "the star is permitted to underact . . . and this underacting produces the effect that the star behaves rather than acts."[164] In the case of great beauties, this means they perform not by impersonating others, but by radiating personal charisma.[165]

The studios bridged the gulf between love goddesses and their admirers by constructing elaborate star personalities, which typically rest on a foundation of "ordinariness." This helped fans to feel a personal connection to their screen idols, a sense of intimacy fostered on screen by techniques like POV shots and close-ups, and outside the cinema by such memorabilia as letters and signed photos—ordinary objects endowed with a numinous presence. Star casting thus connects us with the "real" person of the star, even while presenting her as a mythic figure, unattainable by those who gaze on her beauty from afar. She is a "magical reconciliation of opposites," "at once ordinary and extraordinary, available for desire and unattainable," ideal yet real, generic yet individual, public, yet private; "powerless, yet powerful; different from 'ordinary' people yet . . . 'just like us.'"[166]

Star discourse is thus—like mythology—a means for managing paradox. We can see this at work in the caption describing Joan Crawford in Waterbury's *Photoplay* article (above, figure 1.1). She is "Venus rising from the movies. Just a modern girl, but Joan Crawford . . ." Crawford—who was indeed, in this period, a rising star—is simultaneously a specific named person, a Greek

162. Cf., e.g., the synergy between Elizabeth Taylor and Cleopatra (Wyke 1997: 101–9; Wyke 2002: 307–15; Llewelyn-Jones 2018: 356–68), Rita Hayworth and Salome (Llewellyn-Jones 2017: 206–10), or Hedy Lamarr and Delilah (Barton 2010: ch. 13).

163. G. King 2002: 150. On the way a star's individuality is revealed through performance, see Ellis 1992: 99–100. See further Seldes 1950: 58–59; McDonald 1998: 182–86; McDonald 2012; G. King 2002: 150–52; Maltby 2003: 384–88; Morin 2005: 117–34; Llewelyn-Jones 2018: 307–24; cf. also Braudy 2002: 191–212.

164. Ellis 1992: 104.

165. In part for this reason, big stars—especially icons of beauty—are often considered "bad" actors. See, e.g., Ringgold 1974: 11–12 and Wood 1989: 57 (Rita Hayworth); Babington & Evans 1993: 221 (Susan Hayward); Buckley 2000: 542 (Gina Lollobrigida); Gundle 2007: 250 (Monica Bellucci); Barton 2010: 171, 173 (Hedy Lamarr).

166. G. King 2002: 172; Ellis 1992: 91; Allen & Gomery 1993: 174.

goddess, and a modern American "girl."[167] The star's paradoxical identity also conditions our response to her performances. A contemporary reviewer of *Flesh and the Devil* declared Greta Garbo, as the vamp character, to be "believable" as a real woman, and as an object of male desire, yet at the same time "both real and unreal until she finally becomes a symbol of sexual appeal rather than any particular bad woman."[168]

The recognition essential to stardom might seem to preclude a sense of immersion in the past. There is, however, a sense in which star casting can actually enhance the representation of historical figures.[169] Star power can seduce us into overlooking the "credibility gap" between actor and role, and star status can assist in representing "not *real historical* figures but rather the *real significance* of historical figures."[170] As George Custen explains, when Queen Elizabeth I is played by a star like Bette Davis, "the moviegoer is drawn to resonant aspects of the impersonator as well as the life impersonated . . . One admires Queen Elizabeth I for her statecraft but also because she is Bette Davis."[171]

If this is true of a role like Elizabeth, a historical figure whose appearance is familiar from portraiture, it is far more so of a mythological creature whose likeness exists only in the imagination. Like the gods and heroes of mythology, stars are anthropomorphic divinities, transcending mere mortals in beauty and prosperity (if not morality). They reach us mediated by verbal and visual representations, which perpetuate their renown, while remaining open to endless manipulation and reinterpretation; they serve, in complicated ways, as models or ideals; they shine—both literally and figuratively—with the radiance of heavenly bodies, which is an expression, in turn, of their personal beauty.[172]

The homology is especially compelling in Helen's case. It is no surprise to find a Greta Garbo fan addressing her idol, in a poem, as a goddess who is

167. On Crawford as star, see Allen & Gomery 1993: 176–85; Barbas 2001: 144–51; below, ch. 2.

168. Pratt 1973: 451.

169. Cf. Späth & Tröhler 2012: 41–45. On stars and historical representation, see further Custen 1992: 17–18, 45–47, 60–67, 193–205; Landy 1996: 22–23.

170. Haskell 2016: 128; Sobchak 2003 [1990]: 310.

171. Custen 1992: 34.

172. On beauty and shining, cf. above, n. 138. "Famous people glow, it's often said" (Braudy 1986: 6). Greek gods dazzle the eyes of mortals; several are identified with heavenly bodies (such as the sun or moon); and a number of heroes become stars upon death (including Helen's brothers, the Dioscuri).

Helen reborn.[173] Like a love goddess, Helen is an icon of beauty and glamor, whose looks and love life are an endless source of public fascination, evaluation, and judgment;[174] she is simultaneously superhuman and "real," endowing material objects with a numinous aura;[175] she is identified with her reputation and captivates even by report, or through her intentionally constructed image (*eidolon*); she is not only eternally young and beautiful, but seductive, evasive, and available for fantasy and appropriation by fans and admirers, who may fall in love with her without ever having seen her in the flesh.

These parallels posit Helen, like a movie star, as an *object* of desire, emulation, envy, blame, or gossip. Yet Helen's spell has always depended, in part, on her own erotic agency, exercised in defiance of male authority. The glamor of the love goddesses, similarly, "carries with it the right to romantic domination. . . . [so that] they are free to assert their own sexual desire independent of patriarchal control."[176] As the "trump of trumps" for women in Hollywood,[177] beauty could also be the avenue to a different kind of power. Like the Greeks who created Helen, the film industry shapes star images for its own purposes. Yet "the money, fame, and erotic desirability with which the industry has endowed them" can render them, at times, "more powerful than the men who created them."[178] Among other things, they may gain control of the very image that empowers them.[179] Granted, only the greatest female stars exercised (or exercise) much real power in Hollywood. Yet films like the perennial *A Star Is Born* (1937, 1954, 1976, 2018) continue to dramatize their emasculating threat.[180] A bona fide star who takes on the role of Helen may thus be

173. M. Williams 2018: 36.

174. On the centrality of private lives (especially romance) to stardom, see deCordova 1990: 98–151; Wexman 1993: 24.

175. Ancient shrines displayed the egg from which Helen hatched, plus a sandal she lost during her elopement (Blondell 2013: 44). In the early twentieth century, enthusiasts sought out artifacts that she might have touched (cf. above, p. 11).

176. Wexman 1993: 156. For glamor as an invitation to "flight and transformation and escape," see Postrel 2013: ch. 3.

177. Shields 2013: 12.

178. Wexman 1993: 156.

179. Leading stars had approval of their own publicity portraits (Finler 2012: 45) and a say in their own wardrobe and makeup (examples in Llewellyn-Jones 2002: 294–95; Llewellyn-Jones 2009: 576–77; Llewellyn-Jones 2018: 207, 265–66). Cf. also Haskell 2016: 8–11. On beauty as cultural capital, cf. Shields 2013: 37–38.

180. See Wexman 1993: ch. 2 and 4. On *A Star Is Born*, see Maltby 2003: 146–54 and cf. Douglas 1994: 59.

in a position to appropriate the power that radiates from her iconic beauty and dominate her own film. This means that the story of casting Helen is itself a story about female power, and specifically the ability of women to parlay the passive power of the desirable object into the power of agency. For all these reasons, star casting seems like the perfect solution to the kinds of representational difficulty that she embodies.

Despite this synergy, however, the role has often been filled by a minor player or a complete unknown. The lack of audience recognition is thought to render such performances more "human" and "believable," and thus more "realistic," than a star turn. Casting an unknown helps to reduce the "eternal feminine" to someone with whom any woman can identify and whom any man can aspire to possess. Such treatments tend to focus less on Helen's exceptionalism than on her ordinariness (a form of "realism" often used to humanize mythic figures). To embody transcendent beauty successfully an actor must be not only individual, but iconic; and an unknown is liable to come across as less iconic because more ordinary. In such cases, Helen's mythic supremacy is sacrificed on the altar of Hollywood "realism."

Yet unknowns are not entirely excluded from the star system. As we shall see, such casting is often accompanied by the publicity stunt of a beauty contest or "worldwide search." The lucky winner's performance is not enhanced by a preexisting star aura, but she does come with a (presumptively male) seal of approval, which raises certain audience expectations. This is a risky casting strategy, which fails unless it takes hold via the kind of breakout performance through which a star is "born."[181] No matter who is cast as Helen, however, or how she is shaped by the work of the actor, director, writer, or designers, success in the role depends ultimately on the fickle judgment of that modern Paris, the movie audience.

The rest of this book offers a series of case studies, each examining ways in which the figure of Helen is both shaped and judged in the various contexts laid out in this chapter. For each work, I ask: How does it address the problem of representing extraordinary beauty as an inheritance from Greek antiquity? Who is cast as Helen and how do they look, dress, and act? How is our response to them mediated by such factors as genre, narrative, cinematography, and mise-en-scène? How does each Helen reflect and refract conceptions

181. The first instant (crafted) star was Theda Bara in *A Fool There Was* (1915) (Koszarski 1990: 273–76); but the ascent to stardom was often more gradual (cf., e.g., Allen & Gomery 1993: 176–85 on the rise of Joan Crawford).

of beauty, and anxieties about its impact, within the specific historical and cultural context in which the film was made? How does each work use her to examine female sexuality and erotic agency? How does it craft its appeal to disparate viewers? How does it position itself in face of the alien yet familiar culture that it purports to represent, cuing dialogue between ancient and modern? How does it harness the cultural authority of ancient Greece, and specifically of "Greek" beauty, to flatter, lure, or challenge its intended audiences? And finally, how did audiences respond?

2

A Brilliant Gem in a Finely Wrought Setting

THE PRIVATE LIFE OF HELEN OF TROY (1927)

Advertised for 2700 Years and Now You Get Her

1927 was a pivotal year in Hollywood history. Most notable for the introduction of synchronized sound, it also happens to be the year that saw Hollywood's first feature film centered on Helen: *The Private Life of Helen of Troy*, a silent comedy (now fragmentary) directed by Alexander Korda for First National Studios.[1] The role of Helen, which was "about the most talked-of . . . in Hollywood,"[2] went to Maria Corda, Korda's wife and fellow Hungarian, with whom he had recently arrived in Hollywood.[3]

Audiences of the period flocked to cinemas for blockbuster ancient world epics like *Ben-Hur* (1925).[4] But *Private Life* was different. The script, by Carey Wilson, was loosely based on a 1925 novel of the same title by

1. The script is in the Margaret Herrick Library in Los Angeles. The film was originally 83 minutes long. There are fragments totaling about half an hour in the British Film Archive; a large collection of stills and a music cue sheet in the George Eastman House in Rochester, NY; and a two-page synopsis in the Library of Congress. For full production details, see Kulik 1975: 343.

2. Anon. 1928a.

3. Corda (born Maria Farkas) took her husband's name, but spelled it with a C as a gesture of independence (Kulik 1975: 28–29; Korda 1979: 71). They were recruited together by First National. On imported Europeans in this period, see Everson 1978: ch. 18; Negra 2001; Negra 2002; Horak 2005.

4. There was, however, no existing Hollywood epic about the Trojan War, though several had been made in Europe (Winkler 2007b: 204–5).

John Erskine. The novel displays an intimate knowledge of the Greek literary background while reinventing Helen and her ménage as players in a bourgeois comedy of manners. Erskine, an English professor at Columbia University, was the creator of the influential Great Books curriculum, which, among other things, brought the *Iliad* in translation to a large readership.[5]

Erskine's novel was aimed at a similarly "middlebrow" audience, that is, at "men and women, fairly civilized, fairly literate," who made up the majority of readers in this period and were eager to learn about "high" culture from accessible and entertaining sources.[6] The author—a self-styled feminist—gave Helen "a set of brains,"[7] which she uses to provide extensive ruminations on life and love, couched in contemporary language and peppered with witticisms. She unabashedly defends her pursuit of erotic fulfillment and is openly contemptuous of respectable conformity. Despite "the safety the classical plot provided," some contemporaries found the book "scandalous" and "immoral on the face of it."[8] Whether despite or because of that fact, it became the best-selling American novel for 1926 and enthroned its author, like his Helen, as a dispenser of wit and wisdom concerning "this man-and-woman problem."[9]

As a silent movie, Korda's *Private Life* necessarily dispensed with most of the vaunted "wisdom" that gives Erskine's Helen her distinctive personality.[10] But it retained Erskine's central conceit that Helen and her ménage are "modern" people. The intertitles (which won an Oscar) used colloquial, contemporary language, and the score (by Carl Edouarde) was based on popular songs of the day, such as "Lady Be Good."[11] Though the mise-en-scène was "Greek," the tone had more in common with the social comedies of Lubitsch

5. Rubin 1992: 165–78; Grobéty 2014: 25–56; cf. Schein 2008: 83. On the rise of the cultural and social capital of the classics (especially Homer) in translation after World War I, which resulted in a huge expansion of their readership, see Schein 2007. On Erskine, see further Helena Smith 1927; Rubin 1992: ch. 4; Chaddock 2011; Malamud 2013: 330–33.

6. Rubin 1992: xii (quoting a journalist named Margaret Widdemer).

7. Helena Smith 1927: 28.

8. Rubin 1992: 180; Helena Smith 1927: 28.

9. Helena Smith 1927: 27, 28.

10. Korda later lamented that it had not been a sound picture (Kulik 1975: 46).

11. "The horse was dragged in to the tune of 'Horses, Horses, Horses,' and when Helen returns 'to Troy' [sic] with Menelaus the orchestra played a few bars from 'Home Sweet Home'" (M. Hall 1927a).

or DeMille than with conventional Hollywood treatments of antiquity.[12] But its humor relied heavily on the audience's background knowledge both of antiquity and of epic spectacles like *Ben-Hur.*

Ads for Korda's film capitalized on the novel's suggestive title, declaring that it would reveal "The *private* life of the world's most public woman."[13] But it also one-upped the novel by promising to fulfill a desire the book left unsatisfied. Ads cater unabashedly to the voyeuristic desire to "peep through the keyhole of the past" into Helen's "startling love affairs."[14] Visuals show her sneaking out of a locked book, while copy proclaims, "You've Heard About Her—Read About Her—Now You Can SEE Her—IN PRIVATE!" (figure 2.1). Lobby cards feature cartoon moviegoers ogling Helen within the frame (plate 1). On careful inspection they are gazing at a screen or stage, but the framing strongly suggests spying through a window. One of the salacious, winking viewers is actually using a telescope! Other ads go even further: "Advertised for 2700 years and now you get her" (figure 2.1). All written sources, from Homer to Erskine, are downgraded to mere advertisements, over 2,700 years, for a Helen who has finally arrived.

Like her counterpart in Erskine's novel, this Helen takes a dim view of marriage, which she calls "only exchanging the attentions of a dozen men for the inattention of one."[15] Menelaus is, indeed, an inattentive and socially inept husband. The role was played by Lewis Stone, a well-known comic actor nearly twenty years older than Corda. Helen complains that her husband is too busy for her during the day and too tired to go out in the evening. When she dresses up for the theater, he wants to stay home. He's no fun! Nor is he Helen's match

12. Cf. Horak 2005: 252. DeMille's sex comedies took a light tone concerning marriage and divorce, and focused on consumerism, with "plenty of clothes, rich sets, and action" (Higashi 2002: 301). They were subjected to censorship, but were very popular with audiences (Higashi 2002: 315–17). See further Higashi 1978: ch. 7; Walker 1967: 27–32; Card 1994: 225–29. For specific thematic parallels with *Private Life,* cf. Higashi 2002: 307, 312.

13. Erskine originally planned to call his book *The Argument of Helen* but came to realize that *Private Life* was "the real title" (Helena Smith 1927: 28). He was well aware that the change would attract "those who hoped for the worst" (Wiggins 1926). There is a spread showing many ads for *Private Life* in *Motion Picture News* (February 4, 1928, p. 382). Others mentioned in this chapter are from the author's collection or located via www.newspapers.com or the Media History Digital Library (MHDL).

14. H. Wolf 1927; *Times Recorder* [Zanesville, OH], April 5, 1928.

15. Unless otherwise indicated, intertitles are transcribed from the surviving footage.

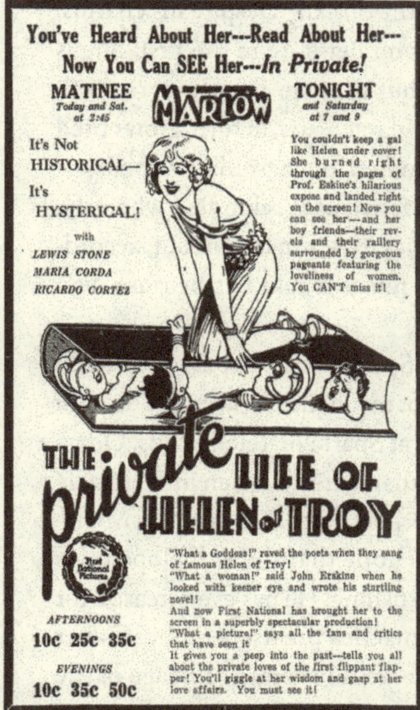

FIGURE 2.1. Newspaper ads for *The Private Life of Helen of Troy*. Reprinted (left) from the *Independent-Record* (Helena, MT), February 17, 1928, and (right) from unknown source.

in age, allure, or temperament. The caption on a publicity still explains, "While Helen dreams on, Menelaos snores contentedly."[16] And a lobby card showing Helen leaving Menelaus's bed is captioned, "When Helen got the idea that the king was getting old." But Helen is not the only character in *Private Life* to take a lighthearted view of love and marriage. Menelaus is already tired of her *before* she elopes and has no wish to get her back. He would much rather go fishing (one of the movie's running jokes) and is only badgered into attacking Troy by his war-hungry generals.

Paris, in contrast, is definitely eye candy, at least by 1927 standards. Ricardo Cortez, who played the role, was two years younger than Corda, and thus Stone's junior by twenty-three years. He was an American Jew (born Jacob Krantz), who had been reinvented by MGM as a "Latin Lover" in the wake of

16. On the spelling of Greek names in this movie, see below, p. 75.

Rudolph Valentino's rise to superstardom as the *Sheik*.[17] Despite his charms, however, Helen's second marriage turns out no better than the first. She is distressed to find out that Paris also snores; but they are already en route to Troy, and it is too late to turn back.[18] During the war, Paris, in turn, grows tired of Helen, and suggests returning her, but is shouted down by his own belligerent generals. Meanwhile Helen's desire for Menelaus is rekindled when she sees him fighting to win her back. She even tries to return to him but, according to the script, is thwarted when the Greeks refuse to take her, because "you must be captured properly."

After the war, Helen is happy to get back to Sparta, where she throws herself into the role of attentive wife. But this does not mean she has seen the error of her ways. The film concludes with the arrival at Sparta of Telemachus, Odysseus's handsome son—who is even younger than Paris.[19] Helen immediately sets about seducing him. Delighted at the prospect of losing her again, Menelaus actively facilitates their flirtation in the hope that she will elope once more, since this would mean he can finally go fishing. He has every reason for optimism, since Helen's dialogue with Telemachus precisely replicates her previous flirtation with Paris (stills of the scene show a mirror image of the latter). The film thus transforms the merest innuendo from a scene in the *Odyssey*, in which Telemachus visits Helen in Sparta, into an outright seduction. It even alludes to the Homeric Helen's drugging of her guests' wine, when Helen offers Telemachus wine that has "magic" in it (to which he replies "the . . . magic is not in the wine").[20]

This distinctive ending, with its Homeric allusion, was taken directly from Erskine's novel. In other respects, however, the film departs dramatically from the book. Wilson's most striking innovation is the central role played by clothes, fashion and shopping. The surviving portion opens with complaints from the Spartan fashion industry that they are going bankrupt, since Helen, followed by the other Spartan women, prefers the latest designs from Troy over those

17. Publicity for *Private Life* refers to Paris as "the sheik of the day" (as in plate 1). An intertitle calls Troy "the big city with the shops, shows and sheiks" (M. Hall 1927b). On Cortez, see Avrech 2009 and cf. Higashi 1978: 91.

18. M. Hall 1927a.

19. The role was played by Bill (Gordon) Elliot, who was six years younger than Corda. All three Greek generals (Achilles, Ulysses, and Ajax) are, in addition, her disappointed suitors.

20. On the *Odyssey* scene, see Blondell 2013: ch. 4.

from provincial Sparta.[21] It is this that causes the war, since Menelaus's generals want to destroy the Trojan fashion industry that is competing too successfully with the locals. As for Helen, she is attracted to Troy not just by Paris but by the city's haute couture, and, when she gets there, upsets her second husband—like her first—with her shopping habit. When conquering Troy, according to *Variety*, Menelaus understandably "[makes] a beeline for Helen's dress-maker to destroy the shop."[22] Back in Sparta, after the war, Helen briefly renounces fashion along with flirtation. But as soon as Telemachus is announced she reverts to form, dressing to the nines in order to seduce him.

This remarkable spin on the traditional tale allows Korda's film to revel in the display of extravagant fashions, transforming Erskine's verbal and intellectual entertainment into a visual and sensory one. It also allows *Private Life* to exploit the age-old equation of erotic beauty with glamorous clothing. As Telemachus explains, he was drawn to visit Helen by reports of "her daring clothes, her dazzling beauty." In so far as the feminine weakness for finery is a coded expression of women's own eroticism, Helen's passion for clothing also reflects the interpenetration of women's desires for sex and adornment. The film satirically deflates the legendary power of her beauty: the Trojan War is not ascribed to that beauty, or even to men's desire to retrieve her. But even though she is not the war's official cause, she is implicated in starting it, thanks to her lust for fashionable attire. The power of female sexuality—of woman as both desirable object and desiring agent—is thus transmuted into the economic power of feminine consumerism. This is of a piece with Helen's unromantic view of sex and marriage, reflecting a sartorial self-indulgence as irresponsible as her erotic exploits.

Private Life also takes aim at male pretensions, mocking ancient epic by presenting the great heroes as bombastic warmongers, not glorious but vainglorious, absurd looking in their "ancient" uniforms.[23] But this does not prevent it from wholeheartedly embracing the spectacular aesthetic integral to

21. On this Helen as a frivolous, narcissistic consumer, see Malamud 2013. The contrast between Sparta and Troy echoes that between Los Angeles and New York (cf. above, p. 6, and Malamud 2013: 337). But the Los Angeles fashion industry was exploding in this period, thanks to the movies (Eckert 1990 [1978]).

22. Anon. 1927b.

23. This is in keeping with the deglamorization of warfare following World War I (cf. Postrel 2013: 13–14). One review opines that setting the film in ancient Greece makes it safe to satirize "the recent World War and many of its chief idols" (Anon. 1928b). Another suggests that the

that genre. As with the grandest of such productions, publicity emphasizes the film's magnificent spectacle and cost. According to one ad, "It took over a year and cost over a million dollars to bring Helen and her playmates to the screen. Hundreds of beautiful women—gorgeous clothes—dazzling pageants of breathtaking splendor."[24]

As this wording implies, women and their wardrobe were an integral part of the film's spectacle. It does, to be sure, cast a satirical eye on the marketing of beauty via clothing, and clothing via beauty, but this was a market in which film itself was deeply implicated. Hollywood had a vested interest in celebrating, rather than disparaging, the fashion industry with which it was so closely allied. In contrast to the broadly parodic male characters' costumes, the film approaches women's fashions with the kind of "knowing humor" that "acknowledges the absurdity of the artifice without sacrificing its allure."[25] According to the *Scranton Tribune*, Helen sports "seventeen distinct costumes, with capes and wigs to match," adding up to "the largest assortment of costumes ever worn by one person in any motion picture."[26] This Helen is not only a model of woman as consumer but a model for women to consume.

Europe's Idea of the Eternal Feminine

Maria Corda was a romantic, ambitious woman who, in collaboration with her husband as director, had become a top movie star in Europe. According to the *Los Angeles Times*, she was cast in the title role of *Private Life* because, "like some of the reports of the fabled Helen," she was "a stunning blond, impressive of bearing and possessed of a lovely figure."[27] The *Washington Post* calls her "ideally suited to the role of the classical maiden," being "above the average height," "slender and artistic," with an oval face, a "Grecian" nose, a fragile mouth, and large blue eyes.[28] *Picture Play* magazine notes her "symmetrical

---

distance of antiquity affords detachment about "the recent struggle" (Anon. Herrick; cf. below, n. 141).

24. *Neosho Daily News*, November 26, 1929. Cf. also figure 2.4. On the promotional rhetoric used for epics, see Sobchak 2003 [1990]; Llewellyn-Jones 2018: ch. 1. Paul speaks usefully of the "rhetoric of numbers" (Paul 2013a: 226).

25. Postrel 2013: 107

26. Anon. 1928e.

27. Whitaker 1927.

28. Anon. 1928a. According to *Screenland*, she was 5′4″ (the perfect height by Waterbury's standards; above, pp. 7–8), weighed 120 pounds, and measured 36–37.5–26.5 inches (M. Martin

limbs" and "classic purity of feature."[29] Drawing on romantic ideas about Greek aesthetics, *Photoplay* dubs her "Europe's idea of the Eternal Feminine," exemplifying "the calm, modelled perfection of the classic beauty."[30]

Corda's star persona also made her a good fit for the role. She was new to Hollywood, thus satisfying the studio's claim to be introducing Helen for the first time (not to mention the industry's thirst for novelty); but she had been recruited on the strength of her star status in Europe, where she regularly played the beautiful, sometimes disreputable, romantic lead who caused conflict among men.[31] This meshed with her off-screen image as a glamorous, flamboyant attention seeker. Korda's biographer Charles Drazin observes that the role would require "very little adjustment to the life she was already leading as one of the most bored and fashion-conscious wives in Hollywood."[32]

Despite these qualifications, Corda was only cast "after much discussion and disagreement."[33] Apparently "everyone in Hollywood" expected the role to go to Billie Dove.[34] Dove was a well-known actor, nicknamed The American Beauty after a film made earlier the same year, whom First National "had gone to great lengths to promote as 'The Screen's Most Beautiful Star.'"[35] Drazin suggests that Corda was cast instead at Korda's insistence; but she was signed for the role at an early stage, before her husband was asked to direct.[36] Given Korda's status as a new arrival, and the control exercised by the studios in such matters,[37] it is unlikely that he was in a position to insist that his wife play Helen over an established American star. It seems more probable that the studio was intentionally tapping into the exoticism of their latest European discovery. *Picture Play* reports that the

---

1928: 97). A contemporary observer says she has "a face distinctly different in type, a face that is ageless, that shows sophistication, innocence, deviltry [sic] and buoyancy" (Barnes 1928). Kulik describes her as "a tall, statuesque dark-blonde with a classical, almost Grecian face" (Kulik 1975: 24, cf. 46; cf. Korda 1979: 57).

29. Oettinger 1928: 74.

30. *Photoplay*, January 33, 1928.

31. For examples, see Kulik 1975: 39–41; Drazin 2002: 47–51.

32. Drazin 2002: 59.

33. Kulik 1975: 45.

34. Drazin 2002: 59.

35. Drazin 2002: 59.

36. For what it is worth, some journalists report that Corda was recruited specifically for this role (Whitaker 1927; Oettinger 1928: 74). Korda replaced the original director, George Fitzmaurice, after they arrived in Hollywood (Kulik 1975: 45; Horak 2005: 252).

37. Korda disliked Hollywood, largely for such reasons, and soon left for England (see Kulik 1975: 48; Korda 1979: 78–83; Malamud 2013: 333–34).

studio wanted her to play the "wicked vamp," in explicit contrast to "'sweet,' 'nice,' proper girls" like Billie Dove.[38] The wholesome Dove was the *American* beauty, but Corda "exude[s] the charm of the true Continental."[39] Like the long-awaited Helen herself, she was *Europe's* idea of the Eternal Feminine.

Corda's European origins are highlighted over and over again in advance publicity. Stills captions speak of the "old world charm" or "old world loveliness" brought to the role of Helen by "Madame" Corda, the "exotic European screen beauty" (figure 2.2). Along with the prestige of old-world culture, this provenance brought an element of risqué old-world sophistication.[40] In costume for the role, we are told, Corda looks "regal, dashing, beautiful and dangerously piquant."[41] A *Photoplay* article recounting her behavior on set presents her as quite literally born to play the part of Helen (figure 2.3). The author, Ruth Biery, reports that, in defiance of the Hays office, Corda exhibits a shocking (and "Greek") refusal to clothe her bare legs with tights; she is not only extraordinarily beautiful and enticing, but willful, wild, spoiled, narcissistic, temperamental, and autocratic—all traits, it is implied, befitting the Greek Helen herself; the disputes she allegedly instigates on set are even likened to "another Trojan War."[42]

Much of this fits well with what we know of Corda's character and personal life. She and her husband were a flamboyant, willful pair. Gossip items present Corda as a snobbish prima donna who will not accept lesser roles, and Korda was known as a controlling director, with "a reputation for being difficult."[43] In their marriage he sometimes comes across as something of a Menelaus, playing second fiddle to a woman who always gets her way, but despite their tempestuous relationship Corda was evidently devoted to her husband. They

38. Whitaker 1927. Cf. the wholesome "American" female entertainers in the Ziegfeld Follies (Glenn 2000: 173–74; Mifflin 2020: 26).

39. Oettinger 1928: 74, who also calls her smile "continental in its subtlety." According to artist and beauty expert James Montgomery Flagg, she "typifies the 'continental type' of femininity at its best" (Reilly 1929: 100). She was often compared to Garbo (cf. below, n. 103).

40. European films were suspect for their "sexual and/or political undertones" (Everson 1978: 318). Cf. also Haskell 1974: 96 on Lubitsch's "European" women, and von Stroheim's use of Middle Europe "as a metaphor for human vanity and sexuality" (McConathy & Vreeland 1976: 90). In 1927 there was a backlash in Hollywood against central European imports; European directors were considered "too demanding" and European women "too exotic" (Horak 2005: 244, 258).

41. Whitaker 1927.

42. Biery 1927a. For Greeks as "bare-legged," cf. above, p. 10.

43. Horak 2005: 253.

FIGURE 2.2. Promotional still for *The Private Life of Helen of Troy*. The caption reads, "OLD WORLD LOVELINESS exemplified by exotic MARIA CORDA, First National Pictures' Hungarian find, who plays Helen in 'The Private Life of Helen of Troy.'"

both remained faithful throughout the marriage, and it was he who eventually initiated their divorce, against her wishes.[44] Since this does not suit the requisite racy portrait, Korda explains to Biery that "of course" his wife has

44. On their marriage, see further Korda 1979: passim; Drazin 2002: 36–40, 48–52. Both could be petty and vindictive (anecdotes at Drazin 2002: 50; Kulik 1975: 49). The tension between them emerged in a magazine interview where she declared, "at home, I am the director" (Kulik 1975: 49; cf. Oettinger 1928: 98); the article's title ("Should Husbands Direct Wives?") speaks to the limitations on the acceptable expression of female power over men in Hollywood, even when the wife is a star.

FIGURE 2.3. Spread from *Photoplay*, November 1927. The photo caption at left reads, "'They vill never make me all a good voman. They vill never all tame theese *Helen*!' We can believe Maria Corda when we look at the temperamental soul portrayed in this picture." The photo above the headline, showing Helen and her handmaids posing as an ancient Greek sculpture, is captioned, "A scene from 'Helen of Troy.' Tights never made a Greek frieze."

infatuations with other men, simply because she *is* Helen; Corda herself suggests that it would be "good publicity" if she fell in love with Cortez, and mentions a duel that her husband supposedly fought over her with an Italian prince.[45]

This emphasis on European exoticism prepares us to perceive Corda's Helen in the persona of "the world's greatest 'vamp.'"[46] The archetypal vamp was dark-haired, dark-eyed, earthy, and sultry. She was notoriously embodied in the teens by Theda Bara, whom one fervent admirer hymns as "peasant . . .

45. Biery 1927a. The caption on one still similarly hints at a triangular relationship between Korda, Lewis Stone (Menelaus), and Helen, "Maria Corda being Helen's other name." The inconsistency between role and actor is finessed by her admission that "I find no man in America" (Biery 1927a: 133), which allows her to retain the chastity officially required of Hollywood stars.

46. Cf. above, p. 13.

goddess . . . eternal woman."[47] By the 1920s, this type had come to exemplify the sexual and economic threat posed by immigrant women. Its most prominent representative was Pola Negri, who, unlike Bara, was "an actual ethnic import with a foreign accent and a well-publicized European past."[48] Filmically constructed as a temperamental old-world "Gypsy," Negri was "earthy and tempestuous," a "flamboyant diva" and femme fatale who flaunted her affairs in defiance of Hollywood mores.[49]

The blonde, blue-eyed, husband-loving Maria Corda was no Pola Negri. As a "classical" blonde representing the "timeless" beauty of ancient Greece, she strikes a sophisticated, aristocratic figure. Yet publicity worked hard to assimilate her to the Negri type. The caption on one still, where she is modelling an imported Hungarian outfit, is headlined "THE TRUE PEASANT." And Biery informs us that, despite Corda's own bright blonde hair and blue eyes, her mother was a "Gypsy," "dusky-eyed" and "raven-haired"; those blue eyes, moreover, can "smoulder" as well as any black ones, radiating "scorching fire" as well as "sparkling water"; in true vamp style she slowly lights her cigarette and closes "the big eyes to a half slant."[50] We are even told, regarding Corda's treatment of a supposed rival, that "she chased the poor thing down the lot with a big black whip."[51] The *Photoplay* headline notwithstanding, Corda assures us in the photo caption, "They vill never make me all a good voman. They vill never all tame thees *Helen*" (figure 2.3).[52] The author adds, "We can believe Maria Corda when we look at the temperamental soul portrayed in this picture."

Such publicity readied viewers of *Private Life* for a Helen combining blonde, blue-eyed, "classical" beauty with the dangerous exoticism of a European vamp. Yet ads also assimilated her to the most modern and American of female types by dubbing her "the first flippant flapper" or "the first flapper queen"

47. Card 1994: 189.

48. Negra 2001: 68–69.

49. Negra 2001: 71, 80; Everson 1978: 201; Horak 2005: 243. Negri was never successfully assimilated to Hollywood ways (Negra 2001: ch. 3; Negra 2002). Though treated harshly by the press, she was enormously popular with audiences, and her "'European' free spirit may have . . . won her admirers among America's modern women" (Horak 2005: 244).

50. Biery 1927a: 133.

51. Biery 1927a: 132. This evokes the memorable climax of Negri's 1925 *Woman of the World*, in which the vamp-heroine takes a bullwhip to her chastened lover.

52. Negri's speech was similarly exoticized in fan magazines (Negra 2001: 66), as was Korda's (e.g., *Motion Picture Magazine*, July 1927).

FIGURE 2.4. Newspaper ad for *The Private Life of Helen of Troy.* Reprinted from the *Winnipeg Tribune,* February 25, 1928.

(e.g., figure 2.1). Then as now, the flapper was the type most emblematic of the 1920s.[53] Flappers embodied the youthful female consumer and were "obsessed with love of dress and gaiety."[54] The cartoons advertising *Private Life* represent a youthful Helen sporting the most notorious markers of flapper style: short hair and short skirts (figures 2.1, 2.4). Short hair (the bob or shingle) was an

53. On the flapper, see especially Conor 2004: ch. 7 and cf. Weinbaum et al. 2008 on the "modern girl," of whom the flapper is a species.

54. Conor 2004: 212.

emblem of freedom, independence and even defiance of men.[55] Short skirts (which often, shockingly, revealed the knees) facilitated a freedom of movement that could be used for sports, but also for seduction.[56] These transgressions of social and sartorial boundaries were perceived by both critics and supporters as a form of resistance to patriarchal control. Inheriting the erotic self-assertion of the traditional vamp, the flapper became a central focus of the period's assumptions and anxieties about female beauty, desire, and sexual freedom.[57] This made her an ideal vehicle for conveying, in a distinctively modern idiom, the ambivalence about female beauty and eroticism that had always been central to Helen's identity. As "a professor" had informed newspaper readers as early as 1922, "the beautiful Helen of Troy was a flapper, attaining that daring, rebellious and impudent sauciness for which the young girl of today is so widely denounced."[58]

The audience was thus prepared, before entering the theater, to respond to Corda's Helen as a "classic" and "exotic" European beauty, a temperamental queen with "Gypsy" roots, and the timeless "eternal feminine," colored in various shades of vamp, all reborn in the up-to-date guise of the flapper. The complexity of this image generates a certain tension. *Photoplay*, for example, predicted that the film would revive an interest in "the calm, modelled perfection of the classic beauty" *as opposed to* the "pert, sharp prettiness of the flapper."[59] And the *Los Angeles Times* comments, praising Corda's physical grace, "it would have been dreadful to have a jerky, flapperish person as Helen of Troy, yanking those classic draperies about."[60] Yet the typology of beauty was not as fixed as such remarks may suggest.[61] Beauty "types" were supposedly based on biological features, but those features were subject to manipulation and enhancement, and, features aside, "types"

55. Anita Loos wrote that bobbing her hair made her feel "secure, free, and capable of taking on the New York press" (1966: 138). For a wife to cut her hair was considered emasculating to the husband (Conor 2004: 242–43). See further Fass 1977: 280–81.

56. Cf. Fass 1977: 281–83; Landay 2002: 232.

57. See, e.g., Anon. 1922c. The "modern" vamp of this period evinces a more innocuous-seeming style than the traditional variety (see, e.g., McEvoy 1924).

58. *San Antonio Evening News*, March 23, 1922. For hostility to flapper style, see especially Latham 2000: ch. 2.

59. *Photoplay*, January 33, 1928 (emphasis added).

60. Whitaker 1927.

61. As early as 1922, there were complaints that the term "flapper" had no fixed meaning (e.g., Anon. 1922d).

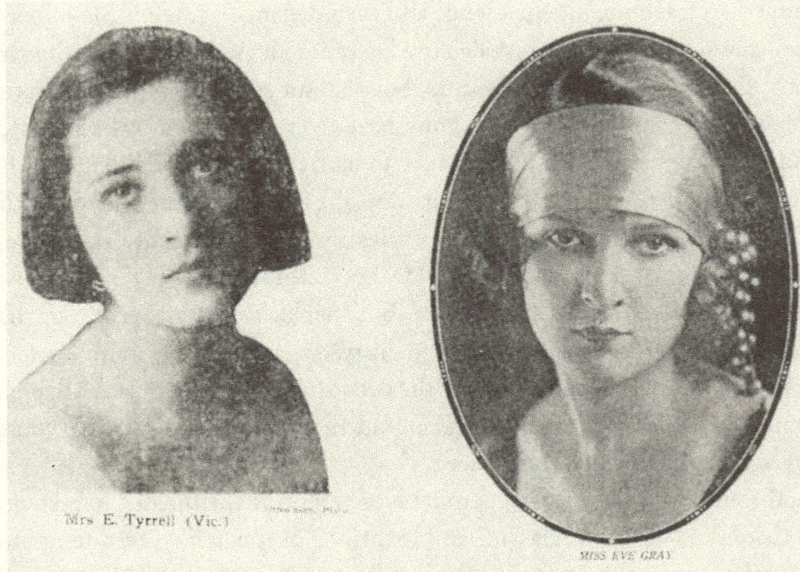

FIGURE 2.5. A "Madonna" (left) and a "Venus" (right) beauty type, both 1922, reprinted from Conor 2004: 143. *The Herald* (Australia), August 17, 1922.

were heavily dependent on dress, makeup, personal style, adornment and demeanor.

There is even a convergence, at times, between the flapper and the "classical" type. Conor, for example, prints paired photos of a Venus type and a Madonna type (figure 2.5). Their features are hard to differentiate in themselves, but the "Madonna" is unadorned, and rolls her eyes upward in a gesture drawing on religious imagery, while the "Venus" wears a bandeau and a self-assured frontal gaze. Given her name, one might expect the Venus type to be more "classical"—yet her look is unmistakably flapper. Waterbury's "Greek" ideal is likewise suspiciously flapper-like: she is "the bare-armed, bare-legged, slender, short-haired girl of beauty and ambition."[62] Moreover the star in her article whose measurements come closest to the Venus de Milo turns out to be none other than Joan Crawford, whom F. Scott Fitzgerald himself called "the best example of the dramatic flapper."[63] Crawford, one of the most prominent flapper stars, had a reputation as a "'party girl' of loose morals."[64] In her

62. Waterbury 1928b; cf. above, pp. 7–10.

63. Pratt 1973: 456.

64. Fuller 1996: 192.

breakout film, *Our Dancing Daughters* (1928), the flapper heroine introduces herself as Diana the Dangerous—a nod to the "Greekness" of the free-spirited modern young woman.[65]

Publicity for *Private Life* finessed the potential dissonance between the classical and flapper types by explaining that this Helen is the culmination of a "timeless" tradition—a tradition that turns out to have been modern all along. The script introduces her as "Helen, the eternal, immortal Helen—the eternal immortal woman." In publicity, she is tagged "the immortal Helen," the "immortal 'vamp,'" "the immortal beauty," and as "loving in a style that hasn't been improved in 2,700 years." At the same time, contemporary references underline the up-to-the-minute nature of her appeal. Earlier that year, for example, the film *It*, based on Elinor Glyn's novel, had made a star of Clara Bow.[66] Publicity for *Private Life* declares, "OH! What a Gal was Helen—You'll learn about 'it' from HER."[67] Other ads allude to Anita Loos's *Gentlemen Prefer Blondes* (the second best-selling novel for 1926, after Erskine's); Helen is "the first preferred blonde," or "the first blonde whom gentlemen ever preferred." As "the most dangerous blonde in history," she also has her own preferences: she is "the dizzy blonde who preferred gentlemen . . . well done." This framing helps to justify the studio's extravagant claim that only now, in the twentieth century, and here, in Hollywood, has this immortal Greek beauty finally arrived.

The First Flapper Queen

This presentation of Helen makes *Private Life* not only a burlesque of ancient world epic but a variation on the flapper film—a popular genre of the 1920s, of which *Our Dancing Daughters* is a quintessential example.[68] Visually, these films reflect the aesthetics of the Jazz Age, with its revealing costumes, lively dance scenes and Art Deco style. Their plots concern "the flapper's pursuit of modern life—independent from parental and other

65. On *Our Dancing Daughters*, see Higashi 1978: 126–28; Card 1994: 132–35; Massey 2000: ch. 1; Landay 2002: 221–24, 234–37.

66. See Walker 1967: 33–41; Card 1994: 199–204; Mellencamp 1995: 215–19; Studlar 1996 [1991]: 281–84; Barbas 2001: 54–56.

67. H. Wolf 1927.

68. See especially Landay 2002; also Haskell 1974: 74–82; Ryan 1976; Higashi 1978: 125–131; Conor 2004: 224–25; Addison 2006: 8.

authoritarian control—and a modern romance in which her defiant actions, unruly behavior, and daring dress are either obstacles or catalysts, or both."[69]

A passion for "daring dress" is, as we saw, both Helen's defining character trait and the engine that drives the plot. This marks her, like the flapper, as a narcissistic and unproductive exhibitionist. In one still she tries on a new outfit, smiling into the mirror held by her handmaiden. As the object of all eyes—her own, her attendants' and the film audience's—she is the very picture of narcissism. To her husband's distress, many of her outfits are scandalously revealing, often displaying the actor's knees, her back, and even her legs and underwear (cf. figure 2.3). A contemporary critic of the flapper speaks grumpily of streets "filled with women who are apparently trying to see how much they can leave off without being arrested."[70] When Menelaus orders Helen to "wear Spartan fashions or none at all," she replies, "the newest frocks from Troy *are* practically none at all." Some stills even hint at nakedness, with decency preserved only by the strategic placement of "mere drapery."

Helen also engages in "unruly behavior," especially where romance is concerned. The still accompanying Biery's article (figure 2.3) evokes a famous scene in *Our Dancing Daughters* where the heroine takes off her skirt and dances in her satin underpants (figure 2.6)—at a time when "taking off her dress in public" was, in Quentin Crisp's words, "the most wicked thing that a girl could do."[71] In her various flirtations, Helen makes liberal use of the look known as "giving the glad eye," which flappers were thought to do much too freely.[72] Flappers further expressed their personal and sexual freedom through lively movement, above all dancing (preferably in an energetic and revealing style).[73] Helen may not have done the Charleston, but we are

69. Landay 2002: 224.

70. Conor 2004: 231.

71. Crisp 1989: 22.

72. Conor 2004: 212, 236–52; see also Landay 2002: 226–30, 237–39. This updates the erotic power of the ancient Helen's eyes, shown most conspicuously at the moment when her beauty makes Menelaus drop his sword (Blondell 2013: 40; cf. figure 2.11).

73. See further Fass 1977: 300–306; Landay 2002: 231–37; Conor 2004: 214–215. Like many stars, Corda began her career as a dancer (Kulik 1975: 24). Biery 1927a claims that she objected to jazz on set, insisting on classical music—another example of the tension between the "classic" and "modern" aspects of Helen's persona.

FIGURE 2.6. Joan Crawford in a still for *Our Dancing Daughters*.

informed that she is "as real and modern as jazz,"[74] and some of her poses evoke flapper dance style (compare figures 2.7 and 2.8). The flapper was also known for her frankness and wit: her charms include "a sense of humor and a

74. H. Wolf 1927. Cf. the wording of the second ad in figure 2.1.

FIGURE 2.7. Still for *The Private Life of Helen of Troy* showing Helen (left) dancing with Aphrodite. The caption, headlined "LIKE A PORTION OF AN ANCIENT FRIEZE," tells us that the two actors "represent the mood of classic dance."

nice line in snappy dialogue."[75] In Helen's case, these qualities are expressed through the intertitles, whose saucy "voice" is enhanced by her body language and the reactions of her listeners.[76]

75. Morey 2002: 340–41. Elsewhere flappers are called "impudent" (Higashi 1978: 126) and "over-frank" (Conor 2004: 231; cf. 240).

76. Devotees of fan magazines might also hear Corda's exotic accent in their heads (cf. above, p. 49). Loos writes interestingly about the comic impact of intertitles, which could rescue a dull film (1966: 98–104). Cf. the inscriptions on ancient statues which allow even these static images to "speak" (Steiner 2001: passim).

FIGURE 2.8. Still for *Our Dancing Daughters*.

As for "defiant actions," Corda's Helen displays far more control over her men, the plot, and her destiny than any Greek Helen ever did. She pursues Paris much more actively than in most versions of the story, whether ancient or modern. Typically, they are thrown together and Paris seduces her, often in the face of considerable resistance on her part, and usually in Menelaus's absence. In *Private Life*, however, after she and Paris spot each other at the theater, Helen persuades her husband to invite Paris to dinner, then flirts with him right under said husband's nose. She is attracted to Menelaus again during the war, and when he threatens to kill her, she "takes good care that her gown is draped effectively."[77] Even the idea of trying out frumpy clothing at Sparta is her own idea (though one she quickly abandons).

The flapper's "hedonistic immaturity" makes her unsuited to marriage; she does not like to get tied down to one man, and her idleness and vanity make her unwilling to undertake housework; yet she is so restless, jaded, and bored that she may marry after all, in order to try "the one social novelty as yet unsampled."[78] Her idea of marriage is, however, "fun and fine clothes. . . . but no work or children," and any husband remains secondary to her continuing interest in a variety of men.[79] This picture of marital instability is illustrated not only by the fickleness of Corda's Helen but by her behavior after the Trojan War. Back in Sparta, as we saw, she briefly plays the good wife, donning modest domestic garb and turning to housework. But this turns out to be just another role, and outfit, to be quickly discarded.

The flapper's obsession with the new and fashionable allows her to play with shifting identities in a way that transcends typing, even as she remains one of the most recognizable of types.[80] Accordingly, Maria Corda's flapper-Helen exemplifies most of the roles available to young women in the 1920s. She is the shopper seeking out the latest fashions and presenting herself as a spectacle, like a living mannequin.[81] She is the gold digger who marries for the clothes.[82] She is the city girl who yearns to leave rustic Sparta for the luxuries of Troy.[83] She is, a fortiori, the beauty contest winner. Above all, she is the movie star. The film's very title evokes the public's gossipy fascination with the stars' private lives. As for Helen herself, she not only has the star's dazzle, and desire for self-display and excitement, but is a conspicuous fashion leader for other women, who flock to emulate her; the sets she inhabits, decorated

77. M. Hall 1927a.

78. Conor 2004: 216, 211, 241.

79. Burton 1925; Conor 2004: 243.

80. Conor 2004: 27, 226, 247.

81. Stills that show her modeling clothes recall the fashion shows that are a striking presence in other early movies (see J. Allen 1980: 488; C. Herzog 1990).

82. The gold-digging flapper—or Flapper Trapper, as she was known—uses her looks to attract men who may serve as a source of treats and presents, especially more clothing and adornment (Conor 2004: 241). See also Glenn 2000: 197–209.

83. In *Private Life*'s Sparta, geese wander the marketplace and the butcher's shop is indicated by a dead pig, whereas Troy has elegant buildings, a dedicated sandal shop, and a bath house.

with antiquities, resemble that "strange luxurious space somewhere between art and life" in which Hollywood's divas were enshrined.[84]

The role of movie star helps put the "queen" into "flapper queen." As far as democratic Americans were concerned, real queens belonged in Europe. Nevertheless, movie audiences loved such political exotica. Accordingly, Helen's royalty, as queen of Sparta, is updated with allusions to the British crown. Intertitles refer to Paris as "H.R.H. Paris"; gossips at Troy mutter, "There's a Queen in Sparta, and if Paris goes there, God save the King."[85] Menelaus's palace—a white, sheer Art Deco castle—is referred to as Sparta's White House, distancing the American viewer from the decadence of "European" Troy. Yet Hollywood was the seat of a new and modern royalty, made up of new and modern men and women in the glamorous persons of the stars. Since high fashion required both wealth and leisure, flaunting one's appearance and one's body—particularly the bare back—became a mark of the idle wealth of the "new(de) rich,"[86] among whom Hollywood royalty took pride of place. Beauty contests, similarly, crowned their winners in a way that fed Americans' "baffling fascination with royalty."[87] These identities merge in the person of Helen of Troy, whom ads label the "ravishing royal renegade."

This movie star persona enrolls Helen not only in the new aristocracy, but in the new pantheon. Publicity insists that she is a (modern) woman, as opposed to an (ancient) goddess. Yet as we saw, it also proclaims her timelessness or immortality. The two coalesce in the identity of the cinematic goddess. As the star who will play Helen, Corda is introduced via both identities. Some stills promoting the film show her wearing suitably "ancient" clothing and accessories; others present her in full-on movie star mode (figure 2.9). Within the film itself she poses, like a Hollywood star, with Aphrodite's statue, paradoxically endowing her "modern" character with the cachet of ancient divinity (figure 2.10).[88] The statue in question is of the Pudica type, indebted to such

84. S. Dixon 2003: 81. See further M. Williams 2013a: 76–79. A photo of "Helen of Troy at Home" (i.e., Corda and her husband in their house in Beverly Hills) mentions the couple's European origin and shows a spacious interior with exoticizing touches (*Motion Picture Magazine*, June 1927).

85. M. Hall 1927a.

86. Conor 2004: 244.

87. Mifflin 2020: 8. Cf. Deford 1971: 7 and see further Banner 1983: 371–78. On the "American queen" in nineteenth-century art, see Banta 1987: 440–47, 469, 516–18.

88. Cf. above, p. 9.

FIGURE 2.9. Publicity cards for *The Private Life of Helen of Troy*. The caption for the still used at right reads, "Sable the gown and plumes and gold the hair of MARIA CORDA exotic European screen beauty [who] will create the role of the immortal Helen in the screen version of John Erskine's brilliant book, 'The Private Life of Helen of Troy.'"

familiar models as the Capitoline Venus and the Venus de' Medici.[89] By posing beside it, Helen becomes the star as a modern luminary glorified by ancient myth; but thanks to her preexisting mythic identity, she is also the mythic figure as star.

These immortalities merge in the film text. When Helen appears at the center of a pedimental arrangement, where one would expect to see a Greek god or goddess, the pose enhances her star quality by making her stand out—both compositionally and sartorially—from a group of otherwise similar beauties.[90] Another still shows Aphrodite dancing with her protégée in a way that, according to the caption on the back, represents "the mood of classic

89. According to M. Williams 2013b: 139, the Venus de' Medici was the slimmer alternative ideal to the Venus de Milo. She also has the benefit of arms.

90. One such still is reproduced above the headline of Biery's article (above, figure 2.3).

FIGURE 2.10. Still for *The Private Life of Helen of Troy* showing Helen at Sparta with a statue of Aphrodite.

dance" (above, figure 2.7). This image equates Helen with the goddess in a different way. Both are blonde, and their poses, hairstyles and outfits are almost identical. The resemblance enhances Helen's beauty by association with her divine patron, a technique familiar from ancient art. In the vase painting shown in figure 2.11, Helen looks like Aphrodite but is clearly subordinate, as

FIGURE 2.11. Helen seeking the protection of Aphrodite when Menelaus threatens her at the sack of Troy. On the right, Menelaus drops his sword, overcome by her beauty. Attic red-figure bell krater, c. 450–440 BCE.

she seeks protection with the goddess on the left. In the still from *Private Life*, Helen remains Aphrodite's dependent, yet the photograph, in contrast to the painting, seems to place them on an equal footing. Aphrodite looks less like her protector than her partner in crime.

As a film goddess, however, Helen is not just Aphrodite's equal but her superior. One lobby card reverses the ancient hierarchy of divine over mortal by tagging the goddesses of the Judgment "the jazz queens of Helen's court."[91] In cinematic terms, this superiority is implied by the contrast between the living star and Aphrodite's marble likeness (figure 2.10).[92] Even while helping to glorify Helen as a "modern" star, the statue is demoted, as an inanimate object, by its juxtaposition with her "living" presence (not to mention the dove perched on the goddess's head). In contrast to the monochrome statue, Helen's dress has flow and texture, complementing the warmth of her skin and softness

91. "Jazz queen" was a slang term for a committed flapper (cf. Studlar 1996: 278).

92. Cf. above, p. 21.

of her hair; though physically subordinate to the marble goddess, she is larger, more decorative, and more present.

This superiority is further conveyed by means of the Pygmalion theme that, as we saw earlier, pervades Hollywood cinema.[93] The caption on the still that shows Helen and Aphrodite dancing (figure 2.7), is headlined "LIKE A PORTION OF AN ANCIENT FRIEZE," suggesting that the actors have animated the frieze in question.[94] In other stills, Helen holds her hand to her breast in a gesture resembling the Venus Pudica pose, familiar from statuary, thus hinting that she is the goddess in human form. One publicity image superimposes this still on a Greek vase, simultaneously turning Corda into a vase painting and implying that her performance will bring to life what ancient art can only show in static form (figure 2.12). Within the film, Helen and her attendants were more explicitly transformed from "ancient" sculptures into living women. Stills show them posing as a pedimental sculpture, frozen in actual motion—an effect to which Greek sculpture and its imitators could only aspire, as the punning caption in figure 2.3 implies ("tights never made a Greek frieze"). But in the film itself (according to the script), they "came to life" and danced in the courtyard.[95]

While such images affirm the superiority of Hollywood's beauties to those of Greek sculpture, one thing remains constant: all these modern avatars of Aphrodite are as white as the Venus de Milo.[96] The transformation of "ancient" sculpture into "modern" dancers reenacts and reaffirms Hollywood's inheritance and appropriation of ancient Greek beauty. It is no coincidence that the "sculptured" dancers are all blonde, like Helen and Aphrodite.[97] As a blonde northern European, Corda in the role of Helen is the bearer of philhellenist traditions that affirm white culture through a racial othering that

93. Above, pp. 21–22.

94. Cf. press descriptions of Isadora Duncan as "an Ancient Greek Bas-Relief Come to Life" (Daly 1995: 101).

95. The same thing happened to the sculptured goddesses in the course of the film. Footage of the Judgment is unfortunately lost, but the script indicates that it took the form of a dream in which three statues came to life.

96. Whiteness has historically been intrinsic to popular conceptions of Greek marble statuary, despite the fact that in antiquity the statues were painted. This is partly due to the enormous influence of Johann Winckelmann, who viewed color as primitive and unsophisticated (Painter 2010: 61–63).

97. On the whiteness and racism of such dance troupes, cf. Mayer 2013: 102. Other stills show some of Helen's attendants with dark hair.

FIGURE 2.12. Still for *The Private Life of Helen of Troy* showing Helen, posing as Aphrodite, superimposed on a Greek vase.

excludes those of genuinely Greek as well as "Gypsy" ancestry. Despite the attempts of publicity to assimilate her to such dark-haired and relatively dark-skinned outsiders as Pola Negri, Corda's whiteness—and that of Paris, her "sheik"—is marked in certain stills by the contrast with her exoticized, jet-black attendants (plate 1).

Helen outshines Aphrodite in one more way—a way that is distinctive to Hollywood. The role of the goddess was cast via a contest mounted by the studio to discover "Hollywood's most beautiful extra girl." An eighteen-year-old named Alice Adair was selected "from among thousands" for the role.[98]

98. Adair went on to a minor film career, with small roles (mostly uncredited) in a dozen films. On beauty contests and early film, cf. above, p. 3.

Korda himself played the part of Paris, publicly bestowing a golden apple on the winner, who wears the outfit of a contemporary "bathing beauty." In so doing, he enacted for the public the role of the director as male connoisseur of female beauty, and consequently as star-maker. The Helen of Troy Contest, as it was called, authorized the studio to designate the most beautiful contestant a divinity, by casting her as Aphrodite. It thereby transformed the Judgment of Paris from a moral tale about the risks posed by beautiful women into a celebration of Hollywood's expertise in identifying the "Greek" ideal of beauty in modern form.

Yet the goddess who personifies that ideal is demoted to a supporting role. The contest was named for Helen (as opposed to Paris), and the winner was not the star but just "the most beautiful extra girl." This positions Maria Corda not as a mere aspirant to ideal beauty but as the ideal itself to which others must aspire. Her primacy is reinforced by promotional contests offering prizes to the "girl most nearly approaching the original Helen of Troy in looks and grace," or to "the eight . . . girls whose photographs and measurements showed them to have forms like that of Maria Corda."[99] Such promotions treat the star the way star discourse treats Venus: as a paradigm of beauty modelling a supposedly timeless ideal.

A Decidedly Classical Turn

The movie star's capacity for ceaseless transformation makes this the persona that ultimately encapsulates Helen's many identities. Just as Maria Corda, qua star, may be found modelling an extraordinary array of fashions, her Helen is free to ring the changes on "Grecian," vamp, or flapper style. This sartorial expression of her chameleonlike persona is her cinematic essence, both as a character and as the manifestation of beauty. It is her kaleidoscopic wardrobe that makes her, arguably, "the only film or stage Helen who looks convincingly like a divine creature."[100]

Most of Helen's many outfits reflect—in one way or another—the prevalent image of ancient Greek clothing as "mere draperies."[101] A few hint at the upscale immigrant peasant look, with its modest headscarves and wraps; others show her swathed in luxuriant, gleaming fabric (figure 2.13). More

99. *Film Daily*, February 7, 1928; *Film Daily*, January 8, 1928.

100. Maguire 2009: 185.

101. Cf. above, p. 10.

often, her "drapery" is a mere wisp. Whatever its extent, however, its "Greekness" is further affirmed by the off-the-shoulder look associated with antiquity, complemented by such recognizable elements as Greek key and wave patterns, headbands, wreaths, and lace-up sandals. Corda's blonde hair is styled in an array of elaborate hairdos, including ringlets or braids evoking the decadent, bewigged aristocracy of Old Europe. It is adorned with an impressive collection of whimsical headgear, which often alludes to antiquity, including a jeweled headband with cameos (figure 2.9) and an extraordinary griffin hat; another, helmetlike, hat and a winged headband both mock the plumage of male warriors, as they appear both in *Private Life* itself and in ancient world epics like *Ben-Hur* (figure 2.14).

Yet Helen's fashion sense is, at the same time, distinctly contemporary.[102] Many of her outfits evoke stars like Gloria Swanson, who showcased lavish costumes and exotic headpieces, both on-screen and off (especially in vamp roles), or Greta Garbo, another fashion leader known for playing the foreign siren or vamp in sexually scandalous roles (figure 2.13).[103] Others confirm Helen's identity as the "flapper queen." Her long hair is sometimes arranged and photographed in ways that give the impression of a bob.[104] Her skimpy costumes incorporate many specifics of flapper style, with its clean lines and flat-chested look. Her dancing dress, for example, as seen in figure 2.7, could easily be a fashionable tennis outfit.[105] Other outfits sport *au courant* details like feathers, fringes, metallic fabrics, and asymmetrical hemlines, and such accessories as headbands, cloche hats, strappy shoes, and conspicuous jewelry. Helen also wears newly fashionable makeup—notably the cupid's bow mouth, in bold lipstick, which was especially popular.[106] When she dresses up to

102. For 1920s fashions, see Steele 1985: 236–42; Laubner 1996; B. Altman & Co. 1999; Fiell & Dirix 2015.

103. For Garbo as fashion leader, see L. Fischer 2003: 113–16. Corda is often likened to Garbo (e.g., Biery 1927a; Waterbury 1928a; Reilly 1929: 100).

104. Women who kept their hair long often wore a chignon, giving the impression of short hair from the front (Laubner 1996: 88). The title character in *The Flapper* (1920) temporarily sports an appropriate do without actually cutting off her long locks. See further Sessions 2013.

105. Tennis stars like Suzanne Lenglen and Helen Wills (a.k.a. "Helen of California") advocated comfortable, incidentally revealing clothes for female athletes (Banner 1983: 407; Laubner 1996: 73).

106. Makeup in the 1920s was "created to be noticed, to suggest independence and modernity" (de Castelbajac 1995: 52; cf. Fass 1977: 283–85).

FIGURE 2.13. Detail of a still for *The Private Life of Helen of Troy* (left) and a publicity card for Greta Garbo (right).

seduce Telemachus, she dons a flimsy minidress with a slanted hem, makeup, and copious jewelry—the sartorial choices of the fashionable flapper.

Many of these costumes literally combine ancient and modern elements: short skirts are worn with "classical" drapery, and a relatively demure Greek-inspired wrap accompanies an up-to-the-minute minidress with a fringed diagonal hem (figure 2.15). The cloche hat, accessorized with plumes, becomes a helmet, and vampy black drapery is trimmed with a laurel leaf design (as in the still shown in figure 2.17 below). Sometimes even Helen's hairdos combine long and short-looking styles for an oddly schizophrenic look. Though eclectic, however, Helen's wardrobe is not a mere grab bag of elements. Fashions of the period were heavily influenced by Art Deco, which was considered

FIGURE 2.14. Details of stills showing (left) Maria Corda in *The Private Life of Helen of Troy* and (right) Francis Bushman in *Ben-Hur*.

modern, sophisticated, decadent, and European.[107] Since Deco in turn was influenced by antiquity, it allowed women to see themselves as simultaneously modern and exotic.[108]

Consequently, many of the "Greek" features of Helen's wardrobe would not have been out of place on a fashionable, wealthy young woman in the 1920s.[109] Headwear was often wreathlike and/or accessorized with feathers or grapes, both of which have ancient associations. One fashion report informs us, "Head bands for the evening coiffure have taken a decidedly classical turn. . . .

107. See L. Fischer 2003: 17–24, 25, 255. Deco connoted luxury and affluence, and was used to attract women consumers via beauty products and fashion (L. Fischer 2003: ch. 2 and 3). In film, it was used to convey the past and future, legend and fantasy (Everson 1978: 311–16).

108. On Art Deco and classicism, see M. Williams 2013a: 13–14.

109. Compare the exploitation of Egyptomania to endow early Cleopatras with contemporary style (Wyke 2002: ch. 8; Llewellyn-Jones 2013a: 322–25).

FIGURE 2.15. Details of stills for *The Private Life of Helen of Troy* showing Helen (left) in a dress shop at Troy and (right) wearing the same outfit but without the wrap.

copying designs such as Helen of Troy herself might have worn.[110] A cloche hat from the same year "somewhat resembles a Greek helmet worn by the warriors who were fighting to recover fair Helen of Troy."[111] Greek key designs were ubiquitous, and "the classic cameo remained in style."[112] As for Helen's footwear, it evokes not only "Greek" sandals but several contemporary types of strappy shoe, including ballet slippers, dancing shoes, elegant evening shoes (which often had long ties), and tennis shoes.[113]

110. *Scranton Republican*, May 21, 1924.

111. Anon. 1924b.

112. Laubner 1996: 149.

113. For examples, see McConathy & Vreeland 1976: 46; Fiell & Dirix 2015: 455. I am grateful to Cameron Kippen, of the *History of Shoes* blog, for correspondence regarding footwear in this period.

"Greek" draperies themselves had modern resonance, thanks to the contemporary craze for "Greek dance." First popularized by dancers like Isadora Duncan and Ruth St. Denis, the look became more widely visible through such media as vaudeville and the Ziegfeld Follies.[114] In *Private Life,* Helen's attendants were played by the Marion Morgan Dancers, a dance troupe that started out in vaudeville and became known for shows on ancient themes.[115] One of these, entitled *Helen of Troy,* was a big hit in the early 20s, and presumably lay behind their casting in this film.[116] But such influences were not confined to the stage. An ad from 1920 informs us that the modern Paris has "stolen from history" fashions as beautiful as Helen of Troy herself (figure 2.16). *Women's Wear Daily* was on board with the trend.[117] Fashion spreads featured not only props such as Greek columns, but statuesque poses, and skirts whose pleats and folds echoed the fluting of such columns.[118] This integration of ancient style with a twenties sensibility reached its apogee with the influential designer Madeleine Vionnet, who drew overtly on Greek as well as modern art.[119]

Thanks to classical revival dance, *Private Life* could use movement to conflate ancient and modern in a similar way. Many stills evoke dance poses used by Duncan and her students. At the same time, as we saw earlier, some of them evoke flapper dance. This is no accident, since flapper dance was itself influenced by the freedom of movement espoused in "Greek" dance.[120] Though inspired by antiquity, "art dance" had become a token of the modern.[121] Marion Morgan, specifically, was interested not just in putting on a show but in "educating modern bodies and minds"; her school "promised that women

114. On "Classical Revival Dance" in the 1920s, see Carden-Coyne 2009: ch. 6.

115. On Marion Morgan and her dancers, see Mayne 1994: 40–45.

116. Stills from this production in the New York Public Library show marked similarities to *Private Life*. NYPL, accessed March 29, 2021, https://digitalcollections.nypl.org/items/510d47e2-7da5-a3d9-e040-e00a18064a99.

117. Kirke 1998: 42.

118. See, e.g., Laubner 1996: 21; Fiell & Dirix 2015: 314–15.

119. Kirke 1998: 41–42. For Vionnet's use of modern art, see L. Fischer 2003: 67.

120. On the mutual influence of Greek dance and flapperdom, see Landay 2002: 233–34; Carden-Coyne 2009: 301, 318–19.

121. See Carden-Coyne 2009: 269–75 and cf. Conor 2004: 165–66. Duncan associated her dance style with both sexual liberation for women and political revolution (Daly 1995: 166 and ch. 6). Antiquity was also used to argue for freeing women from the corset (see, e.g., Anon. 1923b).

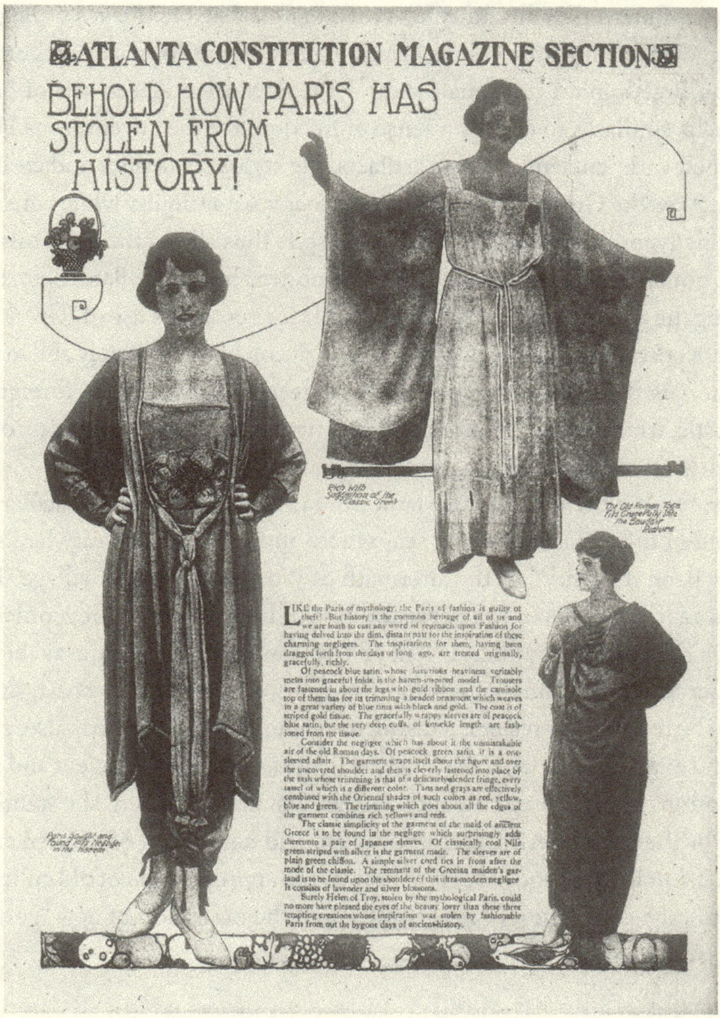

ATLANTA CONSTITUTION MAGAZINE SECTION

BEHOLD HOW PARIS HAS STOLEN FROM HISTORY!

LIKE the Paris of mythology, the Paris of fashion is guilty of theft! But history is the common heritage of all of us and we are loath to cast any word of reproach upon Fashion for having delved into the dim, distant past for the inspiration of these charming negligees. The inspirations for them, having been dragged forth from the days of long ago, are treated originally, gracefully, richly.

Of peacock blue satin, whose luxurious heaviness veritably melts into graceful folds, is the harem-inspired model. Trousers are fastened in about the legs with gold ribbon and the camisole top of them has for its trimming a beaded ornament which weaves in a great variety of blue tints with black and gold. The coat is of striped gold tissue. The gracefully wrappy sleeves are of peacock blue satin, but the very deep cuffs, of knuckle length, are fashioned from the tissue.

Consider the negligee which has about it the unmistakable air of the old Roman days. Of peacock green satin, it is a one-sleeved affair. The garment wraps itself about the figure and over the uncovered shoulder and then is cleverly fastened into place by the sash whose trimming is that of a delicately slender fringe, every tassel of which is a different color. Tans and grays are effectively combined with the Oriental shades of such colors as red, yellow, blue and green. The trimming which goes about all the edges of the garment combines rich yellows and reds.

The classic simplicity of the garment of the maid of ancient Greece is to be found in the negligee which surprisingly adds thereunto a pair of Japanese sleeves. Of classically cool Nile green striped with silver is the garment made. The sleeves are of plain green chiffon. A simple silver cord ties in front after the mode of the classic. The remnant of the Grecian maiden's garland is to be found upon the shoulder of this ultra-modern negligee. It consists of lavender and silver blossoms.

Surely Helen of Troy, stolen by the mythological Paris, could no more have pleased the eyes of the beauty lover than these three tempting creations whose inspiration was stolen by fashionable Paris from out the bygone days of ancient history.

FIGURE 2.16. Story in *The Atlanta Constitution*, August 8, 1920.

could regain their youth through sculptural emulations of feminine grace, beauty, and sensuality"; even "erotic movement" was legitimized "when it looked like classical art," not only "for the benefit of the spectator" but "as an activity of female empowerment."[122]

This fashionable penchant for antiquity affords us the same kind of double vision in regard to other aspects of the mise-en-scène. Deco architecture,

122. Carden-Coyne 2009: 273, 293, 300.

though influenced by antiquity, was used in films like *Our Dancing Daughters* to suggest a protagonist who is "avant-garde and perilous" and to convey a sense of freedom for the female star.[123] The uncluttered Deco sets of *Private Life* help, similarly, to convey a sense of freedom for the adventurous Helen. Adorned with "ancient" art and artifacts, the style's clean lines and choice of decor allow the Greek and Trojan palaces to invoke antiquity while conveying a distinctly modern look. Contemporary style thus allows the film's mise-en-scène not to replace the ancient with the modern but to conflate them, transporting the ancient world into the new and vice versa. The use of "Greek" and modern costumes, hairstyles, gestures, and decor, both separately and in combination, is the matrix for a peculiar synthesis of old and new, foreign and domestic, which enabled Korda and his designers to reinvent the oldest of "old Europe's" femmes fatales as a modern American.

The resulting celebration of Maria Corda's Helen is also a spectacular celebration of the "village near the sea" where ancient Greek beauty had so recently been reborn.[124] In the aftermath of World War I, that "village" had a global reach. Thanks to the pervasiveness of her story, and the iconicity of "Greek" beauty, the mythical Helen of Troy was internationally available. But in order to encapsulate the rebirth of such beauty on the west coast, she too had to be reborn. The result is a distinctively modern figure who is also a "classic" and exotic beauty from the "ancient" world, embodying ancient and modern notions of royalty and divinity. As the "first flapper queen" she stands not only for the consumerism, exhibitionism, and narcissism of women and of cinema, but for the modern cult of beauty, the appropriation of old culture by the new, the coronation of new royalty, and the exaltation of new "gods." In short, she stands for Hollywood.

A Short Cut to Sophistication

The Helen of *Private Life* is not, then, sequestered safely in an ancient, exotic Otherwhere, but conveys a distinctively "modern" style of femininity. When she smiles into the mirror, surrounded by elegant, admiring attendants, the fashionable female viewer is invited to see her aspirational self in the on-screen image. As we have seen, however, many people thought this kind of audience identification posed a moral threat, especially to young women.

123. L. Fischer 2003: 110; Everson 1978: 314.

124. Above, p. 7.

Flapper movies were especially controversial in this regard. Even a staunch defender of the genre, who argues that such films will be beneficial in the long term, acknowledges the "restlessness" they provoke in young women, because they are bringing "the idea of Love and Sex from under cover."[125] In Herbert Blumer's study, reactions to *Our Dancing Daughters* range from censure by adults, who think the movie dangerous, to enthusiasm among the young (especially young women), for whom it embodies modern values and the spirit of their generation.[126] One female respondent wants the protagonist's flapper dress; another says the film inspired her to imitate Crawford's attitude; another admires not her character but Ann, the gold digger played by Anita Page; yet another declares that the film strengthened her rebellion against parental control and the sexual double standard.[127]

Early Hollywood mores required female misbehavior to lead to a bad end—or at a minimum to repentance. In *Our Dancing Daughters*, Ann the gold digger takes to drink and ends up falling down a grand Art Deco staircase to her death. Unlike her dissolute friends, however, Diana, the protagonist, remains virginal and therefore available to be reunited, eventually, with the man she loves. Despite her freewheeling ways, then, the flapper heroine's morals are normally conventional, her virtue preserved by marriage, to "uninteresting males less energetic and more conventional than herself"—marriage, that is, to men like Menelaus.[128] Yet flapper-Helen gets away, unchastened, despite the fact that she behaves deplorably by Hollywood's prim (if hypocritical) standards. Indeed, her transgressive behavior is central to her appeal. *Private Life* was promoted as a "sensational exposé" of her "startling" affairs, which "shocked the world!" As advertisements gleefully declared, "She put the 'Hist!' in History, with a scandal the world has never stopped talking about."

Arguably, the threat posed by Helen's excesses—both sartorial and behavioral—is neutralized through comedy. Humor can serve as a kind of Trojan Horse or alibi—that is, a strategic way of allowing us to enjoy scandalous behavior without endorsing it.[129] By depriving such actions of serious

125. Biery 1927b.

126. Blumer 1933: 183–84. For Blumer's study, see above, pp. 14–15.

127. Blumer 1933: 32, 152, 43, 158.

128. The quotation is from Higashi 1978: 130. Cf. Everson 1978: 200; Ryan 1976: 373. Even in DeMille's sex comedies, "conventional values triumphed in the last reel" (Higashi 2002: 298).

129. In the 1930s, censors (both formal and informal) were alert to the use of humor to smuggle in pernicious messages, specifically in the case of "fallen women" films (L. Jacobs 1991: 66–69, 82–83, 113).

consequences, comedy leaves the film free to revel in the very behavior that it mocks. This alibi allows female viewers to enjoy the self-assertion of flapper-Helen as well as her self-indulgence. By the same token, it allows men (as well as women) to enjoy the film's raciness—and Maria Corda's lovely skin—without facing the seamier implications of their own voyeurism. This approach pervades publicity materials for *Private Life*, where humor is intertwined with raciness as an attraction. By equating the draw of illicit sex with the draw of comedy, for example, ad copy reassures us that men can enjoy the film without being convicted of prurience: "It's the answer to the ancient question—'Why do men leave home?' It is to laugh."

Cartoons are used to similar effect. As we saw, the lobby cards are framed with voyeurs (plate 1). Other ads feature a giant Helen ogled by boys attired as "Greek" warriors, whom she blithely controls as if she were the original 50 Foot Woman; another rather disturbing image shows the gleeful, leering heads of four small boys poking out of a giant book—presumably Erskine's—on which a bare-kneed Helen, adorned with grapes, is posed suggestively, seeming to crush her juvenile admirers between the pages (figure 2.1). This childish rendition of Helen's power over men, whether Greek warriors or the cinematic audience, counteracts any more troubling implications, reassuring us that the film is not an adult sexual threat but a harmless amusement.

The idea that the film was safe even for young children was reinforced by taking advantage of its classical bona fides, which provided a whiff of the classroom. One theater offered a promotion inviting "all pupils of the public and parochial schools of Lawrence county" to compete for free tickets to the show by coloring in one of the ads. For adults, likewise, antiquity had long provided a veil of respectability authorizing an otherwise scandalous eroticism. This classical alibi was assisted by the belief that, as Blumer puts it, "the degree of influence of motion pictures is less in the cultured classes"; these classes consist of "people who have had access to higher institutions of learning," like the college students in his study, whom he calls "a sophisticated and cultured group."[130] Such viewers are capable, on the one hand, of relishing the naughtiness underlying stylized expressions of eroticism, and on the other of resisting their potentially negative influence. If "sophistication" protects audiences from

130. Blumer 1933: 193. "Sophistication" is often a euphemism for erotic content (cf. Anon. 1928d; Evans 1928). Cf. the use of double entendre to appeal to the "sophisticated viewer" under the Hays Code (Maltby 2003: 471–75).

the movies' pernicious influence, then a film pitched to such viewers will, arguably, pose less of a threat.

The film text itself addresses a highly educated audience in unusually specific ways. Aphrodite has her Greek name (rather than the usual Venus), and Menelaos's name is spelled thus (not Menelaus). Ancient Greek lettering is used in the mise-en-scène, spelling out, for example, a Spartan shop sign advertising "dresses and sandals from Troy."[131] Pictorial elements are drawn from real works of art, which provide not only the "authenticity" of antiquarian detail but the pleasure of recognition (for those in the know). The famous statue of Athena from the Athenian Parthenon, which was known as the Athena Parthenos, is portrayed, for example, on a palace wall (figure 2.17). Some of these references are quite obscure. Menelaus's emblem, for example, is a winged boar—a highly specific image clearly taken from an unusual vase painting currently in a museum in Munich.

Classically educated viewers would be flattered by recognition of such details, which appeal to their "high" cultural knowledge. In the first instance, however, *Private Life* was presumably aimed at Erskine's middlebrow audience, who, though they were non-specialists, had due respect for the ancient world and its prestige.[132] The tagline "You've read about her" implies, in the first place, the readership of Erskine's best-selling novel. But the place where "you've read about her" could also be a mythology textbook, Homer, or a column in the local paper; you might have encountered her in college, grade school, or even elementary school (as suggested by that coloring contest).

The film caters to this broader audience by including many more recognizable visual references. As we saw, Helen's statue of Aphrodite is of the familiar Pudica type. The distinctive scene where Menelaus raises his sword against Helen (figure 2.17), which is very frequent in Greek vase painting, also appears as a small drawing on the title page of Erskine's novel, marking it as potentially recognizable to his readership. Such cues would assure a broad range of viewers of their cultural superiority, of privileged access to the world seen through

131. This is very rare in ancient world movies. As Nisbet remarks, "Why torture a mainstream audience with a Greek alphabet and numerals" when Roman equivalents are available (Nisbet 2006: 17; cf. 96).

132. Erskine attended the premiere, and his admiration for Corda in the title role was widely quoted.

FIGURE 2.17. Still for *The Private Life of Helen of Troy* showing Menelaus threatening Helen at the sack of Troy. The wall in the background is adorned with an image of the Athena Parthenos, a famous statue in the Parthenon at Athens.

the window of the past. It's not just a joke, it's a joke about Greeks! And if you're in on that joke, your appreciation of "Helen and her playmates" evinces a sophistication that absolves you of salaciousness while neutralizing the threat posed by her behavior. The film is, in short, is "a panacea for being provincial and a short cut to sophistication."[133]

133. Anon. 1928d.

A New Type of Vampire

These alibis seem to have been largely effective. There is, to be sure, some evidence of censorship. In Ottawa, for example, *Private Life* was shown "in its censored form for Ontario eyes," suggesting that there was at least one censored version in circulation; in Pittsburgh, PA, we are told, "something of the lawless fun and travesty of the pre-Pennsylvania showings was choppily subdued." [134] There is no way of telling where or how often such versions were shown, or the extent of the censorship involved. But another reviewer is surprised that it was not more stringent: "Either [the censors] are becoming more tolerant or some anti-reformer stole the shears."[135] In Salem, Oregon, one proprietor showed the film "over the severe protests . . . of the Salem police department"; the police sergeant's argument that Helen was a "bad influence" is countered by the argument that "the story of Helen is a classic, and . . . every child and adult should be acquainted with her private life."[136]

Most reviews were highly favorable. There are numerous glowing reports in a regular column of the trade weekly *Motion Picture News* (*MPN*), titled Newspaper Opinions of New Pictures, which rounds up brief, positive quotations from around the country.[137] *Private Life* is represented from January to March 1928 by a total of eighteen such entries. Reviewers praised its humor, both for eschewing slapstick ("custard pies") and for the novelty of treating ancient characters as modern people.[138] A few were leery of Helen's "European" misbehavior. *Educational Screen* considers the film "doubtful" for youth and "hardly" suitable for children under fifteen (it "will both please and offend").[139] But most excused it as "good, clean fun"—a bit risqué, perhaps,

134. The first quotation is from the *Motion Picture News* column Key Cities Reports, October 1928 (cf. below, pp. 80–81); the second is from Parry 1928.

135. Anon. 1928f.

136. Anon. 1928g.

137. Reviews from this source are marked *MPN*. Note that they are decontextualized quotations, all positive, and printed without headlines or bylines (though in a few cases I have identified the critics' names from other sources).

138. *New York Graphic* (*MPN*). Novelty in film, that is. A similar treatment in written form, entitled *Ladies in Hades*, had been serialized in *Photoplay* earlier in 1927 and was published as a book in 1928. It treats Helen, among other famous historical vamps, as a fashionable denizen of Hell retelling her earthly exploits (Kummer 1928).

139. Anon. 1928c.

but not "risky."[140] Embracing the promise of the film's publicity campaign, they compared Menelaus and Helen to "Mr. and Mrs." in the Clare Briggs cartoons and to "Helen and Warren," the endlessly bickering middle-class subjects of another popular comic.[141]

The mise-en-scène elicits rapture from nearly every reviewer. The word "beauty" appears over and over again, for all visual aspects of the film. It is "spectacular and strikingly beautiful," with "settings of sweeping beauty and magnificence" and "passages of rare beauty, idyllic and refreshing"; the sets are "formal, dignified and beautiful" and "of unusual beauty"; the photography "enhances all rare beauty that has been put into sets, costumes and action"; the reader "will revel in the real beauty of the sets and costumes, the lighting and play of shadows."[142] Such language evokes Ruth Waterbury's fantasy of ancient Greece, as a world "made by beauty, urged by beauty, producing beauty."[143] She could have been writing about this very film, with its spectacular appropriation of an ideal of ancient Greek beauty for modernity.

Numerous reviewers applauded the incarnation of that beauty in the person of Maria Corda. She is "optically dazzling," "exquisitely beautiful," "brilliantly beautiful," "beautiful, statuesque and decorative enough to carry Helen's reputation," "an amazingly attractive young woman, gifted with grace and poise," "loaded down with . . . 'it,'" and "quite an authentic reason for any old kind of war."[144] She is "pictorially ravishing," "the real work of art in this picture," and "a brilliant gem in a finely wrought setting."[145] That setting includes every aspect of the mise-en-scène, from the architecture to Helen's bevy of elegant handmaids. But its most intimate layer consists of the fantastic

140. *New York Journal* (*MPN*); *New York Herald Tribune* (*MPN*).

141. Briggs's style is comparable to the cartoons framing the lobby cards. Both reviews are cited from a scrapbook held by the Margaret Herrick Library; there are no titles or authors. These sources are cited as Anon. Herrick.

142. *Los Angeles Express* (*MPN*); Anon. 1928c; *Providence News* (*MPN*); *New York Graphic* (*MPN*); *Los Angeles Daily News* (*MPN*); *Educational Screen*. For yet more praise of the film's spectacle, see Malamud 2013: 336. A photospread in the *Illustrated London News* from December 31, 1927 is headlined "Film Art at Its Best."

143. Waterbury 1928b: 34–35; cf. above, p. 000.

144. Anon. 1928d; Regina Cannon, *New York American* (*MPN*); George Gerhard, *New York Evening World* (*MPN*); *Los Angeles Examiner* (*MPN*); Quin Martin, *New York World* (*MPN*); Anon. 1928b.

145. Lusk 1927; Anon. Herrick; *New York Telegraph* (*MPN*). Cf. M. Williams 2013a: 59 on the star as work of art. For the star as a precious jewel, see Morin 2005: 115.

wardrobe used to showcase the jewel of Helen's body. Reviewers speak approvingly of "Maria Corda in various stages of slight clothing," and of "gorgeous, dainty, graceful frocks."[146] One is pleased that "it was too late, fortunately, for [the censors] to do anything with Maria Corda's costumes."[147]

Helen's beauty was produced not only by Corda's figure, face, clothing, and environment, but also by her performance. She is praised for "poise, grace, a sense of dramatic and comedy balance."[148] The eyes are of special importance in silent film acting, and hers, which have "a dazzling warmth," "twinkle merrily as she inveigles her victims over a cup of wine."[149] Others speak of "clinging, earthy, sensuous movements," and praise her "piquant, exotic manner" as "perfect" for the role.[150] One who departs from the chorus of praise for her physical beauty ("not the most beautiful actress on the screen") nevertheless judges her "entirely plausible" in the role because "she is so clever and so glamorous that she gives the effect of amazing beauty."[151]

Corda was evidently successful in infusing her "classical" beauty with "European" exoticism.[152] Nearly every review mentions her Hungarian or European background. Others allude to it. Edwin Schallert, drama critic for the *Los Angeles Times,* speaks of "the piquant paprika of a delightful burlesque"; another reviewer, calling her "a graceful enchantress with a naughty twinkle," opines that no one in Hollywood could have played the role "with the same spirit"; according to a third, any Hollywood star would have looked "out of place," and Corda's "very strangeness to silver screen contributed to her felicitous performance."[153] Running with the allusions to European royalty, Mordaunt Hall's *New York Times* review is entitled "Helen, the First."[154] The word "first" refers to her primacy, as the "first preferred blonde," but also to the novelty of her new incarnation, which matches that of the film itself. As a

146. Anon. 1927b; *New York Daily News* (*MPN*).

147. Parry 1928.

148. *New York Daily News* (*MPN*).

149. *New York Daily News* (*MPN*); M. Hall 1927a. Conspicuous coded eye movements were used in silent film to make the eyes "speak" (cf., e.g., Blum 1953: 15).

150. *New York World*; *New York Evening World* (*MPN*).

151. Anon. Herrick.

152. Hall judges her "just sufficiently classical . . . a combination of the ancient and the modern" (M. Hall 1927b).

153. Schallert 1927; Anon. Herrick; George Gerhard, *New York Evening World* (*MPN*).

154. M. Hall 1927a.

brief *Photoplay* review declares, "Maria Corda as *Helen* has given the screen a new type of vampire and the country is going to rave over her."[155]

There are a few dissenting voices. The trade paper *Film Spectator*, for example, complains grumpily about the number of "meaningless close-ups" of Corda; a reviewer in the *Acron Beacon Journal* protests against the cheapening of Helen from "a symbol of beauty and splendor for all poets and dreamers" to a frivolous modern flapper; *Time*'s reviewer is exceptionally peevish in his contempt for the film's "vulgarizing" of Homer (even though, to his disgust, it still managed "to enrapture most of the people who watch it").[156] Schallert complains about the vulgarity of some of the intertitles, and Donald Thompson, of the *New York Telegram*, likens Corda's performance to that of a seedy burlesque dancer.[157] One female critic calls her "a vapid, vacuous, arch, coquettish creature," and *Variety* complains that the Helen of Troy look-alike contest in the trashy *New York Graphic* is not a good tie-in, since it makes Helen look commonplace: "Miss Corda might [as well] be a bathing girl."[158]

Overall, however, the film was extremely successful with critics. Some reviews suggest that the same was true for the general audience. The *Los Angeles Herald*, for example, declared *Private Life* a "great success with audience which reacted frequently and favorably," while the *New York American* reported, "audience highly amused . . . and enthusiastic."[159] The film did well, if not spectacularly, at the box office.[160] In its column Key Cities Reports, *Motion Picture News* provided regular updates on the box office success (or otherwise) of new

155. *Photoplay*, January 1928.

156. Anon. 1927c; H. Wolf 1927; Anon. 1927a. Briton Hadden, one of *Time*'s founders, "made a habit of printing insulting movie reviews"; the review of *Private Life*, in particular, caused offence to at least one reader who said the film should be reviewed from the audience's perspective (Wilner 2006: 202). Someone calling himself "Mr. Intellect" is also contemptuous (*Variety*, July 11, 1928).

157. Schallert 1927; *Photoplay*, March 1928. Burlesque as a performance genre (in contrast to revues, made respectable by Ziegfeld) was considered low class and vulgar (Latham 2000: 108–112). Cf. also the highbrow hostility of H. Wolf 1927.

158. Ross 1927; Anon. 1927b. The *Graphic* was a tabloid famous for its gimmicky contests and known by some as the "Pornographic" (W. Hunt 1989: 135, 138–39).

159. Both quotes are from *MPN*.

160. It was Korda's most successful Hollywood film and became the first in his series of "private lives," followed by *Henry VIII* (1933) and *Don Juan* (1934). Drazin 2002: 59 reports that it cost $432,000 but returned "what was then a colossal $717,000 at the box-office." *Variety* reported "good" and "satisfactory" sales (March 7, 1928; January 18, 1928). Horak 2005: 252 calls it "a major box office success." For comparanda, see Glancy 1992: 128–32.

movies in various places. For *Private Life,* it includes sales reports from fourteen North American cities. In Albany, "there were hold out crowds each evening"; in Cleveland, "standing room was at a premium"; in Knoxville, "people jammed the sidewalk for a half block attempting to see the show."[161]

Yet Key Cities also reports poor sales for *Private Life* in some locations. At the Troy Theatre in Troy, New York (of all places), the film "did not please a whole lot of people"; in Dallas it "failed to get them"; and in Ottawa, the censored version was "only a fair attraction." Another trade paper, *Exhibitors Herald & Moving Picture World* (*EH/MPW*), which provides brief reports from exhibitors all over the country, is more damning. A few of their comments are positive, but most agree with the exhibitor from Melville, LA, who states that it is "not a small town picture," adding that it was "classed by majority of patrons as very poor and silly"; another exhibitor, from Franklin, Nebraska, explains, "Patrons complained of no action."[162]

This criticism is echoed even by some of the positive reviewers, who found parts of the film boring, slow, or heavy-handed. But the main reason for the film's mixed success with the broader public seems to have been the very absence of slapstick that so pleased the critics. Satire is by its nature exclusionary. The "sophistication" that titillates the middlebrow viewer is understandably alienating to the less educated.[163] As an exhibitor from Logan, Iowa explains, this film "goes right over the heads of small town audiences."[164] In *Variety*'s words, it is not for "pot and pan Annie."[165] There is no way of accessing Annie's opinions, but she seems to have voted with her feet. An exhibitor from Wautoma, Wisconsin reports, "Crowds stay away in gangs after first showing." According to Key Cities Reports, in Atlanta, where the film showed to "average houses," "for the chosen few, [it] met their expectations, but fell down before the masses . . . Audiences did not know whether to laugh or frown." In Seattle, the same source notes, its "subtlety and satire" appealed only to "the wise audiences."

161. With the exception of Ottawa (October 1928), my citations of Key Cities come from the first quarter of 1928.

162. *EH/MPW*, June 1928, March 1928.

163. Michael Korda asserts that the film was "too sophisticated, ironic and 'European' to be a major financial success" (Korda 1979: 79). In general, audiences must be alert to a film's intertexts in order to enjoy it (cf. Staiger 1992: 121). Cf. also Ellis 1992: 86–87 on viewers' aggressive response to films that do not leave them in a position of mastery.

164. *EH/MPW*, March 1928.

165. Anon. 1927b.

The enthusiasm of most professional critics presumably results from their membership in the "wise audiences" or "cultured classes." The *New York Times*, for example, generally treated film reviews as an "extremely low priority," yet its reviewer, Mordaunt Hall, wrote twice about *Private Life*.[166] Significantly, all but two of the eighteen glowing quotations from Newspaper Opinions of New Pictures derive from critics in New York or Los Angeles, as opposed to the "small towns" of the exhibitors' reports.[167] The film was also embraced by journals with certain intellectual pretensions. *Educational Screen* calls it "notable" for intelligent adults, and a column in *Amateur Movie Makers* entitled "reviews for the Cintelligenzia" waxes enthusiastic.[168] A more grudging reviewer, who calls the film "less stimulating than it should be," still thinks it shows that the cinema can be "faintly cerebral."[169]

These various dissatisfactions define the parameters of the film's specific kind of class appeal. *Variety* contrasts "pot and pan Annie" with the "de luxe house loge clientele" who will enjoy the movie; most importantly, it is broad enough "not to be over the heads of the John Held Jr., models here or abroad."[170] John Held Jr. was a well-known illustrator, many of whose cartoons satirized the jazz age.[171] His name is invoked to represent the audience bracketed by "pot and pan Annie" on the one hand, and intellectual snobs like the *Time* reviewer on the other. For this "middlebrow" audience, at least, *Private Life* seems to have achieved the impossible: through judicious casting plus an enthusiastic embrace of contemporary fashions, not to mention Helen's risqué reputation, it succeeded in using distinctively Hollywood resources to generate a plausible rendition of the most beautiful woman in the world.

166. Koszarski 1990: 191; M. Hall 1927a, 1927b.

167. The other two are from Providence, RI. The studio took out magazine ads touting the film's success specifically with New York critics.

168. Anon. 1928c; Anon. 1928b. The latter column was "designed to tell the intelligent movie fan of those photoplays which will appeal to the intelligent person" (*Amateur Movie Makers*, January 1928). It was aimed at viewers who are "intelligent and subtle and who want films above the average as it exists today" (*Amateur Movie Makers*, April 1928).

169. Anon. Herrick.

170. Anon. 1927b.

171. He helped to define the image of the flapper and designed F. Scott Fitzgerald's book jackets (see Held 1972).

PART II

Big Screen Epic

3

An Anticheesecake Doll

HELEN OF TROY (1956)

Olympian Scope and Vastness

Warner Brothers' *Helen of Troy* arrived at the crest of Hollywood's second wave of big budget epics. It appeared in the wake of *Quo Vadis* (1951), the religious extravaganza for which the term "blockbuster" was coined, and *The Robe* (1953), the first film ever presented in widescreen.[1] Ancient themes provided a perfect showcase for this and other postwar technological advances, which enabled the studios to offer spectacles of unprecedented scale, grandeur, and expense.[2] The genre was despised by the highly educated, as the vulgarest form of middlebrow entertainment, but the general public embraced its breathtaking presentation of stories that combined broad familiarity with lofty cultural status.[3]

Publicity for this *Helen* makes much of the fact that its alleged source, the *Iliad*, is both "one of the greatest stories ever written" and "a story we all

1. On *Quo Vadis*, see especially Scodel & Bettenworth 2009; Blanshard & Shahabudin 2011: ch. 2. On *The Robe*, see Babington & Evans 1993: 206–17; Wieber 2016: 227–35.

2. See further Belton 1990; Belton 1992; Eldridge 2006: 56–59. On the centrality of spectacle to the genre, see Paul 2013a: 214–21; Llewellyn-Jones 2009: 574–77; Llewellyn-Jones 2018: ch. 1; Stubbs 2013: ch. 6; and cf. Babington & Evans 1993: 64–65; Theodorakopoulos 2010.

3. On the target audience(s) for ancient world epic, see Llewellyn-Jones 2018: 66–68. On the status appeal of "culture" in this period, see Miller & Nowak 1977: 9. For the scorn of the highly educated, cf. Miller & Nowak 1977: 227–29; Wyke 1997: 11; Jancowich 2004; Jancowich 2011.

know."[4] In keeping with the usual Hollywood formula, the trailer promises not only "All the Storied Wonders of Homer's Immortal 'ILIAD,'" but also "All the Gloried Moments of its Inspired Romance." Like many such productions, it was filmed at the Cinecittà Studios in Rome, with a multinational cast, and aimed at a broad worldwide audience. It opened to enormous fanfare, with a much-heralded global premiere taking place on January 26, 1956 (i.e., 1/26/56) in 126 cities in 56 countries. Presented in WarnerColor and Cinemascope, with an alleged cast of thirty thousand, it was, in the words of the trailer, an enterprise of "Olympian scope and vastness." As such, it was comparable in significance to the Trojan War itself: "Here's a great moment in history, a great moment on the motion picture screen."[5]

The cinematic epic nearly always revolves around a male hero. If he is famous, the film is probably named for him (*Spartacus, Ben-Hur, Attila, Alexander the Great, Ulysses*). Ancient women, in contrast, typically have their agency diminished in favor of their male counterparts.[6] When a woman's name does appear in the title, more often than not it is coupled with a man's as his romantic partner (*Samson & Delilah, Solomon & Sheba, David & Bathsheba*). Yet the occasional epic is named for a famous woman in her own right (*Cleopatra, Salome*). These are usually glamorous but "bad" women, who eventually meet their comeuppance and/or repent their evil ways. Helen's popular image continued to place her in such company. The cover of that year's edition of Erskine's book presents her as a lavishly endowed Monroe-style femme

4. Quotations are from "Sounds of Homeric Troy," one of three promotional telefilms reproduced as extras on the DVD under the title "Behind the Cameras." The other two are entitled "The Look of Troy" and "Interviewing Helen." The screenplay (by Hugh Gray and John Twist) also draws on other ancient sources, as well as creating new material. It was the director's practice to work closely with his writers (Keenan 2007: 43, 170–71) and in this case, Wise says, "we kept . . . re-writing the script" (Cary 1974: 66). Glücklich 2000: 97–108 sees a relationship to the Helen of Ovid's *Heroides*. For other ancient intertexts, cf. Vivante 2013: 23–24.

5. "Sounds of Homeric Troy." For this kind of equation, see Wood 1989: 173; Sobchak 2003 [1990]: 302–13; Eldridge 2006: 59–60; cf. also Paul 2013a: 304–5. On the promotion of epic films, cf. above, p. 44.

6. In *Jason and the Argonauts* (1963), for example, Medea is romanticized by erasing her dark side and given almost nothing to do (Ormand 2013; cf. Paul 2013a: 98–99, 126). Politically powerful women are eroticized, typically showing more interest in romance and beauty than in actually ruling (Wieber-Scariot 1998). Even the virtuous Penelope is reduced (E. Hall 2013). The silent *Judith of Bethulia* (1913), a harbinger of the genre, was a striking exception: though female, Judith is "an archetypal epic hero" (Hirsch 1978: 103).

FIGURE 3.1. Cover of a 1956 edition of John Erskine's novel.

fatale, with copy that speaks knowingly of "the sinful Helen" (figure 3.1). Clearly, she was ripe for epic treatment.

"Sounds of Homeric Troy" informs us that Helen's story is one that "we all know, but that until now no man has ever seen, or heard." In the big-screen frenzy of the period, three studios vied to be the first to tell that story. Cecil B. DeMille planned a Helen of Troy film, possibly starring Hedy Lamarr, and Lamarr did in fact star in *L'amante di Paride*, a three-part Italian epic.[7] But the only such treatment to see the light of day was Warner Brothers' entry,

7. Half an hour of the Helen portion may be seen in *Loves of Three Queens* (1955). But the film was never released in the US and has a chaotic production history. For a detailed account,

directed by the prolific Robert Wise.[8] Wise was a versatile filmmaker who was exceptionally well attuned to the exigencies of genre. By the time he made *Helen*, his twentieth feature, he had already worked successfully in science fiction, horror, historical drama, melodrama, adventure, noir, crime drama, fictionalized biography, western, comedy, and war films. When offered the movie, he was "not mad about the material," but wanted to see if he could pull off an epic.[9]

As a "passionate political liberal," Wise wanted all his films to say something about "social justice, equality, and the need for tolerance," hoping that they would increase international understanding and "aid in bringing the world closer to peace."[10] His science fiction classic *The Day the Earth Stood Still* (1951) is a Cold War parable in which the alien Klaatu, a Christlike figure, tells the human race, "live in peace, or pursue your present course and face obliteration."[11] His war films avoid glamorizing combat and focus on human relationships.[12]

Helen was no exception. Wise was drawn to the "personal and intimate" aspects of the Trojan War story, and it was his choice to center the film on the affair between Helen and Paris.[13] Though well suited to stylization, spectacle, and immersive "realism,"[14] widescreen was on its face inhospitable to close-ups and thus to character development, intimacy, or the subtle

---

see Wingrove 2016; cf. also Wieber 2005: 139; Nikoloutsos 2015: 72–81; S. Shearer 2010: 264, 275–80, 374.

8. Wise was also the de facto producer, since *Helen* has no producer credit—a matter of some irritation to the director (Cary 1974: 68–69; cf. Leemann 1995: 35).

9. Gehring 2012: 168. Wise's biggest hits were to be in yet another genre, the musical: *West Side Story* and *The Sound of Music*.

10. Gehring 2012: xviii; Leemann 1995: 5, 9.

11. On Cold War ideology and American film, see especially Sayre 1982; Biskind 1983; S. J. Whitfield 1996: ch. 6; O'Donnell 2003. On *The Day the Earth Stood Still*, see also F. Thompson 1995: 10; Keenan 2007: ch. 7; Gehring 2012: 141–51. For the generic analogy between science fiction and epic in this period, see Cohan 1997: 130–35. Note too that science fiction costume has owed much to antiquity (cf. Maeder 1987: 97).

12. See Gehring 2012: ch. 9.

13. Cary 1974: 65, 69.

14. Belton 1992: ch. 9; Maltby 2003: 251–55; Eldridge 2006: 65–76; Theodorakopoulos 2010: 3–6, 22–25. On widescreen composition, see Hirsch 1978: 22–24; Bordwell 1985: 199–201; Bordwell et al. 1985: 361; D. Cook 1981: 422–24; Belton 1992: 197–206; Hall & Neale 2010: 155–58.

expression of emotion.[15] But Wise departed from current technique, using traditional editing and "big-head close ups," which would help to engage the audience with the love story.[16] He also wanted his epic to be less "black and white" than films like *Quo Vadis*, and "modern in terms of the acting and delivery of the scenes" as opposed to "overboard and hammed."[17]

In his melodramas Wise often championed victimized women, even when they transgressed the boundaries of normative female behavior.[18] He brought this perspective, along with his pacifism, to the story of Helen, whom he presents as an innocent model of feminine virtue mistreated by cruel, militaristic men.[19] His film goes to extraordinary lengths both to insist on her innocence and to dissociate the love story from the kind of dangerous eroticism standardly associated with her name. This revisionist agenda is spelled out in the promotional telefilm *Interviewing Helen*, where Helen herself appears to inform us that "history lies" about her affair with Paris. Warner Brothers' forthcoming film, she informs us personally, will finally tell the truth about "a woman and her love."[20]

As Wise was well aware, however, a proper epic must have more at stake than personal romance. It requires "big, earthshaking themes," usually related in some way to national or cultural identity.[21] In the Hollywood epics of the 1950s, these themes are usually related to the Cold War conflict, under US hegemony, between communism and the "West."[22] The magnificence of such

15. Miller & Nowak 1977: 323–24; Llewellyn-Jones 2018: 190. Cf. the way *Ten Commandments* shows that "the wide-screen gaze, as well as the social and political power it both projects and signifies, is the property of men" (Nadel 1993: 418). As a general rule, intimacy disrupts spectacle (Llewellyn-Jones 2009: 576; Llewellyn-Jones 2018: 110), and vice versa (cf. Belton 1992: 194–95). On the tension between melodrama and "history" from a design perspective, see Tashiro 1998: ch. 4.

16. Leemann 1995: 126.

17. Cary 1974: 74, 65.

18. See Gehring 2012: 93–94, 135–38, 160–62.

19. Helen's innocence is hammered home by both Cassandra and Hecuba (Helen's bitterest enemy in antiquity). Gehring 2012: 167 equates Wise's Helen with his Delia, the heroine of *Until They Sail* (1957); Wieber 2010: 179 compares the Wise epic to the 1955 Sirk melodrama *All That Heaven Allows*.

20. Promising the "true story" has been a way of introducing a new version or interpretation since antiquity (cf. Blondell 2013: 117–22).

21. Wood 1989: 175. See further J. Russell 2007: 9–15; Burgoyne 2008: 14–15, 19–20, 75–78; Burgoyne 2011: passim.

22. See Eldridge 2006: ch. 4.

films was itself an advertisement for American prosperity and power, along with Hollywood's technological and cultural supremacy.[23] At the same time, their internationalism demonstrated harmonious cooperation among the various nations of the "free world."[24] *Quo Vadis* was promoted as "an artistic Marshall plan,"[25] and in the souvenir brochure for *Helen's* premiere, Jack Warner offered the film "to citizens of the world's great free nations," in the "earnest hope" that it "will help to bring about . . . good feeling and mutual trust among nations."

Mediterranean antiquity is tethered to such concerns primarily as the birthplace of Christianity, which, in turn, was equated both with American patriotism and with morality itself.[26] The religious-themed *Quo Vadis* was not only an artistic Marshall Plan but "an exemplar of Christianity," with a message of "non-violence and a just resistance to a godless aggression."[27] Many such films portray decadent, cruel, and militaristic tyrants visiting the aforementioned godless aggression on humble, innocent Christians or Jews (in the role of Christianity's precursors).[28] The enslaved provide a particularly useful analogue for the victims of communism. In DeMille's *Ten Commandments* (1956), for example, the Jewish Exodus represents religious and political freedom, with Egyptian dictatorship standing in for Russian Communism and "the Hebrews as the free and democratic West."[29] The inevitable ideological

23. Lev 2003: 164, 216; Wood 1989: 169–73; Hirsch 1978: 36–37; Wyke 2002: 318–20; Burgoyne 2008: 75–76. For the importance ascribed to American technological prowess in the 1950s, see Eldridge 2006: 76–77.

24. McLaughlin 1956.

25. Whelan 1951.

26. Sayre 1982: 11; Forshey 1992: 10. In 1954, the words "under god" were added to the Pledge of Allegiance, as a "spiritual weapon" against the soulless "materialist philosophy" of communism (S. J. Whitfield 1996: 89). On anti-communism and religion, see further Miller & Nowak 1977: ch. 3; Cohan 1997: 126–27; J. Herzog 2011; R. Lindsay 2015: ch. 3.

27. Whelan 1951; Wyke 1997: 143.

28. On Jews in biblical epic (typically referred to as "Hebrews") see Babington & Evans 1993: ch. 1 and 199–202. The assimilation was aided by casting non-Jews in Jewish roles (Cohan 1997: 135–36).

29. Lev 2003: 164. Cf. also Wyke 1997: 63. In the film's souvenir brochure, DeMille calls it a "story of the birth of freedom," representing a struggle that "is still being waged today" (cf. also Hall & Neale 2010: 163). On *Ten Commandments*, see further Forshey 1992: ch. 7; Nadel 1993; Higashi 1996; Solomon 2001: 146–58; Stubbs 2013: 97. For these themes in other epics, see Babington & Evans 1993: 54–55, 210–13; Wyke 1997: 71–72, 142–44; Scodel & Bettenworth 2009: 94–95; Lindsay 2015: ch. 3. On the enslaved in epic film, see further Elley 1984: ch. 9.

triumph of the latter—as evidenced by the existence of the audience—made such films into a "'founding story' of Western culture and the Christian religion."[30] As the program for *Quo Vadis* informs us, "A great light is breaking on the world. A new era is being born."

The vaunted superiority of Christianity and "Western" values was firmly grounded in conventional middle-class social structures and the gender norms that sustained them. Communism oppresses women, treating them as "beasts of burden."[31] It is inhospitable, more generally to love, marriage, and the nuclear family.[32] In Red Scare films, which were widely seen (if little admired), communists break up homes and have no children of their own.[33] This deprives their women of the nurturing role that in this period was considered "a woman's only means of completion and fulfillment."[34] Communist women, "bereft of the experience of 'normal' love," were regularly portrayed as "nearly nymphomaniacs."[35] In a period when couples were supposed to stick together at all costs, and even bad marriages were presented as worth saving,[36] marriage to a communist was arguably not a real marriage at all.[37]

In ancient world movies, similarly, the bad guys oppress and objectify women, pursuing them with lust as opposed to love. They offer enslaved women for sex as tokens of hospitality, and their most characteristic form of sexual expression is the drunken orgy. Such films abound in pagan women who are "nearly nymphomaniacs," such as Poppaea in *Quo Vadis*. The cachet of Mediterranean antiquity continued to provide them with an alibi for "a level of sexual display—scanty costume and suggestive scenes—which would have otherwise encountered censorship problems in the United States and many other countries."[38] With her skimpy, shining, or diaphanous draperies, copious jewelry, and decadent, luxurious surroundings, the pagan

30. Lev 2003: 226.

31. Meyerowitz 1993: 1469.

32. Biskind 1983: 169.

33. See Sayre 1982: ch. 3.

34. Miller & Nowak 1977: 152. On hostility to career women in this period, see Miller & Nowak 1977: 131–32, 160–62; Biskind 1983: 263–65; Meyerowitz 1993.

35. S. J. Whitfield 1996: 133.

36. Sayre 1982: 126–27; Miller & Nowak 1977: 329.

37. One woman got her marriage annulled solely because her husband turned out to be a communist (S. J. Whitfield 1996: 185).

38. Lev 2003: 162. Part of the big screen's appeal in this period was that it could be racier than TV (Miller & Nowak 1977: 325; G. King 2002: 30). Religious themes, especially, allowed for

vamp was a conspicuous, titillating embodiment of the desirable and desiring female.[39] She was complemented, at the other pole of desirable femininity, by the proto-Christian heroine, such as Lygia in *Quo Vadis*. Lygia is a paragon of virtuous 1950s femininity: refined, elegant, and romantically desirable, yet modest and demure as opposed to overtly sexy (cf. plate 5).[40] In contrast to pagan decadence, alluring but amoral, such women embody the "Christian" and "feminine" values of peace, compassion, freedom, equality, and above all, love.[41]

A Happy People in Love with Beauty

The Trojan War may not seem like very promising material for this kind of treatment, given its regrettable dearth of Christians or even Hebrews for American identification. Since supernatural material of a non-Judeo-Christian variety is generally eschewed in the "historical" epic, Helen's story also lacks the spectacle of the magical or miraculous, which enlivens many biblicals. Yet it actually has certain advantages when it comes to Cold War allegory. Publicity for Wise's film harks back to a time when "the two great powers of the era . . . fought for world supremacy."[42] This obvious contemporary paradigm is unavailable to stories involving only one "great power," such as Rome or Egypt, which are obliged to reconfigure the Cold War as an asymmetrical struggle between a mighty empire and simple, peaceful underdogs.[43] The Trojan Horse, too, was used widely in anti-communist rhetoric, to express Cold War fears about "the enemy within" in the form of a Soviet fifth column. Over the millennia, moreover, Aeneas's escape from Troy had developed into a foundation narrative not just for Rome but for much of

"a maximum of lust with a minimum of interference from the code" (Schumach 1975: 161). Into the 1960s, biblicals led the fight against censorship (Forshey 1992: 151).

39. On such costumes, see Llewellyn-Jones 2018: 221–25.

40. In *Ten Commandments*, similarly, Sephora is "the American girl next door . . . modestly dressed, well-groomed, and well-spoken—a properly brought up young woman of the American middle class" (Lev 2003: 167). See further Nadel 1993: 421–22.

41. For the "feminization of piety" in this period, cf. Wieber 2016: 226.

42. Anon. 1956a.

43. *Quo Vadis* is a struggle between the proud Roman eagle and the "humble cross" (opening voice-over). The *Ten Commandments* pressbook speaks of "two great opposing forces," of which one turns out to be the Christian god (Eldridge 2006: 80).

Europe. Legends about Troy's survivors served to legitimate the glorious destiny of the "West."[44]

Helen opens on a cityscape of Troy, portentously described by the authoritative (anonymous, British, male) voice-over as a "city of destiny." The main function of this kind of opening voice-over, sometimes called the "voice of history," is to introduce the epic's "big, earthshaking themes."[45] The word "destiny," which had special resonance for Americans in this period,[46] will recur, often on the lips of Aeneas, who is unusually prominent. It is he, in the opening scene, who drives his chariot through the bustling market town where, as the voice-over explains, "the industrious citizens were enjoying the works of peace." Another catchword of both period and genre, "peace" evokes President Truman's words about modern Greece in the 1947 address that initiated the Cold War. Truman characterized Greece (an authoritarian monarchy at the time) as an "industrious and peace loving country" meriting American support against communism. Troy resembles the US itself, however, in its enjoyment of an affluence derived from commerce (as opposed to conquest), which has emerged since the devastation of a recent war. That earlier Trojan war, in which the Greeks invaded under the leadership of Sparta, has created a pressing need for vigilance. Like the "free world," the Trojans know they are under threat, and have taken steps to defend themselves.[47]

The "voice of history" sounds a more distinctive note when it identifies the Trojans as "a happy people in love with beauty." The camera substantiates and aestheticizes this assertion with a panorama of Troy's fine civic architecture, cutting to scenes of "industrious citizens" painting pots and carving sculptures. The palace interior, too, is replete with elegant decorations, including huge statues of the goddesses of the Judgment (figure 3.2). These are aestheticized by the beauty-loving Paris, who calls his devotion to Aphrodite simply "admiration for the beauty of a marble image." This kind of rhetoric posits the Trojans as surrogates for ancient Greeks, who are commonly stereotyped as

44. Cf. Shepard & Powell 2004: 1. See further Görich 2006; Mac Sweeney 2018: ch. 11. Solomon surveys medieval versions of the Trojan War story (2007a: 504–14).

45. See further Babington & Evans 1993: 181–85; and cf. Theodorakopoulos 2010: 30–34; Sobchak 2003 [1990]: 297, 308–9; Stubbs 2013: 20–28.

46. On America's "destiny" as the leader of world civilization during the Cold War, see Miller & Nowak 1977: 10; Higashi 1996: 98–103. For "destiny" as a feature of the historical epic, see Elley 1984: 126; Neale 2000: 62–63.

47. On the need to remilitarize during the Cold War, even though Americans were tired of war and embracing prosperity, see Biskind 1983: 57–58.

FIGURE 3.2. Lobby card for *Helen of Troy* (1956), with statues of Aphrodite (left) and Athena (right) in the background.

cultured and civilized, dedicated to beauty, enlightenment, and art.[48] It is reinforced by the film's "Trojan" art, much of which is recognizably Greek (albeit in a vague, eclectic, and inconsistent fashion). The statue of Aphrodite, for example, is of the archaic Greek *kore* type, and the (very atypical) Athena looks like an exceptionally cranky version of the Athena Parthenos, the famous image of Athena inside the Parthenon.[49]

Wise's Troy thus ironically usurps ancient Greece, and more specifically Athens, as the cradle of "Western civilization." Washed up on the shores of Sparta after a storm, Paris arrives, like Klaatu, as an emissary from a more advanced and peaceful world. The point becomes explicit when he cheekily informs Menelaus that part of his task in sailing there is "to spread civilization." This again echoes Cold War rhetoric, in which the mantle of civilization was

48. See García Morcillo 2008.

49. This is an exception to Athena's usually positive image in film (cf. Maurice 2019: 102–9).

claimed by the US.[50] Hollywood, in particular, remained the home of beauty, still invoking an idealized conception of ancient Greek aesthetics in order to celebrate beautiful women as "love goddesses."[51] The movies had also taken on Troy's civilizing mission, as demonstrated by *Helen*'s worldwide debut. The ideological connection is implicit in Paris's assertion that at Troy they would make "songs" about a beautiful woman like Helen. His words allude both to the *Iliad* and to the film itself, positing Hollywood as the heir of "Trojan" beauty and culture, and as such, superior to Greek antiquity itself.

Troy is also Americanized in other ways. It is, emphatically, a free society: as Hecuba tells Paris, Helen is "not a captive" there. There is no mention of slavery, the few servants are treated kindly, and Paris in particular shows an upstanding disdain for class distinctions, wanting to marry Helen even when he thinks she is enslaved. The regime is not imperialist (there is no reference to subjects or even allies), and Priam is no tyrant. He is, rather, a benevolent patriarch guided by the deliberations of a "royal council," which conducts pointedly civil debates airing diverse opinions. Aeneas, in the opening scene, is on his way to a meeting of that council in order to discuss the best means of achieving peace with the Greeks. Hector, as a family man, is a "man of peace," but the saber-rattling Polydorus favors the nuclear option.[52] Paris is anti-isolationist (he does not want to live "like a crab in a shell") and proposes internationalism as an antidote to toxic paranoia about the enemy within.[53] This view, which happens to be the position most closely aligned with Hollywood's multinational business interests, prevails. But other political options are treated with respect.[54]

50. Cold War texts "depicted American foreign policy as motivated by philanthropy and disinterested good will" (S. J. Whitfield 1996: 57).

51. On the connections between Greek statuary, beauty, and stardom, see above, pp. 8–9; on their persistence in the 1950s, see M. Williams 2018: 11, ch. 5.

52. "I'd take a hundred ships of war and burn the soil of Sparta black." Being anti-war could seem un-American or communistic (cf. Miller & Nowak 1977: 62–64; S. J. Whitfield 1996: 131–32), and some Americans thought the USSR should be nuked in the interests of peace (S. J. Whitfield 1996: 5–9).

53. "We've locked out the understanding of nations, and we've locked in the poison. Trojans jumping at every rumor; pointing figures at each other."

54. Hollywood films generally avoid one-sided political ideology, which risked alienating a segment of the audience (cf. Biskind 1983: 5). Americans who thought the quest for peaceful accommodation with the enemy was a mistake may have taken comfort in the fact that Cassandra turns out to be right. Note too that Polydorus dies happy—like World War II, this is a "good war."

In contrast to Rome's urban decadence, Greece is generally presented in ancient epic as "simple" and rural, with Greeks cast sympathetically as enslaved and/or oppressed (potential) Christians.[55] But the Hellenizing (and Americanizing) of Troy frees *Helen*'s Greeks to assume the generic role of imperialist oppressor. This equivalence is betrayed by some telling slips in advertising. The trailer, for example, speaks of "the legions of imperial Greece"—diction better suited to the Roman Empire.[56] The captions on some publicity stills identify Greek soldiers as "Romans," even as they climb out of the Wooden Horse. While this undoubtedly indicates that the writers of advertising copy either did not know or did not care about differences between these ancient cultures, that fact in itself is indicative of their conceptual equivalence.[57]

This Romanizing of the Greeks turns them into notional communists—a role to which they are in some ways better suited than imperial Rome itself. American disapproval of ancient Rome and other decadent proto-communistic oppressors was attended with some ambivalence.[58] The booming postwar economy was seen as proof of superior American virtue and manifest destiny. This validated the culture of consumerism, making wealth and luxury downright American as compared to communism, which was known for its material austerity, the severity of its art, and its rustic food and clothing.[59] Communist women, in particular, are often stereotyped as ugly or unfeminine by Hollywood standards.[60] In *Silk Stockings* (1957), for example—a remake of the 1939 *Ninotchka*—a dour, plainly dressed communist (Cyd Charisse) resists Fred Astaire's romantic advances until he wins her over with "feminine" clothing,

55. Blanshard 2017: 434; Garcia Morcillo 2013.

56. Cf. the voice-over opening *Quo Vadis*, which speaks of Rome's "conquering legions."

57. The central thesis of Nisbet 2006 is that Greece in film can only be represented and read through Rome.

58. On the multiple points of identification for American viewers of Roman Empire movies, see Fitzgerald 2001; Joshel, Malamud & Wyke 2001: 6–11; Scodel & Bettenworth 2009: 121–23; cf. also Neale 2000: 90. For this kind of ideological tension in *Ten Commandments*, see Higashi 1996: 104–5; Cohan 1997: 136–37. Roman and Egyptian tyrants are also slaveholders—a point of some awkwardness for Americans, to say the least.

59. "The east is cold, austere, its people subject to material deprivation and the dictates of autocratic government; the west is warm, beautiful, and the people live happy and free in material abundance" (Maltby 2003: 65; see further S. J. Whitfield 1996: 69–76). Ayn Rand's *Screen Guide for Americans* (1950) warned against criticizing wealth and "deifying the common man" (Eldridge 2006: 97–98; cf. Sayre 1982: 50; S. J. Whitfield 1996: 130–31).

60. See Lim 2006: 123–27, 157.

perfume, and other extravagances.[61] Her makeover both reenacts the construction of a Hollywood star and demonstrates the superior beauty and happiness of the American woman. In most ancient world films, however, it is the oppressors who evince such luxury and use it to manufacture the spectacle of the feminine. This creates a tension in the equation of the affluent America of the 1950s, where Christianity was thought to promote "success and happiness,"[62] with the Christians of ancient world films, who preach the antithesis of worldly luxury.

The harsh post-Homeric reputation of Sparta, however, makes it a good fit for communist austerity. In Wise's Sparta, there is no commerce, civic life, or public space—only the palace and the wilderness. There are no ordinary citizens—just the king, his army, and the oppressed (women, peasants, and the enslaved).[63] Humble people live in a rustic hut and even the royal palace is a gloomy fortress, whose blank walls and massive Doric columns bear little resemblance to an opulent Roman residence—or to Wise's Troy. In contrast to the bright, bustling Trojan cityscape, we see no built exteriors other than the hut on the beach and close, dark views of the palace. The latter's few interior decorations are militaristic and severe. Helen assures Paris that Menelaus would prohibit any songs in praise of her beauty, evoking the well-known communist crackdowns on "decadent" poets and musicians.

This Sparta betrays no evidence of family life. Indeed, apart from Helen, there are no free women at all (except possibly her old nurse, whose status is unclear). Like communists in the popular imagination, the Greek kings collectively are quarrelsome, violent, vengeful, murderous slaveholders.[64] As imperialist warmongers, they are greedy to seize what the more industrious have amassed through peaceful means.[65] They are cynical, hypocritical,

61. See Lev 2003: 219–20. For the iconic significance of stockings, see Stacey 1994: 128–29.

62. Miller & Nowak 1977: 88.

63. The only exception to these generalizations is the boxing scene at Sparta, where the excited mob includes some women and men of indeterminate status, plus a few children.

64. For this picture of communists, see Sayre 1982: 81, 83; S. J. Whitfield 1996: 135–36. For vengeance as un-American in films of this period, see Biskind 1983: 176. Though not literal slave owners, communists want to enslave America (Sayre 1982: 91; S. J. Whitfield 1996: 134). The only "good" Greek in *Helen* is the ineffectual Nestor, who serves primarily to underscore the villainy of the rest.

65. For communist greed and self-indulgence, see S. J. Whitfield 1996: 134.

treacherous, ill-mannered, rude, humorless, and cruel.[66] Odysseus, creator of what is almost invariably advertised as the "Trojan Horse of treachery," matches the popular image of a communist as "a devious and highly skilled fiend."[67] As for Menelaus, he is a stereotypical tyrant ruling a xenophobic police state. He duplicitously imprisons the innocent Paris, whom he threatens to torture and secretly plans to kill. His desire for Helen is characterized as a violent, possessive lust. Indeed, he almost strangles her out of jealousy, evoking the death of Poppaea at Nero's hands in *Quo Vadis*. As he does so, he declares, "When a king takes spoils he robs no one; when he kills, he commits no murder, he fulfills justice."[68] This too echoes the Rome of *Quo Vadis*, where, as we are told by the opening voice-over, "the individual is at the mercy of the state" and "murder replaces justice."

As a Spartan, of course, Menelaus is devoid of Roman opulence, and with it of the decadent appeal of tyrants like Nero.[69] He does offer sex with enslaved women, Roman style, both to individual visitors and to the assembled company. Yet the resulting orgy—unlike most such spectacles—does not titillate, entice, or invite vicarious thrills. The sexual revelry is crude and violent, the women seem unenthusiastic at best, a brazier sends out thick smoke, and the scene is bathed claustrophobically in a lurid red light.[70] Red is a color with many associations, most of them negative: passion, fire, danger, blood, hell, prostitution, and above all, in this period, the Red Scare.[71] As the film proceeds, red light and smoke will veil the Trojans while they forge weapons for the war; a glaring red light, with smoke, shines on the hideous face of Athena qua war goddess; smoke and flames will rise at the burning of Troy.

66. Even before Helen elopes, Agamemnon says they are planning "a righteous war . . . a war of defensive aggression." The word "sincere," "a key word of the period" (Sayre 1982: 103), is not applicable to communists (S. J. Whitfield 1996: 73). For the communist inability to smile, see S. J. Whitfield 1996: 129–30. Communists are cruel to animals (Sayre 1982: 81) and the script originally had Menelaus killing Helen's dog, but Wise decided that would be going too far.

67. Miller & Nowak 1977: 28; cf. Sayre 1982: 97–98, 198.

68. The scene is discussed by Winkler 2009: 226–28.

69. For the appeal of the decadent emperor figure, see Babington & Evans 1993: 202–5.

70. This recalls the moment in *Quo Vadis* where Nero surveys his own orgy through a ruby eyeglass.

71. The color was a fertile metaphorical field in the rhetoric of anti-communism (e.g., Sayre 1982: 18, who talks of "faucets which dripped red water into film scripts"; more examples in Miller & Nowak 1977: 248; S. J. Whitfield 1996: 29).

The Trojan populace will subsequently welcome the Wooden Horse with an orgy of their own, in which they behave more like an excitable Roman mob than a docile throng of Christians.[72] Though relatively restrained, by the standards of the genre, this celebration fulfills far more effectively than Menelaus's grim soiree the trailer's promise of "orgiastic ceremonies and sensuous rites . . . bacchanalian revels of unbridled abandon." Unlike the tawdry Spartan entertainment, it involves fruit, flowers, musicians, and enthusiastic women, and everyone seems to be having a well-deserved good time. Paris and Helen look on approvingly as our diegetic guides.

Audience identification with Trojan joy is qualified, however, not just because we know the contents of the Horse but because of the connotations of such excess. Troy will, of course, eventually produce the Romans, and the scene suggests that some disturbing aspects of Roman identity are already present within its walls. The scene billows with red smoke, and a sinister cult figure (some kind of masked puppet, evoking a whirling dervish) echoes a scene in *Quo Vadis* portraying what that film's program calls a "pagan rite." The ominous figure of the Horse looms over all, garlanded with flowers like an object of worship. Even though this orgy is modest by DeMillean standards, its best visual comparandum is the Golden Calf scene in *Ten Commandments*, which dramatizes the Hebrews' abandonment of Moses and his divine mandate.

It is, of course, this uncontrolled revelry that allows the Greeks emerging from the Horse to catch the Trojans not just napping but apparently still drunk, or at least seriously hungover. This fatal lapse in vigilance, good judgment, and sobriety results in Troy's total destruction. The sight of that destruction, with its dark, oppressive smoke and flames, evokes any number of images of civilization devastated, from the burning of Rome in *Quo Vadis* to the ruined cities of World War II, or even Cold War fantasies of alien invasion. As we learn from the sci-fi classic *Invasion of the Body Snatchers*—which came out the same year—"falling asleep is dangerous."[73]

72. This aligns them in turn with Hollywood audiences (Fitzgerald 2001: 27–28; Paul 2013a: 275–83). Other scenes also show the Trojan masses in a poor light. Despite his liberal politics, Wise's films, like others of the period, often present an ugly picture of the "common man" (Gehring 2012: 128–29, 141–42; cf. Wood 1989 [1975]: 185–87; Biskind 1983: ch. 1).

73. Biskind 1983: 143.

Another hint of trouble, of a rather different kind, is detectible in the fact that the entire cast speaks with a crisp, upper-class British accent.[74] Given the association of such voices with "authority and aristocracy,"[75] this befits both the Trojans' royal status and Troy's role as the ancestral source of "high" European culture. Yet it departs from the common practice, in Hollywood epic, of using Americans for the good guys (Hebrews or Christians), and British accents for their oppressors (Egyptians or Romans), which helps American audiences to distance themselves from the tyranny and decadence of the latter.[76] The Trojans' Britishness not only deprives the audience of an American hero to identify with but tacitly questions the good guys' wholesome American virtue, subtextually reinforcing the film's political warning against naively trusting the unscrupulous or letting prosperity make your people soft and vulnerable.[77]

Super-Miss America Standards

Dedicated as it is to the love of beauty, Troy is obviously where the world's most beautiful woman belongs. In antiquity, the city's association with erotic beauty cast a shadow over its splendor, giving rise to numerous mythic misadventures as well as, ultimately, its own destruction. In Wise's film, however, Troy's embrace of the American dream requires that affinity to be recast as a celebration of American Cold War ideals, with the beautiful Helen embodying virtuous 1950s femininity.

To play the role of Helen, the studio claimed, in the production notes, to be looking for "the most beautiful woman in the world." In this period, the most obvious contenders for that title were Marilyn Monroe, Kim Novak, Ava

74. Wise felt strongly that the accents in a film should be homogeneous (Cary 1974: 68; Leemann 1995: 33).

75. Fraser 1988: 6.

76. For the association of upper-class British accents with villainy, dubbed by Wyke the "linguistic paradigm," see Wood 1989: 183–85; Wyke 1997: 23, 71, 133, 139; Joshel, Malamud & Wyke 2001: 8–9; Blanshard & Shahabudin 2011: 19; Llewelyn-Jones 2018: 332–36; cf. also Fraser 1988: 5–7. The pattern does not necessarily apply to women (below, p. 105) and is less common in Greek (as opposed to Roman) epics (cf. C. Davies 2019: 39).

77. For the fear that luxury would generate complacency and weakness in the US, see Miller & Nowak 1977: 16–17; cf. S. J. Whitfield 1996: 76, 90, and the use of Troy as a warning in medieval and early modern Europe: "Bluntly, if Troy could fall, so too could they" (Shepard & Powell 2004: 1–2).

Gardner, and Elizabeth Taylor.[78] Monroe, above all, occupied "an almost allegoric position as the symbolic object of illicit male sexual desire."[79] It was standard practice to showcase such stars as the Sirens of ancient world epic,[80] and "most of Hollywood's established love-goddesses," including Monroe, were considered for the role.[81] Unfortunately for Wise, however, she and many other top stars were under contract elsewhere.

Wise especially regretted the unavailability of Grace Kelly, who in his view had the necessary acting ability along with "fine physical qualifications for the part."[82] Kelly, who was soon to marry Prince Rainier of Monaco, was both America's "fairy tale princess" and the epitome of the "classy" star. Characterized by a "distinguished and somewhat restrained elegance," this type is cosmopolitan, sophisticated, cool, ladylike, reserved, and patrician.[83] In contrast to a sex symbol like Monroe, it represents "man's ideal longings within the family."[84] "Classy" stars were often cast in historical epics as the virtuous proto-Christian love interest. Deborah Kerr, who played Lygia in *Quo Vadis*, is another notable example of the type. Though Scottish, Kerr was best known for what she called her "duchess" roles in British films.[85] The camera found in her "an innate gentility."[86] Her star image, much like Kelly's, has been summarized as "moral fortitude" under a "delicate exterior," with erotic passion just below the surface.[87] This is the type suggested by indications in *Helen*'s

78. V. Scott 1956.

79. T. Harris 1991 [1957]: 42. See further Walker 1966: ch. 6; Haskell 2016: 254–60; Dyer 2004: ch. 1; Slide 2010: 175; Higashi 2014: ch. 7.

80. E.g., Hedy Lamarr as Delilah; Gina Lollobrigida as the Queen of Sheba; Susan Hayward as Messalina (in *Demetrius and the Gladiators*); Rita Hayworth as Salome; Lana Turner as the high priestess of Astarte (in *The Prodigal*); Elizabeth Taylor as Cleopatra. See further Llewelyn-Jones 2018: ch. 4.

81. Cary 1974: 65.

82. Wise to Trilling, January 2, 1954. Correspondence between Wise and Warner Brothers' Steve Trilling, and between Trilling and the makeup artist Gordon Bau (below, n. 102), is cited from the Warner Brothers Archive in Los Angeles.

83. Thumim 1992: 53. On star types in the 1950s, see Higashi 2014: 15–25. On Kelly, see further Bruzzi 2000; Higashi 2014: ch. 5.

84. T. Harris 1991 [1957]: 42. For the contrast between Kelly and Monroe, see T. Harris 1991 [1957] and cf. Haskell 2016: 253, 260; de Castelbajac 1995: 120–22.

85. She joked, "I feel naked without my tiara" (Capua 2011: 72).

86. Braun 1978: 156.

87. Deleyto 2001: 120, 128. Cf. also Llewellyn-Jones 2018: 336–39.

script, which mentions, for example, the character's "coolly imperious" demeanor.

Having failed to land a major star, Wise finally settled on a nineteen-year-old Italian named Rossana Podestà. The studio stoked expectations by claiming that she had been selected from hundreds or even thousands of contenders after a yearlong, worldwide search.[88] She was chosen, according to the film's souvenir brochure, because she matched Homer's description of Helen as the "fairest of her kind," who "moves a goddess and looks a queen," emitting "new beauty and radiance from every angle." According to Podestà herself, she was spotted in her recent Mexican film *La Red* (*The Net*), "sent for," and hired without a screen test.[89] *Helen* was Podestà's twentieth film as well as Wise's, but this was her first English-language film and most significant role to date. She was little known outside Italy, and publicity presents her as a newcomer to American audiences. Many viewers would, however, have had a "preview peek" at her as Nausicaa in *Ulysses*, which had just been released in the US.[90]

Italian beauty was stereotyped in the US as exotic, earthy, dark, natural, primitive, passionate, and above all, buxom. Endless newspaper stories discuss the way that moviegoers "have seen the full-bosomed Italian beauties sweep this country with a tidal wave of talent."[91] Podestà is regularly listed among the "lavishly endowed girls" who make up this "covey of voluptuous dames."[92] The magazine *Movie Pix* announced her casting as Helen with an impressive cleavage shot (figure 3.3). In a widely syndicated story on "imported Italian cleavage," Podestà insists that the most important component of a woman's sex appeal is her face.[93] But it was not her face that drew the attention of casting directors. Her career had begun when an Italian producer saw her "ample figure" in a bikini, and she was hired for *La Red* on the basis of a photo in which she was, in essence, performing a striptease.[94] The Mexican film, which landed her the role of Helen, was advertised as "a new kind of

88. E.g., *Cumberland Sunday Times*, February 5, 1956.

89. Parsons 1956: 24.

90. *Ames Daily Tribune*, January 22, 1955. On Podestà's prior image in Italy, see Nikoloutsos 2015: 86–87. Paris was another unknown, Jack Sernas, who was born in Lithuania but grew up in France. The rest of the cast includes several experienced film actors but no big stars.

91. F. Russell 1954. On Italian stars of the period, see Gundle 2007: ch. 7.

92. Anon. 1956b. The press kit stipulates her measurements as 37-21-36, and her height as 5 feet, 1 inch. Her short stature visually enhances her bustiness.

93. E. Johnson 1956.

94. Anon. 1954c; Lane 1954a; Lane 1954b.

FIGURE 3.3. Photo of Rossana Podestà from *Movie Pix* magazine, headlined "The Face that Launched a Thousand Ships." The caption reads, "Warner Bros.' search for 'the world's most beautiful girl' ended when Italian beauty Rossana Podesta was chosen for the title role in Helen of Troy."

ROMANCE that seethes to the boiling point."[95] It includes very little dialogue, but, in the words of one waggish viewer, "The camera spends about 65 [of the film's 70 minutes] roaming around Rossana Podesta's torso."[96] A suitably buxom still from *La Red* was used by *Pageant* magazine to announce her casting in the role of Helen.

Exotic as the Italians seemed in other respects, their buxom figures were decidedly in tune with contemporary American taste. A large bust, contrasted with a small waist, was the primary signifier of female desirability in this period.[97] This enabled publicity for *Helen* to claim that Podestà's figure "measures up with super-Miss America standards."[98] We are assured that, "according to historians, researchers and Homeric scholars, the genuine Helen of Troy . . . couldn't beat the measurements of Miss America, which Miss Podesta meets."[99] Miss America, in the words of the pageant's theme song, is "the queen of femininity," an "ideal" with an "all-American face and form." Many pageant contestants were movie actors; the Italian Podestà was not one of them, of course, but just before *Helen* opened she rode in the prizewinning float at the Pasadena Rose Parade, where Miss America also rides in her "one regular national TV appearance a year."[100]

Podestà thus arrived in Hollywood as a little-known Italian whose vital statistics might make her an American favorite, especially with men. As such, she diverged in several respects from the "classy"—and less voluptuous—star type that Wise originally sought. But the studio did its best to replicate, in Podestà's person, the passage of ancient Greek beauty from its dark, exotic, Mediterranean origins to the aestheticized white ideal produced by northern European philhellenism. Podestà's most visibly Italian feature, her dark hair, was erased by means of a blindingly blonde wig.[101] Makeup was used to

95. *Daily Independent Journal* [San Rafael, CA], June 5, 1957.

96. *Kingsport News* [Kingsport TN], June 23, 1956. Wise mentions how "exciting" he found her in *La Red*, where she made a "terrific impression" on "all of us" (Wise to Trilling, January 23, 1954). Note that Podestà's name typically appears without the accent in contemporary sources.

97. Cf. figure 3.1 above. On "mammary madness," see Rosen 1973: ch. 18; cf. Walker 1967: 115.

98. Anon. 1954a.

99. *Globe-Gazette* [Mason City, IA], February 18, 1956.

100. Deford 1971: 197.

101. This is the period in which blonde hair acquired its "bombshell" associations, but it could also connote the aristocratic elegance of a "fairy-tale princess" like Grace Kelly. In Italy, blonde hair was considered aristocratic and un-Italian, and associated with American

"correct" her olive skin tone,[102] and her voice was dubbed with an upper-crust English accent to match the rest of the cast. In women, this accent was considered intrinsically "classy," and was often used for proto-Christian heroines, in whom it was thought to convey "purity."[103] It further connoted a certain "aloofness and aristocratic reserve," which may be used to "downplay sexiness."[104]

Judging from the underwhelmed reactions of the Hollywood press, this attempt to transform Podestà into a kind of classy Miss America was not entirely successful. After interviewing her on set, Lydia Lane, a syndicated beauty columnist for the *Los Angeles Times*, reported that she had "a classic beauty which increases with familiarity."[105] The United Press International correspondent Vernon Scott describes her, in contrast to other Italian stars, as "no flamboyant beauty"; hers is rather "the olive-skinned, dark-eyed beauty of Italian youth."[106] And the influential gossip columnist Louella Parsons opines, "looking at her closely, she has indeed classic Italian features," but she is "much more attractive with her own dark hair."[107] The studio could do nothing about her dark eyes,[108] but in other respects they did their best to eliminate what these columnists note as the basis of her modest charm.

Along with this makeover, Podestà was given a clearly defined personality. Retaining the Italian association with natural beauty, we are told that she uses olive oil for skin care and prefers to go barefoot; in character she is "unspoiled," sincere, modest, shy, and retiring.[109] Despite her busy career she is a devoted wife and mother, and even "a practical housewife" who does her own housework.[110] The impact of such stories is captured by a gossip item informing us that the "bosomy Italian beauty" will not make good material for the

---

abundance (Gundle 2007: 171–73; cf. Pomeroy 2013: 195). On Helen's blondeness, cf. also Vivante 2013: 24–27.

102. Bau to Trilling, March 18, 1954.

103. Blanshard & Shahabudin 2011: 44.

104. Babington & Evans 1993: 189; Wieber 2016: 231. Kerr's "Englishness" was touted in promoting *Quo Vadis* (Llewellyn-Jones 2018: 338).

105. Lane 1954b.

106. V. Scott 1956.

107. Parsons 1956: 24.

108. Some colorized Japanese advertisements do, in fact, give her blue eyes.

109. Parsons 1956: 24; Lane 1954b; V. Scott 1956.

110. Parsons 1956; Anon. 1954c.

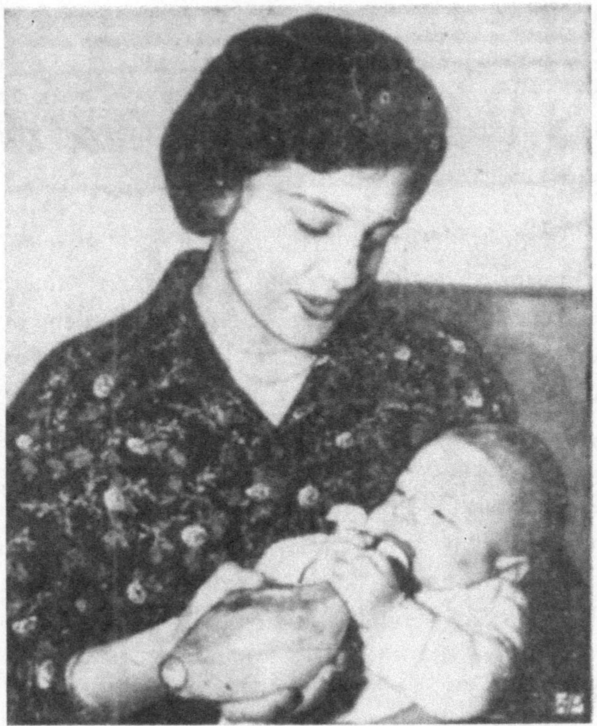

FIGURE 3.4. Publicity still for *Helen of Troy* (1956). The caption reads, "STAR ROLE AHEAD—Rossana Podesta, 19-year-old film actress who'll star in new super-epic movie 'Helen of Troy,' cares for her two-months-old baby in Rome, Italy, home." Reprinted from the *Rushville Republican*, April 30, 1954.

"Marilyn Monroe buildup" of the studio's publicity machine, because of her conservative private life as a married woman and "the mother of a little boy."[111] Publicity photos show a demurely clad Podestà bottle-feeding the infant in question, kissing her husband, or embracing him with a happy smile (figure 3.4). Louella Parsons, who describes her, tellingly, as "nothing like you imagine Helen," says she has "seldom seen two people more in love"—and Louella should know.[112]

111. *Ottawa Journal*, March 11, 1954.

112. Parsons 1956.

Podestà was thus offered up for public scrutiny, as the world's most beautiful woman, not in the form of a sultry, exotic foreigner or a Hollywood love goddess, but as an alternative model of 1950s American femininity: the demure yet voluptuous homemaker, who conveys chaste domesticity while remaining a siren for the right man.[113] This reinforces her fit with the Miss America ideal, since that pageant, unlike other such events, placed enormous emphasis on "respectability." It was insistently wholesome, white, and middle-class, denying its own sexual display, policing the appearance and behavior of participants and audience, and eschewing femme fatale types in favor of nice girls who aspired to marriage and a family in affirmation of "good, old-fashioned *Miss America* values."[114]

This Is Not Goodbye

Those values were also, of course, the values of American Cold War Christianity. The character of the notorious Helen is therefore retooled to transform her into a model of proto-Christian propriety. This Helen prefers the company of humble people, who may be read, in a Cold War context, as oppressed Christians and/or Russian peasants.[115] She tends the unconscious hero (as Lygia does in *Quo Vadis*), then saves him from Menelaus because she "hates cruelty," declaring that she "would have done the same for any slave." When she frees her enslaved attendants—Andraste and Andros—this "Christian" deed is unmotivated except as an expression of her character and values. When Paris mistakes her for an enslaved woman, this is an identity she is happy to embrace. He soon finds out that she is really the queen, but in a nod to the myth of Helen's *eidolon,* the existence of "two Helens" becomes a running theme. Initially, the "slave girl" is the *eidolon* ("the queen's shadow"), but when they kiss on the clifftop, Paris declares her "real." Later, when he lies dying and calls her "that little slave girl," Helen replies, "Oh I am! Whatever your love wishes me to be!"

By abnegating any distinct identity, this Helen performs both the self-abasement and the fictitiousness of femininity, and reminds us that every

113. See Banner 1983: 417–18.

114. Deford 1971: 240. See further Deford 1971: passim; Banet-Weiser 1999: 37–42, 44–47, 71, 79–86; Mifflin 2020. For the pageant's whiteness, see Lim 2006: 125–27.

115. For rural poverty as signifier of Christianity, see Ahl 1991: 48; Forshey 1992: 7–8; cf. also Blank 2015: 68–69.

cinematic Helen, whether goddess, queen, or "slave girl," is equally an *eidolon*. But her "slave" identity—the identity equated with her love for Paris—also has political implications. Menelaus, who has forbidden her to leave the palace, makes her huge bedroom door clang shut like that of a prison cell. Helen herself speaks like a Soviet dissident when she tells Paris, "I despise oppression as do many others here." Echoing her fictitious self-description as "a slave of the palace," Paris calls her "a slave as long as Menelaus possesses you," then begs her to "Come away to freedom!" Her passage to Troy is thus framed less as an elopement than as the escape of an enslaved person or political prisoner, paradigms that transform her from an object of cultural opprobrium—the unfaithful wife—into an American Cold War heroine.

Christianity was considered, above all, the religion of love. In the movies, this encompasses both the transcendent love of god and the human love uniting his followers—most importantly, the heteroromantic love worshipped in Hollywood. At a time when active interest in sexuality was associated with communism, even human love was distanced from the overt expression of erotic passion.[116] In Roman Empire films it is often fused with Christian love, as in *Quo Vadis*, where the hero is claimed for Christianity by means of his love for Lygia and hers for both him and god.[117] Love of Christ elevates such romances above the orgiastic sexuality associated with the decadent Romans—and indeed, above physical sex as such. This dovetails with the requirements of the Production Code, which distinguished between "*pure love,* the love of a man for a woman permitted by the law of God and man," and "the passion arising from this love." "Impure love" (which is tainted by physical passion) must in no way be shown as attractive or justified.[118]

In Wise's Sparta there is no talk of love of any kind. A bit surprisingly, dialogue between Helen and Menelaus indicates that the marriage was not arranged against her will. Yet it is a loveless, childless non-marriage.[119] She might

116. Love might even be recommended as a *substitute* for sexual desire (Miller & Nowak 1977: 158; cf. Thumim 1992: 177). Some thought that Alfred Kinsey's " 'red' tainted" sex research "degraded" American life to the level of "the worst decadence of the Roman era."

117. For the pattern, cf. Babington & Evans 1993: 187–89, 190–92, and cf. 197–99. For women as moral guides in films of this period, see Wood 1989: 65–69; Biskind 1983: 267–71. *Salome* (1953) reverses the genders of the typical conversion plot (Babington & Evans 1993: 185–86). In *Demetrius*, even Messalina fleetingly offers to turn Christian for her lover's sake (cf. Wyke 2002: 372–76).

118. Doherty 1999: 353–56; cf. Seldes 1950: 70, 74–77.

119. Cf. the unhappy marriage as "signifier of evil" in *Ten Commandments* (Nadel 1993: 421).

as well be married to a communist. Nevertheless, when love comes along, in the person of Paris, this Helen shows far more spine than most in the face of erotic passion. She refuses to elope because that would "destroy the hope of peace," vowing instead to stay and "do her small part" to turn the Spartans from war. Like a well-behaved American woman of the 1950s, or a heroine of melodrama, she evinces both self-sacrifice and erotic self-restraint in the service of others. When Menelaus's soldiers threaten them both, however, Paris grabs her and leaps off a cliff down to a waiting ship. Hecuba will later call Helen "a woman of self-determination," but Paris actually *deprives* her of self-determination, at least where her traditionally defining choice is concerned.

The innocence guaranteed by this disempowerment was part of the price Wise had to pay for the privilege of making this particular protagonist an object of sympathy. The director was prohibited by the Motion Picture Association of America (MPAA) from including anything at all that might "justify and romanticize an adulterous sex relationship"; specifically, there must be no implication of actual sex between Paris and Helen.[120] Accordingly, the couple exchange nothing but a few chaste kisses, with only one veiled suggestion of anything further. Helen's love is further desexualized (while suggesting an untapped maternal potential) when she characterizes Paris as just a boy—one she hopes will never grow old.[121] This feeds into a hyperromantic discourse of love as a transcendent, even supernatural force (characterized as "magic" or "a dream"), which unites the couple permanently regardless of any kind of physical contact. When refusing to elope with Paris, Helen declares, "This is not goodbye. You shall always be with me across the sea . . . and always young, Paris!" Like the gods themselves, they will enjoy this eternal youth in a paradise embracing both present and future. Paris promises Helen, "I'll meet you in Elysium," then exhorts, "O goddess come to earth, make me immortal with your kiss, and we'll live on nectar and ambrosia!"

This overwrought romanticism prepares us for the film's conclusion. In ancient world epic, the hero often achieves "transcendental deification" through death, which ensures "his posthumous position at the pinnacle of the social hierarchy."[122] In *Helen* it is, as usual, the male hero, Paris, who is thus

120. Joseph Breen to Warner, March 9, 1954. Correspondence between Joseph Breen (of the MPAA) and Warner is cited from the collections of the Herrick Library.

121. In films of this period men are often presented as fundamentally childish and in need of female care (Biskind 1983: 267–71). On this Helen's lack of sensuality, cf. Vivante 2013: 30.

122. Courcoux 2009: 29.

immortalized. Helen is left in the position of the melodramatic heroine, characterized by Ien Ang as "someone who is forced to give up."[123] Yet tragic melodrama often sustains the fantasy of eternal union by using the magic of cinema to convey "the miracle of communication between the living and the dead."[124] So too, as Helen gazes back at Troy from the stern of Menelaus's ship, we are privy to a voice-over dialogue between her and Paris. Replacing the disembodied male narrator of the opening, the scene bestows the authority of the "voice of history" on an intimate exchange between lovers.[125] After reprising some of their earlier dialogue in Helen's memory ("What has been lived and shared is never lost"), the film ends with the exchange: "This is not goodbye. You shall always be with me!" "And you with me!" The immortality of their love is endorsed by the fact that we too can hear the dead Paris speak, while Helen becomes a spectral image superimposed upon the ship—as if she were on her way to join him in the hereafter.

The immortality of their love is further endorsed by *Helen*'s generic relationship to religious epic. Christianity's promise of literal immortality enables its martyrs to die happy, thanks to the invincible power of eternal love—whether human, divine, or some conflation of the two. *The Robe*, for example, concludes with Marcellus and Diana exiting to their death with a wedding-like walk into the heavens, accompanied by a triumphant chorus of alleluias.[126] In the final shot of Wise's film, similarly, we hear Helen communing with Paris about eternal love, against the background of a cloudy sky,[127] while the romantic theme music swells on the soundtrack, intertextually equating their love with the love of Christ as an immortalizing and redemptive force. If this seems like a stretch, consider the fact that Wise asked one of his writers, the classically educated Hugh Gray, to include a prophecy about the coming of Christ—an idea rejected by the horrified Gray.[128]

In Christian epic, the plot's epochal significance provides a further kind of "happy" ending. In *Quo Vadis*, for instance, Saint Peter himself assures us that

123. Ang 1989: 88.

124. Affron 1991: 114–15; cf. Haskell 2016: 188; L. Williams 2001: 29.

125. On the uncanniness of voice-off (voice outside the frame), see Doane 1980: 40–41.

126. For similar endings, see Fitzgerald 2001: 29; Wyke 2002: 285; Mini 2017: 240; Pomeroy 2008: 34. Spartacus, Christianized through crucifixion, is also "victorious in defeat" (Hirsch 1978: 98; cf. Elley 1984: 112).

127. In Christian iconography, clouds are a mark of heavenly ascent (as, e.g., at the end of *The Robe*).

128. Eldridge 2006: 143.

although Nero may rule today, Christ will rule forever. Helen's story has similarly earthshaking consequences for the history of "Western civilization." It is she who causes the war, planting the seed that will lead to the rebirth, in Hollywood, of both Trojan civilization and Greek beauty. The film bears witness to this rebirth, outdoing the "immortal" *Iliad* not only by bringing it to cinematic life, but by telling the "true" story supposedly for the first time. The story in question is one that not only exculpates Helen but celebrates her, and with her Troy, as the ancestor of American prosperity and the Hollywood cult of beauty.

By glorifying the (male) hero who changes the course of history, the epic endows him with another kind of immortality—the eternal glory (*kleos*) that is a central function of Greek epic and is perpetuated by these films.[129] Helen's own heroic attempt to change the course of history, by preventing the Trojan War, is thwarted dramatically by a man who will not take no for an answer. But she is permitted to reap such glory in a properly feminine form, as an exemplar of "pure" love. In *Interviewing Helen*, she is much concerned with "correcting" her reputation. The script touches on this theme, when Paris remarks that at Troy they would write "songs" about Helen. Their romantic discourse also places great emphasis on the immortalizing function of memory: "What is remembered is forever young." This is dramatized in the final shot, where we are privy to Helen's memories. By remaining "forever young" in Cinemascope and WarnerColor, she and Paris will enjoy not only eternal love but immortal *kleos*—thanks to Hollywood.

Aphrodite! She Does Exist!

This reimagining of Helen's character raises certain expectations about her appearance—expectations that are diametrically at odds with her reputation. Her very name, especially in an epic, primes us for (a particular kind of) spectacle; but satisfying that expectation with the cultural signifiers of the ancient world vamp would raise awkward implications of pagan decadence. As we saw earlier, advance publicity and casting seemed to preempt such decadence. How, then, were the filmmakers to convey her supreme, even supernatural beauty within the film itself without compromising her proto-Christian virtue?

129. On the *kleos* tradition in epic film, see Paul 2013a: 66–85 and cf. Paul 2008b: 160 on the conclusion of *Ulysses*.

We see Helen first through the eyes of Paris, who has been washed up on the Spartan shore after a shipwreck. She emerges from the surf like Aphrodite, in a skimpy pink costume, against the backdrop of a celestial blue sky (plate 2).[130] Such beach scenes, which legitimized minimal and even wet, clinging garments, could be steamy by the standards of the 1950s.[131] *La Red,* for example, was condemned by The Legion of Decency for showing "Rossana Podesta coming out of the briny—scantily clad—with the sea accentuating the positive."[132] Indeed, the entire Mexican film is an ode to Podestà's physique and the eroticism of the seashore. But few Americans would have seen *La Red,* which had not yet been released in the US.[133] Afficionados of the genre would be more likely to recall the beach scene in *Ulysses,* where Podestà plays Nausicaa to the storm-tossed Odysseus, linking Helen intertextually with the innocent virginal princess.[134] Helen's beach outfit is, to be sure, considerably scantier than Nausicaa's; but in contrast to *La Red,* only its trailing hem gets wet.

When Paris awakens to the sight of Helen, he exclaims, "Aphrodite! She does exist!" This invites us to view Helen through the lens of the screen star as "love goddess." More specifically, Paris is identifying her with the statue of Aphrodite at Troy, to which he drew our attention before setting out for Sparta (cf. figure 3.2). Since Podestà was the model for the huge Trojan statue, we are supposed to see Helen, through Paris's eyes, as Aphrodite's image come to life. This trope, which goes back to the beginning of cinema, was still very much alive and well. Both Rita Hayworth and Ava Gardner—two of the period's most prominent love goddesses (see plate 3)—had starred relatively recently as Venus coming to life from a statue: Hayworth in *Down To Earth* (1947) and

130. In the 1958 *Hercules,* the virtuous Iole is likewise first sighted at the beach in a short sporty outfit. According to Pomeroy she was the first female lead in the peplum to wear a "short tunic" (2008: 128 n. 16), but Helen's beach dress is scarcely longer.

131. The most notorious example, in *From Here to Eternity* (1953), has narrative similarities to *Helen* (cf. Vivante 2013: 35–36). On the scandal surrounding it, see Schumach 1975: 62–71.

132. *Kingsport News* [Kingsport, TN], May 29, 1956. On the Legion, see Schumach 1975: 84–93; Lev 2003: 94–97. Foreign films were not bound by the Production Code.

133. There had, however, been some revealing promotional shots in *Life* magazine (September 14, 1953).

134. The intertextuality produced by using the same actors in multiple films is a prominent feature of this genre (Paul 2013a: 155–56).

Gardner in *One Touch of Venus* (1948), which was remade for television in 1955.[135]

The Venus de Milo remained an aspirational model for female beauty. ("I dreamed I was the Venus de Milo," declares a Maidenform bra ad.) In the best Hollywood tradition, both Gardner and Hayworth posed with it for promotions, and stills show Gardner's measurements compared to the statue's. Yet in each case, as with *Helen*, the statue in question is modelled on the actor, to make for a seamless transformation when she comes to life. The ancient Greeks, obsessed with the beauty of statuary, would have appreciated the way in which the art of such statues first imitates life and then becomes an ideal for life to live up to. The practice also makes a perfect metaphor for Hollywood's relationship to "Greek" beauty: film purports to show the modern star in the semblance of antiquity, while really showing an "antiquity" modelled on the modern star. In this case, however, the person posing for the statue was not an established love goddess but the unknown Podestà.

The living statue trope typically leads to trouble. But while, in other epics, Aphrodite serves as an emblem of illicit sensuality, in *Helen* she is no more of a trouble maker than Helen herself.[136] Her statue is archaic and dignified, more stiffly vertical than the Venus de Milo or the Pudica type, with their contrapposto stance, and much more modestly clothed.[137] Famous in antiquity as a cause of strife among men, she is identified at the outset as a goddess of peace ("It was not the goddess of beauty who taught us to arm against our enemies"). Even Cassandra, who equates Helen with the goddess "in mortal form," blames the fall of Troy exclusively on Athena, qua war goddess. Helen's resemblance to this atypical version of her patron goddess renders her beauty restrained, aestheticized, and pure. The erotic threat associated with Aphrodite is further neutralized by the fact that Paris, when he invokes Helen as divine, is suffering from delirium, leading other characters to greet the equation with a deflating touch of humor ("This creature's crazy!" says Helen's old

135. On Hayworth as love goddess, see Sargeant 1947; McLean 2004: 47–61; M. Williams 2018: ch. 4. On Gardner as a love goddess defined by Greek statuary, see Felleman 2006: ch. 3.

136. On the persistence in film of Venus's ambivalence as both pure classical beauty and sexual troublemaker, cf. M. Williams 2018: 110–13.

137. It is, however, bustier than the Venus de Milo, as the pressbook takes pains to inform us.

nurse).[138] The overwhelming impact of Helen's beauty is domesticated by confining it to a single addlepated mate.[139]

The film relies heavily on the impact of this initial view, which is not followed up, during the remainder of the film, by any further display of Helen's beauty as such.[140] She does undergo several costume changes—something typically associated, cinematically, with wealth, status, stardom, and the dazzle of feminine beauty. But in Wise's film, unlike *Private Life*, the accumulation of outfits is not used to express the splendor of Helen's beauty. She quickly exchanges her bathing dress for a long, simple outfit—so simple that it leads Paris to think she is enslaved. This and many subsequent costumes are indeed similar in cut and color to those of Andraste, her enslaved servant, and the unnamed attendant who waits on her at Troy (plate 4). There is a close parallel with Lygia in *Quo Vadis*, who is likewise taken for enslaved by her future lover, while dressed, albeit more stylishly than Helen, in a way that conveys Christian simplicity and a humble affiliation with the oppressed (plate 5).

Like Lygia, Helen wears "the colors of nature" and avoids the intense tones associated with "orientalizing excess."[141] Her outfits are homogeneous and subdued, deficient in contrast, pattern, shine. Their palette includes muted pastels but is predominantly somber (gray, brown, black, and burgundy). Soft, matte, opaque fabrics in earthy solids suggest emotional depth, sensitivity, and sexual restraint. Like Hebrew or Christian women in other films, she often wears several layers, or a heavy wrap or cloak. Her blonde hair is usually styled, like Lygia's, in the girlish "modified ponytail" typical of 1950s epic, which suggests a childlike innocence.[142] Even her grandest outfit, worn for the evening's

138. On three more occasions Paris likens her to a goddess, but this is contrasted each time with her "real" identity as a woman.

139. Only two other characters comment on her beauty, but they are both women. Cassandra equates her with Aphrodite, as we saw, and Hecuba in a private moment suggests that "one so lovely" is not "quite mortal"—a suggestion Helen rejects. Note too that the film elides the traditional wooing of Helen and the oath of the suitors, and with it the renown that brought heroes from all over the Greek world to seek her hand.

140. Spectacle is often marked as such by on-screen spectatorship (Hall & Neale 2010: 31–32). This technique is used elsewhere in *Helen*—for the boxing match, the arrival of a thousand ships, and the orgy welcoming the Horse—but in each case, Helen is a spectator, not the spectacle.

141. Cyrino 2005a: 23; Michelakis 2017: 27. Compare Moses's shift in *Ten Commandments* from bright colors to drab tones as he reclaims his Hebrew birthright (Cohan 1997: 147–48). Cf. also below, p. 000. On Helen's clothes, see also Vivante 2013: 23, 28, 29–30.

142. The phrase is from Maeder 1987: 199. See, e.g., plates 4 and 5.

FIGURE 3.5. Helen's gown for evening wear at Sparta in *Helen of Troy* (1956). The outer cloak is a dull blue, the inner dress a muted pink (visible in plate 4).

festivities at Sparta, is both voluminous and simple by the standards of ancient epic royalty, her jewelry subdued (figure 3.5).[143]

The draperies of antiquity are less easily assimilated to 1950s fashions than to the styles of the 1920s. Yet Helen's costumes often evoke contemporary style by cinching at the waist in a way that draws attention to the bust while firmly containing the figure.[144] Sometimes her famous breasts are seen in profile,

143. Both her crowns, in particular, seem oddly dull. Even Hecuba wears more and brighter jewelry.

144. Cf. Banner 1983: 419–20; Turim 1990. For the influence of 1950s styles on representations of beauty in historical movies, see Maeder 1987: 40. On the interplay of epic costume and 1950s fashion, see Llewellyn-Jones 2018: 249–52.

using what Peter Lev calls the "exploitation shot."[145] But they always remain fully covered. At a time when voluptuous women were dubbed "bombshells," and the memory of Hiroshima was still fresh, the breasts that so preoccupied the American public had to be kept well under control.[146] Joseph Breen, the MPAA censor, was all but obsessed with cleavage, and for *Helen*, specifically, he insisted ad nauseam on full coverage of all female breasts.[147] Helen, like Podestà herself, was thus recreated as a 1950s ideal of desirable but virtuous American womanhood, her voluptuous figure contained in a way that conveyed chaste domesticity.

Thanks to the Production Code, this demure presentation seems to have gone even further than the filmmakers intended. Wise wanted the women's costumes, but especially Helen's, to be "as sexy as possible."[148] Publicity makes much of an elegant, specially designed dress, which Podestà wears in numerous promotional stills. The blurb on the back of one such still (figure 3.6) takes care to inform us that the dress was designed not by Roger Furse (the film's costume designer) but by "famed couturier" Emilio Federico Shuberth. It also announces that "Rossana will wear the dress in some of the major scenes in the movie." In fact, the dress is never seen. It is not unusual for stills to diverge, for various reasons, from the film they advertise.[149] Yet the absence of this ballyhooed dress seems particularly striking. A second outfit that is prominent in publicity likewise appears nowhere in the film. In both cases, the neckline may tell the tale, since these are the only costumes that so much as hint at cleavage. Their prominence in publicity suggests that Wise had hoped to reveal just a shade more of Podestà's principal asset.[150]

But Helen's extreme decorum cannot simply be pinned on the MPAA, since it goes well beyond Breen's restrictions in other ways. As DeMille and others knew so well, it was easy to adhere to the letter of the Code while

145. Lev 2003: 40.

146. May 1989: 163–66.

147. See, e.g., Breen to Warner, September 30, 1952 and cf. Black 1994: 292.

148. Wise to Trilling, February 2, 1954.

149. See Gaines 1990b: 196–97; Finler 2012: passim.

150. There is also some evidence that the script was dialed back. In "Sounds of Homeric Troy," when Paris says, "Come away to freedom," Helen replies, "Yes." But the film as released uses a different take, in which she replies, "And destroy the hope of peace you were taking home with you?"

FIGURE 3.6. Publicity still for *Helen of Troy* (1956). The caption reads, "Italian stylist Emilio Schubert [sic] . . . puts finishing touches on the gown he designed for Rossana Podesta for her title role in 'Helen of Troy.' The clinging dress is made of white and aquamarine silk jersey and is embroidered with pearls and real gold thread. Rossana will wear the dress in some of the major scenes in the movie."

making mincemeat of its spirit.[151] *Helen* not only eschews such techniques but surpasses in drabness even the genre's requirements for feminine virtue. *The Robe*, for example, is short on vamps, but the heroine Diana (who has the advantage of moving in aristocratic Roman circles) is much more elegant,

151. Cf. Gaines 2000 on the use of clothing as "a solution to the problem of sexual representation" (2000: 162). Cf. also DeMille's art of "sexless sex" (Kozlovic 2002; Llewellyn-Jones 2005: 24–26; 2018: 217–21).

colorful, and "sexy" than Helen—at least until Christianity starts to cramp her style. In one long scene, she wears red lipstick and a drapey saffron dress, revealing her bare back, through which her nipples are clearly visible. Even Lygia, when mistakenly thought to be enslaved, wears rosy lipstick that makes Helen look colorless in comparison (cf. plate 5).

Podestà's performance is of a piece with her wardrobe. Her body language is static and statuesque, drawing on ideas about the "classical" as calm and restrained. Needless to say, the film lacks the usual "lingering scene in which the heroine . . . washes and anoints herself in preparation for a feast, an orgy, or perhaps for some less public pleasure."[152] Nor does Helen ever dance, sing, hop, skip, jump, or break into a run. After that first sight of her on the beach, there is only one fleeting view of her legs, in long shot, which lasts about a second. Otherwise, we never see her legs or ankles, her feet, or even her shoes—none of which would have been a problem under the Code. There is a palpable contrast with Brigitte Bardot as her maid, Andraste. Despite her tiny role, the young Bardot is fluid, mobile, flirtatious, and playful.

A Pretty, Innocent-Looking Little Thing

Wise's *Helen* opened strongly, and went on to do reasonably well at the box office.[153] Yet it "never quite became the mammoth blockbuster it was intended to be."[154] Critics were unanimous in their applause for the battle scenes, but less than enthusiastic about the title character.[155] With few exceptions, praise for Podestà's looks is generic or restrained, often employing the word "pretty"—a damning term for a woman who is supposed to be the most beautiful who ever lived (as she is dubbed in the promotional telefilm *The Look of Troy*). One reviewer calls her "a pretty, innocent-looking little thing," another grants her "a suburban prettiness" but denies her the "stunning beauty" called for by the role.[156]

152. Llewellyn-Jones 2018: 158.

153. With a gross of $3.2 million, it came in at number 26 for the year (*Variety Weekly*, January 2, 1957).

154. Soares 2013. This was true of "the vast majority" of such films (Hall & Neale 2010: 179; cf. J. Russell 2007: 27–29). On *Helen*'s box office, see Finler 2003: 301; Keenan 2007: 87; Gehring 2012: 166). On the economics of epics, see Hall & Neale 2010: 155.

155. Ironically, Wise's battle footage was reused, with a "corrected" (i.e., bad) Helen, in *The Story of Mankind* (cf. above, p. 30).

156. D. Williams 1956; Moffitt 1955.

Wise's attempt to focus on the "personal and intimate" aspects of the story also fell flat. According to the *Los Angeles Times*, "the drama of individuals is minimized, almost impersonalized" by the mass spectacle, and when Helen sails home "you don't shed tears"; *Variety* called it "short on heart . . . a cold picture, stirring neither warmth nor compassion . . . there's not much chance to develop a personal intimacy with the lovers."[157] Others were crueler. The *New York Times* mocked the closing dialogue between Helen and "Paris somewhere in the clouds"; the *Mirror-News* (Los Angeles) called the romance "as tepid as a cup of coffee which has sat for too long"; the *New Yorker* likened it to "a summer attachment between a sentimental young lady and a muscular lifeguard."[158]

There are, as always, exceptions. Edwin Schallert of the *Los Angeles Times* calls Podestà "effulgently beautiful," and thinks the romance has "astonishing appeal."[159] Though the sample is too small to determine reviewers' response by gender, women—who were presumably its target audience—happen to provide two of the most positive reactions to the romantic plot. Hazel Flynn, in the *Beverly Hills Citizen,* declares that Helen has not only "great facial beauty" but also "a refined . . . almost spiritual quality," and that she and Paris as a couple have "a dream-like quality that causes their love scenes to be believable."[160] The other, Chaffee Castleton, in the *Valley News* (Van Nuys, CA), calls the love story "tender and believable," declaring that Podestà's face could indeed launch a thousand ships.[161] In some quarters, her costumes achieved the desired effect.[162] But their eschewal of eroticism did not pass unnoticed. One gossip item, remarking that the publicity files show "more leg art of Jack Sernas, who plays Paris," dubs Podestà "an

157. Scheuer 1955; Anon. 1955a.

158. Crowther 1956; D. Williams 1956; McCarten 1956.

159. Schallert 1956.

160. H. Flynn 1956.

161. Castleton 1955. Cf. the *Bridgeport Telegram*, which pronounces the film "torrid, yet tender" (F. Russell 1956), as opposed to *Boxoffice* magazine, which calls it "tender yet torrid" (quoted by Dinan 1956). For the use of words like "tender" as a sign of appeal to women, see Neale 2000: 195.

162. Helen's "long, flowing robes . . . form-fitting from the waist up, give the effect, without the revelation, of a figure any woman could be proud of" (Anon. 1954d). She is "pictorially effective" and has "a distinctive figure that is artistically adorned by some well-draped costumes" (B. Martin 1956).

anticheescake doll," noting the "novelty" of this presentation of "an Italian cutie."[163]

For the most part, even those who admire Podestà's appearance are critical of her performance. In one reviewer's opinion, she is "devoid of expression or passion and so guileless and uninteresting that one can scarcely imagine schoolboys quarreling over her, let alone generals of armies."[164] Another calls her "a young Italian of truly classic beauty who does not yet know how to act."[165] Unfortunately, the director concurred. Wise had serious misgivings about Podestà's ability from the outset, and subsequently acknowledged her inadequacy, considering that the role of Helen called for a "superb actress."[166]

That inadequacy was, however, exacerbated by several factors. Wise's pioneering use of "big-head close ups" raised the stakes regarding both Helen's appearance—especially her face—and the actor's ability to convey the kind of subtle emotion begged for by the script.[167] This is particularly important when it comes to eroticism, in so far as the Code's prudishness necessitated "a suppressed and largely psychological performance" of sexual desire.[168] The problem was compounded by Helen's characterization. Reviewing *La Red*, the *New York Times* equated Podestà with Marilyn Monroe, adding, "she doesn't breathe fire like some of the tempestuous, earthy Italian screen queens. But with the signorina it's not the acting—it's the architecture."[169] In *Helen*, however, appreciation of that architecture was limited by the extreme decorum of her performance, and especially of her costumes. Brilliance, pattern, texture, decoration, and elaborate accessories are not only a source of spectacle in themselves, but guide and distract the eye so that the performer's

163. *Mt. Vernon Register-News*, January 26, 1955.

164. D. Williams 1956.

165. Willing 1956.

166. Wise to Trilling, January 23, 1954; Cary 1974: 74.

167. "We see the strain and shock of topsy-turvy events mirrored in her face." "Camera moves closer looking at the finality in her face." When she sees Menelaus again, we see "the desolation, the emptiness, the hatred in her face." Prior to casting the role, Wise said, "Helen is going to take *a lot of playing*" (Wise to Trilling, January 2, 1954).

168. Haskell 1974: 174.

169. *New York Times*, May 17, 1956. One Italian producer explained that the Italian stars are considered "beautiful because they stay dumb" (Anon. 1954: 55; cf. Buckley 2000: 530).

features—and her acting—have less work to do.[170] Eschewing the code that locates beauty in rich clothing and adornment obliges us to judge the actor herself for her "natural" beauty—and Podestà's beauty, as we saw earlier, is anything but natural in this film.

These difficulties might have been mitigated by casting a major star, enhanced by the aura of her previous roles, for whom "good acting" would be less of an issue; a "love goddess," especially, might have animated the role by bringing to bear her existing image, enhanced by the association of stardom with transcendent love—"a passionate sentiment impregnated with spirituality."[171] Wise claimed that Podestà's lack of a "known image" was a good thing, but when an interviewer observed that he had reduced the superhuman stature of his heroes, he acknowledged that this could have been remedied by casting "stars rather than actors; people who have a presence and magnetism on the screen."[172]

In the same interview, Wise adds that Helen should have been played by someone who "didn't have trouble with the language." Podestà knew virtually no English and Wise no Italian, which severely limited communication between director and star.[173] There were also performance implications, since Podestà had to learn her lines by rote—a procedure imposing a huge handicap on any actor. Wise himself worried that the performance of his foreign actors was impaired by the fact that they had "to concentrate so hard just on getting the English out."[174]

In the finished product, however, we do not hear Podestà's voice at all. Both Helen and Paris were dubbed, making the actors into ventriloquist's dummies in vocal drag. By its nature mechanical and detached, dubbing undermines realism and discourages emotional identification.[175] It also handicaps the

170. Cf. Llewellyn-Jones 2018: 252 on Gina Lollobrigida as the Queen of Sheba. For the "spectacle of detail" (including fabrics), which "invites our attention to surfaces," see K. Thompson 2011: 55 and cf. Babington & Evans 1993: 64–65; Sobchak 2003 [1990]: 297, 301.

171. Morin 2005: 53. On star acting, see above, p. 33.

172. Cary 1974: 66, 74.

173. Wise liked, in general, to work closely with his actors, starting with "a good long discussion" about the script, story, and character (Keenan 2007: 171; cf. Gehring 2012: 160).

174. Wise to Trilling, January 23, 1954.

175. Cf. Elsaesser 1991: 75. In a "unrealistic" genre, like the peplum, dubbing contributes to the films' surreal and disconnected quality, as well as their low reputation (Lucanio 1994: 17–18; Shahabudin 2009: 201; P. Johnson 2018: 33–36). On dubbing in post-WWII Italian cinema, see further S. Davies 2016.

director, in so far as s/he is "in the business of syncing visual physiognomy with sound."[176] Poorly done, it can be acutely alienating.[177] But even when done well, as it is in *Helen*, it deprives the performer of one of her most fundamental resources. One Italian director even remarked—apparently in all seriousness—that the practice of dubbing allowed Italian directors to "put the acting in later."[178] Wise, who was anxious to have very high quality dubbing, explicitly instructed those involved in the process to ignore the actors' own readings.[179] As *Variety* commented, regarding both Podestà and Sernas, the dubbing is "perfect," but "an appraisal of their ability as performers will have to wait until both use their own voices."[180]

Hers the Temptation, Hers the Sin

Clearly, Podestà was the wrong person for the job. But it is hard to see how even Grace Kelly could have survived the constraints imposed by the director's desire to defend Helen's name and reputation within the framework of 1950s gender and political ideology. As a paragon of Christian virtue, she is the kind of woman who may be the romantic center of such epics, but is rarely—if ever—their erotic center.[181] That place is occupied by richly decorative figures, usually scandalous vamps, who allow audiences to revel in their excitement, charisma, and misbehavior. It is scarcely an accident that "good" women—as opposed to a Cleopatra or Salome—rarely have their names on the marquee. It is notoriously difficult to make virtuous characters compelling. Bad, bad Nefretiri, not Sephora, is the woman we remember from *Ten Commandments*.[182] Even Lygia in *Quo Vadis*—a more compelling character than many such heroines[183]—pales beside the magnificent decadence of Poppaea, with

176. Herwitz 2008: 70.

177. Fellini used poorly synchronized dubbing intentionally as an alienation effect (Wyke 1997: 190–91).

178. Anon. 1954b.

179. Wise to Trilling, October 8, 1954.

180. Anon. 1955a.

181. Cf. Llewellyn-Jones 2018: 331 on the failure to make a star out of Haya Harareet in the "thankless" role of Esther in *Ben-Hur*.

182. When DeMille was making his early biblicals, the Catholic censor (and Jesuit) Daniel Lord urged him not to "make your pagans attractive warm-blooded, alive human beings and your Christians plaster saints," but "DeMille ignored him" (Black 1994: 66).

183. See Scodel & Bettenworth 2009: ch. 3 and cf. Mini 2017.

her pet leopards and dress constructed (if we can believe the pressbook) of 14-karat gold lamé.

There are ways of compensating for virtue and its lack of visual interest. Wise's squeaky-clean Helen might have been cast against type by using a love goddess in the role, someone who could bring to the character the frisson of her off-screen reputation. The character of Lygia, for example, would resonate very differently if she had been played by Elizabeth Taylor, as originally planned.[184] *Ulysses* (1954) employs an interesting variation on this technique by casting Sylvana Mangano as both Penelope and Circe, discreetly eroticizing the former via the latter.[185] Not coincidentally, Circe is far more prominent in advertising than the official heroine. (In Italian ads, she is labelled *bellissima*, as opposed to the *dolcissima* Penelope.) Helen's *eidolon* had obvious potential in this regard; yet Wise's film resolutely denies the existence of any evil twin, making Paris declare "both" Helens "wise and good."

Another common approach is to give the romantic heroine a more exciting foil: a Poppaea to her Lygia. *Quo Vadis* throws in an added bonus, in the form of the enslaved entertainer Eunice (Marina Berti), who is displayed shamelessly to the male gaze. In *Demetrius and the Gladiators* (1954), the virtuous heroine lies conveniently unconscious for most of the picture, leaving the hero to cavort with the wicked Messalina. (This allows the hero temporarily to behave badly too, and even denounce Christianity.) But *Helen* includes no such compensating attractions. Bardot, as yet unknown, has a very limited role. Even the possessed Cassandra, played by sixteen-year-old Janette Scott, is more schoolgirlish than arresting.[186] This has the advantage of freeing the "most beautiful woman in the world" of competition for the (male) gaze, but it also deprives that gaze of the kind of erotic spectacle that was central to the genre.

Quo Vadis provides such spectacle not only via its eroticized pagans and enslaved sex objects, but by giving Lygia a temporary makeover, against her will. She is adorned for the emperor's pleasure as a high-class courtesan, with a sparkling sky-blue dress, lavish jewelry, and an elaborate hairdo touted in the

184. See Blanshard & Shahabudin 2011: 43.

185. Paul 2013b.

186. According to the souvenir brochure, she is precocious but "still a normal young girl." Contrast, e.g., Elena Zareschi's exoticized Cassandra in *Ulysses*. Wise's *Helen* is further hampered by the drabness of its male villains, who lack the allure of a Nero and his court.

FIGURE 3.7. Still from *Quo Vadis* showing Lygia, the Christian heroine, being made over to attend the Emperor Nero's orgy.

pressbook as the latest evening look (figure 3.7).[187] So arrayed, she is conveyed to Nero's palace and displayed to his (and our) gaze as a piece of "rare merchandise." Most advertising images of Kerr show her in this outfit, or else burning at the stake in diaphanous drapery (a species of eroticized spectacle compatible with Christian virtue). Other epics find other ways to make the virtuous heroine her own alibi. Salome plays the vamp strategically for righteous moral purposes.[188] In *The Story of Ruth*, the biblical heroine acquires a lavish backstory as an exotic pagan priestess.

This kind of pagan excess is the "primary source of visual pleasure" in ancient world epic, and often a film's "most authentic" quality (even in religious films).[189] It is also central to the epic's ethos of consumerism. Though

187. Comparable temporary makeovers are given to Varinia in *Spartacus* (Jean Simmons) and Lucia in *Demetrius* (an anglicized Debra Paget). Kerr's biographer thought the star was overglamorized as Lygia, and the costumes were "particularly inappropriate" (Braun 1978: 126).

188. Cf. Buchanan 2013.

189. Paul 2013a: 223; Hirsch 1978: 72.

Hollywood no longer influenced fashion as it had in the 1920s, the lavish costumes of ancient world vamps, such as Taylor's Cleopatra and Lamarr's Delilah, still allowed fashion promotions to piggyback on the status of the stars as "idols of consumption."[190] Rita Hayworth's costumes for *Salome* were heavily promoted and allegedly inspired new fashions.[191] In addition to the usual beauty contests, the pressbook proposes an entire "Salome Glamour Week."[192] But promotion could do little with Podestà's wardrobe. *Helen*'s pressbook contains the usual suggestions for beauty contests and fashion displays, but they pale in comparison to the tie-ins for other such films.[193] Wise's film offers almost nothing, either literally or figuratively, for its audience to *buy*.

Reviews of the blockbuster *Quo Vadis* make it clear that spectacle was *the* criterion for evaluating that film. Bosley Crowther praised the "splendor" of the court surrounding Nero and "the evil and voluptuous Poppaea" as "utterly dazzling to the eye," even while damning Kerr's Lygia as "anything but inspired.[194] Those who do praise the latter call her "charming" and "restrained," or grant her a "soft sweetness" that makes her "a great foil to the fiery, glamorous Marina Berti, the slave girl."[195] But others scorn her as "a mincing little Christian."[196] The *Los Angeles Times* suggests that she and Robert Taylor (who played Marcus) may have suffered such "cruel appraisals" because it was difficult for them "to reconcile their young, fresh viewpoint with the spirit of decadent grandeur and not have it appear colorless."[197] But such judgments did not impair the film's success. It was not its Christians but its pagans that made *Quo Vadis* a hit.[198]

190. The phrase is Dyer's (1998: 39). For the influence of cinematic Cleopatras on fashion, see Wyke 2002: ch. 8. For Lamar's Delilah as fashion icon, see Llewellyn-Jones 2005: 27–28. On stars as role models, fans, and consumption in the 1950s, see Higashi 2014. On consumption and the epic generally, see Llewellyn-Jones 2018: ch. 3.

191. Anon. 1953. To promote *Down to Earth*, women were invited to compete for "Rita Hayworth trophies" by posing as Hayworth posing as Venus (M. Williams 2018: 123).

192. Llewellyn-Jones 2018: 72–73, 253–55.

193. The suggested Helen of Troy fashion contest merely involves designing a dress for the modern Helen.

194. Crowther 1951b; 1951a.

195. McClay 1951; Spear 1951; Parsons 1951.

196. A. Knight 1951.

197. Schallert 1952.

198. The MPAA even found it necessary to issue a defensive statement about the importance of Christianity in the film (by Arthur H. DeBra, November 28, 1951; consulted in the Herrick Library).

Filmmakers were well aware that pagan vamps were not merely a useful foil for proto-Christian heroines, but an attraction in their own right.[199] Messalina's carnality helped to give *Demetrius* commercial potential.[200] Trailers for *David and Bathsheba* (a story of adultery, comparable to Helen's) dwell heavily on the couple's sinfulness. Ads for *Quo Vadis* make much of the film's multiple "exciting women," promising "three fiery love-stories against the flaming background of sinful Rome" (figure 3.8).[201] Of these women, Lygia is easily the least exciting. In the souvenir brochure, Poppaea is much more prominent and, literally, far more colorful.[202]

Advertisements for *Helen* raise similar expectations. The Helen of the film text offered little grist to the publicity mill, but countless posters and print ads show "the face that launched a thousand ships" with heavy-lidded eyes and juicy, slightly parted red lips, providing a definite whiff of Marilyn Monroe (plate 6).[203] Others show her skimpily clad, literally abducted (by Menelaus) or running bare-legged from the Greek army. Stills present her in vamp poses, barefoot or wearing fancy sandals, showing her legs and sometimes holding a mirror, none of which occurs in the film itself (figure 3.9).[204] In numerous stills and advertisements, she is wearing the special dress that seems to have been censored from the film.[205] In the trailer, after her name goes up in flames the words "Hers the Face" appear in dramatic lettering, followed by "Hers the Temptation, Hers the *Sin*"—heavily loaded language in this period (figure 3.10). It is hardly surprising if viewers were disappointed to find themselves cheated of the promised sin.

199. On the use of sex to sell epics, see Llewelyn-Jones 2018: ch. 1 passim. This is not only an attraction for male audiences. For examples of women enjoying assertive "bad" women in the postwar period, see Thumim 1992: 122; Black 1994: 80; Stacey 1994: 166–67, 230.

200. Wyke 2002: 370–71.

201. Ads for *Quo Vadis* are cited from the Herrick library collection or the author's collection.

202. Lygia gets just one full color picture, as opposed to Poppaea's four.

203. On posters as the "essence" of the film, designed to draw audiences, see Llewellyn-Jones 2018: 80–102.

204. The studios often used "cheesecake" photos for publicity, even when there was nothing like them in the film (Finler 2012: 125, 140; cf. also Williamson 1986: 180–82). Podestà supposedly received "sacks" of "love letters" connected to the film, even before it opened (Anon. 1955b). If this is true (a big if), it suggests the effectiveness of advance publicity in raising audience expectations.

205. Above, p. 116.

FIGURE 3.8. Newspaper ad for *Quo Vadis*.

In terms of character, the closest parallel to Wise's Helen is Salome, another famous model of female eroticism and misbehavior, who also gets to title her own movie and is sanitized—and eventually Christianized—in defiance of audience expectations.[206] The heroine was portrayed, critics complained, as

206. See Llewellyn-Jones 2017; 2018: 368–81.

FIGURE 3.9. Publicity still for *Helen of Troy* (1956), showing Podestà with a mirror, bare legs, and sandals (a shot that resembles nothing in the movie itself).

FIGURE 3.10. A frame from the trailer for *Helen of Troy* (1956).

"a nice girl who'd gotten a raw deal from love."[207] Unlike Helen, however, Salome was played by a love goddess (Rita Hayworth), and the picture lived up to its advertising, which promised an extravagant display of vampish pagan

207. Llewellyn-Jones 2017: 224.

FIGURE 3.11. Publicity still of Rita Hayworth for *Salome*.

exoticism (figure 3.11). This culminated in Salome's famous dance, which was, as Lloyd Llewellyn-Jones notes "in many respects . . . the movie's only *raison d'être*."[208] The film, which did far better than *Helen* at the box office, was received as "a whale of a spectacle."[209] Yet most of its spectacular elements were quite restrained: the interior settings are modest, and there are no big battles or crowd scenes. Hayworth's biographer actually complains about the absence of the "special kind of vulgarity" that made DeMille's biblical epics "engrossing."[210] But *Salome* relied on a different type of spectacle: the love goddess herself, displayed in no fewer than nineteen exotic, revealing costumes, which made her "the object of all eyes."[211] Salome's character may have been good, but her costumes were *bad*.

208. Llewellyn-Jones 2017: 225.

209. Llewellyn-Jones 2017: 210, who adds, "By and large the press regarded *Salome* as a colourful, entertaining spectacle, and if the movie was not profound, deep, or cutting-edge it was at least, in the words of Orval Hopkins, 'a gee-whiz picture.'" According to *Variety Weekly* (January 13, 1954), it grossed $4.75 million, making it eleventh in the top grossing films of the year (at number one was *The Robe*).

210. Ringgold 1974: 189.

211. Crowther 1953.

Robert Wise was fundamentally opposed to DeMille's "special kind of vulgarity," and specifically to the extravagance of the wildly successful *Quo Vadis*.[212] As a pro-feminist pacifist, he tried to make Helen the center of her own epic in a way that would be intimate, naturalistic, and "modern." He transformed her into a dignified model of contemporary womanhood, resisted objectifying her, and tried hard to give her something to do. But this treatment deprived the epic audience of the decadence they loved to hate. In fairness to the director, he was constrained by many factors, including censorship and the available actors. The production was also dogged by problems, including a serious fire on set, the accidental death of a crew member, and delays caused by enthusiastic extras who kept wounding each other during the battle scenes.[213] In the final analysis, however, the film is most severely handicapped by Wise's conception of Helen and discomfort with ancient world epic as a genre. As a result, the audience is denied one of the central pleasures to be expected from that genre and especially from Helen of Troy as a pagan vamp, namely a decadent eroticism thinly veiled in respectability. Wise gives us too much alibi, not enough crime.

212. Cary 1974: 74.

213. Keenan 2007: 87; see also Cary 1974: 64–87; Gehring 2012: 167–74.

PLATE 1. Lobby card for *The Private Life of Helen of Troy*.

PLATE 2. Our first sight of Helen in *Helen of Troy* (1956).

PLATE 3. Rita Hayworth in *Life* magazine, illustrating Winthrop Sargeant's article "The Love Goddess in America."

PLATE 4. Helen waited on by Andraste in *Helen of Troy* (1956). Note the similar cut of their dresses. In other scenes Helen wears the same shade of blue as Andraste does here and each of them wears a similarly styled brown outfit.

PLATE 5. Still from *Quo Vadis* showing Lygia with her admirer Marcus.

PLATE 6. Poster for *Helen of Troy* (1956) (detail).

PLATE 7. “Shakara as Diana, Goddess of the Hunt,” from the *Sports Illustrated* Swimsuit Issue, 2001. The caption reads “Statue-Esque: These goddesses are used to being bronzed, but that usually refers to their tans.”

PLATE 8. Our first sight of Helen in *Troy* (2004).

PLATE 9. Poster for *Troy* showing a heroically bronzed Brad Pitt. Note the absence of any female stars' names.

PLATE 10. Carolyn in the *Star Trek* episode "Who Mourns for Adonais?"

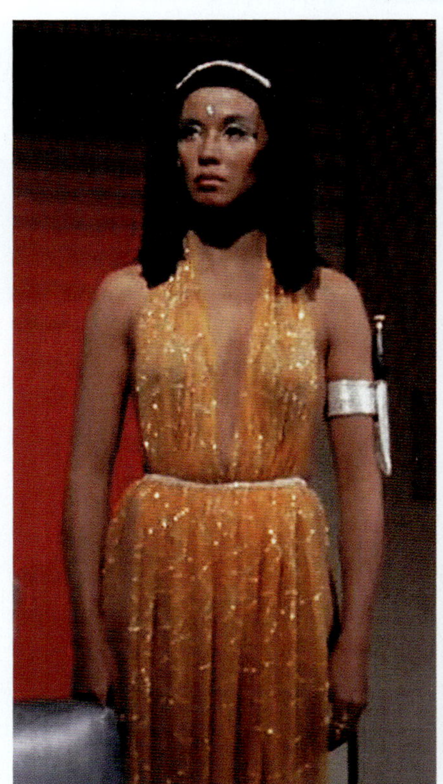

PLATE 11. Elaan's four costumes in "Elaan of Troyius."

PLATE 12.
France Nuyen on the cover of *Life*, October 6, 1958.

PLATE 13.
Elaan of Troyius as fan icon.

PLATE 14. Publicity still of Aphrodite from *Xena: Warrior Princess*.

PLATE 15. Our first sight of Helen in *Helen of Troy* (2003).

4

Helen of Abercrombie & Fitch

TROY (2004)

The Human Thing

It would be half a century before Warner Brothers unveiled its (and Hollywood's) second Trojan War blockbuster.[1] *Troy*, directed by the German Wolfgang Petersen from a script by David Benioff,[2] was released in May 2004, as part of the third wave of ancient world epics initiated by the remarkable success of Ridley Scott's *Gladiator* (2000).[3]

That success—a surprise to many—was driven in part by *Gladiator*'s innovative use of computer-generated imagery (CGI) to "reconstruct" ancient Rome.[4] But technology was not the only thing to have changed since the 1950s. While Hollywood blockbusters still hoped to draw a broad audience, the primary emphasis had shifted towards young males, especially "the all-important teenager."[5] Fortunately for certain segments of this audience,

1. This chapter is a substantially rewritten version of Blondell 2009, which it supersedes.

2. Unusually for a project of this kind there was only one writer, but Petersen was heavily involved in the script (see, e.g., Cohen 2004: 40; Goldsmith 2004: 56; Faraci 2004b; Epstein 2004). Winkler 2007: 4 gives reasons for viewing *Troy* as fundamentally Petersen's work (as opposed to the scriptwriter's or the studio's).

3. The demise of the epic in the 1960s is often attributed to the debacle of *Cleopatra* (1963), but other factors were also in play (see Blanshard & Shahabudin 2011: 216–18; Paul 2013a: 136–45). On the late twentieth-century revival of the genre, see Elliott 2014a; Blanshard & Shahabudin 2011: ch. 10.

4. Paul 2013a: 164–67. For the impact of CGI on epic film, see K. Thompson 2011; Elliott 2014b.

5. Hunter 2007: 159. Cf. G. King 2002: 80, 138–39, 197–201; Maltby 2003: 23; Krämer 2004: 362.

cleavage was no longer off-limits, though female nipples were (at least if younger teens were to be admitted).[6] Yet there was less attention in the new millennium to vamps and orgies, and a more exclusive focus on glorifying the male action hero.[7] Ancient themes still carried a marketable prestige. It was no longer necessary to promote such films as "educational," but the epic continued to take itself seriously, using warfare (as opposed to religious faith) as "the catalyst for change," and replacing Christianity as a driving "spiritual" force with the nostrums of "moral nostalgia," "mystic nationhood," or the "traditional" family."[8] And of course, the Cold War was over, stripping the historical epic of its ready-made template for audience identification. The sociopolitical context was, rather, informed by 9/11 and the subsequent US invasion of Iraq.

Despite these cultural, technical, and historical developments, *Troy* was an avowed heir of the sword-and-sandal movies of the filmmakers' youth.[9] Petersen, who had grown up on the epics of the 1950s and 1960s, liked "larger-than-life people and grand stories," and was drawn to the art of the Hollywood blockbuster.[10] Benioff, who also loved films like *Ben-Hur* and *Spartacus*, said *Troy* was a conscious attempt to "get back" to that tradition.[11] In contrast to Scott, who distanced *Gladiator* from the midcentury epic tradition, Petersen placed his film squarely within it, embracing such generic features as the initial map and grave male voice-over establishing the story's epochal significance.[12] *Troy* does, to be sure, employ CGI, especially for crowds of ships and soldiers,

6. The Code had been replaced in 1968 by the voluntary MPAA film rating system. *Troy* received an R rating, meaning that children under seventeen had to be accompanied by an adult. Petersen was aiming for a PG-13 rating but this was denied because of the corpse-dragging scene, which the director refused to eliminate (Winkler 2015c: 24). The director's cut is both more sexually explicit and gorier (see further La Pay 2007).

7. Ridley Scott found orgies "boring" (Raucci 2013: 143). Like other films of this epic cycle, *Troy* owes much generically to the combat film (C. Davies 2019: 42–48).

8. C. Davies 2019: 13; Pomeroy 2008: 99; Burgoyne 2008: 92; Blanshard & Shahabudin 2011: 233–34; Wieber 2002: 15–16.

9. These films lived on via television, which gave the genre a "bedrock of familiarity" (Blanshard & Shahabudin 2011: 219).

10. M. Russell 2004; Haase 2007: 63–64, 84.

11. Faraci 2004b; cf. Arnold 2004.

12. This time, however, the voice belongs not to history but to Sean Bean's Odysseus (see further M. Williams 2018: 172; C. Davies 2019: 48–50). On Petersen's self-conscious use of "old" Hollywood style, in contrast to Scott, see Shahabudin 2007: 110–18. For *Gladiator*'s relationship to tradition, see Blanshard & Shahabudin 2011: ch. 10; Paul 2013a: ch. 4; C. Davies 2019: 2–3.

but the director downplayed that fact.[13] Even though there were only eight hundred human soldiers and two physical ships, he invoked the traditional "rhetoric of numbers," telling *Variety*, for example, "This is the best kind of epic because you are working on the grandest scale, with 1,000 ships and 75,000 people waging enormous battles."[14]

Unsurprisingly, *Troy* has much in common, specifically, with Wise's *Helen of Troy*.[15] The opening voice-over opposes the film to tradition by insisting that this is what "really" happened; "love" is the Trojans' defining value, as opposed to the Greeks (for whom, Hector tells us, "this is about power, not love"); the Greeks are violent and self-interested, Troy the home of beauty and peace; there are no visible divine agents (as opposed to statues); the treatment of Helen and Paris is heavily romanticized; as usual, there is no Hermione to complicate our judgment, nor does Paris abscond (as he did in antiquity) with any of Menelaus's nonhuman treasure; Agamemnon is a naked imperialist for whom Helen's departure is no more than a convenient excuse (he calls her "a foolish woman" who has "proven to be very useful").

Unlike Wise's film, *Troy* does not deny Helen's agency in the elopement. It does, however, absolve her of responsibility. Benioff claimed that, in his script, "Helen's will is free, the choice is her own, and the consequences on her own conscience."[16] Yet in the film text her key transgression is literally elided from the narrative, both as choice and as action: one moment we see Helen treating the idea of eloping as a joke ("Don't play with me"); the next, Paris is revealing a mere glimpse of her to Hector—and us—in the ship conveying them to Troy. Benioff evaded the moral issue, saying that Helen's elopement is "beyond good and evil," that she does it because "she has to survive."[17] He also said that his script "doesn't judge [Helen] for the choice," merely showing its terrible consequences.[18] But in fact, both the script and its realization on screen do everything possible to judge her, and to find her not guilty.

13. Cf. Shahabudin 2007: 110. Blanshard & Shahabudin argue that this was a strategic mistake (2011: 235).

14. Fleming 2003. For numbers of soldiers and ships, see the Special Features "Creating an Army" and "Creating an Armada," on the DVD of *Troy*, directed by Wolfgang Petersen (Warner Bros., 2004).

15. For *Troy*'s apparent debts to Wise's film, see Wieber 2005: 150; Blank 2015: 69–70; C. Davies 2019: 38.

16. Benioff 2005.

17. Cohen 2004: 39.

18. Benioff 2005.

In contrast to the 1956 Helen's attempted self-sacrifice in the cause of political freedom, the Helen of 2004 is motivated strictly by personal fulfilment.[19] This makes her less heroic and self-denying than Wise's Helen. But she is also much more passive, hapless, and victimized, to a degree that exceeds even the requirements of the modern romantic plot (which typically endows heroines with some degree of feistiness or spunk). Her marriage to Menelaus was arranged, against her will, when she was sixteen, conveniently (if not quite fairly) displacing blame for her predicament onto the patriarchal structures of antiquity.[20] Once at Troy, this Helen suffers no reproach from her new family. Wise's ominous Cassandra has disappeared completely, along with Hecuba, the carping mother-in-law of the *Iliad*, and Helen is evidently on warm terms with Andromache.[21] Even her subsequent attempt to stop the war, by leaving Troy, is thwarted by Hector before it can take place (as if he had seen Wise's film and knew the effort would be futile).

Publicity, as in 1956, took advantage of the prestige of Homeric epic, albeit more cagily. The *Iliad* is named on-screen only as the movie's "inspiration." Benioff acknowledged that his script drew on a variety of ancient sources and distanced himself from any claim of fidelity to Homer.[22] Nevertheless, both he and Petersen invoked the *Iliad* repeatedly in interviews. Benioff stressed his childhood love of the epic, which his mother supposedly read to him "over and over again," and claimed Achilles and Hector as his earliest boyhood heroes.[23] Petersen emphasized his close familiarity with the Homeric text—in Greek—from his school days, and freely acknowledged *Troy*'s debt to his youthful fantasies from those formative years.[24] Discussing the characterization of Achilles, the director explained that he thought of him as "the ultimate rebel" like James Dean or Marlon Brando, because "when you are 15 or 16 that's

19. C. Davies 2019: 44 notes the absence from *Troy* of "freedom" as a political value.

20. In Greek myth she is born in Sparta. In the film, her parents sent her there to marry a Menelaus who apparently lived there already. There is no indication of where she was sent from.

21. At Hector's death, Helen supports the collapsing Andromache; at his funeral, it is she who holds the infant Astyanax, making her iconographically both an Andromache and a Madonna.

22. E.g., Benioff 2005; Epstein 2004.

23. Eimer 2004: 69; Faraci 2004b.

24. Kofler & Schaffenrath 2015: 87. Petersen repeatedly refers to his school days in connection with this film (e.g., M. Russell 2004). On his background, see Petersen & Greiwe 1997; M. Russell 2004; Haase 2007: ch. 3.

what you think."[25] When he justifies directorial choices by appealing to what "sixteen-year-old movie goers . . . want to watch," it is hard not to think he is talking about his teenage self. [26] To be sure, like other action blockbusters, *Troy* includes romance as a way of appealing to girls and women.[27] But Petersen himself, in keeping with his generally masculinist oeuvre, displays zero interest in this segment of his audience.[28]

Chris Davies speculates that it was Petersen's emphasis on his schooling that led critics to "mistakenly assume that *Troy* was an adaptation of the *Iliad*."[29] Yet that "assumption" was encouraged not only by the usual default tendency to equate the Trojan War narrative with the *Iliad*, but also by overt signals from the director (and others), who trumpeted the film's cultural credentials. Petersen told interviewers, "It's Homer, it's *The Iliad* . . . 'One of the great stories of all time,'" or "maybe even the greatest story of all time."[30] He explained, quite misleadingly, "We more or less do the whole Iliad," with the addition of only "a few things."[31] He even presented himself as a modern Homer, doing "the exact same thing" as his august forbear, who, he believed, would have blessed the undertaking, including his controversial elimination of the Homeric gods.[32]

The director claimed, in particular, that *Troy* was "far more faithful to Homer" than Wise's film.[33] This is questionable, considering some of Benioff's innovations (which include the death at Troy of both Menelaus and Agamemnon). Petersen's film is, however, much more Iliadic than Wise's in its central focus on masculine heroism. In contrast to his predecessor's brave, if unsuccessful, attempt to retell the story from a female point of view, he reclaims the Trojan War story for Achilles. This hero is presented as an unequivocally awe-inspiring and admirable—if conflicted—warrior (quite unlike

25. van Beekus 2004: 19.

26. Winkler 2015d: 111.

27. For its appeal to young people generally, see Wieber 2005: 157–62.

28. Cyrino notes that several of his previous films had "largely if not exclusively male casts" (Cyrino 2005b: 10). Discussing the ensemble nature of *Troy*, Petersen says there's "great pleasure and joy from watching a lot of great actors together"; he names six men, "and, of course, our women" (van Beekus 2004: 24). Unlike even Wise's film, *Troy* fails the Bechdel test.

29. C. Davies 2019: 40.

30. Petersen apud Schruers 2004a (similarly Pitt apud Carrillo 2004); Eimer 2004: 68.

31. Eimer 2004: 68.

32. Winkler 2007d: 457; C. Higgins 2004; see further below, p. 137.

33. Eimer 2004: 69.

Stanley Baker's comically villainous Achilles in Wise's version). But all the most substantial female characters in the Trojan War story are reduced. Andromache and Thetis are diminished; Hecuba and Cassandra are excised entirely. As for Helen—the most vocal and compelling female figure in the *Iliad*—her role is truncated in comparison not only with Wise's film but with the epic itself. Where the older film enhanced her Iliadic role, *Troy* significantly reduces it.

It is easy, then, to read *Troy* as a response to the 1956 epic. Yet Petersen claimed never to have seen Wise's version.[34] Claims to originality (and ignorance) are a trope of the genre, but there is no reason to disbelieve Petersen in principle.[35] The workings of tradition and allusion are not linear, but employ multiple correspondences and variations without necessarily involving direct or conscious influence.[36] Elsewhere, however, Petersen shows some awareness of Wise's film, not only judging it less faithful to Homer but dismissing it as "pretty bad."[37] Both he and Benioff, moreover, erased the earlier film by claiming that the story of the *Iliad* had "never been done before," or that there had never been "the grand version the story deserves."[38] Such assertions of primacy—generic as they are—imply that "grandeur" and "real" Homericity require a masculine emphasis: to center Helen's story on Helen is to expel it from the very category of epic.

Such statements use the discourse of authenticity to perpetuate male centrality in a manner that veils *Troy*'s own distance from antiquity, which is in its way as great as Wise's. Leaving aside his drastic changes to the Iliadic narrative, Petersen's overall approach is positively anti-Homeric. As he reiterated in interviews, he wanted to show the Trojan War story "realistically." This did not mean, for example, providing a believable picture of the heroes glorified by Homer, as men who were far greater "than men are now."[39] However "real" those heroes may have been to the oral poets and/or their audiences, they are dismissed by Petersen as "mythical" accretions. He wanted, rather, "to tell the story as it could have happened *in reality*, before it was relegated by the

34. Winkler 2015c: 19.

35. Like other 1950s epics, Wise's film was shown regularly on television; but it had not yet been released on tape or DVD.

36. See further Paul 2013a: ch. 4.

37. M. Russell 2004.

38. Petersen apud Eimer 2004: 68; Benioff apud Cohen 2004: 36.

39. This is a standard Homeric way of referring to the heroes of the past.

centuries to a more mythical realm."[40] He is not referring here to "realistic" recreation of the ancient world—though as usual, considerable effort was devoted to the meticulous (if arbitrary) reproduction of select archeological details—but rather to the way people "really" are. In Benioff's words, he wanted to "see the human thing."[41] Needless to say, this purportedly transhistorical human nature turns out to look remarkably modern. As the writer remarked, "This sort of thing happens every day in America."[42]

Given Petersen's distaste for the "mythical," it is unsurprising to find him invoking "realism" most commonly to explain the film's excision of Homer's divine characters.[43] Using *Clash of the Titans* (1981) as a straw man, he argued that his audience would be alienated by such literal presentation of the gods, claiming that "people would laugh today if you had God entering the scene and fighting and helping out. It's hard to even imagine that."[44] This claim seems quite extraordinary in a period when popular film and television were replete with the supernatural in myriad forms. To cite only the most obvious comparandum, the *Lord of the Rings* trilogy (*LOTR*), released in 2001, 2002, and 2003, was fresh in the public mind. But Petersen wanted his film to be taken seriously in a way that would set it apart from this kind of fantasy epic, which is often deemed frivolous or juvenile.[45] Despite sharing much the same target audience as *LOTR*—and some of the same actors—he claimed that *Troy* was different because it showed "the reality of war."[46] This was not just a matter of eliminating the gods. The highly stylized *300* (2007) has no divine

40. Winkler 2015b: 18 (emphasis added). On *Troy* and the "modern obsession with the historicity of the Trojan War myth," see Dué 2007: 248–55 and cf. Burgess 2009: 168–70.

41. Faraci 2004b.

42. Goldsmith 2004: 57.

43. This was part of Benioff's pitch from the start (Faraci 2004b; Epstein 2004; Benioff 2005). The film denies the gods' power as well as their visibility (see the fine account by Chiasson 2009: 195–203). The only exception is Thetis (Julie Christie), who retains a slight supernatural aura (below) but is not an Olympian (i.e., not one of the "Greek gods" with whom most of the audience would be familiar).

44. M. Russell 2004. He and Benioff asserted repeatedly that the gods are laughable. See, e.g., Special Feature: "Homer: A Story for the Ages," *Troy: Director's Cut*, directed by Wolfgang Petersen (Warner Bros., 2007), DVD; Faraci 2004b; G. Flynn 2004: 28; Higgins 2004; Epstein 2004; Winkler 2015c: 18; Winkler 2015d: 111.

45. Cf. Wieber 2005: 156. For the "juvenile" associations of "non-realist" genres, see Neale 2000: 35–36; Paul 2013a: 94, 104–7.

46. M. Russell 2004; cf. Eimer 2004: 71. Both Sean Bean and Orlando Bloom came to *Troy* from *LOTR* (Susman 2003; cf. Millar 2004b: 24). Several reviewers noted that, at the end of

characters, yet Petersen scorned it as less affecting for a modern audience than his own brand of "realism."[47] His goal was a "serious" war film "in the tradition of the great David Lean films."[48]

Petersen's anxiety about seriousness is crystallized in his oft-expressed fear that "people would laugh"—a (very Greek) sentiment betraying a chink in his transhistorical armor. Yet he underestimates the degree to which viewers can take *anything* seriously, and conversely the degree to which seriousness is synonymous with his particular brand of "realism." In any case, *Troy*'s "realism" is in practice quite selective. Whatever might have happened "in reality, before it was relegated by the centuries to a more mythical realm," it is unlikely—to offer just one example—that the Trojans defended themselves with giant fireballs rolled down the beach at the Greek invaders.[49] The director said he wanted "blood, sweat and tears," "the reality of a fight," and as much gore as possible.[50] Yet *Troy* is a far cry from the "gritty" realism of, for example, Petersen's own *Das Boot* (1981), which has been called "the most convincing war movie ever made."[51]

Nor does Petersen do away with the Trojan Horse, which is not only the most spectacular element of the Trojan War story but also the most ludicrous—a fact that would not be lost on the contemporary audience.[52] Yet the director called *Troy*'s Horse "very realistic" because it appeared to be

---

Troy, the latter "transforms back into Legolas" (Spicciati n.d.) when he uses a bow to kill Achilles.

47. Winkler 2015c: 25. *300* was, however, considerably more successful at the box office (at least domestically). Petersen did treat *Gladiator* as a worthy comparandum, but considered his own film "much bigger" (Eimer 2004: 68; Hiscock 2004).

48. van Beekus 2004: 19; cf. Fleming 2003. Peter O'Toole was cast both because of his star image and as an homage to David Lean (Fleming 2003; van Beekus 2004: 19).

49. This moment owes more to *Gladiator* than to history (Blanshard & Shahabudin 2011: 235). For *Gladiator*'s influence on *Troy*, see also C. Davies 2019: 38–39, 49.

50. Special Features: "Achilles v. Hector" and "The Weapons of Troy," *Troy*, directed by Wolfgang Petersen (Warner Bros., 2004), DVD. See further Haase 2007: 90–91.

51. Haase 2007: 77. *Das Boot* shows, for example, sailors being searched for pubic lice and emerging in terror from the latrine when under attack. As an acerbic IMDb commenter named Agrenish puts it, "Obviously they didn't make [*Troy*] to be realistic; otherwise they would have gone with dirty fingernails, rotten teeth, mud, grime, gore and hair on the women's legs."

52. Even in a promotional article about *Troy*, the *Film Review* "Epics Special" refers to the Monty Python parody, complete with illustration: "Look, if we were to build a large wooden badger . . ." (Anon. 2004a: 30).

put together out of charred timbers.[53] Though supposedly built by the Greeks in twelve days, however, it was forty-two feet tall and weighed twelve tons (despite being made of polystyrene).[54] If one does not laugh at this Trojan Horse, that is not because it "could have happened in reality," but because one is willing to enter imaginatively into the world of the film. The "realism" of other aspects of the mise-en-scène is just as equivocal. Petersen wanted the reconstruction of the city of Troy to be "as authentic as possible"; yet the sets were far more majestic, powerful, and beautiful—and much, much bigger—than warranted by archeology.[55] In the words of historical advisor Lesley Fitton, "The whole setting is glamorized" because, as the production designer explained, an epic film has to have "epic proportions."[56]

The tensions between various conceptions of myth and "reality" engendered by applying Petersen's "realism" to Greek epic—tensions apparent in both publicity and the film text—apply equally to *Troy*'s characters. They are particularly acute in the case of Achilles and Helen, the two semidivine figures produced by Zeus to generate the Trojan War through their preternatural strength and beauty respectively. These characters pose a special challenge to Petersen's ideas about realism and the "human thing"—a challenge the film addresses, as we shall see, in two quite different ways.

A New Face, a Fresh Face

Unlike most epics, *Troy* lacks an eponymous hero. Yet the name most closely associated with the titular city is, of course, Helen's. Petersen described her role as "charged with the grandeur of history and legend,"[57] and publicity featured her conspicuously, either alone or paired with Paris as the second most important couple in the film (the first being Achilles and Hector). The

53. Schruers 2004a: 47.

54. Special Feature: "Making a Decoy," *Troy*, directed by Wolfgang Petersen (Warner Bros., 2004), DVD.

55. Special Feature: "The Real Troy," *Troy*, directed by Wolfgang Petersen (Warner Bros., 2004), DVD. Statues, for example, were up to forty feet high (instead of ten feet), or even fifty feet in the case of Zeus (cf. Fitton 2007: 103–4). At forty feet, the walls of Troy were also far bigger than those of Troy VI, the stratum of Bronze Age remains that are usually identified with Homer's Troy (Special Feature: "From Ruins to Reality").

56. Special Feature: "The Real Troy."

57. Bing 2003.

theatrical trailer and grandiose souvenir brochure both dwell at length on her romance with Paris.

Advance publicity raised high expectations for Helen's appearance, inevitably referring to her as "the most beautiful woman in the world" and/or "the face that launched a thousand ships," and in one case "the most dangerously beautiful woman in the world."[58] According to one pop culture website, "casting notices say whomever [sic] plays Helen must be a 20 on a scale of 1–10."[59] Petersen declared that whoever won the role "had to be . . . a woman thought stunningly beautiful by everyone who saw her, just as Helen was," insisting that "she has to be believable as the face that launched 1,000 ships and caused the Greeks to go against Troy . . . She has to be that beautiful."[60] The Warner Brothers chief confirmed that they were "looking for the thousand."[61]

As usual, we are informed that the studio "held a worldwide search" to fill the role.[62] According to Petersen, they considered three thousand women around the globe, of whom he personally auditioned some two hundred.[63] The casting director, Lucinda Syson, said they were looking for "an actress with the epic beauty of, say, Elizabeth Taylor in *Cleopatra*."[64] It was reported that "established Hollywood stars such as Nicole Kidman and Julia Roberts . . . were . . . eager to play Helen," and the studio was "very interested in Nicole Kidman."[65] Sultry supermodel Kemp Muhl was also considered, but rejected because at sixteen she was too young.[66] Another rumored candidate was Angelina Jolie, *Esquire* magazine's 2004 "sexiest woman alive," whose scandalous image at the time could have been an added bonus.[67]

In keeping with his conception of "realism," however, Petersen wanted his Helen to be just "Helen from Sparta," reasoning that since "no one had ever seen her . . . hidden in Sparta," she should be played by an actor who brought

58. Schruers 2004a: 113.

59. Stax 2002.

60. Anon. 2004c; Fleming 2003.

61. Faraci 2004a.

62. E.g., Fleming 2003.

63. van Beekus 2004: 22.

64. Turner 2003.

65. Anon. 2004b; Desta 2019.

66. Turner 2004.

67. She was involved in a high-profile divorce and would soon be accused of "breaking up" Brad Pitt's marriage to Jennifer Aniston. Compare the way in which the Taylor/Burton scandal enhanced Taylor's image for *Cleopatra* (Wyke 2002: 309–17).

no "baggage" from her previous roles.[68] Unlike Wise, who was clearly putting a brave face on things when he defended casting the unknown Podestà, Petersen rejected Kidman specifically because she was a star.[69] Despite concerns expressed by the studio, he wanted "someone who was unknown, a new face, a fresh face," who "would both surprise a global audience and play on the mythical aspects of the character.[70] This dovetailed conveniently (though not coincidentally) with Hollywood's usual practice of casting male stars first, and paying them much more than women.[71] Petersen initially approached Brad Pitt to play Achilles, then built the movie around him; Helen was the last role cast, just four weeks before the start of shooting.[72]

As with Wise's Podestà, the fresh, new face in question belonged to a young European still unknown to Hollywood. At the time of filming, Diane Kruger was a twenty-six-year-old German with no public visibility in the US. After an abortive career as a ballet dancer, she had been working for a decade as a top European model, and had only recently turned to acting.[73] At first sight, Petersen rated Kruger at only 855 ships, and she had to wait four months for the final decision.[74] But the director explained her last-minute casting as a personal choice, justified via a heteronormative narrative of love at first sight: "As soon as Diane entered the room, I knew I'd found her"; he was attracted, he said later, by the fact that "she was so sweet and so nervous."[75]

The press release called Kruger a "stunning beauty" with "charisma and artistry,"[76] and she appeared on the cover of *Tatler* with the caption "the girl picked from thousands to be Helen of Troy." As with Wise's Podestà, discussions of her casting dwell on her status as a "new face," who "beat" such "established stars" as Roberts and Kidman.[77] Her modeling career is mentioned

68. van Beekus 2004: 22.

69. Desta 2019. For Wise and Podestà, see above, p. 121.

70. van Beekus 2004: 20; Desta 2019.

71. Pitt was reportedly paid $17.5 million (Eimer 2004: 70).

72. G. Flynn 2004; Bing 2003; Faraci 2004a.

73. Kruger's dance career was cut short by injury (Lynn B. n.d.). As a model, she appeared on the cover of major European fashion magazines, including German *Vogue* and French *Elle*. She had been in one English-language TV movie, which she called "terrible" (Freydkin 2004), and three French-language films.

74. van Beekus 2004: 22; Faraci 2004a.

75. Anon. 2004c; Desta 2019.

76. Schruers 2004b: 50.

77. Anon. 2004b.

repeatedly, and fashion spreads add sexual overtones enhancing readers' expectations for her appearance in the film. *Tatler*, for example, posed her enticingly under the headline "Homer Erotic," continuing, "Diane Kruger's fantastic in the sack . . . of Troy."[78]

Kruger had neither the stardom nor the experience of a Kidman or Roberts (let alone an Elizabeth Taylor). As a model, however, she was well used to being scrutinized and appraised for her beauty. That beauty is of a familiar "Western" type: blonde, slender, and white. Fashion models of the period were notoriously thin, and Kruger describes herself as "very skinny" at the time she was cast, even though she had gained 10 pounds for the audition (which made her feel "obese").[79] She has blue eyes and long blonde hair, which Petersen considered a sign of Helen's "otherworldly" appearance, marking her as "a blonde aberration" among the dark-haired Greeks.[80] In modern terms, however, blonde hair, especially with blue eyes, is a well-worn signifier—perhaps *the* signifier—of stereotypical "Western" femininity. At the turn of the twenty-first century, a time when American culture was awash in young and often disreputable celebrity blondes,[81] it could adorn a whole range of types, from the cheerleader to the bombshell, the princess to the power blonde.

Kruger's overall appearance is very Teutonic, a term that, in fashion circles, implies blonde hair, sharply defined features, and a certain coolness or hauteur. The most characteristic expression on her angular face is a slight twist of the lip, suggesting a touch of amused detachment or cynicism. Her bearing is called "aristocratic" or "regal," with some descriptions evoking the blonde princess Grace Kelly: "Cut her and she'd bleed champagne."[82] This "sang-froid 'germanique,'" as Frédéric Martin calls it, is further enhanced by Kruger's

78. Weinberg 2004: 144–45; cf. also Schruers 2004b: 50–51.

79. Faraci 2004a; Weinberg 2004: 146. Fan sites inform us that Kruger is five feet, seven inches tall, weighs 126 pounds, and measures 33-23-35 (Celebrity Facts, "Diane Kruger," accessed June 18, 2020, https://www.celebsfacts.com/diane-kruger/), but IMDb puts her an inch taller. On the Body Measurements site, she is called a "banana," glossed as "Very slim figure, classic supermodel-like look" (Body Measurements, "Diane Kruger," accessed June 18, 2020, http://www.bodymeasurements.org/diane-kruger/).

80. Schruers 2004a: 114; cf. Cyrino 2005b: 11.

81. E.g., Britney Spears, Lindsay Lohan, Paris Hilton, the Simpson sisters, and the Olsen twins (to name only the most obvious).

82. Schruers 2004a: 114; Faraci 2004a; Conrad 2013; on Kelly, see above, p. 101.

accent.[83] Thanks to Winckelmann's indestructible legacy, this kind of "Teutonic" beauty is still associated with ancient Greece. Petersen claimed that he did not know Kruger was German or choose her for that reason.[84] But, aside from the fact that he must have detected her accent, it seems probable that she satisfied the German director's personal vision of "Greek" beauty, just as the male heroes were informed by his childhood fantasies of masculinity.[85]

Greek mythology, as perceived through this Aryan lens, had not lost its currency, far beyond northern Europe, for expressing the idea of unearthly and overwhelming beauty. Kruger's fellow German supermodel Heidi Klum (often described as "Teutonic") features extensively in the "Greece" section of "Goddesses of the Mediterranean," the *Sports Illustrated* Swimsuit Issue of 2001.[86] Besides numerous solo swimsuit shots, Klum, referred to as an "über-model," gets her own multiple-page section posing with American football stars, and appears as Athena in an enormous centerfold. Several of the models are bronzed to evoke ancient statuary (plate 7). The magazine identifies all the models in this special issue as "Babe Goddesses," explaining that this kind of "goddess" exemplifies the Platonic Form of beauty, and is, as such, "a woman so beautiful that she puts a distance between herself and the world, between herself and you," who "floats by, oblivious to you and all other earthly concerns."[87]

Kruger's Teutonic appearance and successful modeling career thus supplied a readily available early twenty-first-century template for representing Helen as a fantasy object of superhuman beauty. This template is invoked, for example, in a fashion article that "takes its cue" from Kruger in *Troy* to promote the "heaven sent" "goddess look," whose gauzy drapery "will make you feel gorgeous, glamorous and utterly worthy of worship."[88] But Petersen's conception of "realism"—which required even Achilles's armor to be less beautiful than in

83. F. Martin 2002: 16. Italians were not considered for the role because "accents were a concern" (Turner 2003: slide 13). Syson explained, "You can't-a have-a Helen talking like-a this." But this caricature seems like a straw man justifying the avoidance of Italian sensuality (as opposed to Germanic "cool").

84. Anon. 2004b.

85. Some Germans, at least, felt that their country had a special claim to ownership of the Trojan War, owing to Schliemann and his successors (cf. Wieber 2005: 148–49).

86. The whole section is overwhelmingly dominated by blondes. A few darker models are presented with their skin colored in the guise of bronze or terracotta.

87. Consagra 2001: 20–21.

88. Anon. 2004d.

Homer[89]—prohibited the use of such associations to present Helen as someone whose godlike beauty makes her a creature of the imagination, not fully of this world. Benioff's script, to be sure, ascribes to Helen an "unearthly beauty," which is "so extreme she seems to exist in a separate realm"; yet his self-appointed task was to give her "the same humanity" as the other characters.[90]

Stripped of supernatural associations, Kruger's blonde, blue-eyed, slender beauty is that of a conventionally attractive model, a young woman who might catch the eye not only of Paris but of Petersen's sixteen-year-old boys, and with whom a (putatively youthful) female viewer might identify. In person, she is described as "an incredibly nice girl . . . easy-going and straightforward," while profiles normalize her by telling us about her cooking skills, her allergies, her penchant for puttering and her "corpulent cat."[91] The word "girl" is used advisedly. A very pink website called A Girl's World ("written and edited by girls and teens"), explains, "This chick is ultra gorgeous, right? Okay, right but, talking with her is like chatting with a girlfriend in the hall before Phys Ed class. She's fall over dead beautiful but . . . normal."[92] Her "baby blue eyes" could "knock over an entire football team . . . but they are friendly too." She is not a femme fatale, but a "Gorgeous Girl Next Door."

Human and Real and Vulnerable

This demythologizing approach is fatal to Helen's archetypal identity. Tellingly, Marlowe's "a thousand ships" line, ubiquitous in surrounding media, appears nowhere in the film text. Nor is there any reference to Helen's supernatural origins, the competition for her hand, or the oath of the suitors. Despite Petersen's view of Helen as "a woman thought stunningly beautiful by everyone who saw her," his film never shows her capturing all eyes.

We first see Helen sitting mute and static at an otherwise riotous table of feasting Greek and Trojan warriors, where she is overshadowed by the bulky

89. Kofler & Schaffenrath 2015: 105; cf. D. Petersen 2015: 28. The stunt coordinator emphasized that getting the weapons right was "really key to keep it all real." Special Feature: "The Weapons of Troy."

90. Cohen 2004: 39. The script can be consulted at Cinefile, accessed April 4, 2022, http://www.cinefile.biz/script/troy.pdf.

91. Weinberg 2004: 146; Freydkin 2004.

92. Lynn B. n.d.

Menelaus (plate 8). Her posture is rigidly dignified, in sharp contrast to the only other women in the scene—a group of lively, sexualized dancing girls, who come running in to entertain the men. She wears a voluminous dark red costume, with no crown or other indicator of royal status. A lavish necklace, seemingly made of gold coins, suggests, rather, the status of a purchased object. Her unsmiling face, downcast eyes, and smudgy eye makeup convey deep gloom. Apart from one sidelong glance by Menelaus, when he mentions her name, she is ignored by everyone but Paris, who fixes puppy-dog eyes on her from across the table. Unlike Sernas's Paris, he is not lying helpless on the ground gazing up at her, nor does he liken her to a goddess.

The scene establishes sadness and passivity as the keynotes of this Helen's character. As Kruger explained, she tried to make her "human and real and vulnerable," in keeping with both script and direction. "The way Wolfgang talked about it, I wanted to show . . . how unhappy she must have been."[93] In her view, this characterization made her Helen more "likeable" than the Homeric original, whom she perceived as "vain and absorbed," because she "does all these horrible things for her own selfish reasons."[94] These traits also undergird her romance with Paris. Kruger thought of Paris as *attracted* to "[Helen's] vulnerability and her aura of sadness"[95]—echoing Petersen's response to the actor's nervousness. Sadness is not typically considered sexy or alluring, whereas smiling is strongly associated with sexual attraction.[96] But Kruger's Helen almost never smiles.[97]

If gloom is erotically appealing to anyone, however, it may be naive young men with delusions of romantic heroism. When Helen slips away unnoticed from the feast, Paris follows her upstairs. We observe her in her bedroom through the eyes of her lover, who watches stalker-like from the doorway. The camera moves in slowly while she removes her jewelry and lets down her hair, oblivious to his (and our) voyeuristic presence. When she does become aware of Paris, she utters low words of resistance (her accent isolating her further from the otherwise anglophone cast). But Paris refuses to accept that no

93. Faraci 2004a.

94. H. Hayes n.d.; Special Feature: "Homer: A Story for the Ages."

95. H. Hayes n.d.

96. See, e.g., Golle et al. 2013 ("the evaluation of attractiveness is strongly influenced by the intensity of a smile expressed on a face").

97. The only exceptions are a tremulous half-smile in response to Paris's suggestion that they run away together and a very restrained smile as she enters Troy (below, p. 149).

means no. He fondles Helen's throat from behind, a moment conveying acute vulnerability.[98] She never verbally assents, but simply unpins her dark red dress so that it falls to the floor and embraces the still-clad Paris. The spectacle of her naked breasts pressed against his armored torso is distinctly uncomfortable. There is no romantic music on the soundtrack—no music at all—to soften the scene. Nor are we privy to any further erotic activity: their putative sex act is excised by cutting away to Menelaus's dalliance with a dancing girl.

Afterwards, we see the nude Helen from behind, reclining in a stylized pose familiar from numerous paintings, her body lit dramatically in the firelight, while Paris (now topless) gazes down at her (figure 4.1). The scene takes advantage of the period's loosened norms around sexuality to present Helen as a naked, explicitly eroticized object, thus satisfying contemporary expectations regarding the assessment of female beauty. But such displays do not necessarily enhance that beauty's impact. Nakedness is a kind of depersonalizing costume, which locates a woman's allure in the surface of her body, exposing her as an object to be assessed and evaluated in its particularity.[99] Kruger's pose evokes the odalisque, a trope arising from the artistic "white slave" tradition.[100] To be sure, nudity as a costume can also express sexual power, or "a kind of unbridled, uninhibited confidence," but this Helen's objectivized body, her averted gaze, and her static, passive nudity, so carefully framed and lit, suggests the opposite of such "bare-assed bravado."[101] The scene conveys not erotic power but exposure to male scrutiny and helplessness in the face of male desire (all the more so because of the heavy costume that Helen has just removed). The effect is reinforced by Kruger's lack of a star image. The scene would play very differently with Kidman or Roberts in the role.

The love affair is further demythologized through the characterization of Paris. Orlando Bloom, who played the role, explained that as a "real" and "human" young man, Paris is consumed with "the seven deadly sins," more specifically "lust."[102] That particular sin is articulated, to Helen in her Spartan bedroom, via an extravagant romanticism designed to elicit her elopement.

98. We have Kruger's word for her sense of vulnerability in this scene (P. Fischer 2004a).

99. "Nudity is the greatest costume because no-one is looking at you as a person—all they see is your body" (Parks 2009, quoting actor Mary-Louise Parker). On nudity (vs. nakedness) as a form of dress, cf. Berger 1972: 54.

100. Cf. Painter 2010: 52–53 and below, p. 239 n. 66.

101. The quoted phrases are from Bari 2016.

102. Schruers 2004a; Millar 2004a.

FIGURE 4.1. Two sex scenes from *Troy*: Paris and Helen (above); Achilles and Briseis (below).

("Men will hunt us and the gods will curse us. But I'll love you. Until the day they burn my body I will love you.") Such language gives credence to the unimpeachable Hector when he tells his little brother that he knows "nothing about love." Later Paris will suggest that he and Helen run away to a fantasy island where they will live off the land in a natural paradise, like the island of Pelagos to which Helen retreats in imagination at the end of Wise's film. *Troy*, however, frames the idea as a childish absurdity. Helen responds, "You're very young, my love."[103]

103. This is a comment on his character, not his actual age (which is supposed to be the same as Helen's). (Kruger is a year older than Bloom.)

Despite—or because of—his flights of juvenile romanticism, Paris's "love" comes across less as a grand passion than as an adolescent crush that just happens to offer Helen a ticket out of Sparta. She herself seems devoid of "sexual avidity."[104] Calling Paris "my love" (which she does just twice) is the closest she comes to actively professing her love for him. The instance just quoted does not suggest passion so much as a detached world-weariness. This is in keeping with the filmmakers' conception of her character. As we saw earlier, Benioff explained the elopement without mentioning Helen's love.[105] Kruger's own account of her character does mention love, but only in the abstract. She describes a "sad," "young" Helen who is "married to a man she hates," adding, "I just hope that people will look and see and believe in that hope of love, that hope of freedom, even if it was just for a limited time"—a freedom that a courageous Helen "dared" to grasp.[106] This wording belies the cinematic presentation of the character, who is portrayed as reactive, a refugee from Greek male oppression, never "grasping" at anything or actively asserting her desire.

Little follows to challenge this impression of Helen as a passive object whose effect on Paris is less a product of her world-shattering beauty than of a specific romantic bond, forged by the circumstances of her victimhood. Menelaus is a stern warrior who never speaks a word about love or beauty.[107] At the feast in Sparta, he does not even bother to ogle Helen, focusing his attention on a dancing girl after his wife has slipped away unnoticed.[108] When Agamemnon is manipulating his brother, he calls Helen "a beautiful woman," but later he tells Menelaus, "I didn't come here for your pretty wife. I came for Troy." This encapsulates her role as the merest "pretty" pretext for a war that is really being fought, in Hector's words, "for one man's greed."[109] The only man in Troy to praise her beauty is the paternalistic Priam. It is true that when Helen first rides into the city with Paris, a group of locals stare and point at her, "mystified by her appearance" (according to the script), but there is no suggestion that the crowd is overwhelmed by her beauty.

104. Cyrino 2005b: 18.

105. Above, p. 133.

106. P. Fischer 2004b.

107. Helen calls him a "great warrior" who "lived for fighting."

108. In the director's cut, he urges Hector to do the same, telling him that "wives are for breeding" and showing no respect for Hector's marital fidelity.

109. On the word "pretty," cf. above, p. 118. It is also used by Hector to mark Paris's immaturity, and by reviewers who disliked Pitt in the role of Achilles (Denby 2004: 109; Reed 2004).

FIGURE 4.2. Still from *Troy* showing Paris and Helen entering Troy.

This grand entrance is the source of the most frequently used publicity images of Kruger in the role of Helen (figure 4.2). She wears a long white dress and a white mantle richly trimmed with gold. (Some stills also give her a long white veil, but this does not appear in the film.) Her accessories, which include Paris's gift of a slender pearl necklace and a delicate golden crown of leaves, flowers, and berries, are airy and festive (as opposed to meretricious or burdensome). The white dress signifies innocence, while the vegetal motif marks Helen's arrival as a Trojan (Andromache has a similar gold crown, Briseis a more rustic version). The scene evokes a royal wedding, with the crowds cheering the procession, throwing flower petals, and dancing in the streets. Helen even wears a slight smile, though she remains a "pale and uneasy bride."[110]

The palette of Kruger's remaining costumes is confined to black and white, in a visual expression of Helen's two most salient characteristics—sorrow and

110. Cyrino 2007: 137.

innocence.[111] Most of them echo the "wedding" outfit, employing white drapery (sometimes accessorized with a veil), gold accents, and simple gold jewelry. But she wears black for an intimate scene with Paris in which they discuss their future, again when she tries to leave Troy, and a third time at Hector's funeral. None of these costumes is especially revealing, except for some plunging necklines. Despite the skeletal thinness of contemporary models, "the 2000's was the decade of boobs," in which women pursued "that almost-unnatural look of perfectly round and overly perky breasts."[112] But Helen's cleavage is shallow and in many cases veiled by her hair or jewelry.[113] Nor do we ever see her and Paris in the throes of passion. After their single, decorously elided, sexual encounter at Sparta, the relationship becomes increasingly bourgeois. The second time that Helen calls Paris "my love," after he fails to go through with his intention to fight to the death for her, she is consoling him with her desire for companionate marriage: "I don't want a hero, my love. I want a man to grow old with."[114] The point is underlined by Menelaus's contempt: "Is *this* what you left me for?"

Paris's adolescent crush on Helen is evolving, at the same time, into something more respectable. When Priam asks his son if he loves Helen, Paris responds by equating his love for Helen with the aged king's love of his country. Priam goes on to give the romantic plot his seal of approval: "I've fought many wars in my time. Some were fought for land, some for power, some for glory. I suppose fighting for love makes more sense than all the rest." *Why* it makes sense is not explained. But the romance between Paris and Helen is progressively legitimized so as to resemble the mature heterosexual "love" that supposedly undergirds the nuclear family (as represented by Hector, Andromache, and the baby Astyanax). Under Helen's influence, Paris matures from excruciating cowardice to the "quite heroic act" of retrieving the Excalibur-like

111. There is an exception in the director's cut, where we glimpse her escaping at the end wearing a dull blue (which in this film is the color of heroism and of Troy).

112. Sims n.d. Cf. Komar 2016; Finnigan 2018. Menelaus's dancing girls wear push-up bustiers.

113. Many stills of her online, which are supposedly from the film, have had the breasts digitally enhanced. It is widely rumored that Kruger subsequently had breast augmentation surgery.

114. The scene was evidently too "realistic" even for Petersen, who eliminated it from the director's cut (Winkler 2015b: 6; 2015c: 23).

sword of Troy from the battlefield.[115] His irresponsible ardor is redeemed by the romantic trope that "love" is a force for personal improvement.[116]

As it turns out, Helen may even get her wish to grow old with him. In the film as released, which ends with the death of Achilles, the fate of Paris is left open. The death of Menelaus, moreover, rules out the traditional thwarting of Helen's doomed desire, allowing for the possibility that she and Paris may live mopily ever after. Both Benioff's script and the director's cut actually show them escaping together, in the company of Aeneas, Andromache, Astyanax, and Briseis.[117] This is the ultimate triumph of Petersenian "realism" over legend, erasing Helen's time-honored role as an emblem of tragic passion and turning her story, instead, into "a romantic comedy."[118]

Everything Is More Beautiful for the Doomed

This demythologizing of Helen stands in sharp contrast with *Troy*'s treatment of Achilles. To be sure, his character, like Helen's, had to retain its "humanity" in order to satisfy Petersen's conception of "realism."[119] The director calls him "a haunted person, driven, pained—a very modern kind of man."[120] As such, he is a familiar antiestablishment heroic type: an idealistic, alienated free spirit, who broods on the meaning of life and tells Patroclus, "Don't waste your life following some fool's orders."[121] This recognizably American identity is reinforced by the fact that Pitt is an American surrounded by an ensemble of foreigners (Australian, British, German), marking him, in the best traditions of Hollywood epic, as the primary hero for modern audience identification.[122] He is also demythologized in more specific ways. When an awestruck boy asks Achilles whether he is really invulnerable, he sardonically replies that, if that

115. The phrase is Petersen's (Schruers 2004: 48).

116. For the upgrading of Paris's character compared to Homer, see Chiasson 2009: 191–93.

117. Cf. Winkler 2015b: 9. On the film's various endings, see also Burgess 2009: 181 n. 33; Salzman-Mitchell & Alvares 2018: 60–62.

118. For the latter, see Morrissey 2004.

119. Anon. 2004a.

120. Bennetts 2004: 171; cf. Horn 2004.

121. This type was produced in part by the Vietnam war (Junkelmann 2005: 94; C. Davies 2019: 27–28).

122. Cf. Ahl 2007: 179–80 (who also notes that Achilles is the only blond male). Supposedly, both Greeks and Trojans use English accents, the Trojans' "slightly more cut-glass" and the Greeks more varied (C. Higgins 2004). But Pitt's wobbly accent was noted by many critics.

were the case, he would not need a shield; this is corroborated by his death, which results from the impact of many arrows—not just one to the heel.[123]

Nevertheless, like the walls of Troy (and unlike Helen), Achilles is endowed in several ways with an "unrealistic" stature, beginning with casting. The director wanted a "big superstar" in the role, because Achilles was "like a rock star of his time"; he was "a pop star of those days," "a half-god . . . a legend," and, therefore, "you need one of the great, great-looking guys from today."[124] Brad Pitt, around whom the role (and the film) was built, was *the* Hollywood megastar of the period.[125] Alan Horn, the president of Warner Brothers, said Pitt was "literally" the only person he could think of for the role: "He had to look like a god."[126] This deft casting choice effected a plausible cultural translation of ancient heroic glory into an approximate modern equivalent. Publicity strongly identified the star with his role, with Petersen describing Pitt as a "dark, edgy . . . tortured soul"—just like his Achilles.[127] Conversely, the script gave Achilles moody reflections on fame befitting the modern star.

Unlike Helen, whose "realistic" character within the film text creates a troubling dissonance with the hype of advance publicity, Achilles is also presented on screen as a hero whose charisma and power far surpass the common run of mortals. The film makes copious use of Pitt's star image as a sculptural "Greek god."[128] And whereas Helen's divine paternity is never mentioned, there are several nods to Achilles's supernatural connections. Most notably, his mother, Thetis (Julie Christie), is the only divinity among the dramatis personae. Though her visible age suggests mortality, it is she who provides the prophecy about her son's death, thereby generating the sense of doom that drives his character. Her status, like his, is enhanced by star casting, and the "rumor" that she is a goddess—a rumor that Achilles does not actually deny—casts a mythic aura over her son. Petersen himself asserted, "In our film, he's sort of like a half-god—it's not totally explained, but his mother's obviously a goddess."[129]

123. On the demythologizing of Achilles's heel, see Shahabudin 2007: 116–18.

124. van Beekus 2004: 20; Spelling 2004: 72–73.

125. The Hollywood star system in its classic form was long gone, but in certain respects the breakup of the studio system increased stars' power (cf. Schatz 1993: 31).

126. Waxman 2004b.

127. G. Flynn 2004. On Pitt's romantic hero image, see Abele 2014. Leslie Bennetts opined that "the words [Pitt] chooses to describe Achilles reflect his own journey" (Bennetts 2004).

128. See M. Williams 2018: 181–88.

129. M. Russell 2004.

In the *Iliad*, the pursuit of glory (*kleos*) in battle lies at the heart of Achilles's heroism. In *Troy*, the fighting is bloody, and Petersen insisted repeatedly that it is "not glorious."[130] (Hector, our exemplary good guy, says of death in battle, "There's nothing glorious about it—nothing poetic.") Nevertheless, *Troy* is unusually concerned with *kleos* for its genre, and especially with the glory of Achilles, which it explicitly perpetuates.[131] Glory gives him a motivation for fighting that is both less offensive and more heroic than Agamemnon's ugly imperialism. It also allows the audience, by remembering him, to participate in Homeric tradition. The casting of Pitt was proleptic. Benioff's script indicates that Achilles's name is not yet well known; he has yet to establish his fame. It will be established, however, through the actions shown in the film itself, which thus becomes the vehicle of his *kleos.*[132] The very end of the movie sounds this note, concluding with the name of Achilles, as Odysseus declares in his final voice-over, "These names will never die. Let them say I lived in the time of Hector, tamer of horses. Let them say I lived in the time of Achilles."

Achilles's glory is perpetuated not only verbally but cinematically. In ancient sources, Helen's superhuman status is grounded in her beauty, Achilles's in his fighting skill. But whereas *Troy* diminishes the former on screen, it enhances the latter, through the repeated insistence that this hero "fights like a god."[133] The fight choreographer noted the difficulty of fulfilling the script's direction "Achilles fights in a god-like manner," and the sword master called the results "very stylistic."[134] Establishing the style in question is a central function of the film's opening scene, where Achilles effortlessly kills a monstrous opponent with an extraordinary leap and dramatic plunge of his sword into the neck. Slow motion is used sparingly in *Troy*, but this moment is slowed just enough that the hero seems to be momentarily floating or flying—a distinctive effect that recurs in his subsequent battles.[135]

130. Special Feature: "Beach Battle," *Troy*, directed by Wolfgang Petersen (Warner Bros., 2004), DVD.

131. See Burgess 2009; Paul 2013a: 70–75. On *kleos* and epic, see above, p. 111.

132. "He wants his name to last through the ages . . . And you know, he was right—because we're making a movie about him" (Petersen apud M. Russell 2004).

133. E.g., M. Russell 2004.

134. Special Feature: "Achilles v. Hector"; cf. Eimer 2004: 71.

135. These moments are marked by "slightly sped-up footage with slow-mo for the climactic bits, sound effects with metal that sings and swooshes at a higher pitch than the weapon clashes of others and thus can be experienced as more elevated and godlike, accompanied by the heroic Achilles music theme" (Futrell 2005).

We might expect the glorification of Achilles—and eclipsing of Helen—to mark a shift away from the romantic aspects of the Trojan War story. Instead, those aspects are coopted for Achilles. When the opening voice-over warns us that "love" will be as central as "fighting" to the movie's epic agenda, this turns out *not* to be primarily the love between Paris and Helen. Rather, "love" and "fighting" become inextricable components of Achilles's manly heroism.[136] This requires considerable adjustment to his Homeric character. Pitt's Achilles does make the proper Iliadic choice—to die at Troy instead of staying home to meet and marry (in his mother's words) a "wonderful woman." But it is "love" for which he meets his death, not revenge or glory. This love is not, alas, the affair with Helen hinted at in some ancient texts. Nor (to the disappointment of many) is it romantic love for Patroclus, who is introduced, in keeping with an obscure mythological tradition, as Achilles's cousin.[137] In an expansion of a different tradition Achilles's true love turns out to be Briseis, the captive Trojan with whom he embarks on an intense affair after reclaiming her from Agamemnon.[138]

Promoted from a tiny role in the *Iliad,* Briseis, as Achilles's love interest, becomes the most significant female character in the Trojan War story.[139] As such, she is a kind of anti-Helen, explicitly eschewing a Helenic role: "I don't want anyone dying for me."[140] The part was played by another little-known actor, the twenty-three-year-old Australian Rose Byrne (who is now, like Kruger, a successful mid-level star). The character is supposed to be only seventeen—a virginal teenager ripe for marriage—but according to Benioff's

136. Heterosexual pair bonding even becomes a tenet of the heroic code, as enunciated by the unimpeachably admirable Hector ("Honor the gods. Love your woman. And defend your country"). On the film's reconfiguration of Homeric heroism, see Chiasson 2009: 186–95 and cf. Winkler 2015d: 151–52.

137. On receptions of Achilles and Patroclus as "the Adam and Adam of Western gay mythology," see T. Jenkins 2015: 78–84. For complaints about *Troy*'s treatment of their relationship, see, e.g., Purves 2014a; Cooper 2014. This does not, of course, eliminate the possibility of subtextual homoeroticism (see, e.g., Krass 2013).

138. For Briseis's ancient role as a love interest for Achilles, see K. King 1987: 172–74. On their relationship in *Troy,* see Proch & Kleu 2013: 182–87.

139. Briseis's only speech in the *Iliad* is her lament for Patroclus (19.282–300). In *Troy,* her character incorporates not only her Homeric namesake—much developed—but elements of the ancient Cassandra, Polyxena, Chryseis, Clytemnestra, and even Athena (see A. Allen 2007: 156–62; Danek 2007: 80–81).

140. She all but steals this line from Euripides's Iphigenia, herself an anti-Helen (*Iphigenia in Aulis* 1417–20).

script she has an "aristocratic demeanor" and even in rags "her noble bearing and authoritative tone command respect." Like Achilles—albeit in a rather different manner—she spurns the "conventional" love ties underpinning the heteronormative nuclear family.[141] This enables her to fulfill the modern stereotype of the feisty heroine that is so conspicuously denied to Helen.[142] Her feistiness reaches a climax when, threatened by the evil Agamemnon, she kills him with a dagger to the neck. The placement of the blow even echoes Achilles's fighting style (though without the slow-motion superhuman leap).

Despite the divergence in the two women's personalities, Briseis also trespasses on Helen's territory as an icon of the desirable female. She is, of course, beautiful, but in contrast to the refinement of the morose, static Helen she is introduced as fresh-faced, girlish, and playful, with "natural" makeup and a big toothy smile (figure 4.3). Her features are soft and rounded compared to Helen's and her lively and (initially) cheerful manner underscores the latter's passivity and powerlessness, while her tousled dark curls, suggesting earthiness, authenticity, and seriousness, render her beauty "natural" and "real." In contrast to Helen, her clothing shows little sign of royal elegance. She is introduced in a simple white gown, referred to as her "virgin robes." It is rustic in style, with a modest gathered neckline (no cleavage), decorated with touches of blue (not gold), and accessorized with a short veil held well away from her face by a white wreath of natural elements. The outfit has a bridal look, suggesting that, like a nun, she is to be "married" to the god Apollo.[143] Unlike Helen's "bridal" dress, however, hers is off-white and made of coarser fabric, with long sleeves and a border of blue stripes.

For her initial encounters with Achilles, Briseis wears the same dress, but it is by now dirtied and torn, and she has lost the veil and crown. Her hair is bedraggled, and her face increasingly marred with dirt and blood as she is manhandled by Agamemnon's men.[144] Deglamorized as she is, however,

141. She has rejected many suitors and chosen permanent virginity as an acolyte of Apollo; when granted her freedom, she returns home out of allegiance to friends and family rather than stay with the man she loves. Achilles's "resistance to social norms" is signaled, on the other hand, by introducing him in a three-way with two women (cf. Proch & Kleu 2013: 182, 191).

142. On Briseis as a formulaic "feisty" heroine, see McGrath 2004; this characterization is further enhanced in the director's cut (Weinlich 2015).

143. Achilles will tell her she's "in love with" a god.

144. In a later scene in Achilles's camp, she wears a rustic looking sack-like dress in sage green. In the film's final scenes, she wears Trojan blue to kill Agamemnon, bid farewell to Achilles, and (in the director's cut) flee Troy.

FIGURE 4.3. Briseis in *Troy*: at home at Troy (left) and with Achilles in the Greek camp (right).

Achilles sees in Briseis a beauty that shines through dirt and blood ("You will never be lovelier than you are right now") (figure 4.3).

This attraction to his grimy captive reflects the modern romantic conception of beauty as lying in the eye of the beholder. As Achilles puts it, after he rejects the supposed bliss of the gods, "Everything is more beautiful for the doomed." It is this knowledge of his fate, as opposed to any objective aspect of Briseis's appearance, which renders her at this moment, for him, supremely beautiful. This (modern) conception of beauty easily trumps the (ancient) notion of "absolute" beauty, so unflatteringly represented by the passive, mopey Helen. (It also helps to explain the latter's peculiar power over Paris.) It is of a piece, too, with Achilles's ideas about mortality and love. He informs Briseis, "The gods envy us. They envy us because we're mortal, because every moment might be our last." Theirs is a love for the moment, to be seized as such. It is both mortal and "realistic"—like Odysseus's preference for Penelope over the goddess Calypso in the *Odyssey*.[145] As such it not only defies a fundamental tenet of Homeric heroism but is diametrically opposed to the kind of "forever" romanticism espoused by Paris.

Like the Roman epic heroes of the 1950s, then, the hypermasculine Achilles succumbs to love for a beautiful woman who belongs on the other side of a conflict—a woman who "teaches the hero of the cruelty and immorality of

145. On this Homeric scene, see Blondell 2013: 92.

imperialism."[146] As in those earlier epics, the woman in question is defined by contrasting her with a version of "ancient" beauty that she supersedes with her more "modern" allure. But the contrast between Helen and Briseis is rather different from the familiar opposition between pagan femmes fatales and the less exotic but ultimately more desirable Christian women. In *Troy*, as opposed to a film like *Quo Vadis*, the ancient femme fatale is displaced not by dramatizing her downfall or even her conversion, but by banning her entirely from the screen.

Why did the filmmakers choose not to endow Helen with the spicy allure of the pagan vamp, which is so prominent in their beloved 1950s epics, as a way of enhancing the contrast between her and Briseis? Presumably because a willfully transgressive Helen would undermine the film's larger romanticism, which depends, like Wise's film, on the notion of Troy as the home of love, peace, and virtue. To vilify Helen would not only undermine Paris (for taking up with a "bad" woman) but tarnish the idea of "love" for which Troy itself stands. Such a Helen would also undermine the redemption of Achilles, who has an innate affinity with Trojans (signaled by his and his mother's blue tie-dyed leisure wear) and ends up embracing their values.

The deglamorizing of Helen also helps to displace her from the erotic epicenter of the Trojan War story. After the very limited sex scene between her and Paris (in which we do not actually see them in bed together), our attention shifts to Achilles and Briseis, whose relationship far surpasses the childish affair between Helen and Paris in both erotic and emotional power. The sex scenes between Achilles and Briseis are not only more frequent but more extensive, more explicit, more passionate, and more intimate, and their conversations much longer and more substantive. In contrast to Helen, the feisty Briseis is more than a passive object. She is never *presented* to us naked, for our admiring gaze. Instead, she actively wields the dangerous and emasculating power of female sexuality, as betokened by the knife with which she threatens Achilles in their first sex scene—a trope for violent, risky, destructive passion.[147] (Note too the swelling background music.) A later scene shows them in bed together engaging in pillow talk: a symmetrical medium shot of the

146. C. Davies 2019: 47.

147. Agamemnon's death will demonstrate that Briseis knows how to use a knife. In the peplum *Fury of Achilles* (1962), Briseis tries to stab Achilles (Solomon 2007b: 96). There is a comparable moment in Oliver Stone's *Alexander* (2004).

couple, face to face, both naked from the waist up, suggests personal and erotic equality. Later they wake up with their naked bodies intertwined.

The affair ends with Achilles first fighting and then dying for love—as Paris so conspicuously failed to do. This is in keeping with the tragic romantic pattern characteristic of ancient world epic, where the hero achieves "transcendental deification" through death.[148] Initially deaf to Briseis's pleas, Achilles does briefly subordinate romance to his revenge for Patroclus; but in the end he sees the error of his homosocial ways and seeks her out amid the blazing ruins, actually killing men on his own side who are molesting her. This exposes him to Paris's arrows, leading to a climactic *Liebestod* in which he accepts his own death, not because he has had his revenge on Hector but because, so he tells Briseis, "You gave me peace in a lifetime of war."

The casting of Brad Pitt was fundamental to this repositioning of Achilles. Despite the luster of Orlando Bloom's then-emerging idol status among teenage girls, Pitt, with his blazing star power and overwhelming sexual appeal, is clearly the primary erotic focus of this film.[149] The only man at the time ever to have been twice named *People Magazine*'s "sexiest man alive" (in 1994 and 2000), he was widely viewed as "the most desired male in the world."[150] Advance publicity made abundant use of Pitt's body, often bathed in bronze like the goddesses in *Sports Illustrated* (plate 9; compare plate 7). On *Troy*'s battlefields, where Achilles reigns supreme, that body is displayed and eroticized as the site of supreme masculine power. This culminates in a death like that of a rather more vigorous St. Sebastian, as Achilles, wearing only a cuirass and short leather skirt, gasps orgasmically while his magnificent body takes one arrow after another.

Ancient world cinema had always been hospitable to the display of the male body in combat or other forms of heroic struggle. It is less usual for the hypermasculine hero to be eroticized in the bedroom. In the Trojan War story this kind of beauty is traditionally the domain of Paris, Aphrodite's protégé. In *Troy*, however, Paris is no competition for Achilles even in bed. In love as

148. Cf. above, p. 000.

149. On Pitt's star image as an "ideal sexual object," see Fuchs 2007. On the eroticizing of Pitt in *Troy*, see Proch & Kleu 2013: 172–82. For Bloom, cf. van Beekus 2004: 24; G. Flynn 2004; Faraci 2004a; Weinberg 2004; Schruers 2004.

150. Anon. 2005. *Vanity Fair* called him "the heartthrob who's perennially at the top of the world's sexiest-man-alive lists" and dubbed him (not Kruger) "the face that launched a thousand tabloids" (Bennetts 2004).

in war, the Greek hero is a model of manhood in a way that the Trojan never achieves. This is not only because he takes over the latter's role as abductor (and lover) of foreign women. For his very first scene, Pitt's Achilles is introduced in an erotic tableau with two women. He is the naked object of our gaze, asleep, passive, and seemingly vulnerable. The departure from the standard Hollywood fetishizing of the naked female is quite striking. As we saw earlier, Petersen also undresses Helen early in the film, exposing her vulnerability in a way that strips her of mystery. But in Achilles's case the vulnerable air is strictly temporary. Erotic objectification turns out to be no impediment to vigorous action: in a startling gesture, the sleeping Achilles suddenly grabs the child who has been sent to fetch him. He proceeds directly from this presumably heroic night of sex with multiple women to the heroic physical conquest of a gigantic opponent.

Pitt's gorgeous physique and celebrity status reinforce the film's sidelining of Helen as the ultimate object of desire. Despite the elevation of Briseis as a kind of counter-Helen, the film uses Achilles's inarguable charisma to reinstate the notion of transcendent beauty, trumping his own insistence on the beauty of the moment. In Greek myth, Achilles is in some ways Helen's counterpart; in *Troy*, he is her replacement. The substitution of Pitt's naked body for Kruger's is conveyed cinematically by trumping Paris and Helen's only sex scene (where we do not actually see them in bed together) with Achilles's first such scene with Briseis. The latter starts with a shot of Achilles's sleeping face, again passive and seemingly vulnerable, while Briseis stands over him with a knife at his throat. But his passivity is, once more, deceptive. He soon turns the tables, rolling, buck naked, on top of the fully clothed Briseis and actively initiating sexual intercourse. In contrast to Paris's seduction of Helen, here the male is naked and the female clothed, reversing the gender dynamic to celebrate the spectacle of the male body (figure 4.1).[151] Yet that body is not, like Helen's, a static, vulnerable object of scrutiny, but a signifier of active eroticism, unpredictable and threatening.[152] Achilles's nudity, unlike hers, expresses sexual power, or "unbridled, uninhibited confidence."[153] Petersen thus allows Pitt to supplant Kruger not only in charisma, star power, dramatic and

151. Both Pitt in this scene and Kruger in her nude scene (described above) reveal another inch or so of skin in the director's cut, but without significantly affecting the contrast that concerns me here.

152. Cf. Dyer's discussion of the difference between male and female pinups (Dyer 1992).

153. Bari 2016. Cf. above, p. 146.

emotional significance, but also as both subject and object of desire. Glorified for his beauty both on-screen and off, the blond, blue-eyed Pitt becomes a male Helen for the turn of the twenty-first century.

Third Cheerleader from the Left

Troy did well, though not spectacularly, at the box office.[154] But if the goal of any blockbuster is to be an "event" movie, defined by Geoff King as "one that gains prominence in the wider culture, beyond the cinema screen; one that everyone seems to be talking about, that is almost impossible to avoid,"[155] then Petersen's film must be accounted a success.

The film was widely reviewed by professional critics and also by bloggers—a group ranging from widely respected critics to amateur writers on tangentially related topics.[156] *Troy's* reviews were "generally average,"[157] but individual critics diverged wildly on key issues, including the film's Homericity,[158] its success as an "old-fashioned, sandal-shod" epic,[159] its effectiveness compared to similar films (whether 1950s blockbusters, David Lean epic, contemporary war films, or *LOTR*),[160] and Petersen's "realism" as a vehicle for epic myth and warfare.[161]

154. On the box office for *Troy* (with comparanda), see Iordanova 2011: 107; Shone 2004: 16–19; B. Gray 2004; C. Davies 2019: 40–41. Warner Brothers' sales manager attributed its success in part to its "young, sexy cast, including Brad Pitt, Orlando Bloom and Eric Bana" (B. Gray 2004; note the absence of women).

155. G. King 2002: 52.

156. As of June 24, 2020, IMDb listed 209 external reviews, many by bloggers, of which about 150 are in English and the vast majority are by men (cf. Lachenal 2015; Bernstein 2016; Pulver 2018). More are available via Rotten Tomatoes and Metacritic. On "mass amateurization" and the difficulty of distinguishing bloggers from journalists, see Shirky 2008: ch. 3. Cf. also Reagle 2015: 35–38 on the uncertain line between the "critic" and the online reviewer.

157. C. Davies 2019: 40.

158. E.g., Ebert 2004; Arnold 2004; and many others. The absence of the Homeric gods is a particularly fraught issue (see especially Winkler 2009: 111–14; Winkler 2015d; Llewellyn-Jones 2013b: 17–18; Purves 2014b). For scholarly discussions of *Troy*'s Homericity, see especially Winkler 2007a; 2015b (on which, see Blondell 2016b).

159. McGrath 2004. See, e.g., Wilmington 2004; McCarthy 2004; Arnold 2004; Edelstein 2004; Hanke 2004.

160. E.g., Hiscock 2004, Villarreal 2004; Larsen 2004; Baine 2004; Denby 2004; O'Sullivan 2004; L. Miller 2004.

161. E.g., Ebert 2004; D. Mendelsohn 2004; Hartman 2004.

Prominent among these polarizing issues was Brad Pitt's casting and performance as Achilles. Reviewers diverged wildly in their liking or loathing of *Troy*'s rendition of the epic hero. Nearly all of them recognized, however, that he was exempt in key respects from Petersenian "realism." Love him or hate him, he is "the Greek army's rock star," or a "petulant movie star" with the narcissism of a modern celebrity, his "celebrity status" rendering him "remote and unapproachable."[162] Reviewers observe that he is "deified" by the "camera eye," and that, playing the role "in all-out movie-god mode," he convincingly "impersonates" a god.[163] One critic calls the film "an exercise in adoration," another speaks of "the cinematic fetishizing of an actor on a virtually unequaled level," observing that Pitt is "lavished with elaborate photographic attention" of the kind usually reserved for the great classical female stars, in an attempt "to turn his character into an icon with godlike status."[164] Many note his "otherworldly skills on the battlefield," where he employs "a lightning style of combat never before seen on earth."[165] "He's deadly poetry in motion, a Diaghilev of a killing machine—so effortlessly charismatic that . . . it would be hard to imagine a more compelling embodiment of Greek mythology's headiest hero."[166]

Helen was a different matter. Despite the controversy swirling around other elements of the film, reviewers were almost unanimous on this particular issue.[167] The vast majority agree that she is not "sufficiently fabulous-looking to be convincing as the face that launched a thousand ships."[168] Echoing Agamemnon's dismissive judgement, the word "pretty" recurs over and over again. A website assembling the "Top 15 Wicked Film Critics' Descriptions"

162. Edelstein 2004; A. Scott 2004; McGrath 2004: 38. For Achilles as rock star, see above, p. 152, and cf. Morrissey 2004 ("Sleeping in with his groupies, he is late for his gig").

163. Wilmington 2004; Larsen 2004; Edelstein 2004.

164. Baine 2004; McCarthy 2004.

165. Baine 2004; Denby 2004. On his fighting style, cf. also Hiscock 2004; Ahl 2007: 179; Purves 2014c.

166. Arnold 2004.

167. Exceptions are for the most part perfunctory. Kruger "shines" as Helen (Hiscock 2004). She has a "delicate beguiling beauty" (Lemire 2004). Stuttaford 2004 rates her at a thousand ships even though he hates almost everything else about the film. Murray 2004 finds her "stunning" but devoid of passion. One blogger thinks "Kruger is a classically beautiful woman who looked the part of a golden-haired princess," but finds her looks outweighed by the character's "lack of any real substance" (Jamie Z. 2012).

168. McGrath 2004: 38.

of Kruger in the role of Helen conveys an overwhelming ordinariness: she resembles "dozens of young women you might see at the mall" or "the third cheerleader from the left at a basketball game."[169] Others concur: she has a "bland sweetness" that makes her "Helen of Troy, N.Y.," or a "stunning vacuity," and looks "more like a waitress than a princess."[170] Such verdicts betray the tension between the ideology of the eye of the beholder and the objectivity on which critics implicitly rely. Collectively, however, the vast majority of these eyes condemn Kruger's Helen as insufficiently extraordinary—whatever that may mean for any given viewer.

Critical judgment of Kruger is frequently framed by her previous (and continuing) career as a model, sometimes neutrally but more often negatively. She is identified as "a German model turned medium-cool actress"; "a statuesque blonde German model" who cannot act; an "uncharismatic former model."[171] She's "blond and pretty, but unremarkable—she'd look at home in an ad for Herbal Essences shampoo"; she "looks like a model for a young woman's magazine, not like a heartbreaker of yore"; she is "distressingly lightweight, as if she were played by a mannequin (and I'm not positive she wasn't)."[172] Despite her weight gain, Kruger appears "glamour-magazine slender, i.e. on the edge of anorexia."[173] Another critic likens Helen and Andromache, lamenting the death of Hector, to "a pair of runway girls mourning a snapped Manolo Blahnik heel."[174]

Particularly telling, for the way it captures Kruger's combination of model-like blonde beauty and bland normalcy, is the comment calling her "pretty enough in a Darien, Connecticut, kind of way—not exactly Helen of Troy, but maybe Helen of Abercrombie & Fitch."[175] Darien, CT is where the original *Stepford Wives* was filmed, making it an icon of bourgeois, gender-normative suburbia. As for Abercrombie & Fitch, at its pinnacle in the early 2000s the company was notorious for its distinctive brand identity—an identity that

169. *The Oregonian; San Jose Mercury News*. For the website, see Anon. n.d.a.

170. Zacharek 2004; LaSalle 2004; Mcfarlane 2005; French 2004. The word "bland" recurs repeatedly (e.g., Travers 2004; Keller 2004; Winkler 2009: 239; Hunter apud Anon. 2004e; Reed 2004; Cyrino 2005b).

171. Morgenstern 2004; P. Green 2004: 183; French 2004.

172. Turner 2004; O'Sullivan 2004; Baine 2004.

173. Nilsen 2004, criticizing all the women in the film.

174. L. Smith 2004.

175. Zacharek 2004.

defined beauty as thin, young, white, and "all-American."[176] According to a teenage critic, "There is no company with as big an impact on the standards of beauty. There are kids starving themselves so they can be the 'Abercrombie girl.'"[177] The crowdsourced Urban Dictionary conveys the stereotype more cynically: Abercrombie shoppers are "Rich, materialsitic [sic], dumb, blonde girls," characterized by "conformity and perceived airheaded-ness," and stereotyped as preppies and cheerleaders.

Paris fared no better than Helen with reviewers. As for their relationship, the lovers are "two of the most vapid characters imaginable," whose "on-screen chemistry is about as convincing as a mime."[178] Their romance is an "undercooked teenage love story," "puppyish," "juvenile and pathetic," with "the depth of a wading pool."[179] "They are so placid they might be a young suburban wife and a handsome lawn man smooching in an afternoon soap opera."[180]

Judging from online review aggregators, general viewers enjoyed (and enjoy) *Troy* more than the critics.[181] Both Rotten Tomatoes and Metacritic indicate that it was more popular with the general public than with professionals.[182] Petersen evidently succeeded in reaching his target audience: according to the demographic breakdown on IMDb, the film is liked most (at the time of writing) by males under eighteen (with an average rating of 7.6 out of

176. These terms recur over and over again in the Netflix documentary *White Hot: The Rise & Fall of Abercrombie & Fitch* (2002).

177. Denizet-Lewis 2006. Deleon 2013 lists some of the company's most egregious sexist and racist, or otherwise offensive, behavior, much of which involves denigrating women who do not fit a thin, blonde, able-bodied, "bimbo" stereotype.

178. Hanke 2004; Murray 2004.

179. Hanke 2004; A. Scott 2004; J. Shearer 2004; Travers 2004.

180. Denby 2004: 109.

181. Several users excoriate the critics as "idiots" out of touch with ordinary viewers (https://www.metacritic.com/movie/troy/user-reviews). One IMDb comment is titled "Proof that critics should be ignored." In what follows, IMDb comments on *Troy* are quoted from https://www.imdb.com/title/tt0332452/reviews/?ref_=tt_ql_urv, accessed October 8, 2019. Note that it is rarely possible to determine the gender or sexual orientation of these writers, though gender is sometimes suggested by usernames.

182. According to Metacritic (on August 10, 2020) its current critical score is "mixed or average" while its user score indicates "universal acclaim." As of October 10, 2019, *Troy* had an audience score of 73 (out of 100) on *Rotten Tomatoes* (based on 824,891 user ratings), with a critics' score of 54 (228 reviews) and top critics score of 63 (49 reviews); a 7.2 on IMDb (based on 459,254 user ratings), a 56 on *Metacritic* (based on 43 critics), plus a "user score" of 8.7 (557 users).

ten) and least by females over thirty and all viewers over forty-five (6.9 out of ten). IMDb also has many positive comments about the film, mostly concerning the action sequences. Where Helen is concerned, however, general viewers are on the same page as the critics. IMDb users seem less concerned than reviewers about Helen's appearance, but those who do mention it nearly always concur that she is "very cardboard," looks like "a mechanical porcelain figurine," or is "pretty in a blonde sort of valley white girl way." Where her romance with Paris is concerned, again they agree overwhelmingly that there is "no chemistry."[183] As always, there are exceptions. (One user even likens her to Sofia Loren.) But pop culture's highest praise is best conveyed by the blogger who explains, "Paris is a stupid little pretty boy who decides to sleep with and steal away the Spartan King's wife, Helen (the very yummy and super duper delicious hottie Diane Kruger), and return to Troy with Helen as his tasty treat of a girlfriend."[184] This kind of accolade does little to dispel the sense that her beauty is not for the ages.

Critics and general viewers alike realized that Achilles supplants Helen as the truly glorious sex-object in this film: "There is indeed a legendary beauty in 'Troy'—a face that brings the ancient world to its knees, a being whose grace is such that grown men feel stupid and ashamed in its presence. I speak, of course, of Brad Pitt."[185] It is his face, not Helen's, that "launched a thousand ships," he who is "the movie's real erotic object."[186] His "looks are integral to the role, the movie's whole sense of heroic beauty," and his over-the-top preening "right for the role."[187] The movie "turns the gender tables, gazing right over the head of the iconic Helen to bask in the blinding mystique of Brad the Rad."[188] Another critic even identified him mockingly with Aphrodite, referring to "Brad Pitt on the half-shell."[189] Female reviewers mention the appeal of "eye candy" in the form of "hot, scantily clad men."[190] IMDb users concur, speaking of "extremely beautiful man flesh," and even dubbing Pitt "The New Brigitte Bardot." Others, including a confessedly heterosexual male, admit to

183. "The two actors have zero chemistry and both have the screen presence of a couple of fruit flies"; "I've seen better chemistry between two rocks."

184. Anon. 2004f.

185. Burr 2004.

186. Gouveia 2004; Edelstein 2004.

187. Wilmington 2004; Larsen 2004.

188. Baine 2004.

189. Burr 2004.

190. Johanson 2004; Dork Droppings 2004.

erotic fantasies about Pitt as Achilles. These responses reveal much about what it takes to present a character as an awe-inspiring mythical beauty, thereby underlining the ways that this treatment has been denied to Helen.

The chorus of disapproval raining down on Kruger's head is grounded primarily in the audience's prior "knowledge" of Helen's appearance and character. Viewers remain undeterred by the idea that in this rendition the war is not really caused by her beauty.[191] Explicitly or not, the vast majority are criticizing the film for failing to match up either to "Homer" or to the viewer's preconceived notion of a familiar character. When a critic complains, for example, that Helen and Paris should be portrayed as "the movie stars of the Trojan War,"[192] he is objecting not to Kruger's and Bloom's performances as such, but to the way in which the filmmakers chose to present these characters. When another opines that Helen's "high-strung, tremulous anxiety makes her less than appealing,"[193] he is objecting less to Kruger's performance than to the filmmakers' conception of her character—and incidentally corroborating the unsexiness of this conception. As one blogger puts it, "She emotes two things during the entire movie: fear and sadness. What man wouldn't want a fun girl like that?"[194]

None of this means, however, that Kruger failed to do her job. The performance that elicited such jeers is an accurate reflection of the character as written, cast, and directed. If Kruger, best known for her modeling, is "little more than scenery,"[195] that is because she is asked to do little more than model. Her looks may be generic and her performance mediocre, but on the whole, this serves rather than undermines the concept of a sad, passive pretty girl rescued by a foolish, infatuated youth. The conditions imposed by the script and director left little leeway for any performer. Within these limitations, Kruger should be accounted a success. Her critics were judging her not by this standard, however, but rather by the single "fact" that most people already know about Helen: her supreme beauty, as measured on a scale of one to one thousand ships. The fact that this particular Helen is not the center of the story, or that she does adequately what is asked of her, is not enough to shake such

191. Thus, one IMDb user opines, "It would have been nice to have a beauty that was truly breathtaking to underpin the story for the viewer as to why she could launch a ten-year war."

192. Denby 2004.

193. McCarthy 2004.

194. Dork Droppings 2004.

195. Jamie Z. 2012.

preconceptions: the audience knows who Helen "really" is and has no hesitation in asserting it.

To destabilize this tradition, by convincing audiences to accept a Helen who is "realistic" in Petersen's sense, would require, at a minimum, considerable advance managing of expectations. As we have seen, however, the filmmakers and the studio's publicity department did nothing to challenge prior assumptions about Helen's transcendent beauty, and actively encouraged them to assess this unknown actor by the starriest of standards. She had to be "realistic" yet, at the same time, "charged with the grandeur of history and legend." As with Wise's film (though in a rather different way), publicity misled the audience regarding the nature and importance of Helen's role. It is scarcely surprising that Petersen's "realism" could not deter a rush to judgment grounded in thousands of years of precedent and fostered by advance publicity. For Kruger, this was a no-win situation. Trapped between audience expectations and the director's conception of "realism," she was set up to fail. [196]

The other central characters were spared this predicament. The case of Achilles makes it clear that Petersen was happy to abandon his conception of "realism" when it suited him. The contrast with Briseis—a little-known character played by another little-known actor—is also instructive. Despite her much greater importance to the film we see virtually nothing of her in publicity materials, and she gets correspondingly little attention in reviews. Kruger, as Helen, was placed in a uniquely difficult position, highlighted by the many, many jokes about how many (or few) ships her face would launch. One says she "couldn't launch a dinghy," but others think she could launch "a rubber dingy [sic] or two," "a paddle boat . . . or a couple of canoes."[197] One dubs her "the face that launched 1,000 golf carts," another "the face that served a thousand lunches."[198] The role that might have been expected to make Kruger a star instead made her an object of derision.

196. She claimed at the time that it "was a really good part for me" (Lynn B. n.d.) but admitted later that she was embarrassed by the film and by the role, which she said offered her no scope as an actor (Reynolds 2008). She told one interviewer, "Personally I wanted to see more of why Paris was willing to sacrifice so much for Helen . . . Her beauty didn't do her any good and she couldn't use it in any positive way or manipulative way" (P. Fischer 2004a).

197. Zacharek 2004; LaSalle 2004. The middle quote is from an IMDb user.

198. Zacharek 2004; French 2004.

Ironically, the filmmakers' conception of Helen turned out to be a disturbingly good fit for its early twenty-first-century geopolitical context. Benioff pitched his script in October 2001, just weeks after 9/11, and filming began a month after the US invaded Iraq.[199] The process of filming was shadowed by the war, which obliged the filmmakers to change locations from Morocco to Mexico. A few weeks before *Troy* opened, the charred corpses of four American contractors were dragged through the streets of Fallujah, eliciting outrage from the American public. By the time the film premiered, however, support for the war was dwindling, as reports emerged of American atrocities such as those at Abu Ghraib.[200] Benioff said *Troy*'s parallels with contemporary events were unintentional, but acknowledged that their influence on the writing process was "unavoidable."[201] Petersen himself compared Agamemnon to George W. Bush; like Benioff, the director denied any deliberate parallelism, but was happy to take advantage of the equation in promoting the film, saying, "It's as if nothing has changed in 3,000 years."[202]

As such remarks acknowledge, the Iraq war was the latest in a history of struggles between East and West that could be traced back to the Trojan War. The American media were replete with the analogy.[203] In the aftermath of 9/11, some Americans identified with Troy as the innocent victims of a foreign invasion, even likening the planes that attacked New York on 9/11 to the Trojan Horse.[204] Shocking events like those at Fallujah encouraged this self-perception of Americans as victims. Since the US was the invading force in the Iraq war, however, it was not easy to equate America with the virtuous, peace-loving Trojans. Post 9/11, moreover, American audiences wanted films where they could identify with winners,[205] which made it hard to avoid seeing themselves in the victorious but unpleasant Greeks. The analogy was therefore used primarily by critics of the war. As an "invasion of antiquity," the invasion

199. Fleming 2003; Cohen 2004: 37; Schruers 2004; G. Flynn 2004; Waxman 2004a. On *Troy*'s relationship to the Iraq War, see C. Davies 2019: ch. 2; and cf. Meier 2006: 191.

200. C. Davies 2019: 29–30.

201. Faraci 2004b.

202. Rothstein 2004.

203. Grobéty 2014: 124–48.

204. Grobéty 2014: 146–47; cf. Burgess 2009: 172; C. Davies 2019: 29.

205. Waxman 2004a.

of Iraq also helped to stimulate a "massive (over)production of classically themed films and pop culture."[206]

It was inevitable, then, that *Troy* would be perceived through the lens of recent events.[207] Sixty years after the end of World War II, when even the Cold War had become history, American audiences no longer felt such an intimate bond with the European countries that traced their lineage to Troy.[208] This helped to keep the analogy between the US and the Greeks front and center. As one article on *Troy* sardonically commenced, "A powerful western alliance makes war on an eastern nation, a shaky pretext concealing an ugly lust for power. The slaughter of thousands follows—and deeply shameful abuse of the defeated. We are, naturally, talking about the Trojan war."[209] Agamemnon's imperialism evoked American policy in the Middle East, with his motive—the seizing of precious "Eastern" resources—equivalent to the Bush administration's thirst for Iraqi oil.[210] Even the Trojan Horse "could be seen as paralleling the hidden agenda of American occupation."[211] The visual echo of Fallujah backfires ideologically since it is, of course, the Greek Achilles who does the corpse-dragging.[212] It is also Achilles who demolishes an imposing Trojan statue of Apollo, evoking both the toppling of Saddam Hussein's statue and the wholesale looting of Iraqi antiquities that was unleashed by the war. There is

206. T. Jenkins 2015: 98. For the impact of 9/11 on American film, see also Prince 2009; McSweeney 2014; McSweeney 2017; C. Davies 2019. Novels about the Trojan War have also seen an "almost explosive increase" since the beginning of the millennium (Bär 2007).

207. For references to Iraq in reviews, see, e.g., McGrath 2004: 38 and cf. Ahl 2007: 180–81; Purves 2014a; Grobéty 2014: 131–34. One IMDb user reads the film as a detailed political allegory. C. Davies argues that the film (which was in pre-production well before the war) should be seen as a "universal" indictment of war, influenced by Vietnam and World War II as well as present circumstances (C. Davies 2019: 50). While this is a fair point, present circumstances are the key to immediate receptions of any film.

208. In Petersen's film, it is Paris, not Aeneas, to whom Priam entrusts the Excalibur-like "sword of Troy," telling him, "So long as a Trojan carries it, our people have a future." In a perfunctory gesture, Paris hands the sword over to Aeneas, but the latter makes only an awkward cameo appearance (cf. Ahl 2007: 175–76).

209. Higgins 2004.

210. Prince 2009: 289.

211. Haas 2004.

212. Benioff considered the analogy "eerie" (Epstein 2004). One reviewer called the scene "a sharp, if unintentional, comment on our current involvement in Iraq" (McGrath 2004). Cf. also Rothstein 2004.

more than one level of irony, then, in Agamemnon's claim to have personally "built the future."

The uneasy position in which the analogy places American viewers is mitigated somewhat by the diversity of leaders in Agamemnon's "coalition of the willing," none of whom is quite as nasty as he is. Of these, Achilles is naturally the most significant. While he could initially be seen as Agamemnon's "Haliburton contractor mercenary,"[213] the fact that he ends up embracing Troy and its ("our") values allows us to identify with the most prominent hero of the winning side without embracing its imperialistic leader. On Helen, however, the analogy forces a symbolic significance of the most diminishing kind. As "the trumped-up cause for a disastrous war in a faraway place," she is analogous with the Iraqi weapons of mass destruction (WMD) that were the pretext for Bush's invasion.[214] Petersen himself exploited the analogy, which was spelled out by many critics, both of the war and of the film.[215]

Yet Helen's functional resemblance to the WMD rests on more than her status as a flimsy pretext. The WMD were, after all, not merely a pretext but a nonexistent one, which the Iraqis could not have surrendered to the Americans even if they had wanted to. This equates them not just with the "real" Helen but with her *eidolon*, the false image created by the gods, making her the perfect mythical embodiment of the Iraq War's bogusness. This more specific analogy informed contemporary productions of Euripides's *Helen*, a tragedy that attributes the Trojan War to Helen's *eidolon* and is widely held to be a comment on the futility of war.[216] Technically, the Helen of *Troy* is an *eidolon* only in the cinematic sense. Yet both the director and the character call her a "ghost" as long as she remains at Sparta. This wraithlike existence is supposed to end with the arrival of Paris, when, in Kruger's words, Helen's life finally starts.[217] Nevertheless, throughout the rest of the film she remains a muted presence, who merely "emerges from the shadows every once in a while like a ghost of guilt."[218]

213. Johanson 2004.

214. S. Huler apud Grobéty 2014: 291.

215. Rothstein 2004; Grobéty 2014: 145, 287–90.

216. See T. Jenkins 2015: 142–46 and cf. C. Davies 2019: 42. On Euripides's *Helen*, see Blondell 2013: ch. 10.

217. Special Feature: "Homer: A Story for the Ages."

218. Larsen 2004.

One of the nasty jibes against Kruger's acting in *Troy,* that it made her "the next best thing" to an *eidolon,*[219] is thus more insightful than was presumably intended. For all Petersen's talk of "realism," he unwittingly restored Helen to the symbolic heart of the millennia-long conflict between East and West. The filmmakers conspired with history and politics to erase her. In so doing, however, they remythologized her for the turn of the twenty-first century.

219. P. Green 2004: 183.

PART III
Television

5

The Plural of Helen of Troy

TWENTIETH-CENTURY TELEFANTASY

Helen Was an Android

Science fiction, horror, and fantasy—genres known collectively as speculative fiction—have always been hospitable to ancient myth.[1] That is because, like myths, they use epistemologically fantastical worlds as a way of talking about the world that produced them.[2] Like myth, too, these genres are all preoccupied, at their core, with what is it to be human. Within this broadly "humanist" concern, women occupy a special place: are they natural or fabricated, animal or object, human or machine? Such anxieties have given birth not only to Pandora, and to Pygmalion's Galatea, but to a legion of fembots and "female" cyborgs with variously problematic relationships to humanity in general and men in particular. Diverse though they are in many ways, however, "whatever the variety of formats, the modern gynoid is always presented as a sexually desirable, perfect woman."[3]

It is scarcely surprising, then, to learn from a pleasingly literal tabloid story that "Helen was an android," as proven by newly discovered ancient

1. Speculative fiction is a term used to avoid becoming bogged down in taxonomic controversies about overlapping subgenres. On antiquity and speculative fiction, see Fredericks 1980; Wieber 2002a: 19–21; S. Brown 2008; Kovacs 2011; Roberts 2016 [2006]: ch. 2; Gloyn 2015; Keen 2017; Weiner et al. 2018.

2. On the mythic status of speculative fiction in popular culture, see Willis 2017 and cf. Gwenllian-Jones 2003: 170–71. This is to be distinguished from the fact that such fiction often uses *material* from prior myths (Keen 2017: 313).

3. J. Brown 2011: 98.

documents, plus "parts of [her] transistorized body" found in her tomb.[4] Her name has been invoked, less literally, in speculative fiction from Lester del Rey's classic *Helen O'Loy* (1938) to John Wright's "The Plural of Helen of Troy" (2014). She has also played a recurring role in television series belonging to genres like science fiction, fantasy, and horror, which fall collectively under the umbrella of telefantasy.[5] Telefantasy has a generic tendency to intertextuality, playfulness, and hybridity, which enables it to bear the burden of "classical" reception more lightly than high-profile cinematic productions. By definition, fantasy is not concerned with what "really" happened but with more free-floating questions about what might happen in an alternate reality. Audiences are committed to the coherence of the show's own world, but not tied down by expectations of fidelity to antiquity as such. This results in a mutually beneficial relationship, in which ancient myth provides the imaginary worlds of telefantasy with a gloss of prestige, familiarity, tradition, and high culture, while the fantastical nature of such worlds helps to free classical receptions from the millstone of "authenticity." As a result, we shall see telefantasy engage more daringly with Helen's mythical identity than many grander, more expensive productions.

In the post-WWII period, television quickly became the dominant screen medium for mass entertainment. In marked contrast to the kind of grand spectacle that increasingly characterized both ancient world epic and science fiction film, early TV was an intimate, domestic medium, whose technical constraints encouraged an emphasis on small-scale human interaction.[6] The series format, in particular, created an illusion of personal intimacy, allowing viewers to develop a sustained relationship with the fictional characters who entered their living rooms on a regular basis.[7] A focus on the personal was further encouraged by low budgets and consequently cheap production values, which shifted the emphasis towards character and narrative. Shoestring budgets freed both producers and audience from expectations of illusionistic realism in regard to the miraculous, inhuman, or ineffable. Budget limitations

4. Anon. 1993.

5. On the broad genre of telefantasy, see C. Johnson 2005.

6. For the dominance of visual spectacle in science fiction film (as opposed to television), see Roberts 2016 [2006]: ch. 12 and 15. On film versus TV speculative fiction generally, see Bould 2003.

7. This was enhanced by reruns, and later the VCR and subsequent technologies. On the impact of rewatching, see H. Jenkins 2000: 172–73; H. Jenkins 2013: 67–75.

also freed TV to be more adventurous than film in certain respects, unburdened as it was by the high financial stakes driving the aesthetic caution that clogs many expensive blockbusters.

American telefantasy shows in which Helen has featured over the past half century include *The Time Tunnel* (1966),[8] *Star Trek* (1968), *Kolchak: The Night Stalker* (1975),[9] *Xena: Warrior Princess* (1996), and most recently the superhero series *Legends of Tomorrow* (2017).[10] In each case, she is configured as a vehicle for fears and expectations about women, sex, and power that are specific to the episode's subgenre (science fiction, horror, fantasy), to the period and context in which the screen-text was produced, and to each show's "universe," or megatext, which extends far beyond any particular episode or season. Given the breadth and diversity of the material, this chapter will focus on her appearance in two contrasting shows: *Star Trek* and *Xena: Warrior Princess.* The Original Series (TOS) of *Star Trek,* the most famous and influential telefantasy show of all time, laid the groundwork for an enduring modern mythology that shows no sign of waning.[11] The feminist telefantasy series *Xena: Warrior Princess* (*XWP*) began life as a spin-off of *Hercules: The Legendary Journeys* (*HLJ*),[12] but quickly outstripped its parent to become (apart from *The X-Files*) "the first cult hit of the Internet age."[13] Like TOS, it exercised a powerful influence on popular culture and continues to enjoy a robust following.

8. *Time Tunnel,* an "educational" series on the Learning Channel (Wieber 2005: 145), was distinctive for its recycling of cinematic spectacle. The episode *Revenge of the Gods* was built around the Trojan Horse footage from Wise's film, with a very different Helen playing a peripheral role (see Grams 2012: 265–73). The show debuted the same week as *Star Trek* but suffered from the comparison and was canceled after a single season (see Grams 2012: 112–48).

9. This short-lived but influential horror series aired on ABC for one season in 1974–1975. Its penultimate episode, *The Youth Killer,* reimagines Helen as a vampiric figure who drains the youth and beauty from healthy young people.

10. In the episode, entitled "Helen Hunt," Helen takes the form of a contested star in 1930s Hollywood who is rescued by our heroes.

11. On *Star Trek* as myth, see Reid-Jeffery 1982; Jewett & Lawrence 1988: ch. 1–2; Wagner & Lundeen 1998; Kapell 2010; Lawrence 2010; Tyrell 2010 [1977].

12. Both shows were produced by Americans Rob Tapert and Sam Raimi for their production company Renaissance Pictures.

13. C. Young 2005. For the meaning of "cult," see Gwenllian-Jones 2003: 164–65 and cf. Gwenllian-Jones & Pearson 2004; Lavery 2010. On *XWP* as a cult show, see Skelton 2010. It is notorious for its following among lesbians, but had a broader core audience of "women and men ages eighteen to thirty-four" (Weisbrot 1998: 156).

In typical telefantasy style, both TOS and *XWP* are dominated not by expensive visuals but by personal relationships, enlivened with engagingly cheesy special effects. Despite the absence of grand spectacle, both use the series format to generate a different kind of epic feel: an Odyssean variety of incident is framed by a portentous male voice-over (like that of the epic film), uniting the series around the core characters' adventures and locating them in a mythic time and space. Both shows blithely plunder global storytelling traditions. Both are playful and irreverent towards the past, yet address important cultural issues and continue to be taken very seriously by a dedicated fanbase. Both make Helen the focus of a single episode, where, as in the *Odyssey*, she is one in a long series of guest characters encountered by the protagonists in the course of their adventures. And each, as we shall see, gives an unsettling twist to her archetypal identity and role.

Starship Earth

In the late 1960s, the United States was convulsed with unrest over the Vietnam War, the civil rights movement, and the stirrings of "second wave" feminism. News coverage of this turmoil was ambivalent, if not downright hostile. Civil rights protesters were presented on television "either as decent but aggrieved Blacks who simply wanted to become part of the American dream, or as threats to the very notion of citizenship and nation."[14] Feminist activists were portrayed as "unruly, rebellious, excessive."[15] Most TV fiction avoided such matters, for fear of alienating advertisers.[16]

Star Trek, in contrast, was designed by its creator, Gene Roddenberry, as a vehicle for the serious exploration of contemporary social, moral, and cultural concerns.[17] Though nominally a series of outer-space adventures aboard the Starship Enterprise, the show's playful tone and futuristic framework were intended to make it a "Trojan Horse" for "important and meaningful things."[18]

14. Herman Gray 1997: 350.

15. Douglas 1994: 159.

16. On American TV in the 1950s and early 1960s, see Miller & Nowak 1977: ch. 13; S. J. Whitfield 1996: ch. 7; Tredy 2017: 3–5.

17. Cf. Asherman 1988: 7; Kovacs 2015: 202. Roddenberry's *Star Trek Writers' Guide* gave the series an exceptionally consistent "authorial" voice, even after he was no longer directly involved (Atkins 1983: 93; Isaacs 2010: 185–86).

18. S. E. Whitfield 1968: 21.

Roddenberry conceived of the Enterprise as "Starship Earth," and thought of his stories as "morality plays," which he used to promote a utopian humanistic vision of racial and sexual equality, shaped by both Cold War politics and the progressive zeitgeist of the 1960s.[19]

At a time when the "space race" was the province of white males, and people of color were routinely portrayed in film and television by Caucasians, the cast as well as the starship's crew was unusually diverse. To be sure, the nominal hero, Captain James Tiberius Kirk, embodied the cultural supremacy of the white American male (though William Shatner, who played him, is Canadian). But his second-in-command, Spock, was an alien "half-breed," played by Leonard Nimoy, who had previously been considered too dark or "ethnic" for leading roles and whose Jewishness informed his "alien" identity.[20] The Communications Officer Uhura, played by Nichelle Nichols, was "the first African American woman to have a featured role on an hour-long television drama."[21] Sulu, the helmsman, was played by the future gay activist George Takei, who is ethnically Japanese. Even the other white male characters—McCoy, Scotty, and Chekov—were of diverse origin, with the accents to prove it (southern USA, Scottish, and Russian, respectively). Race and the civil rights struggle also underpinned many of the episodes' plots. The show's racial politics are certainly not immune from criticism, especially by twenty-first-century standards.[22] But it seems churlish to deny that its heart was in the right place.

The same applied to gender, at least in principle. In Roddenberry's original concept, one-third of the crew of the Enterprise is female, and there is "complete equality between members of the crew, between sexes and races."[23] But he was never as committed to this aspect of his egalitarian vision, and soon

19. Grady 2016; Nichols 1994: 181. On *Star Trek*'s utopian humanism, and its limitations, see Worland 1988; Franklin 1994; Bernardi 1998: ch. 2; Wagner & Lundeen 1998: ch. 3 and 7; Booker 2008; Hark 2008: 33–36, 51–53; Isaacs 2010; Barrett & Barrett 2017: part II.

20. For the latter, see Nagourney 2022, for the former Asherman 1988: 25–26, 97. For "half-breed," see, e.g., D. Alexander 1995: 230.

21. Block et al. 2015: 32. On race and representation in 1960s TV, see Bernardi 1998: 32–34; Pounds 1999: ch. 1–2. Race awareness was, however, on the rise. Racial diversity was NBC policy (Solow & Justman 1997: 75–77), and other shows at the time featured substantive Black (male) characters (notably Greg Morris in *Mission Impossible*).

22. See especially Bernardi 1998. Goulding 1985 provides a lively diatribe against all of *Star Trek*'s politics. For a response to such criticisms, see Wagner & Lundgreen 1998: ch. 9.

23. S. E. Whitfield 1968: 205.

backed away from it (partly under pressure from the studio).[24] In consequence, the series as produced was fundamentally patriarchal and sexist in a very traditional way.[25] Regular female crew members have the kind of subordinate occupations that were uncontroversial for earthbound women at the time (nurse, switchboard operator, waitress, secretary). Guest actors sometimes portray women in more authoritative professions, such as archeologist, historian, or judge, but these are typically confined to a single episode and tend to be "emotionally subordinate to men."[26] The few female leaders in the original *Star Trek* universe are not human at all, but aliens.

The show did take advantage of the "sexual revolution" of the 1960s, which allowed female characters, in the words of one fanboy, "to be suggestively attired to the obvious delight of males everywhere."[27] The female crew members' uniforms, in particular, were at the cutting edge of the "micro mini" trend (figure 5.4). The style was suggested not by William Theiss, the costume designer, but by a female cast member, Grace Lee Whitney.[28] As Nichelle Nichols has pointed out, these outfits were comfortable and functional, and the miniskirt could serve as "a symbol of sexual liberation."[29] But most episode plots neutralize this liberatory potential by stereotyping erotically assertive women, in very conventional terms, as sexually voracious, sneaky, and destructive to male bonding.[30]

24. The first pilot had a female second-in-command but the character was axed. Roddenberry blamed the network's sexism but that was not the whole story (S. E. Whitfield 1968: 124–29; Shatner & Kreski 1993: 69–70; Solow & Justman 1997: 59–61, 157; Cushman & Osborn 2013: 73–76). In contrast to race, there is only one mention of gender equality in Roddenberry's *Writers Guide*—but numerous references to the sexual allure of the female characters.

25. Blair 1983; Cranny-Francis 1985; Goulding 1985: 26–27, 49–52; Helford 1996: 11–12. Most treatments of Roddenberry's "humanism" have little to say about gender (but see Wagner & Lundeen 1998: ch. 5–6).

26. Solow & Justman 1997: 226. For a balanced view of the presentation of professional women in TOS, see Henderson 1994.

27. Reginald D. Garrard, November 1, 2003, Amazon review of *Star Trek: The Original Series*, "Episode 57: Elaan of Troyius," https://www.amazon.com/Star-Trek-Original-Episode-Troyius/product-reviews/6300988589.

28. C. Mansfield n.d. Cf. also Cushman & Osborn 2013: 402.

29. Nichols 1994: 169. Mary Quant, the designer who named and may have invented the miniskirt, believed that it represented "life and tremendous opportunity" (Clarke 2021).

30. Wagner & Lundeen 1998: 104–6. On the show's sexual conservatism, see Wagner & Lundeen 1998: 111–15. For the contemporary TV climate concerning the sexual revolution, see D'Acci 1997.

Roddenberry's personal enthusiasm for women was not limited to gender equity. He was a "compulsive womanizer," who thought of a woman as "a decorative tool," and took an embarrassing amount of personal interest in the female actors and their revealing costumes.[31] These propensities are replicated in Roddenberry's alter ego, the womanizing Captain Kirk. Kirk also evokes the archetypal voyager, Odysseus, another brave, crafty, and impetuous leader who finds a desirable but dangerous female in nearly every port.[32] Homer's Odysseus is temporarily ensnared by Circe, Calypso, Nausicaa, and Helen herself; Kirk has his "disposable females," Karin Blair's phrase for the alluring characters that show up in countless episodes, only to "die, disappear, or remain on the planet of the week."[33] Just as Odysseus always abandons these charmers in the end, to travel home to Ithaca, Kirk always ends up leaving his female lovers for his one true love—not Penelope but the Starship Enterprise.[34] The relative insignificance of each episode's plot to the hero—an artifact of the series format—ipso facto diminishes the guest characters (what is big for them is little in the grand scheme of things). It is the bond between Kirk and his ship, with its crew, that constitutes the show's fundamental romance, gaining increasing authority as it persists from season to season, trumping the disposable women's brief encounters.[35]

It is as one of these "disposable females" that Helen of Troy enters the *Star Trek* universe. The title of the third-season episode "Elaan of Troyius" marks it as one of several drawing on themes from Mediterranean antiquity.[36] The

31. Hark 2008: 36; Solow & Justman 1997: 226. See further, e.g., Solow and Justman 1997: 39, 75, 216–17, 372; Hark 2008: 36–40. The many practical jokes at the studio often involved the sexualization of women (e.g., S. E. Whitfield 1968: 267–68; D. Alexander 1995: 214, 366–67; Solow & Justman 1997: 272).

32. Like the genre of space opera in general, *Star Trek* owes much to the *Odyssey*. For the equivalence of Kirk and Odysseus, see Goulding 1985: 23–25. For the show's pervasive nautical language, see Barrett & Barrett 2017: part I.

33. Blair 1983: 292; cf. Blair 1977: ch. 8; Gerrold 1984: 140–41; Selley 1986: 95–98; Hemmingson 2009. For a full list of Kirk's amours, see Helford 1996: 12.

34. Hark 2008: 38–39; cf. Jewett & Lawrence 1988: 12–14; Lawrence 2010: 100–105.

35. On *Star Trek*'s "fascination with male friendship," see Hark 2008: 31–32; Selley 1986. In general, TOS presents marriage not as a desirable state but as "an escape, a digression, or perhaps a punishment" for its male characters (Wagner & Lundeen 1998: 98).

36. On TOS and antiquity, see Keen 2007; Kovacs 2015. "Elaan" was written and directed by John Lucas. Roddenberry was less involved with season three (Solow & Justman 1997: ch. 23), but the basic idea for "Elaan" was "Roddenberry-approved" (Shatner & Kreski 1993: 265), and he played a large role in shaping the episode, to the point of claiming story credit (Cushman

most strikingly "Greek" of these episodes—entitled "Who Mourns for Adonais?"—presents us with prevailing pop-cultural stereotypes about ancient Greek beauty. It portrays the god Apollo as a powerful alien who is frustrated by the crew's refusal to worship him in exchange for his protection.[37] When he takes a fancy to Carolyn, the ship's archeologist, he expresses his desire by dressing her in long "classical" drapery, with elaborately styled blonde hair, and promising to make her a goddess (plate 10).[38] The made-over Carolyn wears a daringly sexy, backless, "futuristic Grecian gown" of pink chiffon.[39] The upper portion, hanging back over one shoulder, is held in place only by its own weight, exemplifying the costume designer's belief (known as the "Theiss titillation theory") that the sexiness of a costume is proportionate not to its skimpiness as such, but to the perceived likelihood of a wardrobe malfunction.[40] When Carolyn rejects Apollo, she signals her decision by changing back into her functional Starfleet uniform. The god thereupon literally fades away, consigning stereotypical Hellenic beauty to oblivion along with the rest of the culture that he stands for.[41]

Viewers may have expected the title character of "Elaan" to resemble Carolyn. Yet she departs radically from the familiar draped blonde figure of "Greek"

2015: 91). The Helenic storyline is revisited in the Next Generation episode *The Perfect Mate* (1992; cf. Wagner & Lundeen 1998: 102; Hegarty 1995), in which the ideal woman (who is likened to Helen) hatches from "a huge, glowing, golden egg" (Hegarty 1995: 58).

37. Besides the references in the preceding note, the episode is discussed by Winkler 2009: 86–90; Tomasso 2015: 151.

38. A woman dressed as "Helen" in the episode "Squire of Gothos" is likewise a blonde in a long pink gown, as is the Helen of *Time Tunnel* (above, n. 8); cf. also Uhura in "Plato's Stepchildren" (below, pp. 193–94). Pink seems to have become a default color for the drapery denoting "Greek" beauty, presumably because by this period it was well established as the color of femininity (Paoletti 2012: 86).

39. Block et al. 2015: 19.

40. On Theiss and his "titillation theory," see S. E. Whitfield 1968: 360–61; Cushman & Osborn 2013: 47–48; Block et al. 2015: 10–15. Chiffon is a favorite Theissian fabric (Block et al. 2015: 19).

41. See Jewett & Lawrence 1988: 9–11; Wagner & Lundeen 1998: 19–21; Kovacs 2015: 205–9. Similar themes are at play in "Plato's Stepchildren," which offers a very peculiar riff on Plato's *Republic* (see Kovacs 2015: 210–12). The rejection of paradise and/or immortality as stagnant, in favor of the mortal human condition, is a central *Star Trek* theme (Selley 1986: 93–95; Wagner & Lundeen 1998: 120–30; Booker 2008: 205; Tyrell 2010 [1977]: 21–25; Kovacs 2015: 206–12). Since paradise is often presented as feminizing, this theme is interwoven with the show's gender dynamics (Hark 2008: 48–49).

beauty, to convey the threat of the feminine Other in ways more visible to viewers in the turbulent 1960s. This departure is signaled from the outset via the title's distortion of Helen's name, displayed in advance publicity and the opening credits.[42] Despite their gossamer-thin connection to antiquity, "Adonais" and other "Greek" episodes typically incorporate Greek names (like "Apollo") in their familiar forms. The script that became "Elaan" started life similarly, with a title character named Helen. But Roddenberry wanted the names to be made "interesting" and given "more S.F."[43] Elaan's name was therefore exoticized in a way that distances the character from the constraints of her association with the conventional Helen of antiquity.[44] She is no mere relic of the past, to be erased like Apollo, but an ever-present threat (or promise), whose power transcends time and demands eternal vigilance.

Act in a Civilized Fashion

"Elaan of Troyius" first aired in December 1968, at the conclusion of what had been a climactic year of civil strife. In April, much of the country had erupted after the murder of Martin Luther King, Jr.; in September, feminists had protested the sexism of the Miss America Pageant and civil rights activists its racism; in November Shirley Chisholm became the first Black woman elected to Congress. "Elaan of Troyius" configures Helen as one of Kirk's disposable females in a way that engages directly with these powerful social and political currents. The resulting episode serves various *Star Trek* agendas concerning gender, civilization, love, and duty, while furthering the larger *Star Trek* project of promoting American values, science, and the future, at the expense of mythology, alien peoples, foreign cultures, and the past.

The title character is the ruler, or Dohlman, of a planet named Elas, which is at odds with the neighboring planet Troyius. In an obvious allusion to the Cold War, these hostile civilizations have the capacity for mutual nuclear destruction. The Elasian "Council of Nobles" has therefore tried to ensure peace

42. "Elaan" received an unusual amount of advance press coverage, largely because of the title character's outfits (Cushman 2015: 102–3), on which see further below.

43. Roddenberry, note on script of March 20, 1968; Roddenberry to Lucas, April 1, 1968. Script versions, correspondence, other production materials, and fanzines are cited from the Roddenberry Collection housed at the University of California, Los Angeles.

44. Episode titles often have an "implied cultural weight" that "left it incumbent on the reader to infer meaning" (Kovacs 2015: 204). For other examples of significant women's names in TOS, see Henderson 1994: 54.

by arranging a marriage between Elaan and the (unnamed) Troyan ruler, making her, like Vietnam, a pawn in the game played by rival nuclear powers.[45] Elas and Troyius (obvious equivalents of Hellas and Troy) recapitulate some of the stereotypes already associated in popular culture with the Spartans and Trojans. The Elasians are armor-clad, brutal, and authoritarian; Troyius is softer, more peaceful, and more "civilized"—though not entirely admirable, to judge by its petulant and ineffectual ambassador, Petri (another vaguely Greek name). Both peoples, it seems, would benefit from blending their gene pools through marriage, which might help them to achieve the balance of vigor and "civilization" exemplified by the crew of the Enterprise.

The Troyians, in the person of Petri, are physically marked as alien by their green skin and peculiar hair. There is no such visible sign setting the Elasians apart from humanity; but we are informed early on that their women's tears contain what McCoy, the ship's doctor, calls "a subtle mystical power that drives men wild." These magical tears, with their power to disrupt men's autonomy and rational control, exemplify science fiction's well-worn conceptualization of women as "the truly threatening alien."[46] They also update the Egyptian drug used by Helen in the *Odyssey*, which impairs men's emotions and moral judgment in a way that aligns with her erotic power over men.[47] In the course of the episode, Elaan wears four different outfits, all strongly eroticized. In theory, to invoke magic is to externalize the supernatural power of beauty, rendering its user's appearance irrelevant. In practice, however, the magic of Elasian women's tears—like Helen's drug—seems to be, rather, an expression of the power intrinsic in a beautiful woman's self-presentation.[48]

Like Helen, too, Elaan is a member of the ruling class whose marriage has large political implications for war and peace. Despite her status as Dohlman, like most renditions of Helen—and many a female monarch—she had no say in the matter of her marriage, to which she happens to be violently

45. Several episodes of TOS are transparently concerned with the Vietnam War, which bulked large in contemporary speculative fiction, especially the question of whether or not to use nuclear weapons (Franklin 1990). On Elaan as a figure for Vietnam, cf. Bernardi 1998: 64–67 and see further below, pp. 185 and 187.

46. Sobchak 1990: 107.

47. See Blondell 2013: 79–81. There may be an allusion to the use of illegal drugs in the 1960s, a subject on which TOS tends to be puritanical (see, e.g., Cushman & Osborn 2013: 540–41).

48. Elaan has more costume changes than any other female character in TOS except Lenore Karidian (Barbara Anderson) in "Conscience of the King," who has six. But Anderson's are less revealing than Elaan's.

opposed. The Enterprise has therefore been ordered to convey her to Troyius slowly, so that Petri can reconcile her to the marriage and train her in local customs along the way. His task is a challenging one, since the unreconstructed Elaan is an autocratic, violent, ill-mannered, and uncooperative bigot, who refers to her differently colored opponent as "a green pig." In the captain's own words, she is "an uncivilized savage, a vicious monster, an arrogant child in a woman's body."[49] In other words, she is the antithesis of Star Trek's humanistic ideal. As such, like other "primitives" in TOS, she is ripe for "civilizing" by the white male hero.

When Petri tries to introduce Elaan to Troyan ways, she promptly stabs him, obliging the captain to take over her education himself. Kirk proves a very different kind of teacher from the obsequious ambassador. When Elaan physically attacks *him*, for intruding into her room without permission, he pins her to the bed in a way that could portend rape, and threatens to spank her like a "spoiled brat" (a punishment with which he nowhere threatens male adversaries).[50] When she violates his sense of decorum, by drinking a potent alien liquor known as Saurian brandy straight from the bottle and devouring a leg of alien (i.e., green) chicken with her bare hands, he scolds her like a child, showing no respect for her royal status, let alone the possibility of cultural difference. Smugly treating his own experience as absolute, he informs Elaan, "In my experience, the differences between people disappear once they get to know each other." To which she drily responds, "That's not *my* experience."

The bourgeois Kirk thinks Elaan's manners undermine the dignity of her position. Yet their iconic association with the English king Henry VIII makes them, rather, an emblem of monarchical authority.[51] She is not, as Kirk would have it, a savage, a monster, or a child, but the ruler of a planet, who is treated accordingly by everyone but him. In key respects, moreover, she resembles Kirk himself, an alpha male who is used to getting his way. Kirk calls Elaan "impetuous," but he too has an "impetuous" command style that sometimes puts the Enterprise in jeopardy.[52] Throughout the series he issues peremptory

49. The episode was influenced by Shakespeare's *Taming of the Shrew*, and by Shaw's *Pygmalion* via *My Fair Lady* (see, e.g., Lucas to Roddenberry, March 13, 1968; Roddenberry to Freiberger, May 20, 1968). For the Pygmalion (artificial woman) theme in *Star Trek* generally, see Wagner & Lundeen 1998: 101–3.

50. Star Trek's aliens and other adversaries are often infantilized, or are actual children (Reid-Jeffery 1982: 38).

51. According to the script, "Her table manners put Henry the Eighth to shame."

52. Hark 2008: 29.

commands ("Find a solution to that bomb!"), whose spirit is little different from the manner in which Elaan orders people around ("Everything I order is possible!").

In the world of TOS, moreover, a propensity to anger and violence is not intrinsically negative; it is, rather, essential to human civilization as such.[53] In "The Enemy Within," where the captain is temporarily split into his "good" and "evil" selves, Good Kirk achieves nothing, since he will not stop dithering and take decisive action; meanwhile Evil Kirk behaves very much like Elaan, including swigging Saurian brandy from the bottle. The plot makes it very clear that the latter's rage and violence are essential not only to the complete Kirk's personality but to his role as a starship captain—in other words, to effective masculine leadership.[54] In our episode, Kirk underlines the male entitlement of such behavior when Elaan slaps him in the face and he promptly slaps her back—a gesture "traditionally seen as a means of keeping a woman in her place."[55]

Precisely halfway through the episode, however, Elaan changes tactics. Turning on the tears, and adopting submissive body language, she mournfully tells Kirk that she just wants to be liked but doesn't know how. It is no coincidence that tears are the instrument of Elasian women's power, since a woman's tears are not only "weapons in any galaxy, in any time period,"[56] but a way of grounding irresistible eroticism in female submission and self-loathing. Like the Homeric Helen, Elaan is adept at winning men's sympathy through tearful, self-denigrating speech.[57] Sure enough, this strategic performance of femininity elicits the softer side of Kirk's paternalism. He falls, predictably, into the trap, touches her wet cheek, and is instantly overcome with desire. Magic is

53. In "The Apple," for example, the natives are "liberated" by learning violence and aggression (among other human qualities). See further Goulding 1985: 30, 40–43; Hark 2008: 47–49. The alien Spock, interestingly, has more sympathy for peaceful worlds than Kirk does (Blair 1977: 16–17).

54. An early fanzine review of "Cloud Minders" by two female fans, comments that "we finally get a look at the real Captain Kirk . . . When his mind is reduced he is just like a tyrant, or better yet, a madman" (Donna Pace and Sherry Bowen, *Storyteller*, n.d., Roddenberry Collection, p. 35).

55. From a review on the website SF Debris, accessed October 17, 2019, https://sfdebris.com/videos/startrek/s057.php. There was much discussion during production of how to stage the slap scene and what it conveyed (Cushman 2015: 90–91).

56. J. Rodriguez 2008: 65.

57. For Helen in Homer, see Blondell 2013: 64–65.

not normally required to make the womanizing captain fall for an attractive woman, but as we shall see, Elaan is not his usual type. The magic, in this instance, consists in adjustments of demeanor that seem to *make* her his type after all.

Only slightly less predictably, Elaan also falls in love with the captain, betraying the familar Helenic partnership between women's sexual power over men and their own susceptibility to erotic passion. This suggests that the magic inherent in Elaan's tears should be identified with the power of her *own* desire ("I love you, I have chosen you"), and hence with her exercise of erotic agency, expressed as a performance of femininity. As she puts it to Kirk, "You cannot resist my love, my love!" But her love also subjects her, in turn, to Kirk's emotional control, thereby neutralizing the threat their affair poses to his manhood. The joke is on Elaan: she entraps Kirk, but in doing so subjects herself to him. The power reversal is conveyed with disconcerting clarity when their relationship takes a brief turn for the kinky, as Elaan, with a suggestive smile, asks Kirk to teach her more about spanking. The instrument with which he threatened to discipline her as an unruly child is embraced and eroticized by its self-infantilizing target.

Even though we have been informed, repeatedly, that there is no antidote for Elasian tears, when a Klingon ship provokes the Enterprise, Kirk rises to the occasion, subordinating romance to his "duty" as a starship commander. This inspires Elaan to perform her own "duty," since she, like him, has "no choice." She must accept the "responsibilities and obligations" that go with the "privileges and prerogatives" of her title. If Elaan is Vietnam, nuclear war has been successfully prevented by winning her mind in addition to her heart.[58] The concept of "duty" is configured as masculine in *Star Trek* ("That's all you men . . . can speak of . . . duty"). Embracing it therefore allows Elaan to reframe her "manliness" in a way that serves Kirk's—and the show's—patriarchal purposes. This takes the form, however, of a distinctly feminine gesture of self-sacrifice. Sadly but meekly, she beams down to Troyius, to enter on her new role as diplomatic wife. Like Euripides's Iphigenia, who first protests then embraces her literal victimization, Elaan becomes complicit in her own sacrifice.

58. On "winning hearts and minds" as a slogan during the Vietnam war, see Franklin 1990: 347.

Kirk thus successfully inducts the intemperate Elaan into "civilized" values. For both of them, this requires erotic self-denial.[59] In her case, however, "civilization" turns out to entail not only emotional self-control but the renunciation of personal erotic autonomy, in an abject embrace of her own subjection. Earlier, when she refused to be "humiliated" by a forced marriage to the hated Troyan, Kirk replied, "Then act in a civilized fashion." It turns out, however, that "civilization" preserves her only from being dragged to the altar kicking and screaming—not from the humiliation of a loathsome marriage.[60] Kirk too is nominally heartbroken; but he remains free, like Odysseus, to move on to his next mission—and his next love affair—while remaining true to the one he really "loves." McCoy does finally come up with an antidote for Elasian tears, but only after it is no longer necessary.[61] Spock spells out the moral when he tells McCoy, "The antidote to a woman of Elas . . . is a starship. The Enterprise infected the captain long before the Dohlman did."

Ridiculous Female Trappings

France Nuyen, who played Elaan, brought to the role a remarkable racial and cultural complexity. The child of a French mother and a Vietnamese (but ethnically Chinese) father, Nuyen reports that her mother was persecuted by the Nazis because she "looked Jewish."[62] Culturally, Nuyen was entirely French.[63] She arrived in the US speaking no English and retained a distinctive accent. Unusually for *Star Trek*'s disposable females, she also brought to her guest role the image and temperament of a star.[64] She had a personal

59. For this aspect of the Roddenberry world view, see Hark 2008: 38–41.

60. In earlier versions of the script, Elaan's Troyan fiancé turns out to be extremely attractive, "with the face of a Greek (or rather a Trojan) god," which provokes jealousy in Kirk and provides Helen with both a desirable mate and a happy ending (script version March 8, 1968, p. 24; script version March 20, 1968, p. 33; Roddenberry to Lucas, April 1, 1968). The producer Robert Justman objected that this made her character "shallow," but Roddenberry disagreed (Justman to Roddenberry, March 11, 1968; Roddenberry to Lucas, March 13, 1968).

61. It is needed in narrative terms, however, because it shows that the "magic" of the tears derives from a "biochemical agent," indicating, in typical *Star Trek* fashion, the superiority of science over myth.

62. Thomas 2019.

63. She found it a "supreme effort" to fit in with Chinese actors on the set of *Joy Luck Club* (Rampell n.d.).

64. On Nuyen and the mainstreaming of Asian femininity in the late 1950s, see Lim 2006: ch. 5. Her film career sputtered in the 1960s, in part because the escalating Vietnam war put an

reputation for anger, outspokenness, scandal, and even violence (in part because of an affair with Marlon Brando that ended badly), making her an excellent fit for the unreconstructed Elaan.[65] She was also personally involved in the civil rights movement, and was devasted by the murder of Bobby Kennedy, which occurred during the filming of this episode.[66]

Nuyen's career was launched, when she was only seventeen, with the role of the innocent young Tonganese Liat in the film of *South Pacific* (1958). Later the same year she starred on Broadway as Suzie Wong, a Chinese hooker with a heart of gold—a role for which, according to *Life* magazine, she was made up "to emphasize the Oriental cast of her face" (figure 5.1; plate 12). Both roles cast her as a beautiful young Asian woman involved in a problematic affair with a white man (one who, in *Suzie Wong*, was played by none other than William Shatner). She brought aspects of this persona to Star Trek's El*asian* seductress, especially in the episode's second half, which culminates in the kind of romantic self-sacrifice that is a resonant stereotype for Asian women in particular.[67] The role also draws on another eroticized Asian stereotype—the violent, manipulative Dragon Lady, embodied most famously in Anna May Wong.[68] Her ethnic background reinforced the identification of Elaan with Vietnam, at a time when the war had re-racialized Asians as menacing and "primitive."[69]

But Elaan is not *simply* stereotyped as Asian. Rather, she is a walking compendium of racialized and gendered exotica.[70] Her makeup does not

---

end to the "oriental wave" that had launched it (Lim 2006: 185–87). For her intimidating personality, cf. Cushman 2015: 99.

65. Nuyen said, "Playing the spoiled alien princess was a role that had authority and rage—I was throwing knives around the set. Quite different to other parts I had played and opened up a new range of acting emotions for me" (Thomas 2019).

66. Cushman 2015: 97–98.

67. Cf., e.g., the film *Sayonara* (1957) in which a Japanese woman resists "Western" romance on the grounds that "we have duties and obligations."

68. On Nuyen and Asian stereotypes, see Bernardi 1998: 63–67. On the Dragon Lady, see further Prasso 2005; on Wong, see Lim 2006: ch. 2.

69. Lim 2006: 190. Elaan embodies the stereotype of communists as devious and primitive (cf. above, pp. 97–98), which is also reflected in the Klingons and Romulans (Booker 2008: 201–2). On other *Star Trek* Asians, see Bernardi 1998: 39–44, 55–63.

70. Roddenberry was anxious that her appearance, like her name, should be distanced from "straight and exact human development" through "hair color and makeup" (Roddenberry to Lucas, April 1, 1968). In earlier versions of the script "her skin [is] a rich gold color, her hair silver white" (script version April 12, 1968). Ironically, Nuyen lightened her skin as a child as part of "the racialized struggle to achieve personhood" (Lim 2006: 177).

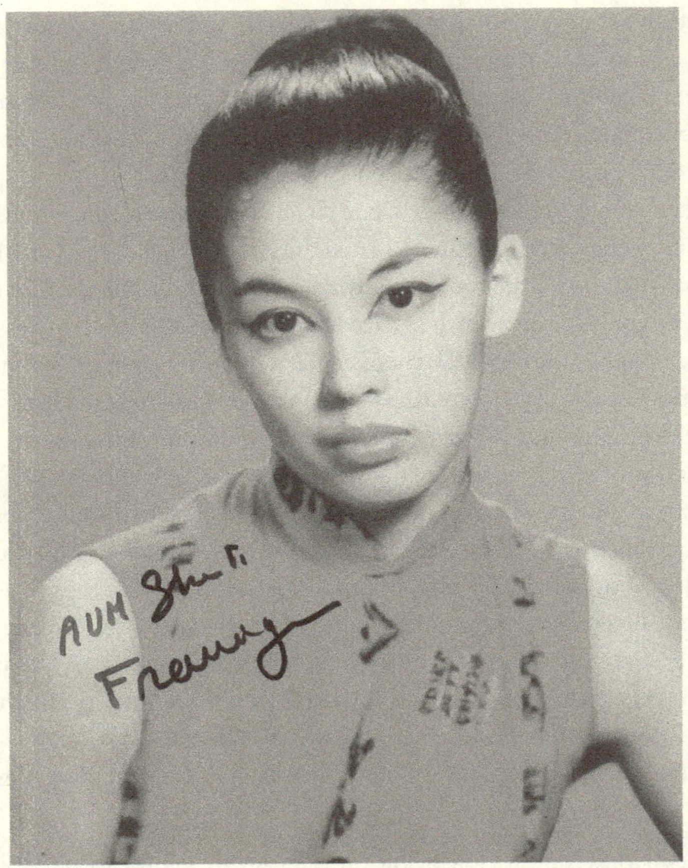

FIGURE 5.1. Publicity still of the young France Nuyen.

"emphasize the Oriental cast of her face." Her features are racially indeterminate, her complexion is darkened, and she wears heavy black braids. This racial complexity is reinforced by a smorgasbord of exoticizing cultural signifiers. Her title, Dohlman, sounds like the Turkish dolman, a kind of robe with "oriental" overtones (and the origin of the dolman sleeves fashionable in this period).[71] There are touches of the Dragon Lady, especially the jeweled dagger in Elaan's sleeve and her long, talon-like fingernails; but she also wears a metallic bindi, of a kind that became fashionable in the counterculture of the late 1960s (especially after the Beatles visited India earlier the same year). Her

71. On the dolman, see Hollander 1978: 286–87. Studio research compared the word "dolman," meaning an ancient tomb, which they thought would be familiar to "many educated people" (De Forest Research, May 20, 1968, Roddenberry Collection).

"gladiator" sandals evoke Apollo's and Carolyn's footwear in "Who Mourns for Adonais?" but also 1960s fashions and *Star Trek*'s alien chic. And of course, she retains her French accent.

Nuyen's racial complexity sets Elaan apart from Kirk's other love objects. The hair on the heads of the disposable females may be blonde, brunette, or green, but those heads typically belong to Anglophone Caucasians.[72] Shahna, in "The Gamesters of Triskelion," is costumed most like Elaan at first appearance, but her outfit is looser, her skin fair, and her hair green-blonde. Miramanee, the dark-haired "noble savage" in "Paradise Syndrome," was played by the Caucasian Sabrina Scharf in redface.[73] Nona, in the Vietnam-themed episode "A Private Little War," resembles Elaan in several respects (she is dark, "savage," and gets her way through aphrodisiac magic); yet she too was played by a white actor (Nancy Kovack). The female character in TOS most comparable to Elaan is the Vulcan T'Pring, played by Tasha Martel, who was an "exotic" looking American Jew. Like Elaan, T'Pring is dark, orientalized, and bereft of moral scruples; but she is a potential mate not for Kirk but for Spock, her fellow alien (played by another dark, "exotic" American Jew).[74]

The unreconstructed Elaan is not only more racially exotic than most of *Star Trek*'s disposable females, but less seductive, more assertive, and more emasculating. Granted, at her first appearance, she is markedly objectified, in keeping with her plot function as an object trafficked among men. Petri has even prepared us by glossing the word "Dohlman" as "a *thing* most feared and hated by our people" (emphasis added).[75] When she is introduced, it is with a cinematic cliché for erotic objectification: the camera moves slowly up her body, inch by inch, culminating in a triumphant chord when we finally see her

72. The captain had three "significant romances" in the past (S. E. Whitfield 1968: 217), all with blondes: Ruth Cartwright ("Shore Leave"), Areel Shaw ("Court Martial"), and Janet Wallace ("The Deadly Years"). Within the time frame of TOS, he has two more significant affairs, one with another blonde, Rayna ("Requiem for Methuselah"), the other with the dark-haired but "angelic" Edith Keeler in "The City on the Edge of Forever" (on whom see Selley 1986: 96–97).

73. On Scharf (born Sandra Mae Trentman in Ohio), see Cushman 2015: 118–19. For the episode's "noble savage" theme, see Bernardi 1998: 44–49. On *Star Trek*'s representation of Native Americans generally, see Wagner & Lundgreen 1998: 177–81; Kanzler 2007.

74. On the "exoticism" of Tasha (born Arlene) Martel, see Asherman 1988: 201–5. Sylvia in "Catspaw" is also darkly exotic (though played by the British-Canadian Antoinette Bowers), but Kirk never really falls under her sway.

75. The word Dohlman was intentionally ungendered, to increase the impact when Elaan actually appears (Roddenberry to Freiberger, May 16, 1968).

FIGURE 5.2. Our first sight of Elaan (left) in "Elaan of Troyius"; one of her guards (right).

as a whole, presented for our viewing pleasure in the stage-like transporter (figure 5.2). But this blatant objectification is quickly challenged by a rebarbative demeanor, especially the scowl on her face with its frontal gaze, her square, unmoving shoulders and firmly planted legs. Nuyen is only five feet, three inches tall, but the low camera angle gives her an authoritative presence, allowing her to look down at the male crew kneeling below her on the floor. Her stance is that of a superheroine, not a seducer. It echoes her male guards, in sharp contrast to such stereotypically seductive *Star Trek* females as the sex workers of "Mudd's Women" (whose beauty has been magically enhanced by a drug), with their swaying hips, soft-focus close-ups, and suggestive, contrapposto stance (figure 5.3). As Ina Rae Hark explains, "A featured guest actress is usually introduced through a gauzy close-up while the soundtrack plays the same syrupy melody, one that quickly became a shorthand for 'look, attractive female here.'"[76] But there is nothing gauzy or syrupy about Elaan's arrival.

76. Hark 2008: 37.

FIGURE 5.3. Our first sight of the sex workers in the *Star Trek* episode "Mudd's Women."

The same may be said for her costume. Admittedly, it is highly revealing (even by *Star Trek* standards), and composed almost entirely of suggestively shaded triangles and arrows (plate 11).[77] Rather than conveying sexual availability, however, its metallic surface repulses the gaze (even while compelling it).[78] There are no skirts or drapery, which might hamper Elaan's freedom of movement or render her vulnerable to the Theiss titillation test (a theory positing women as a passive victims of the male gaze, devoid of bodily autonomy). On the contrary, the armor, which was made of plastic table mats, was literally—and painfully—glued to her skin.[79] Like her posture, the costume distinguishes

77. It has overtones of the Art Deco tradition in speculative fiction style, perceptible in films from *Metropolis* (1927) to *Blade Runner* (1982).

78. Cf. Barthes 2012: 166 on "the diamond- or sequin-covered G-string which is the very end of the striptease: this ultimate triangle, by its pure and geometric form, by its hard and glittering substance, defends her sex like a sword of chastity and definitively repels the woman into a mineral universe." In earlier versions of the script, where Elaan is still named "Helen," she already wears "a scanty metallic costume" with a "barbaric" necklace and carries a dagger (script version March 20, 1968).

79. Cushman 2015: 996. Note that even a bikini is not sexy in a Theissian sense if it appears firmly secured (S. E. Whitfield 1968: 360). Nuyen reports that Theiss "cut [the placemats] into

her sharply from more typical *Star Trek* females like Mudd's women, with their drapey, hippieish style, and assimilates her, instead, to her guards, who wear coordinated armored tunics with samurai overtones.[80] Her sandals echo their footwear, and like them she carries a pointed weapon holstered on her arm in a long metallic sleeve, its phallic shape corresponding to that of their nuclear blasters.

Elaan is thus unusual among Captain Kirk's disposable women in several ways. She is even more exceptional, however, as an incarnation of Helen of Troy. Her jet-black hair, in sharp contrast with Helen's usual blonde, suggests strength, assertiveness, seriousness, evil, or some combination thereof. In an ancient context, it evokes not Helen but Cleopatra. Elaan's braids, in particular (which get a lot of attention from the camera), align her with popular cinematic images of the Egyptian queen and other similar vamps.[81] To aid with mainstream audience identification, such "Egyptians" are typically played by white actors.[82] But Elaan's dark skin and black braids suggest a different kind of identification, racializing her in contemporary American terms as African American.

As such, the fiery, violent Elaan poses a challenge to *Star Trek*'s optimistic racial politics. This is underlined by the sharp contrast with Uhura, the show's normative model of Black womanhood. Uhura is voluptuous but demure, wholesome, neatly coiffed, smooth-haired, self-disciplined, compliant, and relegated to the margins of most episodes (including this one). She belongs securely in the contemporary TV world of "black invisibility structured by the logic of color blindness and driven by the discourse of assimilation."[83] Visually, her Starfleet uniform assimilates her quite literally to the rest of the crew

---

squares and put glitter on one side so when they were clipped together it looked like metal. They were either sewed or glued on me and I lost some skin off my ribs when they were pulled off" (Thomas 2019).

80. Roddenberry thought of the Elasians as a "proud" people like "pre-war Japan" (Roddenberry to Lucas, March 13, 1968).

81. The Cleopatra look was established by the mid-nineteenth century and had recently achieved influential representation in the person of Elizabeth Taylor (see Llewellyn-Jones 2013a). Besides Cleopatra, see, e.g., Nefretiri in *Ten Commandments* (1956) and Nais in the peplum *Lion of Thebes* (1964).

82. Hamer 1993: 105, 118–24, 132; McCoskey 2012: 11–23.

83. Herman Gray 1997: 350. Nichols refused to discuss "the problems of the Negro race as related to acting," saying she wanted "to be considered an actress, nothing more" (*Storyteller* p. 35).

FIGURE 5.4. Spock, Uhura, and Kirk on the bridge of the Starship Enterprise in "Elaan of Troyius."

(figure 5.4). This does not rule out a certain exoticism. Uhura's name is Swahili, she has a personal affinity with the alien Spock,[84] and her quarters are decorated with flowers and "ethnic" *objets d'art* (masks, a zebra bedspread, orientalizing throw pillows). In "The Tholian Web," we see her relaxing there in a colorful but voluminous (non-Theissian) gown. She is orientalized by these touches of exoticism, but in an anodyne, "feminine" fashion.[85]

A few episodes tease us with glimpses of Uhura's potential for the more threatening forms of female self-assertion bound up, in the social fabric of the late 1960s, with the threat of the racial Other. In "Plato's Stepchildren," the evil Platonians force her to wear a long, pink, low-cut gown, with Cleopatran touches in her makeup, hair, and jewelry, and to lounge in an erotic tableau on

84. She is the only non-Vulcan whom he teaches to play the Vulcan lyre (Asherman 1988: 70). In *Charlie X,* she sings a song aimed at Spock warning of the dangerous power of "alien love."

85. For Uhura as "a performance, an icon, of black beauty," cf. Bernardi 1998: 42. Interestingly, Nichols reports that Uhura's regular makeup and the lighting made her look "Asian" to many viewers who saw the show in black and white (Nichols 1994: 160).

FIGURE 5.5. Uhura exoticized in the *Star Trek* episode "Plato's Stepchildren."

the requisite velvet pillows (figure 5.5). This culminates in the notorious kiss between Uhura and Captain Kirk, which was supposedly the first interracial kiss to be shown on national television.[86] In "Mirror Mirror," which posits an alternate world of "brutal, savage, uncivilized, treacherous" people, Uhura temporarily impersonates her "evil" counterpart. The crew's uniforms were adapted for the episode with sashes and glitter, to convey "the hedonistic lifestyle of the alternate universe crew."[87] Uhura's uniform is modified to bare her midriff and accessorized with an "Egyptian" snake bracelet and a knife that she keeps in her thigh-high boot. Though merely playacting her "evil" self, this Uhura is both physically and sexually assertive, wielding her knife with confidence and actively putting the moves on Sulu. Like Kirk in "Enemy Within," she contains conflicting selves, hinting that her assimilated persona may be papering over the disruptive potential of Black women. But both episodes insist on the importance of restraining violent passions. In "Mirror Mirror," Uhura is merely mimicking behaviors from which she personally refrains; in

86. See Asherman 1988: 164–65; Shatner & Kreski 1993: 282–86; Nichols 1994: 193–97; D. Alexander 1995: 317–22; Bernardi 1998: 38–39.

87. Block et al. 2015: 31.

"Plato's Stepchildren," both she and Kirk struggle heroically to resist the external power that forces them into their notorious kiss.

These episodes merely hint at the explosive potential for violence and sexual self-assertion in the exoticized female Other. The unreconstructed Elaan unleashes that potential, manifesting, in both appearance and behavior, the unvarnished female and racialized anger and self-assertion that were of such acute contemporary concern. The contrast with Uhura is dramatized by locating Elaan in the latter's cabin, which is assigned to her as the best available, literally displacing its usual occupant. This is the only episode besides "Tholian Web" to show Uhura's quarters, thereby pointedly opposing the "uncivilized" alien to the assimilated Black woman, with her feminine comforts and gently exoticized *objets d'art*. Elaan rages within the cabin's confines like a trapped animal, tossing her braids and thumping the velvet pillows in frustration. She smashes Uhura's tchotchkes and hurls her dagger at the captain, and when Petri offers her Troyan wedding regalia, consisting of a special dress, slippers, and necklace, she literally throws them back in the ambassador's face, calling these "ridiculous female trappings" an offense to her eyes.

By the end of the episode, however, Elaan has embraced these very trappings. Ironically, as she learns to impose "feminine" constraints upon herself, her costumes become increasingly looser and more Theissian. Her second outfit is softer and more see-through than the first, but still gestures to the look of formfitting metallic armor (as opposed to floating drapery) by means of metallic panels attached to a background of netting (plate 11). Her legs, in loose baggy pants of the same fabric, are still unobstructed, and her body language remains rebarbative—up to the moment when she seduces Kirk by turning on the tears, when she becomes pleading and even smiles. Her success in that endeavor is followed by a third outfit, much more typical of *Star Trek*'s eroticized extraterrestrial couture: a saffron chiffon dress slit from chin to waist, with soft, gleaming drapery, "a unique skirt that is draped through the ankles and open on each side," and no back (plate 11).[88] While she is wearing it, her body language becomes increasingly feminized, aligned in particular with stereotypes of Asian submissiveness. The camera now emphasizes Nuyen's short stature, as she gazes pleadingly at the tall, strong captain, her hands, with their heavy rings and long, polished fingernails, stretching up to embrace him (figure 5.6).

88. See the detailed description at Prop Store, accessed July 2, 2019, https://us.propstoreauction.com/view-auctions/catalog/id/146/lot/32303/.

FIGURE 5.6. Elaan tries to win over the captain in "Elaan of Troyius."

Elaan's ultimate submission is signaled by her voluntary assumption of the hated wedding gown (plate 11). This too is long, drapey, and revealing, in high Theissian style. It also bears a faintly unnerving resemblance to Nuyen's dress in her *Life* cover photo as Suzie Wong (plate 12). It is accessorized with a special necklace, which turns out to be made of dilithium crystals, the material that fuels the Enterprise. Since for complicated reasons they are out of dilithium right now, Elaan gives up part of her necklace to power the ship, making possible her own passage to Troyius and the loathed marriage that awaits. Female submission literally fuels male dominance and the restoration of the patriarchal status quo. Before leaving the Enterprise, Elaan conclusively embraces femininity by giving Kirk her dagger as a keepsake. The phallus is back where it belongs. We last see her trapped and immobilized in the transporter, as she literally fades away before our eyes. The rage of Black Power has been replaced by the decorum and self-effacement of the "model minority."[89] The dragon lady has metamorphosed into Madame Butterfly.

89. On the rise after World War II of "model minority" as a label for Asians, see Lim 2006: 189–90. Historically, the "model minority" myth has been used to pit Asians against Blacks (Kim 1999).

As a barbaric, male-acting, female outsider, who rejects marriage and is "civilized" by subjection to patriarchal authority, Elaan bears a distinct resemblance to the ancient Greek Amazons. Mythology instructs us that such women can be "tamed" by brute force, but ideally should be incorporated into the patriarchal order via their "voluntary" embrace of the institution of marriage.[90] Elaan fades away from the confines of the Enterprise, but unlike Apollo in "Who Mourns for Adonais?," she is not expelled from humanoid society as such. Instead, she is coopted, like an Amazon queen in ancient Athens, to live on as a properly domesticated pillar of *Star Trek*'s supposedly "humanistic" world view.

The episode does follow "Adonais," however, in appropriating, rather than dismissing, Greek heroic masculinity. In the earlier episode, Apollo himself likens Kirk and his crew to the ancient Greek heroes, calling Agamemnon, Hector, and Odysseus their "fathers." In our episode, Kirk gets to play the heroic Greek male role of civilizer, like Theseus or Hercules (both of whom subdued Amazon queens). Yet his erotic self-control aligns him most pointedly with Odysseus, who is immune to Circe's magic, refuses immortality with Calypso, and saves the day for his comrades by resisting the spellbinding power of Helen's voice when they are hidden inside the Trojan Horse.[91]

Kirk one-ups his ancient predecessors, however, in key respects. Homer's Odysseus can only resist Circe's magic because the gods give him a preemptive antidote. To be sure, McCoy eventually comes up with an antidote for Elasian tears, but only after Kirk has already shown that he is man enough not to need it. The captain outdoes Menelaus, too, by refusing to cause a war over the woman he "loves" or succumb in the end to the power of her beauty. Granted, yielding to that power in the first place made him temporarily a Paris figure, risking interplanetary war through his inability to resist *eros*. In the end, however, he becomes a kind of anti-Paris, who sacrifices "love" to shore up the institution of arranged marriage. This enables him to outdo his Greek forebears in the most important way of all. It took the Trojan War to transform the errant Helen into the subdued and dutiful wife of the *Odyssey*; but Kirk domesticates Elaan ahead of time, thus *preventing* an even more terrible war from taking place.

"Elaan of Troyius," whose title alludes transparently to the Trojan War story, thus turns into a reversal of that story. Instead of female desire leading

90. See further Gantz 1993: 282–85, 397–400.

91. Cf. Blondell 2013: 83–84.

to adultery and warfare, peace is produced by maintaining the integrity of a royal marriage, at the price of a beautiful woman's erotic autonomy. Instead of inducing a woman to leave a man she cannot stand, "love" turns that woman into a dutiful but unhappy wife to precisely such a man. Overall, then, Kirk is far more successful than ancient Greek mythology at controlling the dangerous power of female beauty symbolically enshrined in Helen. By racializing that power in contemporary terms, this updated mythical narrative of taming the feminine Other purports to control in one stroke the double threat of female self-assertion and racial fury that was roiling the nation.

Bad Girls Have More Fun

It is difficult to ascertain the reactions of the original audience of "Elaan of Troyius."[92] But the episode's ratings were solid, and among more recent fans, it is generally considered one of the best of the uneven third season.[93]

The nature of Elaan's appeal to some viewers is obvious enough. In the endless online discussions of the hotness of Kirk's conquests, she often makes the short list and sometimes tops it. In the words of one IMDb fan, "Captain James T. Kirk has had a few romantic entanglements. But nothing like France Nuyen as the [sic] Elaan"; another comments, "Trek' has its share of babes, but Elaan is a super-babe." Many viewers appear to approve of the episode's superficial "lesson," summed up in a publication entitled *Captain Kirk's Guide to Women* as: "Spoiled brats need a spanking."[94] But the episode is also widely lambasted, by both women and men, as one of the most unfortunately racist

92. The Roddenberry Collection includes little by way of contemporary fan responses to season three and nothing about this specific episode. The nature of memory makes remembered reactions problematic as evidence for original audience reception (see Spigel & Jenkins 1991 and below, p. 201).

93. E.g., Cushman 2015: 83, 104. For the ratings, see Gross & Altman 1995: 73; Cushman 2015: 102–3. On the ill-fated season three, see Cushman 2015; Shatner & Kreski 1993: 256–98.

94. J. Rodriguez 2008: 64. An Amazon user elaborates: "Kirk, as ever, is the spokesman for liberal democratic values. Meanwhile, the Dohlman represents an ancient mentality which Earth has mostly grown out of . . . an attitude of privilege, arrogance, and war. The Dohlman is Cleopatra, Helen of Troy, and the Queen of Sheba. It is fascinating to see how Kirk, the icon of liberal values, interacts with such an atavistic mentality. Basically, he is the adult and she the child." Brian Overland, June 19, 2007, Amazon review of *Star Trek: The Original Series*, "Episode 57: Elaan of Troyius," https://www.amazon.com/Star-Trek-Original-Episode-Troyius/product-reviews/6300988589.

and sexist in TOS. One blogger calls it "utterly appalling and disgraceful . . . a jaw-droppingly sexist turkey of a story"; another declares that "watching a white man criticize a woman of color for being uncivilized and savage is just . . . painfully terrible."[95]

Yet the choice of Helen of Troy as a mythical reference point renders the episode's racial politics more complex than such reactions might suggest. By appropriating the quintessential high cultural emblem of "Western" female beauty in a way that markedly rejects the associated stereotypes, the episode points to a future in which female beauty may be less racially determined than most of Kirk's conquests might lead us to believe. While this affirmation of "exotic" beauty in the person of the multiracial Nuyen might appeal to any non-white viewer, in the late 1960s it could have had special significance for Asian Americans, who were striving, during the Cold War, to participate in the beauty culture of the "free West." This was a way of showing that they could be "civilized," thus legitimizing their status as true Americans and distancing themselves from communist countries like Vietnam.[96]

At a time when even the anodyne Uhura was an important benchmark for Black representation,[97] Elaan's exoticism would have had a different resonance in American culture more broadly. 1968 was the year of Eve Arnold's photo-essay *Black is Beautiful*. The slogan, which was gathering force as a flashpoint for racial politics, found expression especially in the rejection of straightened hair (like Uhura's), as normative for Black beauty, in favor of "natural" and traditional hairstyles.[98] Cleopatra, too, had long been celebrated as an icon of black empowerment.[99] However threatening Elaan's flying "Egyptian" braids may have been to some viewers, then, they may have been empowering to

95. Marsfelder 2013; Oshiro 2014.

96. See Lim 2006: 49, 162, and ch. 4 passim.

97. Despite the frustrations of her limited role, Nichols stayed with the show at the urging of no less a fan than Martin Luther King, Jr. (Shatner & Kreski 1993: 212–14; Henderson 1994: 52).

98. P. Taylor 2016: 112–13; cf. 118–21. For the history of the Black is Beautiful movement, see Camp 2015. The "natural" style most associated with this period is the Afro, but braids, which had African origins and had been worn by the enslaved, were also starting to be recuperated. Cicely Tyson, who pioneered the Afro, was the first Black woman to wear cornrows on national TV (in *East Side/West Side* in 1962). See further Byrd & Tharps 2014: ch. 3 and 5.

99. Whether or not Cleopatra was "really" Black (a subject of debate among scholars), the idea of her Blackness has had enormous resonance for African Americans (see, e.g., Haley 1995: 27–30). She featured in abolitionist arguments from the early nineteenth century in the popular Black press as well as among intellectuals (Malamud 2016: ch. 4).

others, both personally and politically. The same may have been true for the sight of a "Black" woman exercising erotic power (even temporarily) over the smug, entitled, white male "epic" hero. More recent fans, at any rate, who note the extreme rarity of women of color as love interests in TOS, are well aware of the episode's implications for the politics of beauty. One female blogger deplores the episode's racial stereotyping, but adds "at least she has not just one, not two, but four gorgeous and revealing costumes . . . She was beautiful and captivating in those Cleopatra braids."[100]

The episode's gender politics offer less traction for resistant readings. Astonishing as it may now seem, the producer of "Elaan," Fred Freiberger, intended the episode to attract women.[101] Its writer and director, John Lucas, was pleased with the result, despite his enthusiasm (expressed elsewhere) for using science fiction to "tackle any subject, touch current political issues such as race relations which networks considered dangerous and untouchable."[102] Roddenberry himself expected that "the females in our audience will identify with the strong female being tamed by a real *man*."[103] In some cases, he may have been right.[104] But the endorsement of arranged marriage in 1960s America seems retrograde by any standard, including *Star Trek*'s own.[105]

Looking back decades later, one female fan says she was not bothered at the time by Kirk's "legendary" womanizing, because: "It was the Sixties," and "Kirk's roaming eye was a lot easier to accept because he was Sacrificing His Personal Life for 'My Ship, My Crew.'"[106] Yet early zines indicate that many female fans were sensitive to the show's sexism, though they expressed their concern obliquely, with little more than an occasional eyeroll at Kirk's

100. Doux n.d.

101. *Star Trek* had a strong female following, a fact usually attributed to the show's emphasis on human relationships (Westfahl 2003: 204). But the network's audience research suggested that women generally were not serious science fiction fans, so special efforts were made to attract them (Asherman 1988: 163; Shatner & Kreski 1993: 261–62; Solow & Justman 1997: 64).

102. Lucas 2004: 237; cf. Shatner & Kreski 1993: 243.

103. Cushman 2015: 89.

104. The female authors of *Star Trek Lives!* assert that many women "thrilled" to Kirk's sexual exploits (Lichtenberg et al. 1975: 41; cf. also Nichols 1994: 196). But to Shatner's chagrin it was Spock—not the womanizing captain—who quickly became the most prominent object of female devotion (Cushman & Osborn 2013: 403–5; cf. S. E. Whitfield 1968: 125; Lichtenberg et al. 1975: 78–88; Blair 1983; Cranny-Francis 1985).

105. In "Gamesters of Triskelion," Kirk informs the enslaved population, "On earth we select our own mate."

106. Toner n.d.

behavior.[107] Another online reviewer quotes a fan named Ben P. Duck who writes, looking back from the present, "My memory is of the challenges to racial prejudice and gender inequality being more or less simultaneous. [TOS] really drives home the fact that they were not and that [women's] great victories of the second half of the twentieth century were unrealized in 1968."[108] As Mr. Duck acutely surmises, "These notably misogynistic episodes . . . might reflect awareness that this transformation of our society was on the way, and the deep discomfort that many felt (and still feel) about it."

Yet TV audiences have always used shows selectively, as a way of thinking about their own lives and identities.[109] Female fans, in particular, are adept at appropriating masculinist narratives for their own interests and concerns. This often involves challenging the preferred reading by viewing plotlines from the point of view of a subordinated character. In this vein, one fan sees the Dohlman as "a young woman who is scared to death of marrying a strange man and living on a strange world"; another writes: "asking [Elaan] to uproot her existence to marry a man she's never met but has been trained her whole life to loathe seems shockingly unfair"; as for her table manners, in the words of one (male) reviewer, "If you were having to marry some asshole, wouldn't you drink straight from the bottle?"[110]

Nor has it passed unnoticed that, as we saw earlier for the epic genre, "bad" female characters tend to be more powerful, more memorable, and more exciting than the virtuous. In consequence, women viewers often identify with the former, even if they are demonized and punished by the plot. Female fans of the *Batman* TV series, for example (which ran concurrently with TOS), drew from the villainous Catwoman the lesson that "bad girls have more fun."[111]

107. Cf. Nugent 1991. Kirk was dubbed "Tomcat" by female fans (Toner n.d.). Two women comment in a fanzine, on a different episode, that "for once we did not have to su[ff]er through a Kirk vs. ? love affair" (Suzann Hughes and Sherry Bowen, *Storyteller* p. 34). Another zine indicates that female speculative fiction fans in this period were already tired of Jack the Ripper plots and were fantasizing about female vengeance (*Psychotic*, January 1968). A pair of ten-year-old girls, who liked to role-play as Kirk and Spock, wrote to Roddenberry offering to participate in the show as the two male protagonists' sisters, which would "make it more interesting" (Maureen Dyshere and Kathrine Thompson to Roddenberry, July 11, 1967).

108. Quoted by Doux n.d.

109. Cf. above, p. xvii–xviii.

110. Hayes-Gehrke 2008; Atkinson 2010; Anon. n.d.b (a video review in the form of an amusing pro- and anti-Elaan debate).

111. Spigel & Jenkins 1991: 139.

They used her as "a way of exploring issues of feminine empowerment, of resistance to male constraints and to the requirement to be a 'good little girl.'"[112]

"Elaan" provides plenty of room for this kind of selective and oppositional reading. Of the online episode reviews I have seen, only six are identifiably by women, yet two of these, both ardent feminists, admit that the episode is for them a "guilty pleasure." After calling it "a feminist nightmare," one adds, "[Elaan's] tantrums are colorful, flamboyant and such a charming contrast to Starfleet obedience that it's hard not to root for her," continuing, "Personally, I find Elaan's most criticized qualities—her deplorably indelicate, unfeminine, graceless manners—to be among her more admirable traits"; another of the six remarks, "Even though she ultimately doesn't get her way, she is a powerful character who commands a posse of guys and manipulates Kirk, and I appreciated the amount of screen time she was given."[113] The Elaan who has become iconic in *Star Trek* fandom is not the demure bride, but the scowling, confident figure of her first appearance or the ill-mannered, knife-throwing "savage" (plate 13).

As the *Star Trek* juggernaut rolled on, the characters of TOS remained—and remain—very much alive. Like real people who can never be completely known, they have developed over time in light of viewers' various, partial, and often conflicting perspectives, knowledge, and dispositions. They are sustained by fan activity which, especially in the internet age, functions much as myth did in antiquity, borrowing, reborrowing, and reinventing familiar stories in an ever-expanding "universe."[114] This allows even minor characters to acquire a substantial existence, rescuing many of Kirk's disposable women from being finally disposed of. Accordingly, fans have reclaimed Elaan by imagining her future in a way that defies the gender politics of her episode's conclusion. One wryly comments, for example, that Elaan's future husband "won't be much of a problem . . . once she gets close enough to weep on him," and hopes that Elaan ends up teaching the Troyians to show more respect for women.[115]

112. H. Jenkins 2013: 35; cf. D'Acci 1997: 86.

113. M. Green 2006; Hodge 2014. In the fanzine *IDIC* 14 (1991), Gloria Fry remarks, "What a pleasant change it is . . . to see a woman using the Captain for a change."

114. On media fandom generally, and especially *Star Trek*, see H. Jenkins 2013; Bacon-Smith 1992; J. Gray et al. 2007. On the transformation of fandom via the internet, see Gwenllian-Jones 2000: 407; 2003; Hellekson & Busse 2006; H. Jenkins 2013: xx-xlii; Diak 2018: 11–12.

115. M. Green 2006.

This impulse achieves its most complete expression in the (predominantly female) genre of fan fiction.[116] From the outset, fan stories were used as a vehicle for critiquing *Star Trek*'s sexism and gender normativity.[117] They often rehabilitate negative characters or flesh out underwritten ones by developing "narratives allowing them to achieve their full potential."[118] *Firestorm*, published in 1994 by Julia Ecklar and Karen Rose Cercone (together under the name L. A. Graf), places Uhura—now wearing pants—in command of a planetary mission on the ground. There she must negotiate as an equal with Elaan's sister Israi, the current Dohlman of Elas. Israi closely resembles Elaan in appearance but is presented more sympathetically and with much greater respect for cultural difference. In the course of the novel, we discover what happened to Elaan after she beamed down from the *Enterprise*. Bereft of her dagger, on their wedding night she stabbed her husband with a kitchen knife. He thereupon appointed her admiral of the Troyian space fleet (thus keeping her at a safe distance). After a long career as admiral, she eventually died in combat.

Firestorm allows Elaan to "achieve her full potential" as the equal of Captain Kirk. Indeed, in the novel, Kirk himself is embarrassed by his original attitude, admitting that he did not just teach Elaan but learned from her, specifically "never to underestimate an opponent."[119] At the same time, the novel reaffirms the weakness in the captain's own character by reconceptualizing the power inherent in Elasian women's tears. That power is no longer intrinsically erotic, but is presented, rather, as a way of inspiring utter loyalty or even "enslavement."[120] In the original episode, we only had McCoy's word for the rumor that the tears "drive men wild." But *Firestorm* uses sly references to the past to imply that their specifically erotic effect on Kirk was a reflection of his own character, thereby reinscribing his identity as a Paris-figure. Male weakness and inflated self-importance are both laid at the door of the male character and his creators, where they belong.

116. On *Star Trek* fan fiction, and its almost exclusively female authorship, see Lichtenberg et al. 1975: ch. 9; Bacon-Smith 1992: ch. 6; Tulloch & Jenkins 1995: ch. 10; H. Jenkins 2013: ch. 5.

117. One early story centers on the crew's young female relatives at school together ("Once Upon a Star Trek," by Sam and The Locos, *Storyteller* p. 40); another concerns a race of aliens that has four sexes and three genders ("The Rainbird," by Astrid Anderson and Dorothy Jones, *T-Negative*, January 1971, p. 16).

118. H. Jenkins 2013: 167–68.

119. Graf 1994: 30.

120. Graf 1994: 27.

"Elaan of Troyius" is one of the few pop-cultural receptions of Helen that grasps the nettle of her transgressive identity by showing her violating moral norms valued not merely by the ancient Greeks, but by the target viewership. In its way, it maintains the delicate Helenic balance between desirability and transgression, agency and victimhood. The Elaan of *Firestorm*, in contrast, leaves behind both victimhood and love spells. Female power as such is neither eroticized nor presented as a threat inherent in female beauty. The novel's reclaiming of Elaan seems therefore to come at the expense of Helen's mythical identity as an icon of female beauty and erotic transgression. If she embodies in her essence the problem of women under patriarchy (for both women and men), then a fantasy world transcending patriarchy has no place for her. *Firestorm* frees Elaan of Troyius from her ridiculous female trappings: but without them, what remains of Helen of Troy?

She Was Xena

The year following *Firestorm*'s publication saw the debut of a show offering Helen a very different kind of rehabilitation. Like *Star Trek*'s Original Series, *Xena: Warrior Princess* promoted a politically progressive vision, in this case purportedly of the ancient past rather than the future, but really of a fantastical world transcending time and place.[121] The show ranges freely through that world, providing wildly revisionist narratives that reveal Xena's remarkable but previously unknown role in history and legend.

The titular warrior princess, played by New Zealander Lucy Lawless, was a third-wave heroine for the "girl power" era. Though introduced as a "hero" at the start of each episode by the usual sonorous male voice-over, this hero's pronouns are emphatically female: "*She* was Xena."[122] Though not technically an Amazon, as a warrior woman whose "masculinity" challenges the patriarchal status quo, Xena is, in essence, a reclaimed Amazon princess in the tradition of Wonder Woman.[123] This also makes her, in a sense, *Star*

121. On Xena's relationship to antiquity, see Futrell 2003; Blondell 2005. For the temporal breadth of her world, see Frankel 2018: 115–16, 125. On the show's postmodern, intertextual play with time, myth, and history as storytelling, see Gwenllian-Jones 2000; Lowe 2009: 228; Willis 2017: 112–15.

122. Cf. Haydee Smith 2018: 208.

123. Blondell 2005: 202–4. The Amazons were appropriated early by both modern feminism and speculative fiction (cf. Staley 2006: 228–30; Hall & Stead 2020: 385) and play a prominent role in *XWP* fandom (Gwenllian-Jones 2000: 410–13).

Trek's Elaan unleashed. When we first meet her, in *Hercules: The Legendary Journeys*, Xena, like Elaan, is a stereotypically manipulative femme fatale, who uses her erotic appeal to create strife between male buddies united by a tight homosocial bond. Like Elaan, she wears a variety of sexy costumes, some armored, some more "feminine." Like the unreconstructed Elaan, she is mean, rude, and bossy, "a hissing, spitting vixen who fears nothing."[124] She shares Elaan's propensity for violence, expressed via a facility with weapons that include a phallic knife. And, like Elaan, she has an exotic name, a multicultural style, and a touch of the superhuman.[125] She even eats chicken with her bare hands.

Like Elaan, as well, Xena is reformed by the love of (and for) a good man (Hercules). This time, however, it is the reformed woman who walks away from the amorous man, sacrificing romance to her heroic destiny. That destiny plays out in her self-titled spin-off show, which presents us with a Xena who has been thoroughly chastened, albeit in a very different way from *Star Trek*'s Elaan. Like the Elaan of *Firestorm*, she has learned to use her "masculine" power for good. In the opening credits the camera zeroes in on her body parts one by one, as it did when introducing *Star Trek*'s Elaan; but it is to show her actively buckling on her armor, piece by piece. She still scowls in contempt, like the unreconstructed Elaan; but her anger is righteous. Unlike the domesticated Elaan, moreover, she retains her erotic freedom. Like "Tomcat" Kirk, she has sequential lovers of the "opposite" sex, while maintaining a primary relationship with her same-sex buddy Gabrielle.[126] Above all, as the hero who returns every week, Xena is no mere disposable female, but

124. van Hise 1998: 192.

125. Her name was chosen because the letter X is "mysterious and evocative" (van Hise 1998: 42; cf. Weisbrot 1998: 6). Her war cry was "based on Arabic women ululating" (Abrams 2016). Her weaponry and fighting style are exoticized via Asian martial arts traditions and her signature weapon, the chakram (an ancient Indian weapon) (van Hise 1998: 164–65; Weisbrot 1998: 1, 5–6, 19, 29; K. Hayes 2003: 6, 12, 15; cf. Tasker 1993: 23–26). She has a multicultural backstory (Kennedy 2003: 41) and gets involved in myths worldwide (cf. K. Hayes 2003: 226–31). The show's theme music is also multicultural (K. Hayes 2003: 18–19).

126. Her male lovers include Hercules, Julius Caesar, Ulysses, and at least three entirely fictional characters: Petracles, the warlord Borias/Barias (the father of her son Solan) and Marcus, who is Black (van Hise 1998: 183–84; Helford 2000:150). This adds up to an exceptional degree of promiscuity for a positive female character (Strong 2018). On Xena and Gabrielle, see especially Kennedy 2003, and for the queering of the hero narrative, Haydee Smith 2018.

is endowed with the sustained authority and complexity of *the* hero at the center of the Xenaverse.[127]

As such, Xena often challenges and appropriates the great male heroes of the legendary past, many of whom appear as characters in the show. The most prominent of these is Odysseus. Amongst other things, in the episode "Ulysses," Xena displaces Penelope to become the canonical hero's true love and helps him to string his own bow. But the show is her *Iliad* as well as her *Odyssey*. Achilles himself is conspicuous by his absence from the show's dramatis personae, but he remains subtextually present in the destructive wrath that pervades the show, fueling not only Xena's principal enemies but the bad old Xena herself. This covert presence, signaled by Iliadic echoes, permits the reformed Xena to displace Achilles as the ultimate warrior-hero.[128] She does so not only by struggling against wrath and glory-lust in herself and others,[129] but also by embracing Achilles's pro-social aspects—his loyalty to friends (especially Patroclus) and his overwhelming remorse for harming them.[130] Meanwhile Gabrielle, the "bard" who shares her adventures, appropriates Homer's masculine privilege and cultural status to immortalize Xena by conveying her glory down through the centuries.[131]

The show also revisits ancient female characters, reclaiming notorious "bad" women like Pandora, Clytemnestra, Salome, and Cleopatra. Xena rescues these and also countless ordinary women from the physical and

127. Xena's character is unusually complex by any standard, as she wrestles with a "dark side" that remains essential to her heroism (Caudill 2003; Kennedy 2003: 43; cf. above, p. 184). J. Brown 2011: 61–62 notes the significance of the series format for making female characters into more than sex objects.

128. In "Rheingold," bad Xena offers her army an Achillean choice: "You can surrender and crawl back to your hovels and the everlasting scorn of your kinfolk, or you can go out in a blaze of glory!" Cf. the conversation in "Succession" about achieving immortality through fighting and remembrance. After she is reformed, allusions to Homer ascribe Achillean wrath to Xena's enemies. In "Kindred Spirits," one of Gabrielle's scrolls reads, "I sing the wrath of Callisto." In "Looking Death in the Eye," Joxer says (apparently of Xena), "She continued to sing the rage of her Olympian foes."

129. The series is peppered with characterizations of warfare as, for example, "No glory—no honor—just a monster that needed to be fed" ("A Good Day").

130. The most notorious such scene is the "Gab drag," when Xena drags the (living) Gabrielle behind her galloping horse, echoing Achilles's treatment of Hector's corpse ("The Bitter Suite"). For Achillean echoes in Xena's relationship to Gabrielle, see Breitenfeld 2023.

131. Gabrielle actually coaches the young Homer ("Athens City Academy of the Performing Bards"). She is also a role model for a poet named Virgil (in "Livia" and other episodes).

psychological oppressions (including self-oppression) of patriarchy. The chief beneficiary of this project is Gabrielle, a proxy for the viewer, who develops in the course of the series from a naive, innocent girl into the bearer of Xena's heroic legacy.[132] But the same narrative, writ small, structures many individual episodes, in which women learn to be more like Xena by making their own choices.[133] The show's sole Trojan War episode (season one, episode twelve) presents this theme *in nuce* with particular clarity, making the reimagined story of Helen of Troy, both as a "bad" woman and as the "essential feminine," programmatic for the series as a whole.[134]

Life Lesson Buffet

"Beware Greeks Bearing Gifts" opens on Helen asleep in her boudoir at Troy. We never find out quite how she got there. As usual, Menelaus's mediocrity justifies her unhappiness at Sparta, but we hear nothing about her decision to elope. At Troy, however, things are not going well. Paris is controlling and possessive. He has not tired of Helen sexually, but clearly no longer "loves" her—if he ever did. When the chips are down, and he plaintively protests, "I just wanted to love you," Helen answers, "No—You wanted to own me." At the start of the episode, then, she is a damsel in distress who needs rescuing, not from Menelaus but from Paris. Instead of turning to yet another man, however, she sends a plea for help to her old friend Xena. With that decision, she exits the age-old narrative of the helpless woman saved by the heroic male and embarks on a new kind of adventure.

To cut a long story short, Xena defeats Helen's many enemies (both Greek and Trojan) and ends up smuggling her out of the city in the Trojan Horse. This leaves Helen free to head off into the unknown, after requesting the

132. The filmmakers thought of Gabrielle as a character that the viewer could identify with, who was "traveling along for adventure but finding the hero in herself along the way" (Sears 2018: 221). Her skin (as well as her hair) is fairer than Xena's, to denote "innocence [and] purity" (Weisbrot 1998: 75). See further Weisbrot 1998: 26–28; K. Hayes 2003: 146–48. In "Gabrielle's Hope," she even becomes pregnant without experiencing sex, like the Virgin Mary, except that the father of her child is a demon (oops!).

133. E.g., "Cradle of Hope," "Warrior . . . Princess," "Here She Comes . . . Miss Amphipolis." Xena has a particular affinity for protecting and encouraging little girls (see especially "Little Problems").

134. The episode first aired January 15, 1996. It was directed by T. J. Scott and had multiple writers (Potter 2010: n. 13).

provisional, apparently non-romantic, escort of Gabrielle's ex-fiancé, a young man named Perdicus.[135] In a tradition going back to Euripides's *Helen*, her exceptionality is treated as a burden to be set aside with relief, as she declares her desire "to be treated like a normal person"—an anti-Achillean choice of "ordinary" life over renown. Unlike Euripides's Helen, however, her wish is granted. The episode concludes not with a reassertion of her beauty, her fame, or even her reputation, but the opposite. We will never find out what becomes of her. In rescuing her, Xena offers a new understanding of "feminine" power, leaving us with a Helen who is a blank slate for her own inscription rather than the inscription of men.

Before Helen can embrace this outcome, however, Xena must teach her what it is to be a "real" woman. In marked contrast to Kirk's tutelage of Elaan, Xena educates her protégée not by slaps and insults, barking orders, or even falling in love with her, but, like a therapist, by asking questions about her feelings.[136] When Xena first raises the idea of cutting loose from Troy, Helen asks:

HELEN: But, where would I go? What would I do?
XENA: What do you want to do?
HELEN: I don't know. No one's ever asked me that before.

Xena's questions allow Helen to learn from experience and seek her destiny on her own terms. The next time she asks, "What's next for you?" Helen replies, "I don't know. But for the first time, it's my decision." Using a self-help cliché, she announces that she has learned, "The only person that can make me happy is me." Xena thus restores to Helen the self-determination of which so many of her defenders have deprived her, granting her freedom, autonomy, and maybe even a chance at happiness.

This plot trajectory helps to explain why Helen's role in her own elopement—a seemingly crucial plot point—is never spelled out. If she is only now *learning* to act, under Xena's guidance, then she must never really have exercised agency in the past. If she "chose" to go with Paris, this must not have been

135. There is no indication of romance between Perdicus and Helen, but fans toyed with the idea of "shipping" them, i.e., treating them as a couple (*Xena: Warrior Podcast* episode six: 1x11–12). Cf. also Textbard's fan fiction *Between the Lines* 1.12: "The War of the Exes," Academy of Bards, accessed October 12, 2020, http://www.academyofbards.org/fanfic/t/texbard_thewaroftheexes.html.

136. Cf. the psychotherapeutic reimagining of Hercules in *HLJ* (Blondell 2005).

a real choice, even if she thought at the time that she "loved" him. This renders the question of her culpability moot, leaving the episode's writers in a delicate position. If the script asserted that she went willingly with Paris, that would problematize her status as a victim (who has never before been asked what she wants) and weaken the message of empowerment (which indicates that she is making her own choices for the first time). On the other hand, if it insisted that Paris took her against her will, that would eliminate the love narrative, which is important for other reasons.

Those reasons are not the usual ones. Romance is typically introduced into the Trojan War story as a way of defending Helen's elopement with Paris. But *Xena: Warrior Princess* is less interested in justifying her past than liberating her future. This explains why the shadowy background love narrative is needed: not to elicit our sympathy, but to enable its own repudiation. The episode's distinctive—and unprecedented—version of a happy ending for Helen results not simply from Xena's intervention, but from the radical narrative decision to free her from the romantic ideology clogging most modern renditions of her story. Paris is not the love of her life, but merely the second in a series of dysfunctional relationships (with an exceptionally unpleasant Deiphobus in line to be the third). Her love for him is not eternal, nor does it ultimately give meaning to the heroine's life. As different as this treatment of her story is from Korda's *Private Life*, it is the first we have seen since then to reject romantic closure, leaving Helen free at its conclusion to follow wherever her own desires may lead.[137]

Xena: Warrior Princess is far from opposed to "love" per se. The relationship between Xena and Gabrielle, though scarcely conventional, is deeply romantic (there is much talk of "soul mates"). But the refusal of the clichés of heteronormative romantic love in "Beware Greeks Bearing Gifts" is consistent with other episodes, which, for example, make fun of the idea of love at first sight ("Many Happy Returns"). In "Beware Greeks," this critique is reinforced by Gabrielle and Perdicus's backstory, which is retconned (or reinvented) in a way that diverges from the show's opening episode.[138] There Perdicus appears

137. Not coincidentally, both these versions also show Helen's disillusionment with Paris, echoing the *Iliad* in a way that is very rare for modern popular treatments.

138. This retcon is discussed in *Xena: Warrior Podcast*, episode six. The relationship reappears in "Return of Callisto," in which Perdicus says they "weren't ready" back then, and Gabrielle declares that she fell in love with him at Troy. She marries him, but he is immediately killed by Callisto. This leaves fan fiction to explain that Gabrielle was never "really" in love with Perdicus.

as Gabrielle's arranged fiancé, whom she abandons to go with Xena. Gabrielle informs us explicitly that she does not love Perdicus: she thinks him "dull and stupid" and cannot stand the thought of marrying him. In "Beware Greeks," however, he is played by a new and (fans agree) "much hotter" actor.[139] When they remeet at Troy, Gabrielle tells him, "Those days are over. I'm not a lovesick kid anymore." Perdicus explains that he came to Troy because he had "heard stories about Helen and Paris" and liked the idea of fighting for love, and she replies, "That's all they were—stories."

These deflating words serve to correct not only Perdicus's idealism but Gabrielle's own (and presumably the viewer's) romantic eagerness, expressed at the outset, to see Troy and "the face that launched a thousand ships." The Marlowe line alerts us that the episode is self-consciously rewriting not just any legend, but the most canonical of all.[140] This rewriting is one that decidedly repudiates the epic splendor of the Trojan War. Unlike Gabrielle, Xena is grimly opposed to visiting the city, and when they get there, it turns out to be shockingly inglorious (dark, dirty, and surrounded by skeletons and torture victims). In Helen's words, it is "a city of misery and death." The warriors on both sides (with the exception of the romantic outsider Perdicus) are all equally repellent. There is no sign of Achilles, or of Hector (usually the appealing family man), leaving both these central heroic roles available for Xena's appropriation.[141] She is both the greatest warrior of the Trojan War and the champion of the vulnerable at Troy, especially its women. The latter are represented exclusively by Helen, who carries the full burden of female suffering in war, as both the prize and the price of male glory (there is no sign of Hecuba, Andromache, Cassandra or Briseis). Ethically speaking, this means the war is no longer between Greeks and Trojans but between women and men.

If Gabrielle's romantic view of the Trojan War is shown up as misguided, her vision of Helen's transcendent beauty, conjured by the Marlowe line, turns out to be equally so. When she asks Deiphobus (who has a nasty eugenicist

---

See, e.g., Textbard, *Between the Lines* 2.5: "Fall into Grace," AusXip, accessed October 12, 2020, http://ausxip.com/fanfiction/texbard/2_5_FallIntoGrace.htm. Cf. also Skelton 2010: 334.

139. Lady Business 2015.

140. As one fan puts it, the episode "automatically gains points" because it is about the "universally fascinating" Trojan War (Upperco 2013). Note that it begins, like the *Iliad,* in the tenth year of the war.

141. Agamemnon is also missing. In an earlier episode, "The Reckoning," Ares offered Xena the help of any warrior from history and she described Agamemnon, Hector, and Achilles as all "long gone" (a nod to the ancient trope that the best warriors die first).

streak) what he wants from her, his answer suggests that he lusts for the legend as much as the woman: "What does every man want from Helen of Troy?" But the episode does nothing to endorse the legend in question by (for example) using special effects to enhance the impact of Helen's beauty or highlighting her ties to divinity.[142] This Helen is a strictly mortal victim of strictly human mistreatment, trapped in the all-too-familiar human predicament of a loveless marriage. Her supreme beauty is a mere *eidolon*—an illusory image constructed by male desire and male storytelling traditions.

We have seen this humanizing move in other treatments of Helen's character. It is particularly striking, however, in a show that is generally pervaded with supernatural forces—none of which makes an appearance in this episode. Those forces include the goddess Aphrodite, a recurring character who embodies the vibrant pop culture stereotype of supernatural beauty—a type for whom "being unnoticed is *not* an option."[143] As played by Alexandra Tydings, Aphrodite is a Valley Girl bimbo, with the requisite long blonde hair and an extensive wardrobe of floating pink drapery, seemingly acquired at Victoria's Secret (plate 14). Given Helen's reputation, and personal kinship with this goddess, we might expect her to inspire similar treatment. We might hope, in pop-cultural terms, for a Babezilla: "A Really, Really, Hot Girl! A girl so hot, even if she was a city-wrecking monster, no man could be able to stop her because no one would want to destroy such a hottie."[144] What we get, however, is a thoroughly normalized Helen, who diverges not only from divinity but from "Greek" or any other signifiers of extraordinary beauty.

The role was played by Galyn Görg, a multiracial American actor and dancer whose background includes African American, Native American, Irish, and German, and who reads as racially indeterminate.[145] She was best known in this period as Nancy O'Reilly on *Twin Peaks* (1990) and Lt. Leora Maxwell

142. There is a temple of Aphrodite at Troy, but it is not specially linked with Helen and no gods take part in the story.

143. Superpower Wiki, "Supernatural Beauty," accessed December 12, 2019, http://powerlisting.wikia.com/wiki/Supernatural_Beauty. On Aphrodite in *XWP* and *HLJ*, see Maurice 2019: 116–17.

144. Urban Dictionary, "Babezilla," accessed September 1, 2016, http://www.urbandictionary.com/define.php?term=Babezilla.

145. Her profile on Backstage stipulated that she could play characters of the following ethnicities: "African Descent, Ethnically Ambiguous / Mixed Race, African American, Caucasian, Native American, Southeast Asian / Pacific Islander." Backstage, "Galyn Görg," accessed December 11, 2019, https://www.backstage.com/galyngorg/.

on *M.A.N.T.I.S.*, television's first Black superhero show (1994–1995). She has often been cast in exoticized telefantasy roles,[146] but unlike the multiracial Nuyen in *Star Trek*, she is both humanized and normalized in the role of Helen. Her dark curly hair, light brown skin, and strong features are not used to render her exotic, alien, or evil. Nor are her looks enhanced by any of the clichés marking dark beauty as mysterious, sinister, and/or seductive. In combination with her demeanor and costume, they suggest, rather, the 1990s trend towards ethnic diversity, simplicity, and naturalness.[147]

Our first glimpse of Görg departs markedly from the kind of self-consciously staged introduction used so strikingly in "Elaan of Troyius." The camera glides intrusively in on an anonymous, passive, sleeping female figure, who is suffering nightmares about fighting (to which we are privy). Her identity is never announced (we hear her name voiced by a warrior in her dream). When she wakes in terror, we get our first close-up of her face (figure 5.7). Görg's hair and makeup are natural-looking in the role, her skin and hair seeming no darker or lighter than their natural tone. Her Blackness—or better, her non-whiteness—is neither enhanced nor denied, but treated as "normal"—that is, devoid of exoticizing signifiers. She is wearing a simple white nightgown, modest in cut, which suggests purity and innocence, as opposed to power, status, or passion.[148] Her appearance is explicitly marked as unglamorous, when snarky Paris comments that the nightmares "rob you of your beauty." Even fully dressed she appears innocent and unthreatening, thanks to simply styled hair, a long, chaste, white gown, and restrained jewelry.[149] When she speaks, her ordinariness is reinforced by Görg's American accent (which renders her unique among the Helens in this book).

Helen's boudoir is, to be sure, replete with the accoutrements of femininity. But they are presented as constraints imposed by men, not a source of power to be used against them. We view her in bed through a visually confining tent

146. She played the Egyptian Princess Anuket in the *HLJ* episode "Mummy Dearest," Kendra in *Stargate*, and a couple of *Star Trek* aliens. More recently, she starred as a heavily exoticized fortune-teller in the web series *Miss Gigi*.

147. Cf. de Castelbajac 1995: 167–84. This was a period when, in pop culture, typically "the blonde is the star, while the brunette is either the best friend or the antagonist" (Mulshine 2015).

148. White was intentionally avoided for *XWP* costuming except for special cases, like Gabrielle's wedding dress (Weisbrot 1998: 55) and Xena's rebirth from villainy (Lodge 2009: 224).

149. Contrast, e.g., the elaborate attire and reverential treatment of the Princess Diana (Lawless) in "Warrior . . . Princess," or Penelope's regal gold dress in "Ulysses."

FIGURE 5.7. Our first close-up view of Helen in the *Xena: Warrior Princess* episode "Beware Greeks Bearing Gifts."

of net-like fabric, where she tosses and turns on the kind of luxurious pillows that so disgusted Elaan. The cry for help that she sends Xena takes the form of a tiara (through which we shall be tracing her personal growth). Later the camera moves in on her stone-walled beauty bath of milk and rose petals as if it were a luxurious prison cell, transforming the sexy bathtub cliché into a site of oppression (figure 5.8). The trope of the mirror as an emblem of vanity is also reconfigured. When we first see Helen at her toilette, she wears not a narcissistic smile but a look of despair; her eyes are cast down, and the mirror that frames her face exemplifies the constraint of the feminine (figure 5.9). But then, ta-da! Xena materializes behind her, opening up the imprisoning frame (figure 5.10).

By the end of the episode, the trappings of feminine beauty have been turned against the men who treated Helen as a mere object. Xena will toss one warrior headfirst onto Helen's pillows, and dump another unceremoniously into the bath of milk and roses. As for that tiara, Xena transfers it from Helen's head to that of the unconscious Deiphobus. In the final scene, Helen's new-found autonomy is signified by a plain black cloak which covers her white dress completely, enabling her to hide or display her body at will. She is empowered to take charge of her own to-be-looked-at-ness, and chooses, for the moment, to withhold it. This encourages us to think of her as a woman with

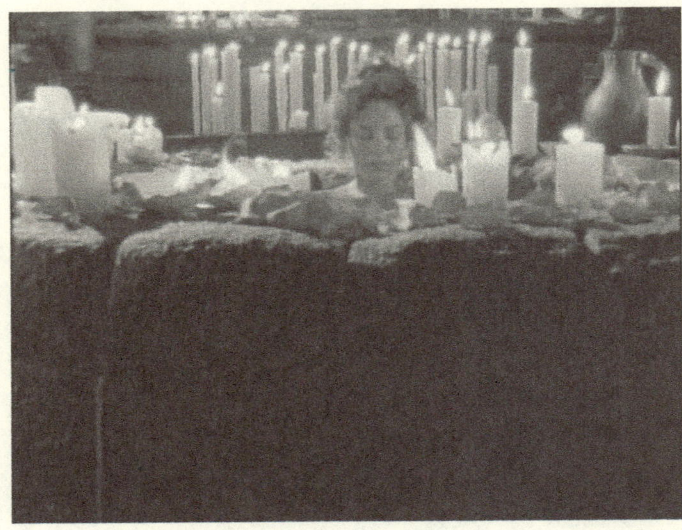

FIGURE 5.8. Helen in her bath in "Beware Greeks Bearing Gifts."

FIGURE 5.9. Helen at her mirror in "Beware Greeks Bearing Gifts."

the potential for strength and autonomy, who may make what use she wishes of her body and its appearance.

Helen's empowerment is reinforced by aligning her visually with the warrior princess herself, who also has dark, strong features, natural-looking makeup, and dark, disheveled, shoulder-length hair. If the figure of Helen normalizes

FIGURE 5.10. Xena appears in Helen's mirror in "Beware Greeks Bearing Gifts."

the racial Other, that of Xena exoticizes the white feminine norm, each in her own way straddling the line between strange and familiar. The Caucasian Lucy Lawless has reassuringly blue eyes, but her light brown hair was dyed black for the role and a sponge-on tan produces a skin tone virtually identical with Görg's.[150] The appearance of Xena in Helen's mirror spotlights the resemblance, even to the smile and slightly tilted head (figure 5.10). Their outfits are also alike, if we look beyond the obvious differences of color and fabric to consider the gold curlicues on Xena's armor, the formfitting nature of both costumes, and of course the bust-enhancing cut (figure 5.11). This similarity grows in the course of the episode, as Helen's dress is gradually accessorized with an armor-like corset and shoulder-pieces that echo Xena's own attire, suggesting that she has the potential to take control of her life, to become strong and independent by modelling herself on the Warrior Princess.[151]

"Beware Greeks" was the highest rated episode of season one.[152] One viewer calls Helen "a real dud" compared to the show's many strong female

150. Lawless said she loved the dye job because people found it intimidating (A. Jacobs 1995: 86; van Hise 1998: 169, who also mentions the tan).

151. Cf. the way Gabrielle's costume develops along with her character. It is hard to imagine Helen ululating and kicking ass, but she does jab Deiphobus with her elbow.

152. K. Hayes 2003: 236.

FIGURE 5.11. Helen with Xena in "Beware Greeks Bearing Gifts."

characters.[153] Another finds the normalized Helen "not as beautiful as she should be."[154] For the most part, however, fans of a show known for its self-conscious subversion of traditional myths, and for challenging gender stereotypes in particular, are not concerned with what Helen "really" looked like or how many ships she can launch. They care about dethroning "Greek" beauty and its oppressive baggage. The light-skinned Görg can easily be read as many different ethnicities, but none of them conveys a stereotypically "Greek" or

153. *Xena: Warrior Podcasts*, episode twelve. For more audience responses to the episode, see Potter 2010: 99–111.

154. Anon. n.d.c.

"classical" conception of beauty. One viewer notes approvingly, "She's not presented as a flaxen-haired bimbo, but rather as an earthy Mediterranean type."[155] Others, presumably aware of her Blackness from her prior roles, praise the fact that "a black woman is considered to be the pinnacle of beauty."[156] One remarks, "Galyn Gorg is skinny as usual, but she's dark-haired, brown-eyed and black which makes a very pleasant change."[157] Another calls the casting of a woman of color in this particular role "a really great trailblazing moment."[158] Viewers also applaud the feminist take on Helen's story. As one blog notes with satisfaction, the episode is "a life lesson buffet for everyone but the evil white dudes, who end up empty handed and/or dead."[159] Because of its message of empowerment, Ms. Magazine declared it "a feminist ending for The Iliad."[160]

The Ultimate Woman

When Xena mentions to Gabrielle that she and Helen have "had our differences in the past," this is easy to interpret as a romantic relationship gone awry. Unsurprisingly, in fan fiction, Helen becomes one of Xena's many exes, thereby challenging Helen's traditional role as the ultimate female object/subject of specifically heterosexual desire. In one story, Xena's recollection of the affair becomes instrumental in her coming out to Gabrielle, demoting the acme of classical beauty to a mere stepping-stone in the show's radical reinvention of "true love." [161] Yet *Xena: Warrior Princess* does not deny the significance of what Helen stands for, namely the power of transcendent female beauty. That essence is, rather, transferred to Xena herself.

As we have seen, Helen echoes Xena visually, in appearance and costume, in a way that suggests her potential for Xena-like autonomy. By the same token,

155. Upperco 2013.

156. Lady Business 2015.

157. Harrisson 2011.

158. *Xena: Warrior Podcast*, episode six.

159. Lady Business 2015.

160. Minkowitz 1996.

161. See Textbard, *The War of the Exes*, Academy of Bards, accessed October 10, 2020, http://www.academyofbards.org/fanfic/t/texbard_thewaroftheexes.html. Elsewhere, Gabrielle's desire for Xena is spurred on by the sight of her having sex with Helen, in maria_eshu's *Karmic Evolution*, Archive of Our Own, accessed April 30, 2019, https://archiveofourown.org/works/10918638.

these similarities encourage us to view Xena as a new and improved incarnation of Helen of Troy. In narrative terms, Xena displaces Helen as the war's most influential female figure in a way that reverses the ancient story's gender dynamics. Like Helen she is a Greek woman who goes to Troy, but she does so as a savior, not a victim or transgressor. She even repurposes the Trojan Horse for feminism. In antiquity, the Horse, which penetrates male defenses with ruinous consequences, is a symbolic equivalent of Helen herself.[162] In *Xena: Warrior Princess* this is reversed by a beneficent use of the Horse, now equated with Xena, who comes and goes as she pleases, making light of the barriers erected by men. Salvation comes not from the Horse's penetration of the city with its burden of warriors, but from its departure, carrying a victimized woman to safety. This twist further reconfigures the Horse's significance as a birth image, making the pregnant body a bearer of safety instead of destruction.

If the legendary Greek heroine has become an ordinary woman, confined like so many others to a single episode, Xena's legendary status is further burnished with every passing week, making her, among other things, a new icon of the supremely desirable, erotically assertive woman. Intended from the outset to convey beauty, sensuality, and charisma, the character was marketed as "every man's fantasy."[163] Within the show, males are drawn to her inexorably, sometimes coming to blows over her (as Hercules and his buddy did in *Hercules: The Legendary Journeys*). Her most aggressive suitor is the god Ares, whose persistent desire positions Xena as an Aphrodite figure.[164] Unlike the goddess or her protégée, however, Xena is—albeit "subtextually"—an icon of beauty and desire for women as well as men.[165] She thus appropriates the role

162. For associations between Helen and the Horse, see Day 2022.

163. Weisbrot 1998: 7; Magoulick 2006: 744. Promotion included sexy cover shots and photospreads of Lawless along with interviews in magazines including *Playboy* (May 1997), *Maxim* (April 1999, August 1999), *Rolling Stone* (October 1998) and *Stuff For Men* (June/July 2000). A video game spin-off "was marketed with the challenge 'Are you MAN Enough to Control the Princess Warrior [sic]?'" (J. Brown 2011: 118).

164. In antiquity, Ares and Aphrodite are notorious lovers, but in *XWP* their relationship is firmly that of siblings. Xena's association with water is also Venus-like (e.g., in "Altared States"). She even becomes a Celtic goddess of sex ("The God You Know"). Note too that it is she, instead of Aphrodite, to whom Helen bears an iconic likeness (cf. above, p. 61).

165. The filmmakers were fully aware of the show's homoerotic "subtext." Although no sexual activity between Xena and Gabrielle is ever shown explicitly, their relationship is openly presented as an ideal love partnership.

of the "essential" feminine in a way that challenges the normative heterosexuality for which Helen typically stands.

Though Xena refuses to be constricted by female trappings, she does not abandon "feminine" decorations, wiles, or skills.[166] Her day-to-day costume may be more robust than the typical action heroine's clinging catsuit, but it remains quite sexy and revealing.[167] She replaces it, moreover, as occasion demands, with countless sexualized disguises, including exotic dancer, concubine, eroticized "sex-slave," sexy pirate queen, and Cleopatra stand-in (complete with braids and bathtub).[168] Like the sword and the chakram, femininity is one of many weapons at her disposal, to be picked up or dropped, as necessary, in the crusade against evil. In one episode she even goes undercover at a beauty pageant, where she provides a humorously conspicuous performance of the feminine, complete with gold dress and long blond wig, set to the song "A Woman's a Natural Thing" (figure 5.12).[169] Such episodes mock the construction of female beauty, yet the significance of such beauty is never denied. Aphrodite, as the embodiment of stereotypical femininity, displays its capriciousness for our amusement.[170] But its power is real, and is ultimately a force for good.

Yet Xena is not limited to the Helenic functions of object and subject of desire: she performs a whole spectrum of female gender roles, including daughter, mother, and spouse.[171] She is even a Madonna figure, mysteriously

166. Cf. Tigges 2017: 142–43. In the episode preceding "Beware Greeks," Xena shows her skill at embroidery ("The Black Wolf"), giving rise to the catchphrase "I have many skills," which became a running joke (van Hise 1998: 209; cf. 188).

167. Cf. G. Knight 2010: 324. The characterization of Xena as "butch" in comparison with the girlish Gabrielle (e.g., Helford 2000: 149–57) is strictly relative. They are, more accurately, a "neo-femme dyad" (Haydee Smith 2018: 2010). Xena's sexualization has distressed some (e.g., Magoulick 2006: 744), but neither male nor female heroism has ever shunned physical beauty and its display (cf. Tigges 2017: 136–38). On the tensions inherent in the sexualization of action heroines, see further J. Brown: 2011.

168. "Cradle of Hope," "Royal Couple of Thieves," "Who's Gurkhan," "Destiny," "Antony and Cleopatra."

169. "Here She Comes . . . Miss Amphipolis." Xena would have been the pageant winner, but when she steps aside, the final winner is a trans woman (Miss Artifice).

170. The idea of irresistible beauty is mocked elsewhere in the show, especially in "Fins, Femmes and Gems," where Joxer dons a frothy pink dress belonging to the delusional Gabrielle, who dubs herself (among other things) "Gabrielle of Troy."

171. Her fulfilment of these roles is unconventional, to say the least, but it is both heartfelt and transformative. On Xena's vexed relation to maternity, see Lodge 2009.

FIGURE 5.12. Xena participating in a beauty pageant in the *Xena: Warrior Princess* episode "Here She Comes . . . Miss Amphipolis."

impregnated with the help of an angel by a higher power known as the "god of light" ("Fallen Angel").[172] Her range is expanded still further by casting Lawless as various Xena lookalikes, notably the ditzy princess Diana, Meg the "tramp," and a priestess named Leah.[173] Each of these personas represents a different type of woman, who makes "different sexual lifestyle and relationship choices."[174] Their physical identity makes Lawless's body the site for a stream of variations on a theme. In "Warrior . . . Priestess . . . Tramp" she plays not only Leah, but "Meg playing Leah, Xena playing Leah, Leah playing Xena and even Leah playing Meg playing Leah."[175]

Yet these "official" doubles are just the tip of the iceberg. Xena's multiple identities transcend the bounds of time, bodily integrity, sex, and gender.

172. Her new (girl) baby, Eve, appears to receive a visit from the Magi, one of whom is female ("Eternal Bonds").

173. "Warrior . . . Princess," "Warrior . . . Princess . . . Tramp," "Warrior . . . Priestess . . . Tramp." On these identities, see K. Hayes 2003: 204–5.

174. Strong 2018: 141; cf. Inness 1999: 174–75.

175. K. Hayes 2003: 83.

Lawless appears not only as Xena and her ancient lookalikes but as a sheltered, scholarly Southern Belle in 1940 ("Xena Scrolls"), and a modern clone of the ancient Xena ("Send in the Clones"). She appears in alternate worlds and/or timelines to become, in one episode, the wife of Julius Caesar and Empress of Rome ("When Fates Collide"), in another a peaceful version of herself ("Remember Nothing"). "Xena" may herself occupy other bodies, as diverse as her nemesis Callisto, Arminestra (an old Indian woman known as the Mother of Peace), and a motherless little girl.[176] In "Succession," she even shares a body with Gabrielle. It is with considerable justification, then, that Xena dubs herself, however humorously, "the ultimate woman" ("Kindred Spirits"). As such, her spirit can empower any woman, be she Helen of Troy or the little girl whom Xena tells to "look in the mirror" if she wants to see her again ("Little Problems").

Paradoxically, this new embodiment of "the feminine" is produced by deconstructing the very notion of essential gender identity.[177] Xena can disguise herself convincingly as a man when necessary ("Many Happy Returns"), but her gender-bending goes well beyond mere role playing. In "The Quest," her spirit, freed from her dead body, enters that of Autolycus (a comic male character), with whom she competes for control of the body in question. The show's ultimate moment of defiance—of time, space, and gender—locates that spirit in the body of a twentieth-century man named Harry (played by Ted Raimi, a.k.a. Joxer), who is the boyfriend of an *XWP* fan named Annie (played by Lawless), who is herself a reincarnation not of Xena but of Joxer ("Deja Vu All Over Again"). If she is a reinvented Madonna, she is also a Christ-figure, repeatedly crucified and resurrected, who becomes the champion of humankind when she takes on and defeats the Olympian gods.[178] She is not only the "ultimate woman," then, but the ultimate (super)human being.

Where does all this leave Helen of Troy? Traditionally, as the male construction of the "essential feminine," she exists as something for men to fight over (physically) or against (psychologically). "Beware Greeks" repudiates this image, unmasking "the most beautiful woman" as a creature of the male

176. "Intimate Strangers," "Ten Little Warlords," "Between the Lines," "Little Problems."

177. On *XWP*'s subversive use of gender masquerade and parody, see Morreale 1998; Sweet 2007; J. Brown 2011: ch. 3 and cf. J. Butler 1990: 174–77, 186–88; Clark 1989: 131–32.

178. Other Christlike features include defeating Satan and resisting temptation by the Satanic Ares to rule the world with him.

imagination. Like *Firestorm,* the episode erases that *eidolon* under the aegis of a particular brand of 1990s feminism. But *Firestorm* replaced the Elaan of *Star Trek* with a warrior whose power was exclusively "masculine," abandoning the association between women's power and erotic beauty—the very premise of Helen's existence. In *Xena: Warrior Princess,* Helen is again displaced by a warrior heroine, but one who restores feminine beauty to a position of power and puts it to work as just one weapon in her arsenal. At the same time, the show presents Helen herself as a new kind of "essential" woman, a figure not for male fear, but for female identification. Beneath the mask imposed by male fantasy lies a new Everywoman, one embodying the victimization that is the essence of woman under patriarchy. Unmasked, that victim is revealed as a blank slate, free to invent herself, drawing inspiration from the overflowing menu of Xena's identities.

6

Not the BBC Version

HELEN OF TROY (2003)

The Greatest Story Ever Told

The revival of ancient world epic at the turn of the twenty-first century is usually credited to Ridley Scott's *Gladiator*. Yet Scott's blockbuster was anticipated by a flurry of "epic" miniseries on the small screen, which was (not coincidentally) no longer quite so small. Classical offerings included both the "historical," like *Cleopatra* (Fox, 1999), *Attila* (USA, 2001), *Julius Caesar* (TNT, 2003), and *Spartacus* (USA, 2004), and the "mythic," such as *The Odyssey* (NBC, 1997) and *Jason and the Argonauts* (NBC, 2000).[1] As a historical tale with mythic elements, *Helen of Troy* has a foot in each camp. Directed by the Canadian John Kent Harrison for USA, a widely watched basic cable network, *Helen* debuted in two ninety-minute parts (two hours each with commercials), at 8pm on April 20 and 21, 2003. After frequent rotation on USA, it was released on DVD as a three-hour film in two parts, just three months after its premiere.

This kind of miniseries is a poor stepsister of the big screen epic extravaganza. As "event-status programming," however, it is more "cinematic"—and thus more "culturally respectable"—than standard TV fare, and much more expensive and spectacular.[2] Though designed, like all commercial TV of the period, to appeal to as many demographics as possible (especially within the coveted 19–49 age group), they also served as "loss leader

1. For the history of the ancient world miniseries, see Solomon 2001: 17; Solomon 2008.

2. The quoted phrase is from Ellis 1992: 116. See further Caldwell 1995: ch. 6; Schulze 1990: 357–58.

showcases," designed to confer cultural prestige on both network and audience.[3] Such prestige was enhanced by harking back to the glory days of the 1950s. Promotion for *Helen* included "epic" taglines ("Desire is War"), a TV Special entitled *Making the Epic,* and a grandiose press kit housed in a faux-leather box. As with the extravaganzas of the Cold War period, publicity claimed both veracity and revisionism,[4] authenticity and originality,[5] "timelessness" and contemporary relevance.[6] More recent cinematic features, like *Gladiator*, were also invoked (for example in *Making the Epic*). The exceptionally grand press kit looks suspiciously similar to the brochure for *Troy*, and publicity sometimes suggests a preemptive challenge to the Brad Pitt vehicle.[7] This Achilles, we are told, will not be a "golden boy" but a "mean, hard-bitten guy."[8]

The network also staked a different kind of claim to epic significance. For fifty years the cultural cachet, "family" decorum, and Christian message of biblical epic had prompted regular re-screenings on television, especially at holiday times. Premiering on Easter Sunday 2003, part one of *Helen of Troy* faced off against the traditional fare of Cecil B. DeMille's *Ten Commandments* on ABC. This prestigious viewing slot positioned it as a grand, potentially uplifting ancient tale appropriate for holiday viewing, while offering a fresher, more contemporary alternative for anyone who had sat through Charlton Heston's Moses one too many times. *Making the Epic* even challenges the primacy of Christianity itself by calling *Helen* "the greatest story ever told"—a phrase

3. Caldwell 1995: 162.

4. In his opening voice-over, Menelaus promises to tell "the real story," which he "knows" because he "was there." (He does not introduce himself, but the mythically informed will identify him from his reference to Agamemnon as "my brother.")

5. "People have heard of it but don't know the real tale . . . We're going to show them the real thing" (Murphy 2003: 12). The producer Ted Kurdyla declared, "No one will have ever have seen [the invasion of Troy] in any movie they've ever seen on the screen" (*Making the Epic*).

6. The director says he "contemporized" the film by casting "energetic, youthful, really fun people" and calls Helen "the first official trophy wife" (*Making the Epic*). Cast members emphasized the "contemporary relevance" of "the emotions and forces which act on a person" as "universal . . . something we can all relate to" (Hart 2003).

7. The miniseries was released a year before *Troy* but the two shows were in production at the same time. *Helen*'s screenwriter, Ronni Kern, was oblivious to *Troy* (personal communication), and *Troy*'s director claimed not to have seen the miniseries (Winkler 2015c: 19). But publicity and public comment often place the two in dialogue.

8. Hart 2003.

familiar to audiences as the title of a 1965 epic about the life of Christ, which flopped in theaters but became another Easter staple.[9]

The *New York Times* opined that since "this pagan saga is played out during Easter week" it "might make monotheistic viewers feel a little superior."[10] But for those in whom monotheism induced different feelings, *Helen* promised pleasures of another kind. The trailer makes clear—briefly but unambiguously—that we will be seeing Helen fully naked. Explicit nudity was a gamble for TV, since it moved the program away from "family" viewing towards "adult" status.[11] By the same token, however, it might serve as what journalists variously referred to as "USA's Trojan horse in the ratings war," "icing on the ratings cake," or the show's "secret weapon."[12] The miniseries was, in addition, "about as bloody as TV gets."[13] Classical antiquity remained a useful alibi in both areas, since, in the words of the *New York Times*, it "gives cable producers a high-brow reason to deliver lust and bloodshed in one extravagant package."[14]

For *Helen*'s scriptwriter, however, lust and bloodshed were themselves a kind of alibi. As a genre, the ancient world miniseries was distinctly masculinist.[15] Unusually, however, *Helen*'s script was written by a woman, and one who was a committed feminist.[16] Born in 1947, Ronni Kern came of age side by side with "second-wave" feminism. She began her career writing feature films but was frustrated by their focus on men, and switched to long-form TV because this was "an arena in which women's stories were not merely tolerated but desired."[17] She had already taken "unconventional, female-centered looks" at women in, for example, the Bible (*Solomon and Sheba*, 1995) and Arthurian

9. See further Forshey 1992: 94–104; Babington & Evans 1993: ch. 7; Hall & Neale 2010: 179.

10. Martel 2003; cf. Owen 2003.

11. Boedeker 2003.

12. McFarland 2003; Shales 2003; Martel 2003.

13. Rosenberg 2003.

14. Martel 2003.

15. *The Odyssey* (1997), for example, has remarkably "reactionary sexual politics" considering its date (E. Hall 2013: 169).

16. IMDb supplies no other female writing credits for any of the ancient world miniseries listed above, with the exception of Margaret George, who is given writing credit on IMDb for *Cleopatra* (supposedly based on her novel).

17. Until quite recently TV was widely thought of as a "feminine" medium, thanks to such mainstay "women's" genres as TV movies (Schulze 1990; Rapping 1992; Gitlin 2000: ch. 9) and soap opera (see further below, p. 229). Quotations from Kern are from my interview with her conducted on September 20, 2016, or from personal correspondence around that time.

legend (*Guinevere*, 1994).[18] Working for USA was, in Kern's words, "very much like working for a frat house," since it was "a guys' network." But she had learned from writing *Solomon and Sheba* for Dino De Laurentiis that "if you gave him enough sex and enough violence, you could do whatever you wanted."[19]

I Don't Want to Say Soap Opera

When USA contacted Kern about the new project, she had already given some thought to Helen, as another legendary woman who deserved a fresh look. She wanted, specifically, to rebut the "received wisdom" that Helen was a "wanton, fickle princess."[20] Adam Shapiro, the executive producer at USA, was open to her approach and, on the basis of a brief story idea, asked Kern to work up a script. He was excited by the idea of offering an "edgy" reinterpretation of a 1950s epic, which would "deconstruct the myth," and be, in his words, "not the BBC version" of the Trojan War.[21] At the same time, he insisted that it was not to be merely "a love story aimed at female viewers," but would have duels, "bloody war," and "Helen's naked backside" to attract men.[22] The trailer reassures us on this point by presenting a rapid montage of clips alternating war and peace, men and women, military and domestic themes.[23]

Part one opens with the trailer, then segues to the birth and exposure of Paris—who quickly grows up—followed by the Judgment, which occurs in a dream. When Aphrodite offers Paris a golden apple as a bribe, he sees Helen's face in it; at the same moment, she is privy to a vision of him gazing at her from the waters of a mountain pool near Sparta; they both fall instantly in love. Next comes Clytemnestra's marriage to Agamemnon, during which Helen is kidnapped by Theseus. After spending an indeterminate period of time with him

18. "Most of my scripts (made and unmade) were fairly revisionist/feminist takes on a whole slew of different women: Guinevere, Queen Esther, Mata Hari, even Lilith for Pete's sake."

19. In TV movies, "feminism and seriousness are sold through sex and violence" (Rapping 1992: 24; cf. Schulze 1990: 364–65). For the relative leeway granted to TV movies, especially on cable, see Read 2000: 159–60; Rapping 1992: 23.

20. Elias 2003.

21. Hart 2003.

22. Keveny 2003; cf. Murphy 2003: 12; Elias 2003.

23. Cf. Shillock 2011: 132.

at Athens, she is "rescued" (against her will) by her brother Pollux.[24] Both Theseus and Pollux are killed in the process, leaving Tyndareus heirless. This leads to the oath of the suitors and a lottery for Helen's hand, which is won, of course, by Menelaus. We then return to Troy, where Paris's identity is revealed and he is dispatched to Sparta on a peace mission. Helen saves him from the machinations of the Greeks (defamiliarized in the script as "Aegeans") but refuses to elope with him. As he casts off for Troy, however, she leaps impulsively into the water and swims to his departing ship. Part one ends with the sacrifice of Iphigenia.

Part two opens on Paris and Helen strolling on an idyllic beach while their ship undergoes repairs from storm damage. We then move to Troy, where the failed embassy of Menelaus and Odysseus is followed by an initial Greek assault. After a ten-year stalemate (indicated through Cassandra's prophetic vision), we witness two duels (Paris vs. Menelaus, then Achilles vs. Hector), Helen's attempt to give herself up, the death of Achilles, the ruse of the Wooden Horse, and the death of Paris. During the sack of Troy, Agamemnon brutally rapes Helen, thereby casting her in Cassandra's ancient role of archetypal wartime rape victim. Shortly afterwards, in another twist, Agamemnon is murdered by Clytemnestra, who has come to Troy for the purpose.[25] Part two ends with Helen's vision of the dead Paris, followed by a reunion—of sorts—with Menelaus. She bares her neck for his sword, but he declines to kill her; when she offers to "follow" him home, he replies, in the final words of the miniseries, "I accept."

This plot has a good deal in common with Wise's homonymous epic.[26] But Kern goes much further in feminizing the narrative, tilting it towards not only the love affair but a whole series of personal relationships that are instrumental in Helen's construction as a woman. She does this by filling out the masculine war narrative with stories tangential to the Trojan War legend (notably Theseus's abduction of Helen), plus tragic material highlighting female concerns. The war does not begin until part two, and even then, Helen

24. According to the press book, "several years" have passed. Castor was omitted for budgetary reasons.

25. Besides serving budgetary and narrative efficiency, relocating the death of Agamemnon to Troy allows Clytemnestra to transgress the boundaries of domesticity and deepens her relationship to Helen (discussed further below).

26. This was not intentional (Kern has no memory of seeing Wise's movie). For brief comparisons of the two, along with *Troy*, see Winkler 2009: 223–42; Martín-Rodríguez 2015: 219–21.

maintains narrative agency to an exceptional degree.[27] Other substantial female roles afford a greater-than-usual emphasis not only on the lives of women (of all ages) but on a broad range of personal relationships. It is true that Andromache is elided, but this allows Iphigenia (a little girl) to replace the little boy Astyanax as the war's iconic child victim, poignantly separated from her same-sex parent. Meanwhile, Andromache's grief for her husband is replaced by Priam's at the death of his wife.[28]

This shift of emphasis helps to blur the usual clear antithesis between Greece and Troy.[29] As in *Xena: Warrior Princess*, the central moral conflict is, in essence, between women and men. All the women, on both sides of the war, are innocent victims subjected to forms of male control that may at any moment become abuse. The Spartans are, to be sure, indicted by grape eating, greed, the presence of Black (presumably enslaved) servants, and other tokens of imperialistic decadence, whereas Troy shows an affinity for the "modern" values of respect, kindness, and compassion. Agamemnon is the undoubted villain of the piece, with the Trojan Paris the romantic hero. Yet the other Greek and Trojan men are not aligned collectively with vice or virtue. The Greek leaders are far more varied than they are even in *Troy*. Menelaus is younger and more sympathetic than usual; Theseus, the violent abductor, turns into a benign father figure; Helen's own brother becomes, in turn, a violent abductor when he "rescues" her against her will. [30]

Troy, conversely, is by no means a haven of admirable manhood. Hector, stripped of his usual role as the ideal husband and father, has a menacing patrician air and, when Paris's identity is revealed, treats his newfound brother with distrust and hostility. Priam, like Tyndareus, is a harsh patriarch. Despite his wife's anguished screams of protest, he has their baby son torn from her arms

27. Notably, it is she who comes to ransom Hector's body with her own. Her prominence is assisted by the absence of any central male action hero.

28. Nagle 2004.

29. This version does not pit a dark, ominous Greece against a more "civilized" Troy, but presents all three locations (Sparta, Athens, and Troy) as bright and appealing. For the unusually urban, panoramic view of Sparta, see Blank 2015: 70–71; it is somewhat more orientalized and "Roman" than the more "classical" Athens (Hanesworth 2015: 70–71), but its exteriors are light and pleasant—a "feminine" style, implicitly asserting the rights of female family members.

30. Cf. Faludi's discussion of "our oldest national myth, the rewrite with the happy ending in which we prevail over the terrorists and save the girl" (2007: 208). In reality, "the girl" often does not want to be rescued (Faludi 2007: ch. 8).

to be thrown to his death from a mountain peak. After Paris is rediscovered—and welcomed ecstatically by his mother—his father sends him to Sparta in the hope that he will meet his death there. As for Cassandra, her father confines her to her room—in the form of an unnecessarily nasty dungeon—for the crime of speaking out when she knows that she is right. Hers is the desperate voice of every adolescent girl who cries aloud unheard.

Shapiro, as producer, was defensive about *Helen*'s "feminine" appeal, demurring, "I don't want to say soap opera."[31] Soap opera is often invoked as "a symbol of the truly awful."[32] It is a metonym for low-status, "feminine" genres, from which more "serious" (i.e., masculine) shows are often anxious to distance themselves.[33] Nevertheless, Kern's dramatis personae do indeed evoke the ultra-dysfunctional families of prime-time soaps.[34] The plot is larded with personal interactions, and often conflict, between husbands and wives, parents and children, and siblings of both sexes. There is even an intimate battlefield conversation between Paris and Menelaus, which self-consciously rewrites a scene from the *Iliad*. In Homer, the goddess Aphrodite, after breaking Menelaus's sword and Paris's helmet strap, sweeps her favorite away from the battlefield in a mist; in the miniseries, the sword and helmet strap break unexpectedly, whereupon the two heroes, veiled in mist, sit and chat until Menelaus comes to see the error of his ways under his rival's therapeutic guidance.[35]

In keeping with this feminized Trojan War narrative, Helen's personal story is introduced with a romanticism that would be expected to appeal primarily to female viewers, especially teenagers. Despite the adult and masculine appeal of nudity and violence, in many respect the miniseries addresses an audience of adolescent girls. Like many a teen film, it centers on coming of age, first love, self-discovery, and rebellion against patriarchal authority.[36] The love affair that subtends these themes is presented as a fairy-tale romance, a genre

31. Hart 2003.

32. Brunsdon 1997: 22.

33. Modleski 2008: 78–79. See further Fiske 1987: ch. 10; Modleski 2008: ch. 4. Cf. also Denby's comment on *Troy* (above, p. 163).

34. For the centrality of the unhappy family to soaps and melodrama, see Ang 1985: 68–72; Modleski 2008: 85.

35. On the association of such discourse with women's genres and female audiences, see White 1992: 35–36. Cf. also above, p. 208.

36. On the teen film, see Neale 2000: 118–25; Driscoll 2002: 216–24.

culturally coded (and scorned) as both feminine and juvenile.[37] The way that Helen and Paris fall in love—at first sight, through divine intervention—literalizes the "magic" of Hollywood romance and marks the affair as "destined."[38] Helen is literally Paris's dream girl, and he literally her fantasy. In contrast both to the traditional story, which makes Helen a "gift" to Paris from Aphrodite, and to *Troy*'s stalkerish courtship by Paris, the mutuality of their silent gaze conveys the essence of romantic love: the "fantasy of oneness, therefore total and effortless communication and mutual understanding."[39] Such love transcends time. It begins before they have ever met or spoken and persists after death, when we share Helen's vision of the dead Paris, in angelic white, as he (like Jesus) tells her, "I've prepared you a place."

This otherworldliness establishes the mythic quality of such romanticism head on, by providing a world in which it requires no "realistic" justification. Helen's superhuman beauty is handled similarly. The press kit designates her not only the most beautiful woman in the world, but "the illegitimate daughter of the most powerful god." In contrast to *Troy*, with its demythologized Helen, such claims are also asserted intradiegetically. Aphrodite herself pronounces Helen (who bears a resemblance to herself) the most beautiful woman in the world, and Theseus informs her personally, "Zeus is your father. That's why your beauty will never be matched." On the downside, the promotional brochure informs us that such beauty is also "a curse from which no one could escape." As Helen puts it, "Loving me causes death and destruction." Once again, she is nominally a mere excuse for the war, but in this version her beauty really is the spectacle that drives the narrative. This supernatural framing marks the miniseries as the kind of "mythological," and therefore "juvenile," rendition of the Trojan War held in such contempt by Wolfgang Petersen.[40]

Establishing the love between Helen and Paris as mystically ordained—long before she was married to Menelaus—is a novel way of legitimizing their elopement. At the same time, Helen's personal agency is much more clearly

37. Cf. Warner 1994: xiii–xiv; Brunsdon 1997: 62–63. The fairy tale per se is fundamental to the enculturation of girls, and the associated romantic conventions "part of our cultural heritage as women" (Modleski 1991: 43).

38. For "destiny" as a theme in so-called chick flicks, see Mellencamp 1995: 93; Negra 2009: 7.

39. Neale 1986: 19.

40. Cf. above, p. 137. Other mythic features include Calchas's prophecy and Cassandra's divine gift, which is on lavish, scenery-eating display. The Judgment is dreamlike, but it is endorsed as supernatural when Helen—who is awake—sees Paris's face in the pool.

acknowledged than it is in *Troy*, both by herself ("What have *we* done?") and later by Paris ("I did not *take* her"). Her active leap into the water is justified, in terms easily legible to the modern viewer, as an act of defiance against patriarchal constraint. At Sparta, she is not only subjected to harsh paternal authority but treated quite literally as an object, first by Theseus and Pirithous, who draw lots for her, then by the Greek kings, who do the same. In the miniseries' most memorable scene, Helen is obliged by Menelaus (at Agamemnon's behest) to parade naked among the assembled kings so that they may judge whether she is worth fighting for (figure 6.1). Like the romantic narrative—albeit in a more sinister fashion—this and Kern's other additions work to make Helen an emblematic figure of the feminine, objectified and helpless as the quintessential object of desire.[41]

The trajectory of the plot seems to confirm the view, voiced by Pollux, that Helen's romanticism is no more than an immature girlish fantasy, which cannot survive the realities of adult life. Her brother and father impose feminine decorum on her tomboyish willfulness, reproving her horseback escapade and making sure she is dressed appropriately for public viewing ("Let's get you bathed and dressed," says Pollux). Though less severe than their father, Pollux is fully on board with the patriarchal program ("Father, I will take her to her room"). The essential object of male erotic obsession—the epitome of female sexual allure—is thus identified as a teenager whose spirit is crushed and romantic impulse denied. To be a "woman" is to be denied both desire and agency.[42] It is little wonder that, when Pollux tells Helen she is "almost a woman," she declares she is "no such thing," and clings onto his back for a piggyback ride like a little kid.

When, at the conclusion, Menelaus asks Helen, "What will you do?" he seems to reverse this arc by acknowledging her agency and leaving the outcome in her own hands. When she responds, "I will follow," she appears complicit in the restoration of the status quo from which she fled.[43] But the absence of any other option makes a mockery of the proffered choice. When she does follow her husband towards the horizon, we are left with a final image combining

41. Kern took the nude scene from the story of Vashti in the biblical Book of Esther. The oath of the suitors and lottery for Helen's hand, though ancient, are absent from most film versions of the Trojan War.

42. On adolescence and "the struggle to retain a sense of self in the face of expected femininity," see Driscoll 2002: 58 and cf. Hudson 1984. Cf. also L. Lewis 1989: 93–97 on the significance of clothing.

43. On this phrase, see George & Duncan 2005: 16–19. Note Guillory's rising intonation, which conveys questioning or uncertainty (below, p. 234).

FIGURE 6.1. Helen displayed nude to the assembled Greek kings in *Helen of Troy* (2003).

submission to patriarchal authority with resistance to its reinscription as romance.[44] The brief exhilaration of teen escape, dramatized in Helen's opening scene, ends up in entrapment and despair. She starts out a naive, girlish heroine of romance, but graduates, like Wise's Helen, as a melodramatic heroine of the kind we so often find in soap opera—one who "is forced to give up."[45]

An Untamed and Disrespectful Child

In time-honored fashion, a network executive informed *Variety* that they were "looking at either trying to lure a big name, known for her beauty and her acting prowess—or at launching a worldwide search for the perfect Helen"—or

44. Contrast the "classic" romantic ending, which shows "lovers turning from the camera and walking into their future, leaving us behind" (Bordwell & Thompson 2011: 220).

45. Cf. above, p. 110.

both.[46] Just three weeks from filming, the role was assigned to Sienna Guillory, a blonde, green-eyed, twenty-seven-year-old English woman who had been modeling and acting, mostly on television, since she was sixteen. Guillory had already starred in the BBC series *Take a Girl Like You* (2000), in which she played an ingenue who has to fight off men—a suitable enough preparation for the role of Helen—and in 2001, readers of *Esquire* UK had voted her "Britain's Most Eligible Woman"; but she was little known to Americans and certainly no "big name." As with Kruger, however, this awkwardness was finessed by reframing the casting narrative in romantic terms. Shapiro came across Guillory in an in-flight movie and told *TV Guide*, "She was only in it for 10 minutes . . . but I couldn't get her out of my head. She was fantastically beautiful"; he tracked her down the next day and "that was it, we hired her."[47]

The filmmakers had to convince more than one man, however, of this unknown actor's fantastic beauty. One way they did so was by presenting Helen intradiegetically as the object of desire for many men—not just Paris and Menelaus, but Theseus, Peirithous, Agamemnon, the assembled Greek kings, and even her own brother. At Agamemnon's wedding feast, when both the groom and his brother gaze hungrily at Helen, we hear eerie extradiegetic music inviting us to share their experience of the psychic impact of her beauty. Such music recurs when she is presented naked to the partying kings, who cheer and toast her ("breathtaking"), and again in another striking scene, when Helen appears on the walls of Troy to look down at the fighting. Menelaus has his back to the ramparts, yet his gaze is drawn to her as if by magic; the action freezes and the camera circles up and around to present the battlefield from a god's-eye point of view, suggesting that the sight of Helen stops time in the mind of the beholder—or at least of Menelaus.[48] The flashy technique used here (known as "bullet time") distances the viewer from the action by making the effect itself—as opposed to Helen—the spectacle.[49] Like the supernatural framework, such techniques arguably excuse Helen's beauty from judgement by distancing us from concerns about "realism."

46. Grego 2002.

47. Murphy 2003: 12.

48. Winkler 2015d: 129–30 describes the scene in detail.

49. Cf. Purse 2005: 156–58. Judging from the number of comments in reviews (both positive and negative), the scene succeeded in this respect. The show won an award for Outstanding Visual Effects in a Television Miniseries, Movie or Special from the Visual Effects Society.

The miniseries demystifies its own mythology, however, in the many scenes presenting Helen as a particularized young woman, where she appears less a figure of timeless, divine beauty than a modern teenager on the cusp of adolescence. Guillory was twenty-seven when she was cast but looks much younger in the role.[50] Like Kruger she is a "banana," very thin, small-breasted, and delicate looking.[51] We first see her in medium close-up, peering from behind long unkempt bangs. Her loose, untidy locks convey a youthful innocence, especially in combination with her abundant (and very un-Greek) freckles (plate 15).[52] Her dress is pale pink, her makeup "invisible," and her only accessory simple sandals. The look is unsophisticated, innocent, and casual. When she opens her mouth, we hear not the upper-crust English commonly associated with both ancient world movies and "quality" television, but the kind of sub-posh accent often adopted by the young in order to distance themselves from upper-class hauteur. This features glottal stops and rising intonation at the end of sentences (a.k.a. "up-talk" or "high rising terminal"), which sounds particularly girlish, modern, and distanced from tradition and high culture.[53]

In a period that was anxiously preoccupied with girls, their freedom and their nascent sexuality,[54] Helen is introduced not as a dignified queen but as

50. Judging from internet comments, few viewers had trouble accepting Guillory as an adolescent. Many would be aware that teen characters are often played by young adults (cf. Driscoll 2002: 218). In general terms, adolescence is best defined not by age or menarche, but as a stage that one passes through to become a woman (cf. Driscoll 2002: 6).

51. Body Measurements, "Sienna Guillory," accessed August 20, 2022, https://www.bodymeasurements.org/?s=guillory). For Kruger, see above, p. 142. Studio publicity no longer trumpets the vital statistics of female stars, but some celebrity websites say Guillory is five feet, six inches tall, weighs 105 pounds, measures 34-23-34, and has green eyes (e.g., Measurements, "Sienna Guillory," accessed March 10, 2020, http://www.measurements.me/sienna-guillory-height-weight-bra-size-net-worth-salary/). Others vary slightly.

52. In popular culture, freckles signify "youthful energy" and "girlish innocence" (see, e.g., TV Tropes, "Youthful Freckles," accessed December 27, 2019, http://tvtropes.org/pmwiki/pmwiki.php/Main/YouthfulFreckles).

53. This mannerism is strongly associated with teenage girls; it suggests lack of confidence and is looked down on by adults as annoying and unprofessional (P. Warren 2016). In person, Guillory uses modern, youthful diction: Helen is "kind of cursed . . . because everybody fancies her" (*Making the Epic*).

54. For the rise of girl studies, see, e.g., Inness 1998; Driscoll 2002; A. Harris 2004 and cf. Tasker & Negra 2007b: 18–19. For the difficulty of defining "girl," see Driscoll 2002: ch. 1 and cf. A. Harris 2004: 191–93.

an Everygirl on the model of the romance novel heroine: spirited, childlike, innocent, and naive about her own allure.[55] Her sighting of Paris in the magic pool is followed by a kind of reverse *teichoscopia*, in which Helen has to ask her brother about the visitors she sees arriving at Sparta and stumbles over Agamemnon's name.[56] She is the baby of the family (Tyndareus calls her "my youngest, still a child"), with squirmy body language and the rebelliousness popularly associated with youngest siblings.[57] Like the stereotypical adolescent girl (ancient and modern) she is wild and willful, or in Tyndareus's words "an untamed and disrespectful child." In contrast to her statuesque cinematic forebears, she and her flimsy garments are in constant motion.[58] She defies the boundaries set for her at Sparta by riding out beyond the city walls ("Father is furious!"). When kidnapped by Theseus, she saws away at her bonds ("I'm not some kind of prize"), spits in his face, and declares that unlike her sister she does not "do what anybody says." It is made very clear that she is still a child, and he old enough to be her father, giving their relationship a distinctly Lolita-ish whiff.[59]

Helen's unconventional characterization lays the foundation for a coming-of-age story in which an innocent girl who rebels against patriarchal gender norms learns the hard way how to be a woman.[60] In her childish persona, she is unaware of herself as an object of the male gaze—that is, as a woman. Her restlessness suggests a teenager discovering her nascent sexuality, but her eroticism is innocent, unintentional, "natural," and non-manipulative, untouched by "third wave" notions of beauty and sexual agency as sources of female empowerment. After "seeing" Paris in the mountain pool, she gallops bareback through the hills, in slow motion, smiling blissfully, to swelling romantic music. Since antiquity, horses and wilderness have been emblems of sexual freedom for adolescent girls. The same is true of Helen's loose, abundant red-gold locks, which blow in the

55. Cf. Radway 1991: 123–27; Modleski 2008: 43. In Kern's original script, Helen was less infantilized and given more to do.

56. *Teichoscopia* is a technical term for a famous scene in the *Iliad* where Helen looks down at the Trojan War and identifies the Greek heroes for Priam.

57. Cf., e.g., Owens 2019.

58. "The director's idea was that there was something agitated about her" (Elias 2003: 5). Cf. Shillock 2011: 134.

59. Stellan Skarsgård, who played the role, was born June 13, 1951, making him old enough to be Guillory's father (let alone her teenage character's).

60. The coming-of-age theme is enhanced by the presence of other girl children (Iphigenia, Cassandra) who are mistreated in parallel ways (see further below).

wind as she rides.[61] Her shapeless dress enhances her girlishness by avoiding cleavage; but it seems minimally attached and swirls around her, revealing as well as concealing her slender body. Pink was by now overwhelmingly *the* "girl" color.[62] But it had also become a mark of the uncertain line between child and woman, the ever-expanding territory of the "girl"—from Disney Princesses to Barbie dolls to Victoria's Secret.[63]

This fresh, arresting characterization stands in some tension with the diegetic assertions of Helen's superhuman beauty and its impact on the internal audience. That tension is not evaded, however, but confronted head-on. For Helen's first scene, the miniseries cuts directly from the Judgment, where Aphrodite declares her The Most Beautiful Woman in the World, to a close-up of her distinctively freckled face, underscoring the individuality of both performer and character (plate 15). The two perspectives are juxtaposed most strikingly, however, in Helen's scenes with Theseus. When he informs her that she is Zeus's daughter, and as such the most beautiful woman in the world, we see her in tight close-up, deglamorized as a scared kid with a dirty face and eyes red from weeping (figure 6.2).

Subsequently, at Athens, Helen rides in on another horse, this time in bridal white, and offers herself to Theseus with the declaration, "I'm a woman."[64] This caps a brief conversation about the "best" kind of honey, during which her flirtatious manner and his yearning gaze make clear that honey is not what is at issue.

HELEN: How do you know it's the best?
THESEUS: Well, I suppose I don't.
HELEN: Then there's always a chance you may find something better.
THESEUS: No.

The scene spells out the conundrum of supreme beauty: how *could* one know if someone was objectively the most beautiful woman in the world? The answer is, of course, that one could not. But Theseus's confident response is grounded in the essential irrationalism of the romantic: "love" brings its own certainty, as it did when Helen locked eyes with Paris in the mountain pool.

61. On the erotic connotations of maidens' loose hair, see Warner 1994: ch. 22.

62. Orenstein 2011: ch. 3; Paoletti 2012: ch. 5.

63. See further below, p. 244.

64. The line is intended to convey menarche—something about which Kern had wished to be much more explicit.

FIGURE 6.2. In *Helen of Troy* (2003), Helen has tried to run away but fallen on her back in the forest; Theseus lies above her staring into her scared and dirty face.

In ancient Greek terms, Helen's arrival at "womanhood" makes her ripe for marriage, but in modern American terms she remains jailbait. Certainly, she is little changed in appearance or behavior. In the Athenian scenes, her hair is tied up with a narrow band, but it is still far from neat, and she still rides horses in filmy garments and dashes off on her own two feet when her will is thwarted. Meanwhile Theseus is as paternalistic as ever. He declines her offer, in part because he has come to realize that he is not worthy of her, but also because, as an experienced adult man, he knows she is not yet ready for "love." She remains an adolescent, subject to the wisdom of the father. In keeping with even the most liberal modern parenting advice, physical maturity does not mean Helen should rush into sex. She should wait for the right boy to come along.

Little does Theseus know that he has already done so, at least in fantasy. But even after meeting Paris in the flesh (and presumably consummating their passion), this Helen remains girlish. She continues to wear filmy, lightly accessorized shifts, in clear, simple solids, which often cling or flutter in revealing ways. At several key moments (including the elopement, and strolling idyllically on the beach with Paris), she again wears pink. We see less of that color, however, as the story darkens, and a series of more distinctive, less girlish outfits marks Helen's progress towards womanhood.

FIGURE 6.3. On the left, Helen dressed up by the Trojans to be returned to her husband, Menelaus, in *Helen of Troy* (2003). On the right, Sophie Schliemann wearing jewelry discovered at Troy by her archeologist husband—jewelry that he thought had belonged to Helen of Troy.

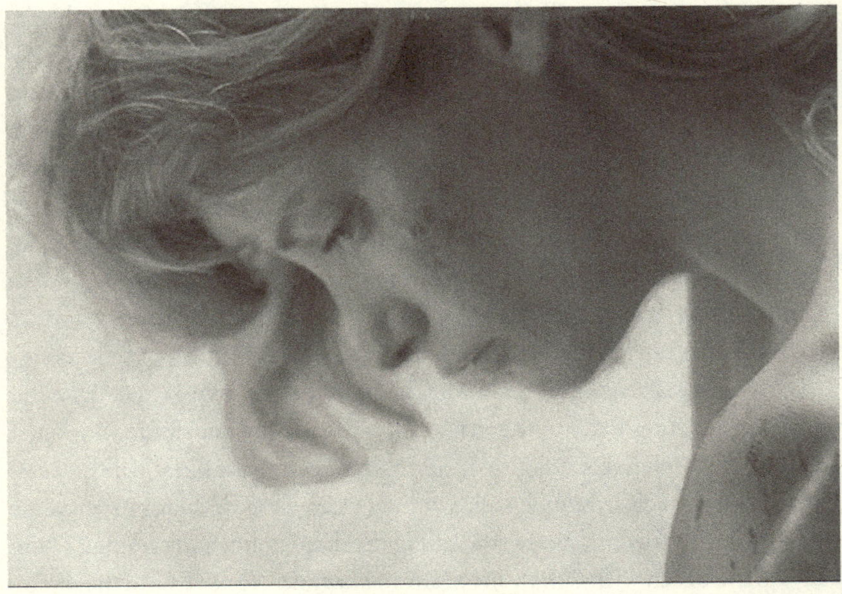

FIGURE 6.4. Close-up of Helen in *Helen of Troy* (2003) after she has been raped by Agamemnon.

When Menelaus wins the lottery, he (and we) see Helen, through the flames from Pollux's funeral pyre, in a striking outfit conveying the threat of her nubility. She is wearing a black veil with a dull gold tiara and a translucent dark mauve dress, through which her nipples and small breasts are clearly visible. Shortly afterwards, she is displayed to the Greek kings in the "costume" of nudity, as a naked object of the male gaze (figure 6.1).[65] Her pale body, standing out against the dark background, vividly evokes the Greek statue tradition and its high cultural progeny, in a way that highlights its complicity with the idealization of female beauty via "white slavery."[66]

A strikingly different outfit marks her presentation at Priam's court: a voluminous yellow dress, accessorized with a substantial gold necklace and a gold headdress modeled on the so-called Jewels of Helen (one of Schliemann's famous finds at Troy) (figure 6.3). She walks at a dignified pace and her hair is braided up, its usual flightiness weighed down under the heavy headdress. She has been burdened with the prestige of antiquity for return to her rejected husband. But her dress still flies in the wind, and her freckles are still evident in tight close-up. After the rape, in painful contrast, we see her naked again, hunched over, with bedraggled hair and bruised face, displaying the ugly subtext of her earlier "artistic" nudity (figure 6.4). Clytemnestra covers her in a heavy dark green throw, which Helen is still wearing when she emerges slowly into the street. As she follows Menelaus into the distance, the fluttering of her garments has finally ceased.

The Most Quintessentially Feminine of Experiences

It is rape that finally makes Helen a woman. For, as Carol Clover puts it, "if Jennifer is raped because she is a woman, she is also, according to the logic of popular culture, a woman because she is raped."[67] This is because, as feminist scholars have argued, "Rape and rapability [are] central to the very construction of gender identity," and rape "the most quintessentially feminine of

65. On nudity as a costume, see above, p. 146.

66. For the role of "white slavery" in the construction of female beauty as "Caucasian," and the artistic idealization of the white enslaved girl "stripped for examination by buyers," see Painter 2010: ch. 4 (quotation from p. 54). Cf. also the use of rape narratives to legitimize nudity in nineteenth-century American art (J. Lewis 1992).

67. Clover 1992: 160.

experiences."[68] Helen thus remains, as she has always been, the essential feminine, as the essential object—and victim—of male desire.

Agamemnon's assault is not merely the unfortunate consequence of one man's lust. It is presented, rather, as the inevitable climax to a story of coming of age in rape culture.[69] Intradiegetically, this is conveyed by presenting rape as the inevitable consequence of female beauty. When Theseus explains her paternity to Helen, he tells her that her mother was raped "because she was beautiful." The result of that rape was, in turn, a child sentenced to supreme beauty by the ur-patriarchal-rapist, Zeus himself. If beauty is a curse, it is one imposed on women by forces beyond their control. When Helen tells her sister, "They can look all they want, but they'll never see me," she implies that her beauty is not her "self" but an identity constructed for her by men and their desires. This gives a different coloration to Theseus's remark about the honey, with its irrational implication that supreme beauty can be simply perceived as such. Such beauty is, it seems, a romantic fantasy on the part of the enamored male. The miniseries thus reframes the idea of absolute beauty from a female perspective as absolute victimhood, from which there is no rational or practical escape. To be Helen (to be beautiful, to be a woman) is to be rapable, and as such to be unsafe, always uncomfortable, in the patriarchal world.

In the person of Sienna Guillory, Helen perfectly exemplifies the stereotypical rape victim dubbed by Projansky "the most vulnerable girl": she is "young and white, with blue, green, or hazel eyes and blond (or occasionally light brown) hair."[70] Like victimized women in countless movies, as well as real life, Helen lives in "a continuously assaultive world," where "sexual threat is everywhere" and rape only a matter of time.[71] Summoned home from a rustic world of freedom and romance, she is subjected to reproof, containment, and the lustful male gaze. This reaches its climax in the nude scene, a visual assault in close proximity to rape, which is shot as an excruciating, nightmarish rendition of what every young woman has experienced walking alone

68. Higgins & Silver 1991: 3; Clover 1992: 154.

69. In rape culture, "individual acts of domination add up to pervasive structural misogyny" (Clover 1992: 144; cf. also Projansky 2001: 9). On rape culture's saturation of popular media, see Higgins & Silver 1991; N. Wolf 1991: 136–37; Rapping 1992: 15, 110–14; Douglas 1994: 209–11, 302–3; Cuklanz 2000; Projansky 2001; Heller-Nicholas 2011.

70. Projansky 2007: 50.

71. Projansky 2001: 127 (on *Thelma and Louise*); Heller-Nicholas 2011: 15 (of Gilda in *Safe in Hell*). "For young women and girls, the 2000s truly were a cursed era . . . It was open season on young women" (Kale 2021).

at night through a crowd of drunken, catcalling men.[72] It is scarcely surprising that Helen responds by dissociating her "self" from her body, seeking safety in the cliché that the true self lies within.

The assaultive male gaze is also responsible, both indirectly and directly, for Helen's abduction by Theseus. At the wedding feast, both Atreidae gaze at her so intently that she abruptly leaves the company, in evident discomfort. This sends her running straight into the arms of her abductor. Though the expectation that Theseus will rape her is not fulfilled, camerawork and script make sure that it remains a constant and entirely plausible threat.[73] After delivering the news that her mother was raped, Theseus picks her up bodily, and the terrified Helen asks, "Is that what you intend with me?" Theseus replies, "I don't rape children. Or are you a woman?"—to which she responds in terror, "No! No! No!" The transition from childhood to womanhood could not be more clearly defined as the transition to rapability, held in check only by the questionable power of male self-control. On hearing, in addition, that she is a product of rape, Helen runs away from her captor, but trips and falls on her back in the forest. Theseus lies over her staring into her face from just inches away. That face, seen in close-up, has been dirtied by her fall in a way that foreshadows Helen's eventual rape by Agamemnon.

In most films, sexual assault is presented as "real" rape (as opposed to acquaintance rape or date rape), that is, as violent, manifestly nonconsensual, and perpetrated by strangers.[74] The miniseries makes it abundantly clear, however, that in rape culture, sexual threat is not confined to drunken kings or passing adventurers. The danger is everywhere, even in the heart of the nuclear family: *all* men are implicated.[75] Helen's own brother speaks of the "madness" her beauty induces in "all men, every one." When she asks, "Even you?" his eyes flicker in tacit acknowledgment, and she runs off fearfully. As for her brother-in-law, Rufus Sewell's Agamemnon eyes Helen voyeuristically every chance he gets. When Helen tries to stop the war by offering herself to

72. Guillory said the extras were "shocked and embarrassed for me" (Murphy 2003: 11). In case we think the Greek men's admiration and "compliments" make it acceptable, an indignant Paris will spell out their significance, speaking of a Helen "forced to walk naked among Aegean kings who leer and spit obscenities." On the assaultive male gaze, see especially Clover 1992: 182–91.

73. The mythically informed will also notice that Peirithous is heading off to abduct Persephone.

74. See further Cuklanz 2000: 30–43.

75. Projansky 2001: 60.

him, he rejects her voluntary submission, showing that his lust is predicated precisely on her withholding of consent. The rape itself is filmed in tight close-up, urging us to identify with Helen as a powerless, terrified victim.[76] It takes place, moreover, in the heat of violent conquest, the surrounding carnage contextualizing the rape in a way that equates it with masculine combat at its most savage.[77] As such, it is produced by male camaraderie: Odysseus holds back Menelaus and forces him to watch, as helpless as Helen herself. The next time we see her, Helen is suffering the symptoms of post-rape shock, which renders a woman "mute, passive, and vulnerable."[78] The "rape of Helen," as her abduction used to be called, has become the rape of Helen in the most brutal modern sense, exposing the misogynistic substructure of the original tale.[79]

This savage assault is the logical conclusion of the surveillance by men that has targeted Helen from the start. It is also the pinnacle of victim-blaming—a key component of rape culture. Coming of age, for a girl, means not only being made aware of the threat that the sight of her body poses to herself and others, but being held personally responsible for the consequences—regardless of her own desires or agency.[80] We are informed that Leda committed suicide out of shame at her rape by Zeus. Her husband Tyndareus hates Helen, in turn, because she was conceived through that rape, and blames her openly not just for her abduction by Theseus but for all its consequences. It is because she has internalized this victim-blaming, reified as the "curse" of her beauty, that she submits voluntarily to the naked public display. When Agamemnon does finally rape her, it is not only out of lust but in revenge for Iphigenia, blaming Helen for the crime that he himself perpetrated to make this moment possible.

76. On the use of POV shots in rape scenes, see Projansky 2001: 215–18.

77. "In fantasies of war, sexuality is manifested in violence, and violence carries an explosive sexual charge" (Modleski 1991: 62). For films treating rape in the context of war and other forms of violence against women, see Projansky 2001: 209–14.

78. Cuklanz 2000: 156. See further Cuklanz 2000: 35, 99–105.

79. Cf. George & Duncan 2005: 16, 17. On reading the physicality of rape back into texts where it has been deflected or disguised, see Higgins & Silver 1991: 4. In the miniseries, Helen is treated by three different men in ways that refract the ambiguities of the Greek word *harpagê* (literally "abduction"): she is kidnapped by Theseus, elopes with Paris, and is raped by Agamemnon.

80. "If it is femininity that makes women 'rapable,' then it is also femininity that makes them 'not rapable' . . . [by calling] into question whether [a woman] was raped or whether she consented" (Read 2000: 93).

Agamemnon's brutal lust, inextricable from the lust for power that drives him to kill his daughter, stitches together the two halves of the miniseries. The equivalence of rape to other forms of patriarchal violence is reflected in the show's bipartite structure: the two halves conclude with paired scenes of horrific violence against women by the very patriarch who should be protecting them. It is reinforced by clear parallels between Agamemnon's victims. Like the carefree Helen of her first scene, Iphigenia is presented as a "beautiful, bouncing, loving pre-schooler,"[81] wearing a pink dress in which she will soon skip playfully to her sacrifice. Clytemnestra, a mother figure to Helen, even tells her that Iphigenia "reminds me of you." The murder is echoed in a different way when Clytemnestra kills Agamemnon using repeated thrusts from a phallic knife. Though she kills him "for Iphigenia," it is clear that she is also avenging the rape we have just witnessed, reinforcing the equation of murder and rape as destroyers of the girl in every woman.[82]

All told, this miniseries is exceptionally realistic about sexual assault. Many films present rape judgmentally as a result of female independence. This is, arguably, what happens to Helen, who is raped in the public square at Troy as a consequence of her elopement. But that is not the whole story. Her initial resistance to patriarchal control does not, in fact, expose her to threatening men. On the contrary, when she defies her father to leave the city of her own free will, she finds not only personal freedom but true love. When she *is* forcibly abducted, it is from within the "safe" space of the palace; yet the kidnapping reaches a happyish ending. The threat within the family, on the other hand, is palpable, and culminates in sexual assault by an intimate acquaintance and family member. It is presented, moreover, as "real" rape. Unlike the stereotypical rapist, Agamemnon is not "visibly abnormal," freakish, or marginal.[83] Nor is he marked by any special variety of personal psychosis. Far from "freakish," his treatment of Helen epitomizes both the patriarchal basis of rape culture and the normality of rape, especially in wartime.

81. Wroblewski n.d.

82. Vengeance is a frequent feminist response to rape in popular culture (cf. Hallam & Marshment 2000: 141; Projansky 2001: 60). On rape-revenge films, see further Clover 1992: ch. 3; Read 2000; Projansky 2001: 58–61; Heller-Nicholas 2011; Hess 2017. The avenger is usually the rape victim herself, or a man outraged on her behalf, but sometimes a meek woman—a sister, mother, or friend—is transformed into an avenger (for examples, see Clover 1992: 137–38; Rapping 1992: 143; Read 2000: 207–8; Heller-Nicholas 2011: 156).

83. For this stereotype, see Cuklanz 2000: 69–74.

This refocusing of Helen's story through the lens of rape culture presents something of a challenge to the ethos of the period in which the film was made. Popular culture had by then been reconfigured not only by "third wave" feminism, but by the antifeminist backlash and associated rise of "postfeminism." Postfeminism, in its various forms, depoliticized the movement that started in the 1970s by declaring the battle won.[84] The emphasis shifted from women's victimization to personal responsibility, individual choice, and therapeutic solutions. As Bonnie Dow puts it, in postfeminist discourse, "the problems of women are no longer located in the external battle against patriarchy but in women's internal struggle to define themselves."[85] At the same time, a nostalgic conservatism suggests that "modifying their expectations and behaviors in line with patriarchal ideological precepts gives women the best chance of achieving fulfillment and intimacy."[86] The postfeminist woman must "unlearn" feminism, adjust her romantic expectations, and "be prepared to live without the man she loves"; women were urged by the media to "settle," as opposed to holding out for "the one."[87]

In some respects, Guillory's girlish Helen is clearly a postfeminist figure. Postfeminist popular culture is epitomized, in Projansky's words, by "girlness—particularly adolescent girlness."[88] It is especially preoccupied with "womanly girls and girlish women," a confusion of girlhood and womanhood that Diane Negra calls "quintessentially postfeminist."[89] Clytemnestra starts out as a different kind of postfeminist figure; she encapsulates the ideal

84. See further Faludi 1991; 2007; Douglas 1994: ch. 9; Dow 1996: 203–17; Brunsdon 1997; Projansky 2001: ch. 2; Tasker & Negra 2007a; Negra 2009; cf. also Whelehan 2000: ch. 4; Hagelin 2013: 11–12.

85. Dow 1996: 182.

86. Negra 2009: 138.

87. Negra 2009: 33, 138–40.

88. Projansky 2007: 45. Cf. Sands 2019 for a discussion of Britney Spears and other "thin, white, heterosexual teens [who] eagerly capitalized on the idea of a 'teen queen' who could embody the ideals of postfeminist girlhood. Their lucrative popularity was grounded in a requisite youthful innocence that necessitated protection and upkeep, including a close surveillance of their sexuality and virginity" (Sands 2019: 69).

89. Negra 2009: 12. Women's fashions of the period evinced "a sweet, romantic, girlish sensibility," featuring loose flowing curls, ruffles and flounces, diaphanous chiffon, and virginal white (Faludi 2007: 136–37). On the "perpetual girlhood" of women in postfeminist culture, see Negra 2009: 12–14, 73, and cf. Wearing 2007. For the girlishness of even the postfeminist action heroine, see J. Brown 2011: ch. 6. On the persistence of the word "girl" and its ambiguities in recent fiction, see Wasserman 2016; Mandel 2016.

woman of the period, who is "undemanding, uncompetitive, and, most of all, dependent."[90] As Helen's sensible big sister, and the dutiful daughter of the family, she is the very picture of a meek suburban mom, who endures her husband's harshness and allows him to silence her, until, in Kern's words "the worm turns." Cassandra occupies a different niche, giving the lie to postfeminist ideas about "girl power."[91] Her superpower might have saved the day, had anyone listened, but she is far from empowered by her special gift. It is used, rather, by men in the most traditional way, "to set and police the boundaries of female normality and acceptability by punishing female power and outspoken-ness."[92]

The miniseries rebukes the adequacy of all these models of femininity as responses to patriarchy. Postfeminist solutions, such as a feisty spirit and the exercise of individual "choice," are glaringly inadequate in both Helen's case and Cassandra's. Clytemnestra's violence, though viscerally satisfying, does nothing to redeem or resolve Helen's personal story, or her own.[93] Postfeminist rape films often "resolve" the rape by (re)incorporating the independent or vulnerable woman "into a stable heterosexual family setting."[94] But Helen merely accepts the protection of a man whose love she cannot reciprocate. The free spirit is tamed, the good daughter driven to homicide, the truth teller jailed.

Arguably, this miniseries' representation of rape culture is defanged by displacing it into an exotic time and place.[95] Postfeminist popular culture "blithely assumes that gender equality is a given,"[96] reassuring us that "we" don't treat women like that, because feminism has "won." But as we saw earlier, the makers of *Helen* emphasized the universality—and modernity—of their own rendition. In any case, "historical" films always resonate with the period in which they are made—an effect supported, in this case, by a script that for the most part uses simple modern English, eschewing the kind of sub-Shakespearean

90. Faludi 2007: 131.

91. On "girl power," see Whelehan 2000: ch. 2. On fantasies of girls' empowerment in films of this period and the contrast with real adult life, see Negra 2009: 12–14.

92. Moseley 2002: 411.

93. In rape-revenge films, the maternal avenger is usually put in her place, in the service of backlash politics (Read 2000: ch. 7). But Clytemnestra simply disappears.

94. Projansky 2001: 30. This exemplifies the broader Hollywood tendency to recuperate problematic women (Kuhn 1993: 31–35).

95. Cf. Projansky 2001: 42, 47, 53, 87, 201–2.

96. Tasker & Negra 2007b: 12.

formality that weighs down so many ancient world films. No viewer can miss the fact that the behaviors this miniseries projects onto the past are disturbingly familiar in the present. Agamemnon's toxic brew of violence, misogyny, lust, and power is as "timeless" as Theseus's frat-boy antics. Like countless real women, Clytemnestra has no legal recourse for Iphigenia's death, Helen no choice but to remain married to a man she does not love. Women and children are still abused by husbands and fathers, and locked away, like Cassandra, if they speak up.

In her discussion of rape-revenge films, which typically portray the legal system as unsympathetic or worse, Carol Clover observes, "One cannot quarrel with civilization, but it is sometimes useful to look past its comforts to see the stories we tell ourselves, as a culture, for what they really are"; such films have a "perverse simplicity" that "leaves us staring at the lex talionis unadorned."[97] The *Helen* miniseries functions similarly. By projecting a narrative of female victimization onto a time and place devoid of modern social institutions, it allows us to view patriarchal structures in the starkest possible terms. The mask of alterity enables the film to dramatize a world where women are subjected nakedly to the power of patriarchy, exposing the unvarnished experience of women in rape culture everywhere.

There is an instructive contrast here with *Troy*'s treatment of sexual assault. Petersen's "realistic" *Troy* is, ironically, far *less* realistic than the miniseries when it comes to rape and the fate of women in war. *Troy* makes unambiguous use of the arty classical alibi for the nude Helen.[98] In the miniseries' nude scene, however, the wailing soundtrack, and Helen's blurred, erratic point of view, give us access to the "real" person behind the image in a way that insists on her victimization. *Troy*'s Briseis, like Helen, is a victim of patriarchal violence who is at constant risk of rape. Yet she is not merely rescued by superior male strength but ends up having enthusiastic sex with her captor. When Agamemnon assaults *her* at the sack of Troy, she succeeds in fighting him off and even killing him. The dirt and bruises associated with sexual assault are even deemed, by her lover, to contribute to Briseis's beauty.[99] However "unrealistic" the miniseries may be in Petersen's terms, then, it offers a far more truthful view than his big-screen movie of the realities of rape culture and what

97. Clover 1992: 151. On the rape-revenge film's "rejection and circumvention of the law" (Read 2000: 169), see Clover 1992: 119–24, 144–51; Heller-Nicholas 2011: 30, 65.

98. Above, p. 146.

99. Above, p. 156.

war means for women. Devoid of *Troy*'s distancing pretensions (such as its ponderous pronouncements about fame), this *Helen* uses its legendary setting not to detach us from the realities of sexual assault but to strip away the smug postfeminist veneer of feminist victory.

What little hope the film does offer depends on the education and "feminizing" of men, more specifically of Menelaus, the only central male character to survive. No amount of personal therapy could have helped Helen, but in his battlefield tête-à-tête with Paris, Menelaus learns to respect his wife by listening to another "sensitive" man (they "could have been friends"). This enables him to evolve, from a "soft" man held firmly under his brother's thumb, to one who has become aware of his own complicity in rape culture and offers his wife autonomy. Like a TV movie villain, he is both repentant and forgivable.[100]

It is this reformed Menelaus, a failure of patriarchal masculinity,[101] whose point of view frames the miniseries as a whole by providing the opening voiceover and its bookend. In marked contrast to *Troy*'s portentous, self-glorifying conclusion, Menelaus's tone is more gloomy than authoritative. His final words accompany a view of the raped Helen moving slowly through the chaotic violence of the defeated city. He ends with a little sermon on the power of love, which presumably expresses Menelaus's commitment to being a better husband in future.[102] But first, he summarizes the consequences of rape culture for men and women alike: "For those of us who survived, we are left with the memory of shame, and misery, and bloodshed."

The *Iliad* Was Not a Love Story

The ratings for the miniseries were "high but not record-breaking."[103] *Variety* reported that it "averaged" 4.1 million viewers (compared to *Attila*'s seven million) and was "the top rated cable program on Sunday night."[104] This was despite largely negative newspaper reviews published during the week prior to the premiere.

100. For the TV movie villain, see Rapping 1992: 146 and cf. Schulze 1990: 369.

101. He does not even evince the hegemonic masculinity of the postfeminist "new man" (on which see Cuklanz 2000: 18–19, ch. 3).

102. "In these dark times, the only thing we have to hold onto is love. The one true gift of the gods. And it is through love that we hope, and pray, the gods will send us peace." For *Troy*, cf. above, p. 153.

103. B. Gray 2004.

104. Oei 2003.

Far fewer professional reviews are published for any TV show than for a big-screen blockbuster like *Troy*. For the miniseries, I found a total of thirteen that were both American-based and contemporaneous. As usual, the authors are predominantly male: nine of the thirteen could plausibly be identified from their names (or a little research) as male, and two as female, while two were indeterminate.[105] Two of those identifiable as male, plus the two of indeterminate gender, praise the film, albeit without great enthusiasm ("a decent, entertaining production").[106] The other male-authored reviews range from lukewarm endorsement ("moderately entertaining at times") to blunt condemnation ("a total failure").[107] Some liken it (disparagingly, of course) to soap opera.[108] Others find it boring ("likely to launch a million naps"), a seemingly neutral judgement that may veil gendered preferences.[109] The misty conversation between Paris and Menelaus incurs special scorn ("ridiculous").[110] The two identifiably female critics are also unenthusiastic, but for different kinds of reasons. One, enraged by the nudity, calls it "simply very bad cable softcore," while the other objects to Helen's traditional blonde beauty as such ("Hitler would have understood perfectly").[111]

None of the male critics applies the lens of gender politics to Helen's looks. Some admire Guillory's beauty in the role, albeit in relatively restrained terms ("could easily set off a small fleet"), while others emphatically did not ("won't float a boat, much less a fleet").[112] A few complain about the disparity between Guillory's appearance and the intradiegetic claims of supreme beauty.[113] Many more fall into the trap set by the nude scene, which invites viewers to judge the ship-launching potential not only of Helen's face but of her naked body.[114] Male critics outdo each other in smirking references to what is called,

105. My gender determinations are based on any of the following: conventionally male/female byline/username; conventionally male/female photo; self-reference indicating a male or female gender identity.

106. Owen 2003.

107. Bark 2003; Bianculli 2003.

108. Martel 2003, Shales 2003.

109. Bianculli 2003. Cf. similar male complaints below, pp. 251 and 254.

110. Bark 2003.

111. McFarland 2003; Newmark 2003.

112. Pardi 2003; Boedeker 2003.

113. Rosenberg 2003; Shales 2003.

114. Note that the trailer's voice-over replaces her *face* with her *beauty* as the launcher of a thousand ships.

among other things, Helen's "bare assets," her "globular gluteal epidermis," and "the hips that launched a thousand ships."[115] Puns, snark, and alliteration are, to be sure, the stock-in-trade of media criticism. Yet this demeaning coyness, from presumably adult male viewers armed with professional power and cultural authority, underscores the contemporary relevance of the film's central theme: the vulnerability of young women to the assaultive male gaze. Like the leering Greek kings, these authoritative male reviewers do not really "see" Helen.

Most critics also disliked the portrayal of Helen as a recognizably contemporary adolescent. One man calls her "Babette of Troy,"[116] and thinks she has an "oddly contemporary" characterization that breaks the movie's "spell"; another refers to her and Paris as "Ken and Barbie of Troy," and Helen as "a headstrong nymphet"; a third calls her "sullen and pouty" and likens her to a "strung-out hippy"; one of the women refers to her, with overt disgust, as "a carefree sprite of a woman-child. (Ugh.)."[117] As usual, such judgments imply that despite the eye of the beholder, there is, in fact, a "right" way to portray Helen. She should apparently be dignified, physically mature, mentally healthy, not "too" young or thin, and somehow noncontemporary.

There are, however, two outliers. One male reviewer likes Helen's portrayal as "a flaky emotional wreck," and concludes that, "resembling a young Mia Farrow, her wispiness belies a hard edge that makes totally credible the dangerous allure she presents to a set of suitors."[118] Another, of indeterminate gender, writes, "She's all pouty, come-hither attitude and mischievous eyes, the kind of perpetually troubled lass who would be popping Prozac like they were Tums if this were the 21st century."[119] Their appreciation is grounded in the specificity of Guillory's performance, as opposed to generic conceptions of beauty or preconceptions about what Helen "should" be like, leaving them receptive to the filmmakers' idiosyncratic vision.

115. Bark 2003; Shales 2003; Martel 2003. One of the women uses similarly demeaning language (Helen's "headlights shone the way to Troy, and her bumper encouraged them to follow"), but does so to express rage at the sexualization of someone she calls "a hero to many women," comparing Helen to Monica Lewinsky as "the focal point of a nation's anger and derision" (McFarland 2003).

116. Presumably to be pronounced Babe-ette, a surfer-slang term for a Southern California beach blonde.

117. Boedeker 2003; Rosenberg 2003; Shales 2003; McFarland 2003.

118. Speier 2003.

119. Anon. 2003.

The film has also been reviewed, over the years, by a number of bloggers.[120] Owing to the much smaller number of such reviews in the present case—as compared with *Troy*—it is possible to attempt a more fine-grain analysis. Despite the wide variety of writers who fall into this category, and the uncertainty of such boundaries, they are presumably more representative, collectively, of the viewing public, than are the professional critics. The position of blogger requires no special knowledge, has no gatekeepers, and is not constrained by professional goals (such as the need to address the public at large or give guidance to "family" audiences). It is presumably in part for these reasons that women, at least, are much better represented among the bloggers than the critics. The twelve such accounts that I discovered include five men, five women, and two of indeterminate gender.[121]

Many bloggers, regardless of gender, echo the negative critics in their lukewarm assessment of Guillory ("beautiful, blond, and boring"), and their objections to the show's "feminine" aspects ("more like one of those romantic Harlequin novels than an epic adventure").[122] A feminist woman complains about "contemporary psychobabble."[123] Yet only one blogger (discussed further below) eviscerates the show, and those who like it, regardless of gender, are much more inclined to express such feelings vehemently than are the critics. This may be in part because they are more likely to have seen and reviewed the miniseries by choice, out of enthusiasm for the subject or genre (not just because it is their job). But they are also, presumably, less inhibited than reviewers by their own cultural capital, less invested in their own expertise, and less affected by the fact that the film belongs to a critically scorned genre.

Whatever the reason, while the same percentage of bloggers as reviewers (four out of twelve) liked the film, they expressed their feelings far more effusively. One woman calls it "enthralling . . . stunning . . . breathtaking," with "incredible" acting and a "fantastic script."[124] A blogger of unknown gender says it is "not my type of film . . . but I was enthralled beginning to end. It was epic in every way."[125] The same applies to their assessment of Guillory as

120. Many are undated, but the most recent dated blog post is from 2012.

121. Note, however, that in the case of this kind of internet content, my criteria for determining gender (above, n. 105) are less reliable, given the possibility of cross-gender or ungendered usernames and fictitious identities.

122. Mahon 2011; Beyond Hollywood 2003.

123. Johanson 2003.

124. Bishop n.d.

125. This quote is from someone called Tuna, apud Wroblewski n.d.

Helen. One woman opines, for example, that she "has the right stunning facial features and golden hair to play the quintessential Helen."[126] Collectively, the bloggers are far less hung up than the critics on Helen's nudity, and almost entirely devoid of their coy or demeaning language. Instead, a male connoisseur is happy to give it his stamp of approval ("Nice female nudity").[127]

Where Helen's character is concerned, "pout" and "petulant" remain key words.[128] One woman complains that she is "insipid" and too "passive . . . in her own story."[129] Yet the bloggers are more willing than the critics, regardless of gender, to see Helen's feistiness as a feminist statement in itself. One woman likes that Guillory's Helen had "spirit and wit" instead of being "an insipid milksop or just a wretched, faithless woman."[130] The same applies to Kern's addition of more "feminine" material. One man objects to the first hour (prior to the war) as largely "superfluous," but more than one woman applauds the extension of Helen's story beyond its usual limits.[131]

For a larger sample of audience reactions, I turn to IMDb.[132] Data from such sources are, to be sure, rife with uncertainties.[133] Used with caution, however, they may offer further insight into the miniseries' reception by a broader audience.

In raw numbers, *Helen of Troy* scored on the low side compared to other ancient world miniseries of the period (table 1).[134] At 5,373, the total number of ratings is quite high, but the mean, at 6.3 (on a scale of one to ten), is lower than *The Odyssey*, *Spartacus*, *Attila*, *Caesar*, or *Cleopatra*. The only entry that falls

126. Jamie Z. 2012.

127. Wroblewski n.d.

128. Wroblewski n.d.; Mahon 2011; Johanson 2003.

129. Mahon 2011.

130. Need Coffee Dot Com 2004. Scholars who have written about the film also tend towards this view (Nagle 2004; Winkler 2009: 234, 236). She is "energetically curious, not conventionally feminine," and "a spirited and rambunctious adolescent" (Shillock 2011: 133).

131. Beyond Hollywood 2003; Jamie Z. 2012; Mahon 2011.

132. Among the many available movie review sites, I focus on IMDb because it is the most widely used and comprehensive, and also because it breaks down respondents by age and gender.

133. The writers are often anonymous; there is only limited indication of gender, age or other social or cultural variables; they are self-selected; they are from all over the world; they are posted over many years; they reflect various viewing contexts (broadcast, DVD, classroom, continuous, episodic, with or without ads).

134. These ratings date from August 12, 2016, except for *Spartacus*, which was added on January 6, 2017.

lower is *Jason and the Argonauts*. If we look at the numbers by gender, however, *Helen* was apparently much more successful with women than men. In every case, many fewer women cast votes than men but their mean rating is higher (even when the title and content focus on men). The two films named for female heroes stand apart, however, falling low in the overall rankings but showing a significantly higher percentage of female voters. Almost sixty-eight percent of those who rate *Cleopatra* are women, and their mean is nearly a full point higher than the men's. The numbers for *Helen* are less dramatic, but it too has a greater percentage of female voters (forty-one percent), who rate it 0.4 higher than the men. These numbers are consistent with the documented fact that women are more tolerant of male-centered shows than men are of female-centered ones, resulting in a statistical demotion of shows aimed at women and girls.[135] We may therefore suspect that *Helen* was more successful, compared to its peer group, than the raw numbers suggest.

Some of the underlying reasons for these ratings may be gleaned from the IMDb comments section. Since only a tiny percentage of responders include comments, this sample is much smaller. In *Helen*'s case, the total number is 162, but in order to produce a sample more comparable to the Anglophone reviews and blogs, I begin with those who identify themselves as located in the United States, for a total of fifty-eight comments.[136] Thirty-seven of the fifty-eight also assign the film a star rating, for a mean score of 5.48. Eleven of the thirty-seven could plausibly be identified as male and ten as female; it was impossible to surmise a gender for the remaining sixteen. For those identifiable as male, the mean rating was 4.27; for the indeterminates, it was 5.06; but for the women, it was much higher, at 8.4.[137] The contrast is especially marked if we look at those who rated the film at either ten stars (best) or one (worst): four men gave the miniseries a one, and only one of them a ten, whereas only

135. Cf. Hickey's analysis of responses to the all-female *Ghostbusters* remake: "Essentially, male users were more likely to rate television shows with a female-heavy audience lower than female users would rate male-centric television. Men were tanking the ratings of shows aimed at women" (Hickey 2016; cf. N. Lang 2016).

136. IMDb does not collect information about nationality, race, or ethnicity, but commenters may supply their location. The site locates 916 *Helen* raters in the US, with a mean score of 6.5 (as against 3,063 non-US users, with a mean of 6.3). Many of the commenters who do not indicate their location are presumably also Americans.

137. These numbers are also much higher than the overall women's numbers for all respondents (8.4 vs. 6.6).

TABLE 1. IMDb Star Ratings for Ancient World Miniseries 1997–2004

Title	total votes	mean rating	male voters	female voters	% female	male mean	female mean	+/–
Odyssey (1997)	11,015	7.0	7559	1630	22.5	7.0	7.1	+.1
Spartacus (2004)	4,822	6.8	3491	614	17.5	6.8	7.3	+.5
Attila (2001)	8,692	6.7	5728	1587	27.7	6.6	7.3	+.7
Caesar (2002)	2,154	6.7	1370	370	27	6.6	7.4	+.8
Cleopatra (1999)	3,241	6.6	1572	1063	67.6	6.3	7.2	+.9
***Helen* (2003)**	**5,373**	**6.3**	**3096**	**1264**	**41**	**6.2**	**6.6**	+.4
Jason (2000)	3,998	5.9	2630	651	24.7	5.9	6.3	+.4

Arranged in order of overall mean rating

one woman gave it a one, and six a ten. In this admittedly modest sample, then, the film was *far* more successful with women than men.

Like the bloggers, these "American" commenters are happy to express forceful judgments, whether positive or negative, and are almost entirely devoid of coy or snarky remarks about Guillory's body. The only notable exception is the sole woman to rate the film at one star.[138] Otherwise Helen's nudity excites only occasional comment ("gratuitous but enjoyable," says one male writer). Some disparage Helen as a "blonde bimbette," or "waif-like . . . pouty and distraught," but others applaud her beauty ("gamine, coltish, pure and innocent"), her "personality and strength," or her "indomitable and chameleon spirit." A few even like the fact that the film is, in the words of one enthusiastic male, "definitely told as a love story."

These are outliers, however, in a torrent of vitriol. The show is "a load of stinking tripe!!!," "a steaming pile of horrendous crap," and "one of the most appauling [sic] movies I have every [sic] laid eyes upon." Such remarks illustrate the ease of criticizing popular culture as such, thanks to its supposedly self-evident inferiority.[139] Several writers further display their cultural superiority by comparing the miniseries to higher status films, including Wise's, now sanctified by time. As "typical Hollywood tripe" it is comparable, rather, to a variety of low-status genres and products. One male

138. She headlines her review "The Fanny that Launched 1000 Ships," and speaks of Guillory's "bodacious bottom." Quotations from these putatively American commenters are taken from IMDb comments made between April 2003 and January 2006, and accessed August 16, 2016, https://www.imdb.com/title/tt0340477/reviews.

139. Ang 1985: 88–89, 94–96.

condemns the horse-riding scene as "videoke," Helen's leap into the water after Paris as "cheesy," and both as "really pointless." Several users compare the show to TV series that just happen to be popular with girls, namely *Xena: Warrior Princess* and Joss Whedon's *Buffy the Vampire Slayer*.[140] One conveys the full force of his opprobrium by refering to *Mutant X*, *Buffy*, CliffsNotes, Homer Simpson, and McDonalds.[141]

Contempt for the influence of "feminine" genres and tastes is palpable. Many writers, regardless of gender, object to the focus on romance and personal relationships at the expense of "other important historical, social, economical aspects of that time." It is "a load of fluff," or "movie of the week drivel." One complains that the Theseus plot "looks like padding," another sneers at Menelaus's "sensitivity training," a third complains that "the melodrama" is "overdone," a fourth declares, "*Even* as a *mere* love story, it fails" (emphasis added). Even positive reviews sometimes betray the film's failure to fulfill viewers' generic expectations: "*Although* more love story than epic, miniseries *still* entertaining" (emphasis added). One woman is "a little ashamed of myself for sticking out the whole four hours" yet "not really sorry I watched it"—a response characteristic of many who enjoy low-status "feminine" genres.[142]

The primary reason supplied by these IMDb users for their hostility is concern about the film's "accuracy," or lack thereof. Professional critics rarely judge *Helen* by this criterion, presumably because they are more confident in their own intellectual and cultural capital, and so feel less need to affirm and display it.[143] General viewers of such adaptations are much less likely to judge them as autonomous works, typically perceiving them, rather, as *versions* whose first duty is a perceived "authenticity" to canonical sources. This attests to a particular kind of pleasure afforded to viewers of the historical miniseries as a species of "event-status" TV. In John Caldwell's words, "When viewers are told by

140. One blogger also compares the show derisively to *XWP* (Wrobleski n.d.).

141. This Floridian writer's username (asteri) suggests that he is of Greek origin and therefore may be exceptionally invested in the *Iliad*'s canonicity.

142. Cf. Ang 1985: 106–7; Brunsdon 1997: 149–51.

143. The few professional scholars who have written about the film seem to enjoy engaging with it as an adaptation and have little interest in "accuracy" as such (cf. above, n. 130). The same is true of the blogger Dindrane, who identifies herself on Need Coffee Dot Com as a "prudish academic," and Wroblewski, whose IMDb bio calls him a "Former stage actor and English professor." A few lay commenters also display their sophistication by scoffing at nitpickers.

television to stop what they are doing in order to come watch 'the motion picture of a lifetime,' they are also told to bring to the screen their proven skills at narrative and history."[144] The canonicity that is used to attract viewers promises the further pleasure of exercising such skills, thereby legitimizing one's taste and judgment. It is no coincidence that such films are routinely promoted for educational use.[145]

The world of Greek legend is especially rich in such opportunities thanks to its settled place in childhood education, which bestows a sense of personal ownership on an unusually broad swathe of potential viewers. This allows those viewers to acquire both personal gratification and social capital by displaying their knowledge of antiquity, which they often do online in considerable detail. Many comments on this miniseries complain about historical specifics (e.g., Troy's proximity to the beach), or opine in detail on such topics as ancient weaponry. Others are concerned with mythological "inaccuracy" (e.g., Cassandra should not have the gift of prophecy before encountering Apollo).

The "accuracy" criterion underlies nearly all of the most rabidly hostile IMDb comments on this *Helen*. The show is condemned, among other things, as "bastardizing," "raping," or "blaspheming" against "the true story," as enshrined in "mythology" or "history." The most vitriolic comments are often directed not (just) at the film, but at its audience. One viewer opines, "People who watch it are killing off brain cells." Another concludes, "If you think this was an amazing piece of cinema, get the coloring book version of the Iliad, and prepare to be amazed. Remember not to eat the crayons though." The sheer nastiness of such remarks is an assertion of cultural superiority over anyone who might enjoy the film. In so far as "publicly assessing others . . . is a gesture of social power,"[146] the degree of vitriol is a measure of the cultural capital felt to inhere in one's personal capacity to make such judgments.

This investment in the author's own cultural capital is further betrayed by the many comments judging the miniseries as a source of knowledge about antiquity in itself—a role in which it inevitably fails: "If you want to know about Helen—read the Iliad, for Pete's sake." This is just one of many, many

144. Caldwell 1995: 191–92; cf. Corrigan 2002: 177–78.

145. Rapping 1992: 118.

146. Reagle 2015: 141. "There are always issues of power at stake in notions such as quality and judgement" (Brunsdon 1997: 130).

complaints about the film's supposed failure specifically to live up to the *Iliad*. In particular, there are countless objections to Achilles: his characterization ("absolutely scandalous"), the minimizing of his role ("barely mentions Achilles"), and his appearance ("there was no reason for him to be bald"). Unlike the cinematic epics, however, the miniseries was not promoted as based on or even "inspired by" the *Iliad*, which in fact supplies relatively little of its material. It is hardly surprising, then, that judging by this criterion, it is "the worst version of The Illiad [sic] ever told."

Another angry IMDb user apostrophizes the filmmakers, "What? Homer didn't do a good enough job for you?" At first sight, such remarks seem to rest on a weird blindness to genre, medium, and cultural context. In what sense could viewing this telefilm possibly qualify as an experience comparable to reading the *Iliad*, and why on earth should we expect it to? Most viewers are well aware, however, that such a reception *must* be in some sense "untrue" to the *Iliad*, if only because it is subjected to different generic and formal constraints ("What else do you expect from the USA channel?"). Assertions about "authenticity" turn out to be, rather, a way to convey not only the writer's knowledge, but their personal feelings or opinions about (what they recall of) "the *Iliad*" and how such a film "should" be made. In other words, claims about fidelity, as a purportedly objective measure of quality, are really claims to authority.

This is betrayed by the fact that assertions about "authenticity" are often a matter of interpretation, at best, and sometimes demonstrably wrong.[147] Nevertheless, with few exceptions, the writers show fierce confidence in their own version of events, often seasoned with righteous indignation. As Timothy Corrigan puts it, in an age of multiple screen adaptations, "fidelity," as a criterion for preferring one version over another, means being "faithful to one's own self, desires, tastes, imagination, and inclinations (provoked perhaps by a memory of or desire for the ghostly palimpsest of a literary text)."[148] The point is clearly demonstrated by the way that viewers who disparage the miniseries for "inaccuracy" will attribute accuracy, in contrast, to a preferred version. "For accuracy watch Troy. In Troy it truly makes you feel as if you are reading the Illiad [sic]." *Troy*, of course, diverges wildly from the *Iliad*, but it evidently captures this (male) viewer's "memory of or desire for the ghostly palimpsest

147. "Helen was not kidnapped by Theseus! Clytemnestra had three children, and Orestes and Elektra helped her wreak her vengeance for the death of Iphigenia."

148. Corrigan 2002: 167–68.

of a literary text." In *Helen*'s case the ten-star reviewers as a group are far less concerned than the naysayers with "accuracy." Yet some of them actually applaud the show on these grounds, insisting, for example, that (unlike *Troy*) it follows "the real storyline" and Achilles is cast "perfectly." Like the haters, these fans use their personal preconceptions and preferences to judge the film and opine on its authenticity. Such judgments are problematic, not because of their subjectivity, but because they are so often framed as "objective" by citing perceived "inaccuracies."

All historical films are subjected to complaints about "accuracy." But reframing a masculine classic in feminine terms makes it especially vulnerable. For *Helen*, this is exemplified by the male blogger who is sick of classics "being revised with a feminist slant," in this case by showing Helen as "a strong character who makes her own decisions."[149] He questions whether it is "appropriate to alter a defining work of literature thousands of years old and an integral part of western heritage just to ensure that it will be inoffensive to . . . a particular generation." This blogger is using the criterion of "fidelity"—decorously veiled as "appropriateness"—to discourage contemporary, and specifically feminist, reinterpretations. A similar attitude is reflected in the IMDb comments using claims about "accuracy" to convey scorn for the film's more "feminine" aspects. "The overall focus on Paris and Helen . . . doesn't do service to the true scope of the Iliad." Or, as one outraged comment is headlined, "The Illiad [sic] was not a love story."

Such viewers are, of course, objecting to precisely the adaptations that were most central to the writer's agenda. This demonstrates the high price exacted from filmmakers by the prestige of classical antiquity: the same cultural heft that is used to draw in audiences also empowers and even encourages those audiences to judge the results from precisely the privileged perspective of canonicity that writers like Kern are trying to decenter. The resulting insistence on "accuracy" militates against creative reimaginings as such, preventing viewers from evaluating or even "seeing" innovative treatments on their own terms. This kind of investment in canonicity is therefore inherently elitist and conservative, both intellectually and artistically. The film's tendency (preferred reading) may be to subvert canonical views of the classical tradition, yet it will be seized on as aiming to promote such views regardless—and failing in that goal.

149. Stoddard n.d.

One of the First Feminists

In *Helen*'s case, the burden of canonicity was exacerbated by a misfit between the audience addressed by publicity and scheduling (fans of epic, a masculine genre) and the audience addressed by the miniseries as text, which, as we saw, is far more hospitable to women and girls than most such "epics." More specifically, as I argued earlier, it is addressed in key respects to teenage girls. It is probably a safe bet that none of the film's reviewers or bloggers falls into this category, and regrettably, we cannot tell the age of most who rate it on IMDb.[150] An obvious place to find teenage viewers would, however, be the classroom.

In a telling departure from the rhetoric of old Hollywood, *Helen*'s producer actively disavowed the film's educational benefits, hastening to assure prospective viewers, "This is not the BBC version of Helen of Troy. It's not homework."[151] But this did not prevent USA from promoting the film for school use. Lesson plans for *Helen* were supplied by Cable in the Classroom, a (now defunct) division of the National Cable & Telecommunications Association dedicated to helping cable networks promote their programs in schools.[152] Some IMDb comments, too, indicate that this is how the user was exposed to the film. A viewer in Chicago, for example, writes, "So I saw this movie in school and I thought it was just going to be another stupid crappy boring thing, but it wasn't. This is seriously one of the best movies that I have seen. I absolutely love it."

There is no indication of that writer's gender, but another, in a review dated August 3, 2004, identifies herself as "a 15-year old, fourth year student at Assumption Antipolo," which is an elite private Catholic girls' school in the Philippines. She even names her English teacher (Karen Manahan), who screened the film in class and had her students write IMDb reviews as an assignment. About sixty-nine of the comments on *Helen*—more than half—derive from

150. Of the 5,373 who rated the film, only two males and three females identify themselves as under 18 (though there are presumably others). Their mean star ratings are 6.5 and 7.0 respectively.

151. Hart 2003. By implying that the BBC version is "homework," Shapiro is flipping the anti-Americanism inherent in contemporary notions of "quality" TV (Brunsdon 1997: 113; cf. Maltby 1989: 17–18). Ironically, the BBC has since produced its own Trojan War series, *Troy: Fall of a City*, which handles ancient sources at least as freely as does USA's (if not more so).

152. Cf. J. Jacobs 2003. Lesson plans may still be found or purchased online.

this source.[153] Many indicate that Ms. Manahan's students viewed the film on DVD, in several class sessions during the last week or two of July 2004 or 2005, and were asked to rate it on a scale of one to five. They have read the *Iliad* (in some form or other) and have quite a detailed familiarity with Greek and Roman mythology.[154] As upper- and middle-class urban Filipinas, they are fluent in English. As students in a Catholic school, they have learned to frame their responses in terms of Catholic values.

Many caveats obviously apply to treating these Filipina schoolgirls as an audience sample. Unlike my other sources they are not based in the US; their reviews, which are far longer than the average, are repetitive and similar, often clearly responding to specific prompts or issues raised in class.[155] They viewed the film in a mandatory, culturally authorized context, specifically the classroom of an elite Catholic school with close ties to European educational traditions and the associated cultural imperialism.[156] Their ratings may have been affected by the educational context, personal feelings about the teacher, or peer pressure (for which some evidence may be seen below). Nevertheless, they provide a unique set of reactions from a significant number of teenage girls who viewed the telefilm soon after its release. All viewers, and indeed the actors and filmmakers, are, in one way or another, perceiving the film through the filter of schooling and other forms of acculturation, but in this case, we can observe the impact of childhood education at its source.

Thirty-three of these young Filipinas assign the miniseries IMDb star ratings, for an average score of 7.9. Those who rate it on their own scale (of one to five) give it an average of 4.1, for an equivalent of 8.2. Their ratings are thus

153. An exact count is not possible, since not all such students identified themselves. I include all comments posted in early August 2004 or 2005 that fulfill two or more of these additional criteria: self-identified as being from Philippines; name looks female; mentions school or appears to be addressing the same generic set of questions; rates the film on a scale of one to five instead of the IMDb's one to ten. Quotations in what follows are drawn from this set of comments, accessed August 16, 2016, https://www.imdb.com/title/tt0340477/reviews.

154. They name-check not just the usual suspects but also, for example, Sinon, the Palladium, Oenone, and Memnon. They have read Edith Hamilton's Mythology and seen other film adaptations, including *Troy*. I am grateful to Ms. Manahan—now Karen Singson—for providing me with background information about her students and her class.

155. Virtually all of them compare the film with ancient sources (especially the *Iliad*) and include a few facts about the production (date, director, producer, genre, casting), plus some comment on plot, characters, acting, music, lighting, setting, and/or cinematography.

156. The school was founded by Congregation of the Religious of the Assumption, a French religious order that reached the Spanish Colonial Philippines in 1892.

comparable to the numbers we saw earlier for American females of all ages (table 1, above). Five give the film ten stars (the maximum) on the IMDb scale, nine more give it the equivalent on their own scale (five), and two do both.[157] None of them hates it (the lowest IMDb rating is four stars), and many affirm their "love" for it, often in the most emphatic terms, calling it a "must see!," "an amazing film," "a great movie," and "one of the rather remarkable films of all time."

One of the most arresting differences between the Filipinas and the "American" IMDb users is that the former are *much* less likely to complain about "inaccuracy." They dutifully list discrepancies between the film and the *Iliad,* and/or the larger mythic background, but show little of the obsession with minute detail that pervades the American comments. Their teacher has clearly coached them to understand that, as one of them puts it, "myths are to be read with imagination and not ponder on the details." As a result, most of them think that the changes are appropriate, and/or that the film "captured the essence of the Iliad." Even when troubled by divergences, they usually acknowledge the filmmakers' right to adapt their source material and make "necessary changes," such as altering the characters for their own purposes.

The other most salient difference is the girls' enormous enthusiasm for this telefilm, for which they offer two main reasons. The first is that the film brought them "closer to the 'reality' of the Iliad". "Reality" in such contexts refers not to archeological or even mythical accuracy, but to what the students regard as "real"—i.e., their own experience. Because of the gulf dividing that experience from antiquity, they do not generally expect to *enjoy* educationally approved cinematic treatments of "classics." As one of them puts it, "We always have a connotation that historical movies are boring and just for the oldies." But *Helen,* she explains, is an exception: a film that "the whole family especially the youth will enjoy." Another recommends it "*even though* the story is considered old or classic" (emphasis added); a third opines, "*Although* it's an epic [the filmmakers] made it really interesting for the viewers of our time" (emphasis added); yet another, speaking for the group, declares, "*Though* the story was antique, the script made its way to every viewer's heart and soul" (emphasis added).

This last comment illustrates the second main reason for the girls' enjoyment, which is imbricated with the first. It is the film's emotional impact that

157. The equivalence is complicated by the fact that two of them give it ten stars on IMDb but a four on their own scale.

enables them to understand the *Iliad* better by making it "real" in their terms. One source of emotion stands out above all. The Filipinas are *far* more likely than the average IMDb user to write about love and romance. As one of them explains, "People have a passion for love and this is the reason why they enjoyed the movie." Another confesses, "I even felt in love after seeing it." A third attributes this reaction to the class as a whole, declaring, "We were all in love and at the same time depressed by the end of the movie." They are well aware that love and romance are not central to the *Iliad*. In their view, however, the film's focus on love did not "lessen its quality." Indeed, this shift of emphasis is precisely what makes the film "interesting" to them, or even *more* "interesting" than the epic. For as one of them puts it, the Trojans "were fighting for the most important thing in this world—love."[158]

Not coincidentally, these schoolgirls are *far* more interested than the average IMDb user in Matthew Marsden in the role of Paris. A few of the American viewers do comment on Marsden's sex appeal. One woman calls him "a gorgeous actor," while another opines that he was "great . . . and hot!!" But the young Filipinas outdo each other in declaring him "charming," "charismatic," "handsome and gorgeous." As a result, "It is almost impossible not to fall in love with Paris." This was evidently manifested during the classroom showings, where Paris "definitely did not fail in making his female audience yelp every time his face would appear on screen." In reacting this way, the girls are identifying with Helen as a subject rather than an object of desire—a significant departure from the usual preoccupation with judging her beauty and desirability to men.[159] They are often quite explicit about this: "It was easy to relate with Helen because she portrayed the type of woman who, like most of us, tend to let our feelings overpower us." Her elopement is "selfish," "morally wrong," and even "sinful," but "we could not blame her," and could still "connect," since "almost everyone knows how love can cause people to do almost anything."[160]

158. This naive romanticism echoes Guillory in *Making the Epic*: "Love is at stake, which is the most important thing in the world." One outlier finds the romantic scenes "dull," and another intrusive, but both still give the film nine stars.

159. The Filipinas have very little to say about her physical appearance. Just a few praise her beauty in generic terms. Only one echoes the adult critics in saying she is too thin.

160. Their judgmental language, absent from other user comments, presumably reflects the Catholicism of the girls' education.

Love is not the only aspect of this Helen that appeals to the Filipinas. They also praise her as "an intelligent, emotional, strong-willed girl who refused that her spirit and rights should be trampled upon," or even "one of the first feminists who challenged the status quo."[161] In contrast to Homer's Helen, she is "a woman who knew what she wanted." Another opines, "Unlike the women of her time, she was not submissive and she stood for her beliefs." The girls are outraged and disgusted by the rape (it is a "sin"), yet aware that it has broader meaning in its military context. They have little to say about the nude scene, but one praises the sense of self demonstrated by Helen's internal resistance to such humiliation: it is this that shows her to be not "just some object in men's eyes . . . [but] a strong and admirable woman, a fighter."

The educational use of such materials is anathema to certain self-appointed guardians of the classics. A Fox News story, headlined "Teenager of Troy," complains bitterly about Cable in the Classroom's lesson plans for *Helen*, especially their use of pop-cultural references.[162] The author quotes a blog post by Mike Antonucci, a conservative blogger, who denounces classroom use of *Helen* as "educating to the lowest common denominator."[163] He sneers, specifically, at the notion that the film fleshes out Helen's character, and mocks a writing prompt asking students which character most reminds them of themselves. By way of contrast, he mentions his own experience reading the *Odyssey* in Greek as a high school junior. Those without the ability, the opportunity or—most importantly—the desire to follow a similar path apparently have no right to participate in the reception and interpretation of classical texts. Yet the kind of pedagogy that Antonucci scorns is not only valuable but essential. Comparing oneself to fictional characters is, in the first place, an inescapable part of reading. More than that, though, it is a natural and legitimate way of entering into a discussion of cultural difference, tradition, and reception. It is a struggle for anyone to enter the Homeric world and be moved by what she finds there, and if she succeeds, it will always be through her own set of lenses.

161. A number applauded the fact that female roles are in general more prominent and "stronger" in the miniseries than in the *Iliad*. In particular, many more Filipinas than Americans comment positively on Cassandra's histrionics.

162. J. Jacobs 2003.

163. Antonucci is the founder of the Education Intelligence Agency, "a private, for-profit, one-man contract research firm focused on the inner workings of the teachers' unions." Center for Education Reform, "Education Intelligence Agency," accessed March 11, 2020, https://edreform.com/edreform-university/resource/education-intelligence-agency/.

If we follow Antonucci's logic to its conclusion, no one should be exposed to Homer in any form, since it is impossible for any modern person to acquire the necessary complete and perfect expertise. In practice, of course, it means restricting ownership of the text to those endowed with at least as much educational and cultural capital as the speaker. But unless one aspires to be a classical scholar, a childhood education in the classics is not (just) about learning Greek or getting the *Iliad* "right," but becoming *invested* in such texts and understanding their continuing role as bearers of cultural meaning. The educational function of a film like *Helen* is not to "deliver" the *Iliad* as such to young people (or adults), but as the Filipina schoolgirls would say, to make it "real" for them. The goal is not, ultimately or exclusively, to introduce students to Homer per se, but to expose them to canonical stories in ways that engage with their own lives. In doing so, it contributes actively to the formation of those lives, often in specifically gendered ways.[164]

In their study of Homer, these girls are in the process of acquiring cultural capital and ways to display it. They dutifully endorse the *Iliad*'s importance as a "timeless" and "educational" "classic," internalizing and perpetuating both its canonicity and the colonial reach of "Western" "civilization." Thanks to the film (and their teacher), however, this reverence is just one strand in a more complex and subtle interpretive stance. Their comments clearly demonstrate the value of the kind of pedagogy despised by Antonucci. Studying the film, in tandem with the *Iliad,* under a good teacher's guidance, has taught them to detect ways in which both the medium of film and the viewer's perspective shape our understanding of texts, whether ancient or modern. By viewing the film not as a failed equivalent of the *Iliad* but as a legitimate interpretation on its own terms, they are learning that texts are adaptable and subject to interpretation; that even a "classic" can be reread in multiple ways; that there is no such thing, really, as timelessness. They are learning not to carp about accuracy (in a way that is ultimately meaningless) but to interpret what they find. They are learning how the viewer's (or filmmaker's) perspective, and the medium, shapes understanding. In short, they are acquiring a much more sophisticated understanding of mythology, canonicity, and tradition than the Antonuccis of the world.

164. In one recent study, for example, women who watched films depicting male aggression were less likely to accept romanticized notions about stalking as a sign of "true love" (Lippman 2018).

This is of special importance where gender is concerned. Women and men have a different *kind* of stake in antiquity. It is very different for a girl, rather than a boy, to be exposed to the *Iliad* as "timeless" and unassailable in its cultural importance. That lesson may all too easily come at the price of demeaning not only their "feminine" tastes (e.g., for romance), but themselves as girls. The students in Ms. Manahan's classroom, in contrast, are learning what "history" leaves out, and ways for women to reclaim it. It is both ironic and satisfying that an "edgy" reinterpretation of the Trojan War myth, designed to give Helen a voice, should be used in making the canonical *Iliad* more palatable to teenage girls. It was precisely because it was "not the BBC version"—not the version hostile critics would have found more acceptable—that these young viewers liked it so much.

Not surprisingly, the girls sometimes struggle to articulate the complexity of what they are learning, a struggle often expressed by wrestling with the issue of "accuracy." One declares, "No one would dare alter this great classic which has influenced our world today," but goes on to explain that the movie does not count as altering it: "People just changed and modified [it] to make it more interesting and understandable." Others seem to have trouble distinguishing the film from the *Iliad* itself. One thinks it "proves that great books are tested by time and they are for people of all era and race [sic]." In consequence, the film is a classic by association: "This movie will last forever . . . It is a classic that will remain in our hearts and minds." Though superficially less than coherent, such comments show the girls wrestling with complex ideas about reception, authenticity, canonicity, and cultural influence.

I argued earlier that, as a TV miniseries on an ancient theme with a female hero, the film is burdened with expectations—generic, institutional, pedagogical, cultural—that work against both the writer's original intention and the commercial success of the product. The Filipinas' response confirms that, despite those expectations, the film succeeded in reaching an audience that values the "feminine" modes of romance and melodrama over the "masculine" heroic mode. Though they cannot stand for all teenage girls (let alone all women), they reinforce other evidence for the film's success with a female audience—a success concealed by ratings and contemptuous reviews, which obscured its greater popularity with women than men.[165] Young girls are

165. Reactions similar to the Filipinas' may be found scattered sparsely through the American comments (cf. above, p. 261).

perhaps, historically speaking, the least prestigious of audience segments. As such, they are arguably the demographic in greatest need of a critical stance towards the authority of the classical tradition and the epic genre. Ms. Manahan's students are not learning to misread Homer. What they are learning is that feminists—and teenage girls—are as entitled as anyone else to read the classics in their own way and use them for their own purposes.

BIBLIOGRAPHY

Aaron, Michele. 2005. "Looking On: Troubling Spectacles and the Complicitous Spectator." In *The Spectacle of the Real: From Hollywood to 'Reality' TV and Beyond*, edited by Geoff King, 213–22. Bristol, UK and Portland, OR: Intellect.

Abele, Elizabeth. 2014. "Romantic Hero." In *Deconstructing Brad Pitt*, edited by Christopher Schaberg and Robert Bennett, 21–35. London: Bloomsbury.

Addison, Heather. 2006. "'Must the Players Keep Young?': Early Hollywood's Cult of Youth." *Cinema Journal* 45: 3–25.

Adriaensens, Vito. 2013. "From Hephaestus to the Silver Screen: Living Statues, Antiquity and Cinema." *Cineaction* 91: 41–49.

Affron, Charles. 1991. "Identifications." In *Imitations of Life: A Reader on Film & Television Melodrama*, edited by Marcia Landy, 98–117. Detroit: Wayne State University Press.

Ahl, Frederick. 1991. "Classical Gods and the Demonic in Film." In *Classics and Cinema*, edited by Martin M. Winkler, 40–59. London: Bucknell University Press.

———. 2007. "*Troy* and Memorials of War." In *Troy: From Homer's Iliad to Hollywood Epic*, edited by Martin M. Winkler, 163–85. Malden, MA: Blackwell.

Alexander, David. 1995. *Star Trek Creator: The Authorized Biography of Gene Roddenberry*. New York: Roc Books.

Alexander, Sally. 1989. "Becoming a Woman in London in the 1920s and 1930s." *Metropolis, London: Histories and Representations since 1800*, edited by David Feldman and Gareth Stedman Jones, 245–71. London: Routledge.

Allen, Alena. 2007. "Briseis in Homer, Ovid, and *Troy*." In *Troy: From Homer's Iliad to Hollywood Epic*, edited by Martin M. Winkler, 148–62. Malden, MA: Blackwell.

Allen, Jeanne. 1980. "The Film Viewer as Consumer." *Quarterly Review of Film Studies* 5: 481–99.

Allen, Robert Clyde. 1985. *Speaking of Soap Operas*. Chapel Hill: University of North Carolina Press.

Allen, Robert Clyde, and Douglas Gomery. 1993. *Film History: Theory and Practice*. New York: McGraw-Hill.

Ang, Ien. 1985. *Watching Dallas: Soap Opera and the Melodramatic Imagination*. Translated by Della Couling. London: Routledge.

———. 1989. "Melodramatic Identifications: Television Fiction and Women's Fantasy." In *Television and Women's Culture: The Politics of the Popular*, edited by Mary Ellen Brown, 75–88. London: Sage.

Annas, Alicia. 1987. "The Photogenic Formula: Hairstyles and Makeup in Historical Films." In *Hollywood and History: Costume Design in Film*, edited by Edward Maeder, 52–77. London and Los Angeles: Thames and Hudson and Los Angeles County Museum of Art.

Anon. n.d.a. "The Top 15 Wicked Film Critics' Descriptions of Diane Kruger, AKA 'Helen of Troy.'" *No Apologies Press (blog)*. Accessed September 27, 2005. http://www.noapologiespress.com/presents/kruger.html.

———. n.d.b. "Star Trek (TOS): Elaan of Troyius." SF Debris. Accessed October 10, 2020. https://sfdebris.com/videos/startrek/s057.php.

———. n.d.c. "Beware Greeks Bearing Gifts Reviewed." Xenaville. Accessed April 12, 2022. http://www.xenaville.com/eps/s1/rev_beware.html.

———. 1911. "Seven Famous Beauties: No. 1. Helen of Troy." *Washington Herald*, January 1, 1911.

———. 1916. "America, Home of Beauty." *Kansas City Star*, February 21, 1916.

———. 1920a. "Who's the World's Most Beautiful Woman?" *Atlanta Constitution*, May 2, 1920.

———. 1920b. "Behold How Paris Has Stolen from History." *Atlanta Constitution*, August 8, 1920.

———. 1921a. "Helen of Troy Stirs Mischief for Mr. Wein." *Chicago Tribune*, January 7, 1921.

———. 1921b. "And That's What They Call 'Los Angeles Love.'" *Charleston Mail*, December 11, 1921.

———. 1921c. "News Notes from Movieland." *Kansas City Kansan*, May 21, 1921.

———. 1922a. "New Discovery of Science Clears and Whitens Your Skin Almost Over-Night." *Cincinnati Enquirer*, September 17, 1922.

———. 1922b. "Neysa McMein's 12 Prize Beauties." *Ogden Standard-Examiner*, October 1, 1922.

———. 1922c. "Ancient Vampires Played Active Part in History." *Topeka Daily Capital*, February 19, 1922.

———. 1922d. "Why Not Let 'Em Be Girls Again?" *Winnipeg Tribune*, August 22, 1922.

———. 1923a. "Every Woman's Duty to Make Herself Attractive." *San Francisco Chronicle*, September 23, 1923.

———. 1923b. "*No!* to Fashion's Wasp-Waist Revival." *Daily World* [Vancouver, BC], February 3, 1923.

———. 1924a. "Helen of Troy Real—*Not a Myth*." *Zanesville Times-Signal*, June 29, 1924.

———. 1924b. "Dainty Hats from Paree." *Evening Review* [East Liverpool, OH], February 23, 1924.

———. 1925. "Dredging for Relics of the World's Greatest 'Vamp.'" *News-Herald* [Franklin, PA], August 1, 1925.

———. 1926. "Summer Tresses." *Springfield Leader*, June 17, 1926.

———. 1927a. "The New Pictures." *Time*, December 26, 1927.

———. 1927b. "Helen of Troy." *Variety*, December 14, 1927.

———. 1927c. "The Private Life of Helen of Troy." *Film Spectator*, November 26, 1927.

———. 1928a. "Maria Corda Keen about First Role." *Washington Post*, February 11, 1928.

———. 1928b. "Helen of Troy." *Amateur Movie Makers*, February 1928.

———. 1928c. "Theatrical Film Reviews for March." *Educational Screen*, March 1928.

———. 1928d. "This Is No Week to Take Grandma to the Movies." *Kansas City Star*, January 29, 1927.

———. 1928e. "Helen of Troy." *Scranton Tribune*, February 1, 1928.

———. 1928f. "'Helen of Troy' Escapes Censors' Shears; Winning Laughs at Colonial." *Harrisburg Telegraph*, March 13, 1928.

———. 1928g. "Even if Jailed Guthrie Offers Helen of Troy." *Capital Journal* [Salem, OR], February 1, 1928.

———. 1953. "'Salome' Costumes Inspired New Fashions By Jean Louis." *Rocky Mount Telegram*, September 27, 1953.

———. 1954a. "New Star Said Most Beautiful." *Statesville Record and Landmark*, May 22, 1954.

———. 1954b. "Hollywood on the Tiber." *Time*, August 16, 1954.

———. 1954c. "'Helen of Troy' Discovers Stardom Interferes with Her Domestic Life." *Albuquerque Journal*, March 23, 1954.

———. 1954d. "Bare-Chested, Bare-Legged Heroes Cavorting on Screen." *Brooklyn Daily Eagle*, October 24, 1954.

———. 1955a. "Helen of Troy." *Variety*, December 21, 1955.

———. 1955b. "Star Wants to Look in Your Eyes." *Pasadena Independent*, December 26, 1955.

———. 1956a. "Film 'Helen of Troy' Is Spectacular." *Mason City Globe-Gazette*, February 15, 1956.

———. 1956b. "Italian Model in Indian Film." *Pampa Daily News*, January 8, 1956.

———. 1993. "Helen Was an Android: 'World's Most Beautiful Woman was Plastic.'" *The Sun*, November 9, 1993.

———. 2003. "Helen of Troy." *Hollywood Reporter*, April 17, 2003.

———. 2004a. "The Making of Troy: The Tale of a Kingdom and a Horse." In "Epics Special." Special issue, *Film Review* 51: 28–35.

———. 2004b. "The Unknown Face That Launched a Thousand Ships." *Sydney Morning Herald*, May 13, 2004.

———. 2004c. "Just Gorgeous." *People*, May 10, 2004.

———. 2004d. "Heaven Sent: 15 Looks for the Goddess in You." *Arizona Republic*, May 7, 2004.

———. 2004e. "A Cartoonish Joke of a Film." *The Guardian*, May 14, 2004. https://www.theguardian.com/film/2004/may/14/news2.

———. 2004f. "First Review of a Test Screening of TROY—Sounds Utterly Fantastic!" Ain't It Cool News, February 13, 2004. http://legacy.aintitcool.com/node/17009.

———. 2005. "Trojan Looks." *Channel Guide Magazine*, February 2005.

Antonucci, Mike. 2003. Review of *Helen of Troy* (2003). *Betsy's Page* (blog). Accessed March 12, 2020. http://betsyspage.blogspot.com/2003/04/education-intelligence-agency-has.html.

Arnold, William. 2004. "'Troy' is a Beauty of an Epic." *Seattle Post-Intelligencer*, May 13, 2004.

Arscott, Caroline, and Katie Scott. 2000. "Introducing Venus." In *Manifestations of Venus: Art and Sexuality*, edited by Caroline Arscott and Katie Scott, 1–23. Manchester, UK: Manchester University Press.

Asherman, Allan. 1988. *The Star Trek Interview Book*. New York: Pocket Books.

Atkins, Dorothy. 1983. "*Star Trek*: A Philosophical Interpretation." In *The Intersection of Science Fiction and Philosophy: Critical Studies*, edited by Robert E. Myers, 93–108. Westport, CT: Greenwood Press.

Atkinson, Torie. 2010. "*Star Trek* Re-Watch: 'Elaan of Troyius.'" The Viewscreen, December 30, 2010. https://www.theviewscreen.com/elaan-of-troyius/.

Avrech, Robert J. 2009. "Hollywood Unmasked: Latin Lover Is Kosher Butcher's Son." *Breitbart*, July 14, 2009. http://www.breitbart.com/Big-Hollywood/2009/07/14/Hollywood-Unmasked--Latin-Lover-is-Kosher-Butchers-Son.

B. Altman & Co. 1999. *1920s Fashions from B. Altman & Company*. Mineola, NY: Dover.

Babington, Bruce, ed. 2001. *British Stars and Stardom: From Alma Taylor to Sean Connery*. Manchester, UK: Manchester University Press.

Babington, Bruce, and Peter William Evans. 1993. *Biblical Epics: Sacred Narrative in the Hollywood Cinema*. Manchester, UK: Manchester University Press.

Bacon-Smith, Camille. 1992. *Enterprising Women: Television Fandom and the Creation of Popular Myth*. Philadelphia: University of Pennsylvania Press.

Baine, Wallace. 2004. "The Passion of the Brad: War Epic 'Troy' Basks in the Fabulousness of Star Brad Pitt." *Santa Cruz Sentinel*, May 14, 2004.

Banet-Weiser, Sarah. 1999. *The Most Beautiful Girl in the World: Beauty Pageants and National Identity*. Berkeley: University of California Press.

Banner, Lois W. 1983. *American Beauty*. New York: Knopf.

Banta, Martha. 1987. *Imaging American Women: Idea and Ideals in Cultural History*. New York: Columbia University Press.

Bär, Silvio. 2007. Review of *The War at Troy: A True History*, by Barry B. Powell. *Bryn Mawr Classical Review*. Accessed August 18, 2020. https://bmcr.brynmawr.edu/2007/2007-06-38.html.

Barasch, Moshe. 1985. *Theories of Art: From Plato to Winckelmann*. New York: New York University Press.

Barbas, Samantha. 2001. *Movie Crazy: Fans, Stars, and the Cult of Celebrity*. New York: Palgrave.

Bari, Shahidha. 2016. "Female nudity is powerful—but not necessarily empowering." *Aeon*, September 12, 2016. https://aeon.co/ideas/female-nudity-is-powerful-but-not-necessarily-empowering.

Bark, Ed. 2003. "USA's Helen Pretty Thin Fare." *South Florida Sun-Sentinel*, April 19, 2003.

Barnes, Eleanor. 1928. "Blonde Film Actress Has Counterpart of Face That Launched Thousand Ships." *Tacoma Daily Ledger*, January 15, 1928.

Barrett, Michèle, and Duncan Barrett. 2017. *Star Trek: The Human Frontier*. 2nd ed. New York: Routledge.

Barthes, Roland. 1986. "The Reality Effect." In *The Rustle of Language*, 141–48. Translated by Richard Howard. New York: Hill and Wang.

———. 1981. *Camera Lucida: Reflections on Photography*. Translated by Richard Howard. New York: Hill and Wang.

———. 2012. *Mythologies*. Translated by Richard Howard and Annette Lavers. New York: Hill and Wang.

Barton, Ruth. 2010. *Hedy Lamarr: The Most Beautiful Woman in Film*. Lexington: University Press of Kentucky.

Baudry, Jean-Louis. 1999 [1970]. "Ideological Effects of the Basic Cinematographic Apparatus." In *Film Theory and Criticism: Introductory Readings*, edited by Leo Braudy and Marshall Cohen, 345–55. New York: Oxford University Press.

Bazin, André. 1997 [1946]. "The Life and Death of Superimposition." In *Bazin at Work: Major Essays and Reviews from the Forties and Fifties,* edited by Bert Cardullo, translated by Alain Piette and Bert Cardullo, 73–76. New York: Routledge.

———. 1967. *What Is Cinema?* Vol. 1. Translated by Hugh Gray. Berkeley: University of California Press.

Bean, Jennifer M., and Diane Negra, eds. 2002. *A Feminist Reader in Early Cinema.* Durham, NC: Duke University Press.

Belton, John. 1990. "Glorious Technicolour, Breathtaking Cinemascope and Stereophonic Sound." In *Hollywood in the Age of Television,* edited by Tino Balio, 185–211. Boston: Unwin Hyman.

———. 1992. *Widescreen Cinema.* Cambridge, MA: Harvard University Press.

Benioff, David. 2005. "Web Access . . . David Benioff." BBC, September 20, 2005. http://www.bbc.co.uk/films/webaccess/david_benioff_1.shtml.

Bennetts, Leslie. 2004. "Aspects of Brad." *Vanity Fair,* June 2004.

Berger, John. 1972. *Ways of Seeing.* London: Penguin.

Berlant, Lauren Gail. 2008. *The Female Complaint: The Unfinished Business of Sentimentality in American Culture.* Durham, NC: Duke University Press.

Bernal, Martin. 1987. *Black Athena: The Afro-Asian Roots of Classical Civilization.* London: Free Association Books.

Bernardi, Daniel. 1998. *Star Trek and History: Race-ing Toward a White Future.* New Brunswick, NJ: Rutgers University Press.

Bernstein, Paula. 2016. "'Thumbs Down' Study Shows Gender Imbalance Among Critics." *Filmmaker,* June 24, 2016. https://filmmakermagazine.com/98958-thumbs-down-study-shows-gender-imbalance-among-critics/#.X0QfZ0l7myE.

Beyond Hollywood. 2003. "Helen of Troy (2003) Mini-Series TV Review." Accessed December 9, 2017. http://www.beyondhollywood.com/helen-of-troy-2003-mini-series-tv-review/.

Bianculli, David. 2003. "Trojan Horsefeathers and the Dame, Nothin' Special." *Daily News* [New York, NY], April 18, 2003.

Biery, Ruth. 1927a. "The Taming of Helen." *Photoplay,* November 1927.

———. 1927b. "Judge Ben Lindsey Defends Flapper Movies." *Photoplay,* November 1927.

Bing, Jonathan. 2003. "WB's 'Troy' finds Helen." *Variety,* April 10, 2003. http://variety.com/2003/film/markets-festivals/wb-s-troy-finds-helen-1117884496/.

Bishop, Charity. n.d. "Helen of Troy (2003)." Charity's Place. Accessed August 18, 2020. http://www.charitysplace.com/review/helenoftroy.htm.

Biskind, Peter. 1983. *Seeing Is Believing: How Hollywood Taught Us to Stop Worrying and Love the Fifties.* New York: Pantheon Books.

Black, Gregory D. 1994. *Hollywood Censored: Morality Codes, Catholics, and the Movies.* Cambridge: Cambridge University Press.

Blair, Karin. 1977. *Meaning in Star Trek.* Chambersburg, PA: Anima Books.

———. 1983. "Sex and 'Star Trek.'" *Science-Fiction Studies* 10: 292–97.

Blank, Thomas. 2015. "Utopia: Cinematic Sparta as an Idea (Not a City)." In *Imagining Ancient Cities in Film: From Babylon to Cinecittà,* edited by Marta García Morcillo, Pauline Hanesworth and Óscar Lapeña Marchena, 65–90. New York: Routledge.

Blanshard, Alastair J. L. 2017. "High Art and Low Art Expectations: Ancient Greece in Film and Popular Culture." In *A Companion to Ancient Greece and Rome on Screen*, edited by Arthur John Pomeroy, 427–47. Hoboken, NJ: John Wiley & Sons.

Blanshard, Alastair J. L., and Kim Shahabudin. 2011. *Classics on Screen: Ancient Greece and Rome on Film*. London: Bristol Classical Press.

Block, Paula M., Terry J. Erdmann, and Robert Blackman. 2015. *Star Trek Costumes: Five Decades of Fashion from the Final Frontier*. San Rafael, CA: Insight Editions.

Blondell, Ruby. 2005. "How to Kill an Amazon." In "Ancient Mediterranean Women in Modern Mass Media," edited by Ruby Blondell and Mary-Kay Gamel. Special issue, *Helios* 32, no. 2 (2005): 183–213.

———. 2009. "'Third Cheerleader from the Left': From Homer's Helen to Helen of *Troy*." *Classical Receptions Journal* 1 (January): 4–22. Reprinted in *Ancient Greek Women in Film*, edited by Konstantinos P. Nikoloutsos. Oxford: Oxford University Press, 2013.

———. 2013. *Helen of Troy: Beauty, Myth, Devastation*. Oxford: Oxford University Press.

———. 2016a. Review of *Classical Myth on Screen*, edited by Monica Silveira Cyrino and Meredith Safran. *Classical Review* 66, no. 1 (April): 282–84.

———. 2016b. Review of *Return to Troy: New Essays on the Hollywood Epic*, by Martin M. Winkler. *Bryn Mawr Classical Review*. Accessed August 19, 2020. http://bmcr.brynmawr.edu/2016/2016-04-44.html.

Blum, Daniel C. 1953. *A Pictorial History of the Silent Screen*. New York: Putnam.

Blumer, Herbert. 1933. *Movies and Conduct*. New York: MacMillan.

Boedeker, Hal. 2003. "PBS Crafts a Fine Story of the Beloved Animal, but USA Network Stumbles with Its Tale of Troy." *Orlando Sentinel*, April 20, 2003.

Booker, M. Keith. 2008. "The Politics of *Star Trek*." In *The Essential Science Fiction Television Reader*, edited by J. P. Telotte, 195–208. Lexington: University Press of Kentucky.

Bordwell, David. 1985. *Narration in the Fiction Film*. Madison: University of Wisconsin Press.

Bordwell, David, and Kristin Thompson. 2011. *Minding Movies: Observations on the Art, Craft, and Business of Filmmaking*. Chicago: University of Chicago Press.

Bordwell, David, Janet Steiger, and Kristin Thompson. 1985. *The Classical Hollywood Cinema: Film Style and Mode of Production to 1960*. New York: Columbia University Press.

Bould, Mark. 2003. "Film and Television." In *The Cambridge Companion to Science Fiction*, edited by Edward James and Farah Mendlesohn, 79–95. Cambridge: Cambridge University Press.

Bourdieu, Pierre. 1984. *Distinction: A Social Critique of the Judgement of Taste*. Cambridge, MA: Harvard University Press.

Braudy, Leo. 1986. *The Frenzy of Renown: Fame and Its History*. New York: Oxford University Press.

———. 2002. *The World in a Frame: What We See in Films*. 25th anniversary ed. Chicago: University of Chicago Press.

Braun, Eric. 1978. *Deborah Kerr*. New York: St. Martin's Press.

Breitenfeld, Sarah Brucia. 2022. "Never Bury My Bones Apart From Yours: *Iliad* Reception in *Xena: Warrior Princess*." In *The Routledge Companion to the Reception of Ancient Greek and Roman Gender and Sexuality*, edited by K. R. Moore. London: Taylor & Francis.

Brown, Jeffrey A. 2011. *Dangerous Curves: Action Heroines, Gender, Fetishism, and Popular Culture*. Jackson: University Press of Mississippi.

Brown, Sarah Annes. 2008. "'Plato's Stepchildren': SF and the Classics." In *A Companion to Classical Receptions*, edited by Lorna Hardwick and Christopher Stray, 415–27. Malden, MA: Blackwell.

Brunsdon, Charlotte. 1997. *Screen Tastes: Soap Opera to Satellite Dishes*. London: Routledge.

Bruzzi, Stella. 2000. "Grace Kelly." In *Fashion Cultures: Theories, Explorations, and Analysis*, edited by Stella Bruzzi and Pamela Church Gibson, 205–8. London: Routledge.

Buchanan, Judith. 2013. "Judith's Vampish Virtue and Its Double Market Appeal." In *The Ancient World in Silent Cinema*, edited by Pantelis Michelakis and Maria Wyke, 205–28. Cambridge: Cambridge University Press.

Buchman, Herman. 1973. *Film and Television Makeup*. New York: Watson-Guptill.

Buckley, Réka C. 2000. "National Body: Gina Lollobrigida and the Cult of the Star in the 1950s." *Historical Journal of Film, Radio and Television* 20 (October): 527–47.

Burgess, Jonathan. 2008. "Recent Receptions of Homer." *Phoenix* 62: 184–95.

———. 2009. "Achilles' Heel." In *Reading Homer: Film and Text*, edited by Kostas Myrsiades, 163–77. Madison, NJ: Fairleigh Dickinson University Press.

Burgoyne, Robert. 2008. *The Hollywood Historical Film*. Malden, MA: Blackwell.

———, ed. 2011. *The Epic Film in World Culture*. New York: Routledge.

Burr, Ty. 2004. "Pitt Looks Pretty, but the Star Makes a Strained Achilles in Lumbering 'Troy.'" *Boston Globe*, May 14, 2004.

Burton, Beatrice. 1925. "The Flapper Wife." *Reading Times*, May 19, 1925.

Butler, Judith. 1990. *Gender Trouble: Feminism and the Subversion of Identity*. New York: Routledge.

Byars, Jackie. 1991. *All That Hollywood Allows: Re-Reading Gender in 1950s Melodrama*. Chapel Hill: University of North Carolina Press.

Byrd, Ayana D., and Lori L. Tharps. 2014. *Hair Story: Untangling the Roots of Black Hair in America*. New York: St. Martin's Griffin.

Caldwell, John Thornton. 1995. *Televisuality: Style, Crisis, and Authority in American Television*. New Brunswick, NJ: Rutgers University Press.

Camp, Stephanie M. H. 2015. "Black Is Beautiful: An American History." *Journal of Southern History* 81, no. 3 (August): 675–90.

Capua, Michelangelo. 2011. *Deborah Kerr: A Biography*. Jefferson, NC: McFarland & Co.

Card, James. 1994. *Seductive Cinema: The Art of Silent Film*. New York: Knopf.

Carden-Coyne, Ana. 2009. *Reconstructing the Body: Classicism, Modernism, and the First World War*. Oxford: Oxford University Press.

Carrillo, Jenny Cooney. 2004. "Pitting Himself Against the Job." *Urban Cinefile*. Accessed August 19, 2020. http://www.urbancinefile.com.au/home/view.asp?a=8891.

Carroll, Noël. 1985. "The Power of Movies." *Daedalus* 114, no. 4 (Fall): 79–108.

Cary, John. 1974. *Spectacular! The Story of Epic Films*. London: Hamlyn.

Castleton, Chaffee. 1955. "The Play's the Thing." *Valley News* [Van Nuys, CA], March 29, 1955.

Caudill, Helen. 2003. "Tall, Dark, and Dangerous: Xena, the Quest, and the Wielding of Sexual Violence in Xena On-Line Fan Fiction." In *Athena's Daughters: Television's New Women Warriors*, edited by Frances Early and Kathleen Kennedy, 27–39. Syracuse, NY: Syracuse University Press.

Chaddock, Katherine. 2011. "The Making of a Celebrity President: John Erskine and the Juilliard School." In *Iconic Leaders in Higher Education*, edited by Roger L. Geiger, 115–36. London and New York: Routledge.

Chiasson, Charles C. 2009. "Redefining Homeric Heroism in Wolfgang Petersen's *Troy*." In *Reading Homer: Film and Text*, edited by Kostas Myrsiades, 186–207. Madison, NJ: Fairleigh Dickinson University Press.

Christie, Ian. 2013. "Rome in London." In *The Ancient World in Silent Cinema*, edited by Pantelis Michelakis and Maria Wyke, 109–24. Cambridge: Cambridge University Press.

Church Gibson, Pamela. 2008. "Concerning Blondeness: Gender, Ethnicity, Spectacle and Footballers' Waves." In *Hair: Styling, Culture and Fashion*, edited by Geraldine Biddle-Perry and Sarah Cheang, 141–149. New York: Berg.

Clark, Danae. 1989. "*Cagney & Lacy*: Feminist Strategies of Detection." In *Television and Women's Culture: The Politics of the Popular*, edited by Mary Ellen Brown, 117–33. London: Sage.

Clarke, Cath. 2021. "Quant review—Sadie Frost's Starry Fashion Doc on Miniskirt Queen." *The Guardian*, October 27, 2021. https://www.theguardian.com/film/2021/oct/27/quant-review-sadie-frosts-starry-fashion-doc-on-miniskirt-queen.

Clay, Jenny Strauss. 2011. *Homer's Trojan Theater*. New York: Cambridge University Press.

Clover, Carol J. 1992. *Men, Women, and Chain Saws: Gender in the Modern Horror Film*. Princeton, NJ: Princeton University Press.

Cohan, Steven. 1997. *Masked Men: Masculinity and the Movies in the Fifties*. Bloomington: Indiana University Press.

Cohen, David S. 2004. "*Troy*: From Script to Screen: An Interview with David Benioff." *Scr(i)pt* 10, no. 3 (May/June 2004): 36–40.

Comolli, Jean-Louis. 1980 [1971]. "Machines of the Visible." In *The Cinematic Apparatus*, edited by Teresa de Lauretis and Stephen Heath, 121–42. New York: St. Martin's Press.

Conor, Liz. 2004. *The Spectacular Modern Woman: Feminine Visibility in the 1920s*. Bloomington: Indiana University Press.

Conrad, Laurel. 2013. "Diane Kruger's 10 Hottest Moments." *Daily Caller*, July 15, 2013. http://dailycaller.com/2013/07/15/diane-krugers-10-hottest-moments-slideshow/.

Consagra, Pier. 2001. "The Babe Goddesses." *Sports Illustrated*, Winter 2001, 18–26.

Cook, David A. 1981. *A History of Narrative Film*. New York: Norton.

Cooper, Anneliese. 2014. "'Troy' Is Ridiculously Inaccurate, & Here's Why." *Bustle*, May 14, 2014. https://www.bustle.com/articles/24095-troy-turns-10-why-im-still-mad-at-period-epic-and-brad-pitts-hair-isnt-the.

Corrigan, Timothy. 2002. "Which Shakespeare to Love? Film, Fidelity, and the Performance of Literature." In *High-Pop: Making Culture into Popular Entertainment*, edited by Jim Collins, 155–81. Malden, MA: Blackwell.

Courcoux, Charles-Antoine. 2009. "From Here to Antiquity: Mythical Settings and Modern Sufferings in Contemporary Hollywood's Historical Epics." *Film & History* 39, no. 2 (Fall 2009): 29–38.

Cranny-Francis, Anne. 1985. "Sexuality and Sex-Role Stereotyping in 'Star Trek.'" *Science-Fiction Studies* 12, no. 3 (November): 274–84.

Crisp, Quentin. 1989. *How to Go to the Movies*. New York: St. Martin's Press.

Crowther, Bosley. 1951a. "'Quo Vadis,' Based on Sienkiewicz Novel and Made in Rome, Opens at Two Theatres." *New York Times*, November 9, 1951.

———. 1951b. "Whither Bound? 'Quo Vadis' Raises a Question as to the Way of the Spectacle Film." *New York Times*, November 18, 1951.

———. 1953. "'Salome,' at Rivoli, Stars Rita Hayworth as Enchantress of the Biblical Story." *New York Times*, March 25, 1953.

———. 1956. "'Iliad' Revisited; Helen's Face Launches Ships at Criterion." *New York Times*, January 27, 1956.

Cuklanz, Lisa M. 2000. *Rape on Prime Time: Television, Masculinity, and Sexual Violence*. Philadelphia: University of Pennsylvania Press.

Currie, George. 1925. "'The Face That Launched a Thousand Ships'—The Steamer Book for Tourists." *Brooklyn Daily Eagle*, June 28, 1925.

Cushman, Marc, and Susan Osborn. 2013. *These Are the Voyages. TOS, Season One*. San Diego: Jacobs Brown.

———. 2015. *These Are the Voyages. TOS, Season Three*. San Diego: Jacobs Brown.

Custen, George. 1992. *Bio/pics: How Hollywood Constructed Public History*. New Brunswick, NJ: Rutgers University Press.

Cyrino, Monica Silveira. 2005a. *Big Screen Rome*. Malden, MA: Blackwell.

———. 2005b. "She'll Always Have Paris: Helen in Wolfgang Petersen's *Troy*." *Amphora* 4: 10–11, 18.

———. 2007. "Helen of *Troy*." In *From Homer's Iliad to Hollywood Epic*, edited by Martin M. Winkler, 131–47. Malden, MA: Blackwell.

———. 2014. "Ancient Sexuality on Screen." In *A Companion to Greek and Roman Sexualities*, edited by Thomas K. Hubbard, 613–28. Oxford: Wiley-Blackwell.

Cyrino, Monica Silveira, and Meredith Safran. 2015. "Introduction: Cinemyths: Classical Myth on Screen." In *Classical Myth on Screen*, edited by Monica Silveira Cyrino and Meredith Safran, 1–11. New York: Palgrave Macmillan.

D'Acci, Julie. 1997. "Nobody's Woman? Honey West and the New Sexuality." In *The Revolution Wasn't Televised: Sixties Television and Social Conflict*, edited by Lynn Spigel and Michael Curtin, 73–93. New York: Routledge.

Daly, Ann. 1995. *Done into Dance: Isadora Duncan in America*. Bloomington: Indiana University Press.

Danek, Georg. 2007. "The Story of Troy through the Centuries." In *Troy: From Homer's Iliad to Hollywood Epic*, edited by Martin M. Winkler, 68–84. Malden, MA: Blackwell.

Daugherty, Gregory N. 2013. "Glenn Close Channels Theda Bara in *Maxie* (1985): A Chapter in the Social History of the Snake Bra." In *Screening Love and Sex in the Ancient World*, edited by Monica Silveira Cyrino, 183–94. New York: Palgrave Macmillan.

Davies, Chris. 2019. *Blockbusters and the Ancient World: Allegory and Warfare in Contemporary Hollywood*. London: Bloomsbury.

Davies, Sam. 2016. "Misread My Lips." *Sight & Sound* 26, no. 10: 52–53.

Day, Kirsten. 2022. "Looking a Gift Horse in the Mouth: Helen of Troy and the Trojan Horse." In *Ancient Epic in Film and Television*, edited by Amanda Potter and Hunter Gardner, 98–115. Edinburgh: Edinburgh University Press.

de Castelbajac, Kate. 1995. *The Face of the Century: 100 Years of Makeup and Style*. New York: Rizzoli.

deCordova, Richard. 1990. *Picture Personalities: The Emergence of the Star System in America*. Urbana: University of Illinois Press.

Deford, Frank. 1971. *There She Is: The Life and Times of Miss America*. New York: Viking.

Deleon, Jian. 2013. "Controversy & Fitch: A History of Abercrombie's Most Flagrant F**k-Ups." *Complex*, May 22, 2013. https://www.complex.com/style/2013/05/controversy-fitch-a-history-of-abercrombies-most-flagrant-fuck-ups/.

Deleyto, Celestino. 2001. "The Nun's Story: Femininity and Englishness in the Films of Deborah Kerr." *British Stars and Stardom: From Alma Taylor to Sean Connery*, edited by Bruce Babington, 120–31. Manchester, UK: Manchester University Press.

Denby, David. 2004. "Heroes: Wolfgang Petersen's 'Troy.'" *The New Yorker*, May 17, 2004.

Denizet-Lewis, Benoit. 2006. "The Man Behind Abercrombie & Fitch." *Salon*, January 24, 2006. http://www.salon.com/2006/01/24/jeffries/.

Derbew, Sarah F. 2022. *Untangling Blackness in Greek Antiquity*. Cambridge: Cambridge University Press.

Desta, Yohana. 2019. "*Troy*: The Secret Impact of Brad Pitt's Sword-and-Sandal Epic." *Vanity Fair*, May 14, 2019.

Diak, Nicholas, ed. 2018. *The New Peplum: Essays on Sword and Sandal Films and Television Programs since the 1990s*. Jefferson, NC: McFarland & Co.

Dinan, Patsy. 1956. "'Helen' Opens at Paramount." *Amarillo Globe-Times*, February 16, 1956.

Dion, Karen, Ellen Berscheid, and Elaine Walster. 1972. "What Is Beautiful Is Good." *Journal of Personality and Social Psychology* 24, no. 3: 285–90.

Dixon, Bryony. 2013. "The Ancient World on Silent Film: The View from the Archive." In *The Ancient World in Silent Cinema*, edited by Pantelis Michelakis and Maria Wyke, 27–36. Cambridge: Cambridge University Press.

Dixon, Simon. 2003. "Ambiguous Ecologies: Stardom's Domestic Mise-En-Scène." *Cinema Journal* 42, no. 2 (Winter): 81–100.

Doane, Mary Ann. 1980. "The Voice in the Cinema: The Articulation of Body and Space." *Yale French Studies* 60: 33–50.

———. 1987. *The Desire to Desire: The Woman's Film of the 1940s*. Bloomington: Indiana University Press.

Doherty, Thomas Patrick. 1999. *Pre-Code Hollywood: Sex, Immorality, and Insurrection in American Cinema, 1930–1934*. New York: Columbia University Press.

Donati, William. 2012. *The Life and Death of Thelma Todd*. Jefferson, NC: McFarland & Co.

Dork Droppings. 2004. "Troy (2004)." Accessed August 18, 2020. http://dorkdroppings.com/troy-2004/.

Douglas, Susan J. 1994. *Where the Girls Are: Growing up Female with the Mass Media*. New York: Times Books.

Doux, Billie. n.d. "Star Trek: Elaan of Troyius." Doux Reviews. Accessed August 20, 2020. https://www.douxreviews.com/2012/08/star-trek-elaan-of-troyius.html.

Dow, Bonnie J. 1996. *Prime-Time Feminism: Television, Media Culture, and the Women's Movement since 1970*. Philadelphia: University of Pennsylvania Press.

Drazin, Charles. 2002. *Korda: Britain's Only Movie Mogul*. London: Sidgwick & Jackson.

Driscoll, Catherine. 2002. *Girls: Feminine Adolescence in Popular Culture and Cultural Theory*. New York: Columbia University Press.

Dué, Casey. 2007. "Learning Lessons from the Trojan War: Briseis and the Theme of Force." *College Literature* 34, no. 2 (Spring): 229–62.

Dyer, Richard. 1992. "Don't Look Now: The Male Pinup." In *The Sexual Subject: A Screen Reader in Sexuality*, edited by Mandy Merck, 265–76. London: Routledge.

———. 1997. *White*. London and New York: Routledge.

———. 1998. *Stars*. 2nd ed. London: British Film Institute.

———. 2004. *Heavenly Bodies: Film Stars and Society*. 2nd ed. New York: St. Martin's Press.

Ebert, Roger. 2004. "Troy." *RogerEbert*, May 14, 2004. http://www.rogerebert.com/reviews/troy-2004.

Eckert, Charles. 1990 [1978]. "The Carole Lombard in Macy's Window." In *Fabrications: Costume and the Female Body*, edited by Jane Gaines and Charlotte Herzog, 100–129. New York: Routledge.

Edelstein, David. 2004. "War is Hellenic: The Blood and Eroticism of Troy." *Slate*, May 13, 2004. https://slate.com/culture/2004/05/the-blood-and-eroticism-of-troy.html.

Eimer, David. 2004. "One or the Other Shall Spill His Life's Blood." *Empire*, June 2004, 66–77.

Eldridge, David. 2006. *Hollywood's History Films*. New York: I. B. Tauris.

Elias, Justine. 2003. "Helen Overcomes Bad Men and Bad Press." *New York Times*, April 20, 2003.

Elley, Derek. 1984. *The Epic Film: Myth and History*. London: Routledge.

Elliot, Andrew B. R., ed. 2014a. "Introduction: The Return of the Epic." *The Return of the Epic Film: Genre, Aesthetics and History in the Twenty-First Century*, edited by Andrew B. R. Elliot, 1–16. Edinburgh: Edinburgh University Press.

———. 2014b. "Special Effects, Reality and the New Epic Film." In *The Return of the Epic Film: Genre, Aesthetics and History in the Twenty-First Century*, edited by Andrew B. R. Elliot, 129–44. Edinburgh: Edinburgh University Press.

Ellis, John. 1992. *Visible Fictions: Cinema, Television, Video*. London: Routledge.

Elsaesser, Thomas. 1981. "Narrative Cinema and Audience Aesthetics." In *Popular Television and Film: A Reader*, edited by Tony Bennett, 270–82. London: British Film Institute and Open University Press.

———. 1991. "Tales of Sound and Fury: Observations on the Family Melodrama." In *Imitations of Life: A Reader on Film & Television Melodrama*, edited by Marcia Landy, 68–91. Detroit: Wayne State University Press.

Epstein, Daniel Robert. 2004. "David Benioff's Epic Adaptation, TROY." Screenwriter's Utopia, June 1, 2004. http://www.screenwritersutopia.com/article/d158312f.

Evans, Delight. 1928. "The Private Opinion of John Erskine of a Certain Famous Heroine." *St. Albans Daily Messenger*, January 30, 1928.

Everson, William K. 1978. *American Silent Film*. Oxford: Oxford University Press.

Faludi, Susan. 1991. *Backlash: The Undeclared War Against American Women*. New York: Crown.

———. 2007. *The Terror Dream: Fear and Fantasy in Post-9/11 America*. New York: Metropolitan.

Faraci, Devin. 2004a. "Interview: Diane Kruger." Ka-Bloom, May 8, 2004. http://www.ka-bloom.org/forum/index.php?/topic/6327-diane-kruger-interview/.

Faraci, Devin. 2004b. "Interview: David Benioff." *Cinematic Happenings Under Development*. Accessed October 31, 2005. http://www.chud.com/news/may04/may11troy3.php3.

Fass, Paula S. 1977. *The Damned and the Beautiful: American Youth in the 1920's*. New York: Oxford University Press.

Felleman, Susan. 2006. *Art in the Cinematic Imagination*. Austin: University of Texas Press.

Ferstl, Paul, and Keyvan Sarkhosh. 2014. *Quote, Double Quote: Aesthetics Between High and Popular Culture*. Amsterdam: Rodopi.

Fiell, Charlotte, and Emmanuelle Dirix. 2015. *1920s Fashion: The Definitive Sourcebook*. London: Goodman Fiell.

Finler, Joel W. 2003. *The Hollywood Story*. 3rd ed. London: Wallflower.

———. 2012. *Hollywood Movie Stills: Art and Technique in the Golden Age of the Studios*. London: Titan.

Finnigan, Kate. 2018. "Underwear Revolution: How Lingerie Grew Up and Put Women's Comfort First." *The Guardian*, December 9, 2018.

Fishbein, Leslie. 1989. "The Harlot's Progress in American Fiction and Film, 1900–1930." *Women's Studies* 16: 409–27.

Fischer, Lucy. 2003. *Designing Women: Cinema, Art Deco, and the Female Form*. New York: Columbia University Press.

Fischer, Paul. 2004a. "Interview: Diane Kruger for 'Troy.'" *Dark Horizons*, May 6, 2004. http://www.darkhorizons.com/features/1230/diane-kruger-for-troy.

———. 2004b. "Diane Kruger Launches International Career with 'Troy.'" *FilmMonthly* (blog). May 14, 2004. http://www.filmmonthly.com/Profiles/Articles/DianeKruger/DianeKruger.html.

Fiske, John. 1986. "Television: Polysemy and Popularity." *Critical Studies in Mass Communication* 3 (May): 391–408.

———. 1987. *Television Culture*. London: Routledge.

———. 1991. "Popular Discrimination." In *Modernity and Mass Culture*, edited by James Naremore and Patrick Brantlinger, 103–16. Bloomington: Indiana University Press.

———. 1992. "British Cultural Studies and Television." In *Channels of Discourse, Reassembled: Television and Contemporary Criticism*, edited by Robert C. Allen, 284–326. 2nd ed. Chapel Hill: University of North Carolina Press.

Fitch, Walter M. 1910. "The Motion Picture Story Considered as a New Literary Form." *Moving Picture World*, February 19, 1910.

Fitton, J. Lesley. 2007. "*Troy* and the Role of the Historical Advisor." In *Troy: From Homer's Iliad to Hollywood Epic*, edited by Martin M. Winkler, 99–106. Malden, MA: Blackwell.

Fitzgerald, William. 2001. "Oppositions, Anxieties, and Ambiguities in the Toga Movie." In *Imperial Projections: Ancient Rome in Modern Popular Culture*, edited by Sandra R. Joshel, Margaret Malamud, and Donald T. McGuire Jr., 23–49. Baltimore: Johns Hopkins University Press.

Fleming, Michael. 2003. "Director Firms 'Troy' Shoot." *Variety*, February 24, 2003. https://variety.com/2003/film/markets-festivals/director-firms-troy-shoot-1117881153/.

Flynn, Gillian. 2004. "Men and Myths." *Entertainment Weekly*, May 14, 2004.

Flynn, Hazel. 1956. "Warner Can Laugh at Them!" *Beverly Hills Citizen*, February 3, 1956.

Forshey, Gerald Eugene. 1992. *American Religious and Biblical Spectaculars.* Westport, CT: Praeger.

Fowles, Jib. 1992. *Starstruck: Celebrity Performers and the American Public.* Washington, DC: Smithsonian Institution Press.

Frankel, Valerie 2018. "Hercules, Xena and Genre: The Methodology behind the Mashup." In *The New Peplum: Essays on Sword and Sandal Films and Television Programs since the 1990s,* edited by Nicholas Diak, 115–34. Jefferson, NC: McFarland & Co.

Franklin, H. Bruce. 1990. "The Vietnam War as American Science Fiction and Fantasy." *Science-Fiction Studies* 17 (November): 341–59.

———. 1994. "*Star Trek* in the Vietnam Era," *Science-Fiction Studies* 21, no. 1 (March): 24–34.

Fraser, George MacDonald. 1988. *The Hollywood History of the World: From One Million Years B.C. to Apocalypse Now.* New York: Beech Tree.

Fredericks, Sigmund Casey. 1980. "Greek Mythology in Modern Science Fiction: Vision and Cognition." In *Classical Mythology in Twentieth-Century Thought and Literature,* edited by Wendell M. Aycock and Theodore M. Klein, 890–105. Lubbock: Texas Tech University Press.

French, Philip. 2004. "Troy." *The Guardian,* May 15, 2004. https://www.theguardian.com/film/2004/may/16/philipfrench.

Freydkin, Donna. "'Troy' Co-Star Doesn't Want Excessive Attention." *Journal News* [White Plains, NY], May 16, 2004.

Fuchs, Cynthia. 2007. "'What all the fuss is about': Making Brad Pitt in Thelma & Louise." In *Thelma & Louise Live! The Cultural Afterlife of an American Film,* edited by Bernie Cook, 146–67. Austin: University of Texas Press.

Fuller, Kathryn H. 1996. *At the Picture Show: Small-town Audiences and the Creation of Movie Fan Culture.* Washington, DC: Smithsonian Institution Press.

Futrell, Alison. 2003. "The Baby, the Mother, and the Empire: Xena as Ancient Hero." In *Athena's Daughters: Television's New Women Warriors,* edited by Frances Early and Kathleen Kennedy, 13–26. Syracuse, NY: Syracuse University Press.

———. 2005. "Troy the Film." Paper presented at the annual meeting of the American Philological Association.

Gaines, Jane M. 1990a. "Introduction: Fabricating the Female Body." In *Fabrications: Costume and the Female Body,* edited by Jane Gaines and Charlotte Herzog, 1–27. New York: Routledge.

———. 1990b. "Costume and Narrative: How Dress Tells the Woman's Story." In *Fabrications: Costume and the Female Body,* edited by Jane Gaines and Charlotte Herzog, 180–211. New York: Routledge.

———. 2000. "On Wearing the Film: *Madam Satan* (1930)." *Fashion Cultures: Theories, Explorations, and Analysis,* edited by Stella Bruzzi and Pamela Church Gibson, 159–77. London: Routledge.

Gaines, Jane and Charlotte Herzog, eds. 1990. *Fabrications: Costume and the Female Body.* New York: Routledge.

Gans, Herbert J. 1975. *Popular Culture and High Culture: An Analysis and Evaluation of Taste.* New York: Basic Books.

Gantz, Timothy. 1993. *Early Greek Myth: A Guide to Literary and Artistic Sources*. Baltimore: Johns Hopkins University Press.

Garcia, Lorenzo F. 2013. "G. W. Pabst's Hesiodic Myth of Sex in *Die Büchse der Pandora* (1929)." In *Screening Love and Sex in the Ancient World*, edited by Monica Silveira Cyrino, 11–24. New York: Palgrave Macmillan.

García Morcillo, Marta. 2008. "Graecia Capta? Depictions of Greeks and Hellas in 'Roman Films.'" In *Hellas on Screen: Cinematic Receptions of Ancient History, Literature and Myth*, edited by Irene Berti and Marta García Morcillo, 219–35. Stuttgart: Franz Steiner Verlag.

Gehring, Wes D. 2012. *Robert Wise: Shadowlands*. Indianapolis: Indiana Historical Society.

George, Lisa Rengo, and Anne Duncan. 2005. "Helen of Troy Reloaded." Diotima. Accessed August 21, 2020. https://diotima-doctafemina.org/essays/.

Geraghty, Christine. 2000. "Re-Examining Stardom: Questions of Texts, Bodies and Performance." In *Reinventing Film Studies*, edited by Christine Gledhill and Linda Williams, 183–201. London: Arnold.

Gerrold, David. 1984. *The World of Star Trek*. New York: Bluejay.

Gitlin, Todd. 2000. *Inside Prime Time*. 3rd ed. Berkeley: University of California Press.

Glancy, H. Mark. 1992. "MGM Film Grosses, 1924–28: The Eddie Mannix Ledger." *Historical Journal of Film, Radio and Television* 12, no. 2: 127–44.

Gledhill, Christine. 1988. "Pleasurable Negotiations." In *Female Spectators: Looking at Film and Television*, edited by E. Deidre Pribram, 64–89. London: Verso.

———, ed. 1991. *Stardom: Industry of Desire*. London: Routledge.

———. 2000. "Rethinking Genre." In *Reinventing Film Studies*, edited by Christine Gledhill and Linda Williams, 221–43. London: Arnold.

Glenn, Susan A. 2000. *Female Spectacle: The Theatrical Roots of Modern Feminism*. Cambridge, MA: Harvard University Press.

Gloyn, Liz. 2015. "In a Galaxy Far, Far Away: On Classical Reception and Science Fiction." *Strange Horizons*, April 27, 2015. http://strangehorizons.com/non-fiction/articles/in-a-galaxy-far-far-away-on-classical-reception-and-science-fiction/.

Glücklich, Hans-Joachim. 2000. *Die schöne Helena: Von Sparta über Troja nach Europa und Amerika*. Göttingen, Germany: Vandenhoeck and Ruprecht.

Goldhill, Simon. 2007. "Naked and O Brother, Where Art Thou? The Politics and Poetics of Epic Cinema." In *Homer in the Twentieth Century: Between World Literature and the Western Canon*, edited by Barbara Graziosi and Emily Greenwood, 245–67. New York: Oxford University Press.

Goldsmith, David F. 2004. "Troy: David Benioff's Trojan Horse Screenplay Conquers Hollywood." *Creative Screenwriting* (May/June): 54–57.

Golle, Jessika, Fred W. Mast, and Janek S. Lobmaier. 2014. "Something to Smile About: The Interrelationship between Attractiveness and Emotional Expression." *Cognition and Emotion* 28, no. 2: 298–310.

Gordon, Joel. 2017. "When Superman Smote Zeus: Analysing Violent Deicide in Popular Culture." *Classical Receptions Journal* 9, no. 2 (April): 211–36.

Görich, Knut. 2006. "Troia im Mittelalter—der Mythos als politische Legitimation." In *Der Traum von Troia: Geschichte und Mythos einer ewigen Stadt*, edited by Martin Zimmermann, 120–34. Munich: C. H. Beck.

Goulding, Jay. 1985. *Empire, Aliens, and Conquest: A Critique of American Ideology in Star Trek and Other Science Fiction Adventures*. Toronto: Sisyphus Press.

Gouveia, Georgette. 2004. "The Human Stain." *The Journal News* [White Plains, NY], May 13, 2004.

Grady, Constance, 2016. "Watch George Takei's Ode to Star Trek's Groundbreaking Legacy of Diversity." *Vox*, September 9, 2016. https://www.vox.com/2016/9/9/12861480/george-takei-star-trek-50th-anniversary-stephen-colbert.

Graf, L. A. 1994. *Firestorm*. New York: Pocket Books.

Grams, Martin. 2012. *The Time Tunnel: A History of the Television Program*. Duncan, OK: Bear-Manor Media.

Gray, Brandon, 2004. "'Troy' Rises with $46.9M, but Not Immortal." *Box Office Mojo*, May 17, 2004. https://www.boxofficemojo.com/news/?id=1381&p=s.htm.

Gray, Herman. 1997. "Remembering Civil Rights: Television, Memory, and the 1960s." In *The Revolution Wasn't Televised: Sixties Television and Social Conflict*, edited by Lynn Spigel and Michael Curtin, 349–58. New York: Routledge.

Gray, Hugh. 1956. "When in Rome . . . (Part II)." *Quarterly of Film Radio and Television* 10, no. 4: 344–53.

Gray, Jonathan, Cornel Sandvoss, and C. Harrington. 2007. *Fandom: Identities and Communities in a Mediated World*. New York: New York University Press.

Graziosi, Barbara. 2013. "The Poet in the Iliad." In *The Author's Voice in Classical and Late Antiquity*, edited by Anna Marmodoro and Jonathan Hill, 9–38. Oxford: Oxford University Press.

Green, Michelle Erica. 2006. "Elaan of Troyius." *Trektoday*, November 3, 2006. https://www.trektoday.com/reviews/tos/elaan_of_troyius.shtml.

Green, Peter. 2004. "Heroic Hype, New Style: Hollywood Pitted against Homer." *Arion* 12, no. 1: 171–87.

Grego, Melissa. 2002. "USA Ships Helen Mini as Quite a Knockout." *Variety*, March 13, 2002. https://variety.com/2002/tv/news/usa-ships-helen-mini-as-quite-a-knockout-1117863886/.

Grig, Lucy. 2017. "Introduction." In *Popular Culture in the Ancient World*, edited by Lucy Grig, 1–36. Cambridge: Cambridge University Press.

Grobéty, Gaël. 2014. *Guerre de Troie, guerres des cultures et guerres du Golfe: Les usages de l'Iliade dans la culture écrite américaine contemporaine*. Bern: Université de Lausanne.

Gross, Kenneth. 1992. *The Dream of the Moving Statue*. Ithaca, NY: Cornell University Press.

Gross, Edward, and Mark A. Altman. 1995. *Captains' Logs: The Unauthorized Complete Trek Voyages*. Boston: Little, Brown.

Gundle, Stephen. 2007. *Bellissima: Feminine Beauty and the Idea of Italy*. New Haven, CT: Yale University Press.

Gunning, T. 1999 [1989]. "An Aesthetic of Astonishment: Early Film and the (In)credulous Spectator." In *Film Theory and Criticism: Introductory Readings*, edited by Leo Braudy and Marshall Cohen, 818–32. Oxford: Oxford University Press.

Gwenllian-Jones, Sara. 2000. "Histories, Fictions, and *Xena: Warrior Princess*." *Television and New Media* 1, no. 4 (November): 403–18.

———. 2003. "Web Wars: Resistance, Online Fandom and Studio Censorship." In *Quality Popular Television: Cult TV, the Industry and Fans*, edited by Mark Jancovich and James Lyons, 163–77. London: British Film Institute.

Gwenllian-Jones, Sara, and Roberta E. Pearson. 2004. *Cult Television*. Minneapolis: University of Minnesota Press.

Haag, Pamela S. 1992. "In Search of 'The Real Thing': Ideologies of Love, Modern Romance, and Women's Sexual Subjectivity in the United States, 1920–40." *Journal of the History of Sexuality* 2, no. 4 (April): 547–77.

Haas, Michael. 2004. "*Troy*." *Political Film Society*, May 15, 2004. https://politicalfilmsociety.com/troy/.

Haase, Christine. 2007. *When Heimat Meets Hollywood: German Filmmakers and America, 1985–2005*. Rochester, NY: Camden House.

Hagelin, Sarah. 2013. *Reel Vulnerability: Power, Pain, and Gender in Contemporary American Film and Television*. New Brunswick, NJ: Rutgers University Press.

Haley, Shelley 1993. "Black Feminist Thought and Classics: Re-membering, Re-claiming, Re-empowering." In *Feminist Theory and the Classics*, edited by Nancy Sorkin Rabinowitz and Amy Richlin, 23–43. New York: Routledge.

Hall, Edith. 2013. "Why is Penelope Still Waiting? The Missing Feminist Reappraisal of the *Odyssey* in Cinema: 1963–2007." In *Ancient Greek Women in Film*, edited by Konstantinos P. Nikoloutsos, 163–85. Oxford: Oxford University Press.

Hall, Edith, and Henry Stead. 2020. *A People's History of Classics: Class and Greco-Roman Antiquity in Britain and Ireland 1689 to 1939*. Oxford: Routledge.

Hall, Mordaunt. 1927a. "Helen, the First." *New York Times*, December 10, 1927.

———. 1927b. "Sparta's Busy Queen." *New York Times*, December 18, 1927.

Hall, Sheldon, and Stephen Neale. 2010. *Epics, Spectacles, and Blockbusters: A Hollywood History*. Detroit: Wayne State University Press.

Hallam, Julia, and Margaret Marshment. 2000. *Realism and Popular Cinema*. Manchester, UK: Manchester University Press.

Hamer, Mary. 1993. *Signs of Cleopatra: History, Politics, Representation*. London: Routledge.

Handel, Leo A. 1950. *Hollywood Looks at Its Audience: A Report of Film Audience Research*. Urbana: University of Illinois Press.

Hanesworth, Pauline. 2015. "Monuments, Men and Metaphors: Recreating Ancient Athens in Film." In *Imagining Ancient Cities in Film: From Babylon to Cinecittà*, edited by Marta García Morcillo, Pauline Hanesworth and Óscar Lapeña Marchena, 91–112. New York: Routledge.

Hanke, Ken 2004. "Troy." *Mountain Xpress*, May 19, 2004. https://mountainx.com/movies/reviews/troy-php/.

Hansen, Miriam. 1985. "Universal Language and Democratic Culture: Myths of Origin in Early American Cinema." In *Mythos und Aufklärung in der amerikanischen Literatur: Zu Ehren von Hans-Joachim Lang*, edited by Dieter Meindl and Friedrich W. Horlacher in collaboration with Martin Christadler, 321–51. Erlangen, Germany: Universitätsbund Erlangen-Nürnberg.

———. 1991. *Babel and Babylon: Spectatorship in American Silent Film*. Cambridge, MA: Harvard University Press.

Hark, Ina Rae. 2008. *Star Trek*. Basingstoke, UK: Palgrave Macmillan.

Harris, Anita. 2004. *Future Girl: Young Women in the Twenty-First Century*. New York: Routledge.

Harris, Paul. 2012. "Cod-Damn Gorgeous! The Girl Who Works in a Chip Shop Who Has 'Britain's Most Beautiful Face.'" *The Daily Mail*, April 20, 2012. http://www.dailymail.co.uk/femail/article-2132896/Florence-Colgate-Girl-Britains-beautiful-face.html.

Harris, Thomas. 1991 [1957]. "The Building of Popular Images: Grace Kelly and Marilyn Monroe." In *Stardom: Industry of Desire*, edited by Christine Gledhill, 40–44. London: Routledge.

Harrison, John Kent, dir. 2003. *Helen of Troy*. USA Cable Entertainment LLC. DVD.

Harrison, Stephanie. 2017. "It's Official, Amber Heard's Face Is Perfect." *Beauty Crew*, May 25, 2017. https://www.beautycrew.com.au/amber-heard-scientifically-perfect-face.

Harrisson, Juliette. 2011. "Xena Warrior Princess: Beware Greeks Bearing Gifts." *Pop Classics* (blog). September 23, 2011. http://popclassicsjg.blogspot.com/2011/09/xena-warrior-princess-beware-greeks.html.

Hart, Hugh. 2003. "A Myth with Muscle/Marsden's Buffed-Up Paris at Heart of Trojan Love Story." *SFGate*, April 20, 2003. https://www.sfgate.com/entertainment/article/A-myth-with-muscle-Marsden-s-buffed-up-Paris-at-2621538.php.

Hartman, Forrest. 2004. "Hollywood Action-Epic 'Troy' Is Good Enough for the Gods." *Reno Gazette-Journal*, May 14, 2004.

Haskell, Molly. 2016. *From Reverence to Rape: The Treatment of Women in the Movies*. 3rd ed. Chicago: University of Chicago Press.

Hatfield, Henry. 1974. *Clashing Myths in German Literature from Heine to Rilke*. Cambridge, MA: Harvard University Press.

Hayes, K. Stoddard. 2003. *Xena Warrior Princess: The Complete Illustrated Companion*. London: Titan Books.

Hayes-Gehrke, Melissa. 2008. "Episode Review of *Star Trek—The Original Series* Season 3: 'Elaan of Troyius.'" *Dr. Melissa N. Hayes-Gehrke's Homepage* (blog). October 10, 2008. https://www.astro.umd.edu/~avondale/Reviews/TOS/s3-elaanoftroyius.html.

Hegarty, Emily. 1995. "Some Suspect of Ill: Shakespeare's Sonnets and 'The Perfect Mate.' (Repressive Use of Shakespeare in 'Star Trek: The Next Generation')." *Extrapolation* 36, no. 1 (Spring): 55–64.

Held, John. 1972. *The Most of John Held, Jr.* Brattleboro, VT: S. Greene Press.

Helford, Elyce Rae. 1996. "'A Part of Myself No Man Should Ever See': Reading Captain Kirk's Multiple Masculinities." In *Enterprise Zones: Critical Positions on Star Trek*, edited by Taylor Harrison, Sarah Projansky, Kent Ono, and Elyce Rae Helford, 10–31. Boulder, CO: Westview Press.

———. 2000. "Feminism, Queer Studies, and the Sexual Politics of *Xena: Warrior Princess*." In *Fantasy Girls: Gender in the New Universe of Science Fiction and Fantasy Television*, edited by Elyce Rae Helford, 135–62. Lanham, MD: Rowman & Littlefield.

Hellekson, Karen, and Kristina Busse, eds. 2006. *Fan Fiction and Fan Communities in the Age of the Internet: New Essays*. Jefferson, NC: McFarland & Co.

Heller-Nicholas, Alexandra. 2011. *Rape-Revenge Films: A Critical Study*. Jefferson, NC: McFarland & Co.

Hemmingson, Michael. 2009. "Sex and Star Trek: Amorous Androids, Interstellar Promiscuity." *Science-Fiction Studies* 36, no. 3 (November): 572–77.

Henderson, Mary. 1994. "Professional Women in Star Trek, 1964–1969." *Film and History* 24: 48–59.

Hendrick, Susan, and Clyde Hendrick. 1992. *Romantic Love*. Newbury Park, CA: Sage Publications.

Herwitz, Daniel. 2008. *The Star as Icon: Celebrity in the Age of Mass Consumption*. New York: Columbia University Press.

Herzog, Charlotte. 1990. "Powder Puff Promotion." In *Fabrications: Costume and the Female Body*, edited by Jane Gaines and Charlotte Herzog, 134–59. New York: Routledge.

Herzog, Jonathan P. 2011. *The Spiritual-Industrial Complex: America's Religious Battle against Communism in the Early Cold War*. Oxford: Oxford University Press.

Hess, Amanda. 2017. "How Movies and TV Address Rape and Revenge." *New York Times*, January 12, 2017.

Hickey, Walt. 2016. "'Ghostbusters' Is a Perfect Example of How Internet Movie Ratings Are Broken." *FiveThirtyEight*, July 14, 2016. http://fivethirtyeight.com/features/ghostbusters-is-a-perfect-example-of-how-internet-ratings-are-broken/.

Higashi, Sumiko. 1978. *Virgins, Vamps, and Flappers: The American Silent Movie Heroine*. St. Albans, VT: Eden Press Women's Publications.

———. 1996. "Antimodernism as Modern Representation in a Consumer Culture: Cecil B. DeMille's *The Ten Commandments*, 1923, 1956, 1993." In *The Persistence of History: Cinema, Television, and the Modern Event*, edited by Vivian Sobchack, 91–112. New York: Routledge.

———. 2002. "The New Woman and Consumer Culture: Cecil B. DeMille's Sex Comedies." In *A Feminist Reader in Early Cinema*, edited by Jennifer M. Bean and Diane Negra, 298–332. Durham, NC: Duke University Press.

———. 2014. *Stars, Fans, and Consumption in the 1950s: Reading Photoplay*. New York: Palgrave Macmillan.

Higgins, Charlotte. 2004. "Troy Stars Speak Out at 'Futility Of War.'" *The Guardian*, May 14, 2004.

Higgins, Lynn A., and Brenda R. Silver, eds. 1991. *Rape and Representation*. New York: Columbia University Press.

Hirsch, Foster. 1978. *The Hollywood Epic*. South Brunswick, NJ: Barnes.

Hiscock, John. 2004. "Troymendous Exclusive." *The Mirror*, May 3, 2004.

Hodge, Jarrah. 2014. "TOS 3X13 'Elaan of Troyius.'" *Trekkie Feminist*, January 5, 2014. https://trekkiefeminist.tumblr.com/post/72395355289/tos-3x13-elaan-of-troyius.

Hollander, Anne. 1978. *Seeing Through Clothes*. New York: Viking.

Horak, Jan-Christopher. 2005. "Sauerkraut and Sausages with a Little Goulash: Germans in Hollywood, 1927." *Film History* 17, no. 2/3: 241–60.

Horn, John. 2004. "A Troy Story." *Los Angeles Times*, May 9, 2004.

Hudson, Barbara. 1984. "Femininity and Adolescence." In *Gender and Generation*, edited by Angela McRobbie and Mica Nava, 48–72. Basingstoke, UK: Macmillan.

Hunt, William R. 1989. *Body Love: The Amazing Career of Bernarr Macfadden*. Bowling Green, OH: Bowling Green State University Popular Press.

Hunter, I. Q. 2007. "Post-Classical Fantasy Cinema: *The Lord of the Rings*." In *The Cambridge Companion to Literature on Screen*, edited by Deborah Cartmell and Imelda Whelehan, 154–66. Cambridge: Cambridge University Press.

Huyssen, Andreas. 1986. "Mass Culture as Woman: Modernism's Other." In *Studies in Entertainment: Critical Approaches to Mass Culture*, edited by Tania Modleski, 188–207. Bloomington: Indiana University Press.

Inglis, Alison. 2001. "Deathless Beauty: Poynter's Helen, Lillie Langtry and High Victorian Ideals of Beauty." In *Love & Death: Art in the Age of Queen Victoria*, edited by Angus Trumble, 71–82. Adelaide: Art Gallery of South Australia.

Inness, Sherrie A. 1998. *Millennium Girls: Today's Girls around the World*. Lanham, MD: Rowman & Littlefield.

———. 1999. *Tough Girls: Women Warriors and Wonder Women in Popular Culture*. Philadelphia: University of Pennsylvania Press.

Iordanova, Dina. 2011. "Rise of the Rest: Globalizing Epic Cinema." In *The Epic Film in World Culture*, edited by Robert Burgoyne, 101–23. New York: Routledge.

Isaacs, Bruce. 2010. "A Vision of a Time and Place: Spiritual Humanism and the Utopian Impulse." In *Star Trek as Myth: Essays on Symbol and Archetype at the Final Frontier*, edited by Matthew Kapell, 182–96. Jefferson, NC: McFarland & Co.

Jacobs, A. J. 1995. "Toys in Babeland; Lucy Lawless of 'Xena.'" *Entertainment Weekly*, November 24, 1995.

Jacobs, Joanne. 2003. "Gender Bias, Banned Words, Helen of Troy." *Fox News*, May 2, 2003. https://www.foxnews.com/story/gender-bias-banned-words-helen-of-troy.

Jacobs, Lea. 1991. *The Wages of Sin: Censorship and the Fallen Woman Film, 1928–1942*. Madison: University of Wisconsin Press.

Jamie Z. 2012. "A History of Helen of Troy on Film." *Funk's House of Geekery* (blog). July 27, 2012. https://houseofgeekery.com/2012/07/27/a-history-of-helen-of-troy-on-film/.

Jancovich, Mark. 2004. "Dwight Macdonald and the Historical Epic." In *Action and Adventure Cinema*, edited by Yvonne Tasker, 84–99. London: Routledge.

———. 2011. "An Italianmade Spectacle Film Dubbed in English: Cultural Distinctions, National Cinema and the Critical Reception of the Postwar Historical Epic." In *The Epic Film in World Culture*, edited by Robert Burgoyne, 161–67. New York: Routledge.

Jeffares, A. Norman. 1989. *Yeats the European*. Gerrards Cross, UK: Colin Smythe.

Jenkins, Henry. 2000. "Reception Theory and Audience Research: The Mystery of the Vampire's Kiss." In *Reinventing Film Studies*, edited by Christine Gledhill and Linda Williams, 165–82. London: Arnold.

———. 2013. *Textual Poachers: Television Fans and Participatory Culture*. 20th anniversary ed. New York: Routledge.

Jenkins, Thomas E. 2015. *Antiquity Now: The Classical World in the Contemporary American Imagination*. Cambridge: Cambridge University Press.

Jenkyns, Richard. 1980. *The Victorians and Ancient Greece*. Cambridge, MA: Harvard University Press.

Jess, Carolyn. 2005. "Achilles vs. Jason (and the Argonauts): Review of *Troy* (Petersen, 2004)." *Literature/Film Quarterly* 33, no. 1: 79–80.

Jewett, Robert, and John Shelton Lawrence. 1988. *The American Monomyth*. 2nd ed. Lanham, MD: University Press of America.

Johanson, MaryAnn. 2003. "Helen of Troy (Review)." *FlickFilosopher*, September 15, 2003. https://www.flickfilosopher.com/2003/09/helen-of-troy-review.html.

Johanson, MaryAnn. 2004. "Troy (Review)." *FlickFilosopher*, May 14, 2004. https://www.flickfilosopher.com/2004/05/troy-review.html.

Johnson, Catherine. 2005. *Telefantasy*. London: British Film Institute.

Johnson, Erskine. 1956. "Italian Star Denies Cheesecake Claim." *Long Beach Independent*, January 11, 1956.

Johnson, Paul. 2018. "Adapting to New Spaces: Swords and Planets and the Neo-Peplum." In *The New Peplum: Essays on Sword and Sandal Films and Television Programs since the 1990s*, edited by Nicholas Diak, 21–43. Jefferson, NC: McFarland & Co.

Jordan, Anne. 1922. "Vivid Vamps of History." *Cincinnati Enquirer*, May 21, 1922.

Joshel, Sandra R., Margaret Malamud, and Maria Wyke. 2001. "Introduction." In *Imperial Projections: Ancient Rome in Modern Popular Culture*, edited by Sandra R. Joshel, Margaret Malamud, and Donald T. McGuire Jr., 1–22. Baltimore: Johns Hopkins University Press.

Jowett, Garth, I. C. Jarvie, and Kathryn Fuller-Seeley. 1996. *Children and the Movies: Media Influence and the Payne Fund Controversy*. Cambridge: Cambridge University Press.

Junkelmann, Marcus. 2005. "Am Strand der Unsterblichkeit." *Antike Welt* 36, no. 5: 91–95.

Kale, Sirin. 2021. "'I was worried Lindsay, Paris or Britney would die': why the 00s were so toxic for women." *The Guardian*, March 6, 2021. https://www.theguardian.com/culture/2021/mar/06/why-the-00s-were-so-toxic-for-women.

Kanzler, Katja. 2007. "'A Cuchi Moya'—Star Trek's Native Americans." *American Studies Journal* 49, no. 6.

Kapell, Matthew, ed. 2010. *Star Trek as Myth: Essays on Symbol and Archetype at the Final Frontier*. Jefferson, NC: McFarland & Co.

Keen, Tony. 2006. "The 'T' stands for Tiberius: Models and Methodologies of Classical Reception in Science Fiction." *Memorabilia Antonina* (blog). April 10, 2016. http://tonykeen.blogspot.com/2006/04/t-stands-for-tiberius-models-and.html.

———. 2007. "'T for Tiberius': The Original *Star Trek*." *Memorabilia Antonina* (blog). April 23, 2007. http://tonykeen.blogspot.com/2007/04/april-23rd-is-apparently-international.html.

———. 2017. "Prometheus, Pygmalion, and Helen: Science Fiction and Mythology." In *A Handbook to The Reception of Classical Mythology*, edited by Vanda Zajko and Helena Hoyle, 311–21. Malden, MA: Wiley-Blackwell.

Keenan, Richard C. 2007. *The Films of Robert Wise*. Lanham, MD: Scarecrow Press.

Keller, Louise. 2004. "Troy." *Urban Cinephile*. Accessed August 24, 2020. http://www.urbancinefile.com.au/home/view.asp?a=8892.

Kennedy, Kathleen. 2003. "Love is the Battlefield: The Making and Unmaking of the Just Warrior in *Xena, Warrior Princess*." In *Athena's Daughters: Television's New Women Warriors*, edited by Frances Early and Kathleen Kennedy, 40–52. Syracuse, NY: Syracuse University Press.

Keveny, Bill. 2003. "USA's 'Helen' Launches Grand Return to Epics." *USA Today*, April 17, 2003.

Kim, Claire Jean. 1999. "The Racial Triangulation of Asian Americans." *Politics & Society* 27, no. 1: 105–38.

King, Geoff. 2002. *New Hollywood Cinema: An Introduction*. New York: Columbia University Press.

———, ed. 2005. *The Spectacle of the Real: From Hollywood to 'Reality' TV and Beyond*. Bristol, UK: Intellect.

King, Katherine Callen. 1987. *Achilles: Paradigms of the War Hero from Homer to the Middle Ages*. Berkeley: University of California Press.

Kirke, Betty. 1998. *Madeleine Vionnet*. San Francisco: Chronicle Books.

Kirwan, James. 1999. *Beauty*. Manchester, UK: Manchester University Press.

Knight, Arthur. 1951. "Spectacle, Spectacular, Colossal." *Saturday Review*, November 24, 1951.

Knight, Gladys L. 2010. *Female Action Heroes: A Guide to Women in Comics, Video Games, Film, and Television*. Santa Barbara, CA: Greenwood.

Knippschild, Silke. 2013. "Seduction and Power in Postclassical Reception: Traditions and Trends." In *Seduction and Power: Antiquity in the Visual and Performing Arts*, edited by Silke Knippschild and Marta García Morcillo, 311–23. London: Bloomsbury.

Kofler, Wolfgang, and Florian Schaffenrath. 2015. "Petersen's Epic Technique: *Troy* and Its Homeric Model." In *Return to Troy: New Essays on the Hollywood Epic*, edited by Martin M. Winkler, 86–107. Leiden, Netherlands: Brill.

Komar, Marlen. 2016. "The Evolution of Cleavage 'Ideals.'" *Bustle*, January 20, 2016. https://www.bustle.com/articles/136569-the-evolution-of-cleavage-ideals-because-boobies-are-complicated-things-photos.

Konstan, David. 2014. *Beauty: The Fortunes of an Ancient Greek Idea*. Oxford: Oxford University Press.

Korda, Alexander, dir. 1927. *The Private Life of Helen of Troy*. First National Pictures.

Korda, Michael. 1979. *Charmed Lives: A Family Romance*. New York: Random House.

Koszarski, Richard. 1990. *An Evening's Entertainment: The Age of the Silent Feature Picture, 1915–1928*. Berkeley: University of California Press.

Kovacs, George. 2015. "Moral and Mortal in *Star Trek: The Original Series*." In *Classical Traditions in Science Fiction*, edited by Brett M. Rogers and Benjamin Eldon Stevens, 199–216. Oxford: Oxford University Press.

Kozlovic, Anton Karl. 2002. "The Whore of Babylon, Suggestibility, and the Art of Sexless Sex in Cecil B. DeMille's *Samson and Delilah* (1949)." In *Sex, Religion, Media*, edited by Dane S. Claussen, 21–31. Lanham, MD: Rowman & Littlefield.

Krämer, Peter. 2004. "'It's Aimed at Kids—The Kid in Everybody': George Lucas, Star Wars and Children's Entertainment." In *Action and Adventure Cinema*, edited by Yvonne Tasker, 358–414. London and New York: Routledge.

Krass, Andreas. 2013. "Over His Dead Body: Male Friendship in Homer's *Iliad* and Wolfgang Petersen's *Troy* (2004)." In *Ancient Worlds in Film and Television: Gender and Politics*, edited by Almut-Barbara Renger and Jon Solomon, 153–73. Leiden, Netherlands: Brill.

Kuhn, Annette. 1993. *Women's Pictures: Feminism and Cinema*. London: Verso.

Kulik, Karol. 1975. *Alexander Korda: The Man Who Could Work Miracles*. London: W. H. Allen.

Kummer, Frederic Arnold. 1928. *Ladies in Hades*. New York: Dell.

La Pay, Trevor. 2007. "DVD Review: Troy–Director's Cut." *Cinematic Happenings Under Development*. Accessed August 24, 2020. http://www.chud.com/12005/dvd-review-troy-directors-cut/.

Lachenal, Jessica. 2015. "Meryl Streep Reveals an 'Infuriating' Gender Imbalance in Rotten Tomatoes Reviews." *The Mary Sue*. October 9, 2015. http://www.themarysue.com/meryl-streep-rotten-tomatoes/.

Lady Business. 2015. "Xena: Episode 112, 'Beware Greeks Bearing Gifts.'" August 26, 2015. https://ladybusiness.dreamwidth.org/2015/08/26/xena-episode-112-beware-greeks-bearing-gifts.html.

Lahr, John. 2019. "Todd Haynes Rewrites the Hollywood Playbook." *The New Yorker*, November 4, 2019.

Lamarr, Hedy. 1966. *Ecstasy and Me: My Life as a Woman*. Greenwich, CT: Fawcett.

Landay, Lori. 2002. "The Flapper Film: Comedy, Dance, and Jazz Age Kinaesthetics." In *A Feminist Reader in Early Cinema*, edited by Jennifer M. Bean and Diane Negra, 221–48. Durham, NC: Duke University Press.

Landy, Marcia, ed. 1991. *Imitations of Life: A Reader on Film & Television Melodrama*. Detroit: Wayne State University Press.

———. 1996. *Cinematic Uses of the Past*. Minneapolis: University of Minnesota Press.

Lane, Lydia. 1954a. "Young Italian Film Star Planned Medical Career." *Ottawa Journal*, July 24, 1954.

———. 1954b. "Importance of Diet Is Stressed by Star." *Paris News* [Paris, TX], August 8, 1954.

Lang, Harry. 1930. "Would You Like a New Nose?" *Photoplay*, August 1930.

Lang, Nico. 2016. "The Growing Gender Divide over 'Ghostbusters': Why Movies Starring Women Get Slimed by Male Critics." *Salon*, July 13, 2016. https://www.salon.com/2016/07/12/the_growing_gender_divide_over_ghostbusters_why_movies_starring_women_get_slimed_by_male_critics/.

Larsen, Josh. 2004. "Battle Stars: Strong Cast Elevates Epic 'Troy.'" *The Sun*, May 19, 2004.

LaSalle, Mick. 2004. "It's No Classic, but Brad Pitt Swashbuckles Up a Storm in Lively 'Troy' / No Clear Rooting Interest in 'Troy.'" *San Francisco Chronicle*, May 14, 2004.

Latham, Angela J. 2000. *Posing a Threat: Flappers, Chorus Girls, and Other Brazen Performers of the American 1920s*. Hanover, NH: University Press of New England.

Laubner, Ellie. 1996. *Fashions of the Roaring '20s*. Atglen, PA: Schiffer.

Lawrence, John Shelton. 2010. "*Star Trek* as American Monomyth." In *Star Trek as Myth: Essays on Symbol and Archetype at the Final Frontier*, edited by Matthew Kapell, 93–110. Jefferson, NC: McFarland & Co.

Leemann, Sergio. 1995. *Robert Wise on His Films: From Editing Room to Director's Chair*. Los Angeles: Silman-James.

Lemire, Christy. 2004. "'Troy' Could Be Shorter, but the Film Is Worth the Time." *GoUpstate*, May 14, 2004. https://www.goupstate.com/news/20040514/troy-could-be-shorter-but-the-film-is-worth-the-time.

Lev, Peter. 2003. *The Fifties: Transforming the Screen 1950–1959*. Berkeley: University of California Press.

Levin, Sam. 2016. "A Beauty Contest Was Judged by AI and the Robots Didn't Like Dark Skin." *The Guardian*, September 8, 2016. https://www.theguardian.com/technology/2016/sep/08/artificial-intelligence-beauty-contest-doesnt-like-black-people?mc_cid=34ef87bb0c.

Lewis, James R. 1992. "Images of Captive Rape in the Nineteenth Century." *American Culture* 15, no. 2 (June): 69–77.

Lewis, Lisa A. 1989. "Consumer Girl Culture: How Music Video Appeals to Girls." In *Television and Women's Culture: The Politics of the Popular*, edited by Mary Ellen Brown, 89–101. London: Sage.

Lichtenberg, Jacqueline, Sondra Marshak, and Joan Winston. 1975. *Star Trek Lives!* New York: Bantam Books.

Lim, Shirley Jennifer. 2006. *A Feeling of Belonging: Asian American Women's Public Culture, 1930–1960*. New York: New York University Press.

Lindner, Martin. 2005. "Zwischen Anspruch und Legitimation: Legitimationsstrategien des Antikfilms." In *Drehbuch Geschichte: Die antike Welt im Film*, edited by Martin Lindner, 67–85. Münster, Germany: LIT.

Lindsay, Richard. 2015. *Hollywood Biblical Epics: Camp Spectacle and Queer Style from the Silent Era to the Modern Day*. Westport, CT: Praeger.

Lippman, Julia R. 2018. "I Did It Because I Never Stopped Loving You: The Effects of Media Portrayals of Persistent Pursuit on Beliefs About Stalking." *Communication Research* 45, no. 3: 394–421.

Llewellyn-Jones, Lloyd. 2002. "Celluloid Cleopatras, or, Did the Greeks Ever Get to Egypt?" In *The Hellenistic World: New Perspectives*, edited by Daniel Ogden, 275–304. London: Gerald Duckworth.

———. 2005. "The Fashioning of Delilah: Costume Design, Historicism and Fantasy in Cecil B. DeMille's Samson and Delilah (1949)." In *The Clothed Body in the Ancient World*, edited by Liza Cleland, Mary Harlow, and Lloyd Llewellyn-Jones, 14–29. Oxford, UK: Oxbow.

———. 2009. "Hollywood's Ancient World." In *A Companion to Ancient History*, edited by Andrew Erskine, 564–79. Malden, MA: Wiley-Blackwell.

———. 2013a. "'An Almost All Greek Thing': Cleopatra VII and Hollywood Imagination." In *Ancient Greek Women in Film*, edited by Konstantinos P. Nikoloutsos, 305–20. Oxford: Oxford University Press.

———. 2013b. "Ray Harryhausen and Other Gods: Greek Divinity in *Jason and the Argonauts* and *Clash of the Titans*." In *Animating Antiquity: Harryhausen and the Classical Tradition*, edited by Steven Green and Penny Goodman, 3–20. New Voices in Classical Reception Studies Conference Proceedings. Vol. 1. Maidenhead, UK: Open University Press.

———. 2017. "'Salome, Nice Girl': Rita Hayworth and the Problem of the Hollywood Biblical Vamp." In *The Reception of Ancient Virtues and Vices in Modern Popular Culture*, edited by Eran Almagor and Lisa Maurice, 206–30. Leiden, Netherlands: Brill.

———. 2018. *Designs on the Past: How Hollywood Created the Ancient World*. Edinburgh: Edinburgh University Press.

Lodge, Mary Jo. 2009. "Knocked Up, Not Knocked Out: Xena: Warrior Princess, Pregnant Action Hero." In *Heroes of Film, Comics and American Culture: Essays on Real and Fictional Defenders of Home*, edited by Lisa M. DeTora, 218–33. Jefferson, NC: McFarland & Co.

Loos, Anita. 1966. *A Girl Like I*. New York: Viking.

Loraux, Nicole. 1993. *The Children of Athena: Athenian Ideas about Citizenship and the Division between the Sexes*. Princeton, NJ: Princeton University Press.

Lovell, Alan, and Gianluca Sergi. 2009. *Cinema Entertainment: Essays on Audiences, Films and Film Makers*. Maidenhead, UK: Open University Press.

Lowe, Dunstan, and Kim Shahabudin, eds. 2009. *Classics for All: Reworking Antiquity in Mass Culture*. Newcastle upon Tyne, UK: Cambridge Scholars.

Lowe, Nick. 2009. "Metamorphoses of Genre in Fictions of Antiquity." In *Crimina: Die Antike im modernen Kriminalroman*, edited by Kai Brodersen, 217–39. Frankfurt am Main, Germany: Verlag Antike.

Lowenthal, David. 2015. *The Past Is a Foreign Country—Revisited*. Cambridge: Cambridge University Press.

Lucanio, Patrick. 1994. *With Fire and Sword: Italian Spectacles on American Screens, 1958–1968*. Metuchen, NJ: Scarecrow Press.

Lucas, John Meredyth. 2004. *Eighty Odd Years in Hollywood: Memoir of a Career in Film and Television*. Jefferson, NC: McFarland & Co.

Lusk, Norbert. 1927. "'Helen' Makes New York Hit." *Los Angeles Times*, December 18, 1927.

Lynn B. n.d. "Diane Kruger: Gorgeous Girl Next Door." *A Girl's World* (blog). Accessed October 28, 2005. http://www.agirlsworld.com/rachel/hangin-with/dianekruger.html.

Mac Sweeney, Naoise. 2018. *Troy: Myth, City, Icon*. London: Bloomsbury.

Maeder, Edward. 1987. "The Celluloid Image: Historical Dress in Film." In *Hollywood and History: Costume Design in Film*, edited by Edward Maeder, 9–42. London: Thames and Hudson.

Magoulick, Mary. 2006. "Frustrating Female Heroism: Mixed Messages in *Xena, Nikita*, and *Buffy*." *Journal of Popular Culture* 39, no. 1: 729–55.

Maguire, Laurie E. 2009. *Helen of Troy: From Homer to Hollywood*. Malden, MA: Wiley-Blackwell.

Mahon, Elizabeth Kerri. 2011. "On Page and Screen: Helen of Troy." *Scandalous Women* (blog). July 8, 2011. http://scandalouswoman.blogspot.com/2011/07/on-page-and-screen-helen-of-troy.html.

Malamud, Margaret. 2013. "Consuming Passions: Helen of Troy in the Jazz Age." In *The Ancient World in Silent Cinema*, edited by Pantelis Michelakis and Maria Wyke, 330–46. Cambridge: Cambridge University Press.

———. 2016. *African Americans and the Classics: Antiquity, Abolition and Activism*. London: I. B. Tauris.

Maltby, Richard, ed. 1989. *Dreams for Sale: Popular Culture in the 20th Century*. London: Harrap.

———. 2003. *Hollywood Cinema*. 2nd ed. Malden, MA: Blackwell.

Mandel, Emily St. John. 2016. "The Gone Girl with the Dragon Tattoo on the Train." *FiveThirtyEight*, October 27, 2016. https://fivethirtyeight.com/features/the-gone-girl-with-the-dragon-tattoo-on-the-train/?ex_cid=newsletter-top-stories.

Mansfield, Catherine. n.d. "Minis Are Maximum Fashion in Star Trek—The Original Series." *Heritage Auctions Blog*. Accessed January 17, 2022. https://blog.ha.com/minis-are-maximum-fashion-in-star-trek-the-original-series/?ctrack=2990422.

Mansfield, Elizabeth C. 2007. *Too Beautiful to Picture: Zeuxis, Myth, and Mimesis*. Minneapolis: University of Minnesota Press.

Marciniak, Małgorzata. 2007. "The Appeal of Literature-to-Film Adaptations." *Lingua ac Communitas* 17: 59–67.

Marsfelder, Josh. 2013. "'I'm spunky!': Elaan of Troyius." Eruditorum Press. Accessed August 25, 2020. http://www.eruditorumpress.com/blog/im-spunky-elaan-of-troyius/.

Marshall, Mildred. 1921. "What's in a Name?" *Wichita Daily Times*, March 13, 1921.

Martel, Ned. 2003. "After All These Eons, She's Still a Tunic-Ripper." *New York Times*, April 19, 2003.

Martin, Boyd. 1956. "Legend Comes to Life in 'Helen of Troy.'" *Courier-Journal* [Louisville, KY], February 10, 1956.

Martin, Frédéric. 2002. *L'Antiquité au Cinéma*. Paris: Dreamland.

Martin, Martin. 1928. "What Size Glory?" *Screenland*, January 1928.

Martín-Rodríguez, Antonio M. 2015. "The Fall of Troy: Intertextual Presences in Wolfgang Petersen's Film." In *Return to Troy: New Essays on the Hollywood Epic*, edited by Martin M. Winkler, 228–47. Leiden, Netherlands: Brill.

Massey, Anne. 2000. *Hollywood beyond the Screen: Design and Material Culture*. Oxford, UK: Berg Publishers.

Maurice, Lisa. 2019. *Screening Divinity*. Edinburgh: Edinburgh University Press.

May, Elaine Tyler. 1989. "Explosive Issues: Sex, Women and the Bomb." In *Recasting America: Culture and Politics in the Age of Cold War*, edited by Lary May, 154–70. Chicago: University of Chicago Press.

Mayer, David. 2013. "Architecture and Art Dance Meet in the Ancient World." In *The Ancient World in Silent Cinema*, edited by Pantelis Michelakis and Maria Wyke, 91–108. Cambridge: Cambridge University Press.

Mayne, Judith. 1993. *Cinema and Spectatorship*. London: Routledge.

———. 1994. *Directed by Dorothy Arzner*. Bloomington: Indiana University Press.

McCarten, John. 1956. "The Current Cinema." *The New Yorker*, February 4, 1956.

McCarthy, Todd. 2004. "Troy." *Variety*, May 5, 2004.

McClay, Howard. 1951. "'Quo Vadis.'" *Daily News* [Los Angeles, CA], December 30, 1951.

McConathy, Dale, and Diana Vreeland. 1976. *Hollywood Costume: Glamour, Glitter, Romance*. New York: H. N. Abrams.

McCoskey, Denise Eileen. 2012. *Race: Antiquity and Its Legacy*. Oxford: Oxford University Press.

McDonald, Paul. 1998. "Supplementary Chapter: Reconceptualising Stardom." In *Stars*, by Richard Dyer, 175–211. 2nd ed. London: British Film Institute.

———. 2012. "Story and Show: The Basic Contradiction of Film Star Acting." In *Theorizing Film Acting*, edited by Aaron Taylor, 176–90. New York: Routledge.

McEvoy, Merely. 1924. "Vamps." *Davenport Democrat and Leader*, February 14, 1924.

McFarland, Melanie. 2003. "Helen of Troy, Monica Lewinsky have much in common." *Seattle Post-Intelligencer*, April 17, 2003. https://www.seattlepi.com/ae/tv/article/Helen-of-Troy-Monica-Lewinsky-have-much-in-common-1112519.php.

McFarlane, Brian. 2005. "Size Doesn't Matter: Big Stupid Films." *Metro* 144: 58–64.

McGrath, Charles. 2004. "Brad Pitt's Big Fat Greek Toga Party." *New York Times*, May 9, 2004.

McLaughlin, Will. 1956. "Studio and Screen." *Ottawa Journal*, March 10, 1956.

McLean, Adrienne L. 2004. *Being Rita Hayworth: Labor, Identity, and Hollywood Stardom*. New Brunswick, NJ: Rutgers University Press.

McQuire, Scott. 1998. *Visions of Modernity: Representation, Memory, Time and Space in the Age of the Camera*. London: Sage.

McSweeney, Terence. 2014. *The 'War on Terror' and American Film: 9/11 Frames Per Second*. Edinburgh: Edinburgh University Press.

———. 2017. *American Cinema in the Shadow of 9/11*. Edinburgh: Edinburgh University Press.

Meier, Mischa. 2006. "Troia im Film." In *Der Traum von Troia: Geschichte und Mythos einer ewigen Stadt*, edited by Martin Zimmermann, 179–93. Munich: Beck.

Mellencamp, Patricia. 1995. *A Fine Romance: Five Ages of Film Feminism*. Philadelphia: Temple University Press.

Mendelsohn, Daniel. 2004. "A Little *Iliad*." *New York Review of Books*, June 24, 2004.

Meyerowitz, Joanne. 1993. "Beyond the Feminine Mystique: A Reassessment of Postwar Mass Culture, 1946–1958." *Journal of American History* 79, no. 4: 1455–82.

Michelakis, Pantelis. 2013. "Homer in Silent Cinema." In *The Ancient World in Silent Cinema*, edited by Pantelis Michelakis and Maria Wyke, 145–65. Cambridge: Cambridge University Press.

———. 2017. "Greece and Rome on Screen: On the Possibilities and Promises of a New Medium." In *A Companion to Ancient Greece and Rome on Screen*, edited by Arthur John Pomeroy, 15–35. Hoboken, NJ: John Wiley & Sons.

Michelakis, Pantelis, and Maria Wyke. 2013. "Introduction: Silent Cinema, Antiquity and 'The Exhaustless Urn of Time.'" In *The Ancient World in Silent Cinema*, edited by Pantelis Michelakis and Maria Wyke, 1–24. Cambridge: Cambridge University Press.

Mifflin, Margot. 2020. *Looking for Miss America: A Pageant's 100-Year Quest to Define Womanhood*. Berkeley, CA: Counterpoint.

Millar, John. 2004a. "Paris in the Spring." In "Epics Special." Special issue, *Film Review* 51.

———. 2004b. "A Greek Odysseus." In "Epics Special." Special issue, *Film Review* 51.

Miller, Douglas T., and Marion Nowak. 1977. *The Fifties: The Way We Really Were*. Garden City, NY: Doubleday.

Miller, Lisa. 2004. "'Troy' Is Loaded with Lots of Boy Toys." *Advocate-Messenger* [Danville, KY], May 20, 2004.

Mini, Panayiota. 2017. "Representations of the Christian Female Virtue in Roman Film Epics: *The Sign of the Cross* (1932) and *Quo Vadis* (1951)." In *The Reception of Ancient Virtues and Vices in Modern Popular Culture*, edited by Alan Almagor and Lisa Maurice, 231–52. Leiden, Netherlands: Brill.

Minkowitz, Donna. 1996. "Xena: She's Big, Tall, Strong—and Popular." *Ms. Magazine* 7, no. 1: 74–77.

Modleski, Tania. 2008. *Loving with a Vengeance: Mass-Produced Fantasies for Women*. 2nd ed. New York: Routledge.

———. 1991. *Feminism Without Women: Culture and Criticism in a Postfeminist Age*. New York: Routledge.

Moffitt, Jack. 1955. "'Helen of Troy.'" *Hollywood Reporter*, December 21, 1955.

Mohanram, Radhika. 2007. *Imperial White: Race, Diaspora, and the British Empire*. Minneapolis: University of Minnesota Press.

Momigliano, Nicoletta. 2013. "Modern Dance and the Seduction of Minoan Crete." In *Seduction and Power: Antiquity in the Visual and Performing Arts*, edited by Silke Knippschild and Marta García Morcillo, 35–55. London: Bloomsbury.

Morey, Anne. 2002 "'So Real as to Seem Like Life Itself': The *Photoplay* Fiction of Adela Rogers St. Johns." In *A Feminist Reader in Early Cinema*, edited by Jennifer M. Bean and Diane Negra, 333–46. Durham, NC: Duke University Press.

Morgenstern, Joe. 2004. "Homer, Run: Epic 'Troy' Hectors Us about History; A Tin Ear for the Bronze Age." *Wall Street Journal*, May 14, 2004.

Morin, Edgar. 2005. *The Stars*. Minneapolis: University of Minnesota Press.

Morreale, Joanne. 1998. "*Xena: Warrior Princess* as Feminist Camp." *Journal of Popular Culture* 32, no. 2: 79–86.

Morris, Meaghan. 1990. "Banality in Cultural Studies." In *Logics of Television: Essays in Cultural Criticism*, edited by Patricia Mellencamp, 14–43. Bloomington: Indiana University Press.

Morrissey, Christopher S. 2004. "'Pomo Homer': A Review of the *Troy* Movie." *Chronicles of Love and Resentment* (blog). June 26, 2004. http://www.anthropoetics.ucla.edu/views/vw304.htm.

Morton, Ella. 2016. "100 Years Ago, American Women Competed in Intense Venus de Milo Lookalike Contests." *Atlas Obscura*, January 15, 2016. https://www.atlasobscura.com/articles/100-years-ago-american-women-competed-in-serious-venus-de-milo-lookalike-contests.

Moseley, Rachel. 2002. "Glamorous Witchcraft: Gender and Magic in Teen Film and Television." *Screen* 43, no. 4: 403–22.

Mosse, George L. 1988. *Nationalism and Sexuality: Middle-Class Morality and Sexual Norms in Modern Europe*. Madison: University of Wisconsin Press.

Mulshine, Molly. 2015. "What Does It Mean When the World's Most Famous Brunette Goes Platinum Blonde?" *The Observer*, March 6, 2015.

Mulvey, Laura. 2009 [1975]. "Visual Pleasure and Narrative Cinema." In *Visual and Other Pleasures*, 14–26. 2nd ed. New York: Palgrave Macmillan.

Murnaghan, Sheila. 2011. "Classics for Cool Kids: Popular and Unpopular Versions of Antiquity for Children." *Classical World* 104, no. 3: 339–53.

Murphy, Mary. 2003. "To Helen and Back." *TV Guide*, April 12–18, 2003.

Murray, C. Alison. 2004. "Lots of Candy for the Eye, but a Shortage of Passion for the Heart." *Star-Democrat* [Easton, MD], May 28, 2004.

Nadel, Alan. 1993. "God's Law and the Wide Screen: *The Ten Commandments* as Cold War 'Epic.'" *PMLA* 108, no. 3: 415–30.

Nagle, Betty Rose. 2004. "For What Purpose? The Treatment of Women in *Helen of Troy* (USA Miniseries 2003)." Paper presented at the annual meeting of the Classical Association of the Midwest and South.

Nagourney, Adam. 2022. "To Boldly Explore the Jewish Roots of 'Star Trek.'" *New York Times*, January 4, 2022. https://www.nytimes.com/2022/01/04/arts/design/star-trek-exhibition-skirball.html?action=click.

Nead, Lynda. 2007. *The Haunted Gallery: Painting, Photography, Film c. 1900*. New Haven, CT: Yale University Press.

Neale, Steve. 1986. "Melodrama and Tears." *Screen* 27, no. 6: 6–23.

———. 1990. "'You've Got to Be Fucking Kidding!': Knowledge, Belief and Judgement in Science Fiction." In *Alien Zone: Cultural Theory and Contemporary Science Fiction Cinema*, edited by Annette Kuhn, 160–68. London: Verso.

———. 2000. *Genre and Hollywood*. London: Routledge.

Need Coffee Dot Com. 2004. "Helen of Troy (2003)—DVD Review." January 17, 2004. http://www.needcoffee.com/2004/01/17/helen-troy-dvd-review/.

Negra, Diane. 2001. *Off-White Hollywood: American Culture and Ethnic Female Stardom*. London: Routledge.

Negra, Diane. 2002. "Immigrant Stardom in Imperial America: Pola Negri and the Problem of Typology." In *A Feminist Reader in Early Cinema*, edited by Jennifer M. Bean and Diane Negra, 374–403. Durham, NC: Duke University Press.

———. 2009. *What a Girl Wants: Fantasizing the Reclamation of Self in Postfeminism*. London: Routledge.

Newmark, Judith. 2003. "Beauty Contested." *St. Louis Post-Dispatch*, April 27, 2003.

Nichols, Nichelle. 1994. *Beyond Uhura: Star Trek and Other Memories*. New York: G. P. Putnam's Sons.

Nikoloutsos, Konstantinos P., 2015. "From Text to Screen: Celluloid Helens and Female Stardom in the 1950s." *Cambridge Classical Journal* 61: 70–90.

Nilsen, Richard. 2004. "Films Like 'Troy' Are 'the Present Masquerading as Past.'" *Arizona Republic*, May 16, 2004.

Nisbet, Gideon. 2006. *Ancient Greece in Film and Popular Culture*. Exeter, UK: Bristol Phoenix.

Nugent, Gary. 1991. "James T. Kirk: Playboy of The Western Quadrant." *Federation Times*. Accessed August 25, 2020. https://www.thefederationtimes.com/james-t-kirk-playboy-of-the-western-quadrant/.

O'Brien, Daniel. 2014. *Classical Masculinity and the Spectacular Body on Film: The Mighty Sons of Hercules*. New York: Palgrave Macmillan.

O'Donnell, Victoria. 2003. "Science Fiction Films and Cold War Anxiety." In *The Fifties: Transforming the Screen 1950–1959*, edited by Peter Lev, 169–96. Berkeley: University of California Press.

Oei, Lily. 2003. "USA's 'Helen' Launches Solid Ratings." *Variety*, April 22, 2003.

Oettinger, Malcolm H. 1928. "Helen of Troy in Hollywood." *Picture Play*, February 1928.

Olsson, Jan. 2008. *Los Angeles before Hollywood: Journalism and American Film Culture, 1905 to 1915*. Stockholm: National Library of Sweden.

O'Neal, Sean. 2012. "The First Lawsuit Has Been Filed in the Drake-Chris Brown Fight, Forcing Us to Pay Attention to It." *The A.V. Club*, June 22, 2012. https://news.avclub.com/the-first-lawsuit-has-been-filed-in-the-drake-chris-bro-1798231899.

Orenstein, Peggy. 2011. *Cinderella Ate My Daughter: Dispatches from the Front Lines of the New Girlie-Girl Culture*. New York: HarperCollins.

Ormand, Kirk. 2013. "Medea's Erotic Text in *Jason and the Argonauts* (1963)." In *Ancient Greek Women in Film*, edited by Konstantinos P. Nikoloutsos, 75–94. Oxford: Oxford University Press.

Oshiro, Mark. 2014. "Mark Watches 'Star Trek': S03E13—Elaan of Troyius." *Mark Watches* (blog). December 31, 2014. https://markwatches.net/reviews/2014/12/mark-watches-star-trek-s03e13-elaan-of-troyius/.

O'Sullivan, Eleanor. 2004. "'Spartacus' It Isn't." *Asbury Park Press*, May 14, 2004.

Owen, Rob. 2003. "TV Review: 'Helen of Troy' offers new diversion on Easter." *Pittsburgh Post-Gazette*, April 20, 2003. https://old.post-gazette.com/tv/20030420owen2.asp.

Owens, Molly. 2019. "The Surprising Ways Your Birth Order Impacts Your Personality Type." *Truity*. February 13, 2019. https://www.truity.com/blog/birth-order-and-personality-study.

Painter, Nell Irvin. 2010. *The History of White People*. New York: W. W. Norton.

Paoletti, Jo Barraclough. 2012. *Pink and Blue: Telling the Boys from the Girls in America*. Bloomington: Indiana University Press.

Pardi, Robert. 2003. "Helen of Troy." *TV Guide*. Accessed August 26, 2020. https://www.tvguide.com/movies/helen-of-troy/review/137454/.

Parks, Tim. 2009. "Nudity is the greatest costume." Digital Spy, November 7, 2009. https://www.digitalspy.com/showbiz/a164529/parker-nudity-is-the-greatest-costume/.

Parry, Florence Fisher. 1928. "They Got What They Wanted." *Pittsburgh Press*, May 8, 1928.

Parsons, Louella O. 1951. "'Quo Vadis' Fine Spectacle." *Los Angeles Examiner*, November 30, 1951.

———. 1956. "Dark Haired Actress Was Helen of Troy." *Cumberland Sunday Times* [Cumberland, MD], March 25, 1956.

Paul, Joanna. 2008a. "Working with Film: Theories and Methodologies." In *A Companion to Classical Receptions*, edited by Lorna Hardwick and Christopher Stray, 303–14. Malden, MA: Blackwell.

———. 2008b. "Homer and Cinema: Translation and Adaptation in Le Mépris." In *Translation and the Classic: Identity as Change in the History of Culture*, edited by Alexandra Lianeri and Vanda Zajko, 148–65. Oxford: Oxford University Press.

———. 2010. "Cinematic Receptions of Antiquity: The Current State of Play." *Classical Receptions Journal* 2, no. 1: 136–55.

———. 2013a. *Film and the Classical Epic Tradition*. Oxford: Oxford University Press.

———. 2013b. "'Madonna and Whore': The Many Faces of Penelope in Camerini's *Ulisse* (1954)." In *Ancient Greek Women in Film*, edited by Konstantinos P. Nikoloutsos, 139–61. Oxford: Oxford University Press.

Petersen, Daniel. 2015. "Live from Troy: Embedded in the Trojan War." In *Return to Troy: New Essays on the Hollywood Epic*, edited by Martin M. Winkler, 27–47. Leiden, Netherlands: Brill.

Petersen, Wolfgang, dir. 2004. *Troy*. Warner Brothers. DVD.

———, dir. 2007. *Troy: Director's Cut*. Warner Brothers. DVD.

Petersen, Wolfgang, and Ulrich Greiwe. 1997. *Ich Liebe die grossen Geschichten: Vom "Tatort" bis nach Hollywood*. Cologne, Germany: Kiepenheuer & Witsch.

Pierson, Michele. 2005. "A Production Designer's Cinema: Historical Authenticity in Popular Films Set in the Past." In *The Spectacle of the Real: From Hollywood to 'Reality' TV and Beyond*, edited by Geoff King, 145–55. Bristol, UK: Intellect.

Pollitt, J. J. 1974. *The Ancient View of Greek Art: Criticism, History, and Terminology*. New Haven, CT: Yale University Press.

Pomeroy, Arthur John. 2008. *Then It Was Destroyed by the Volcano: The Ancient World in Film and on Television*. London: Duckworth.

———. 2013. "The Women of Ercole." In *Ancient Greek Women in Film*, edited by Konstantinos P. Nikoloutsos, 189–205. Oxford: Oxford University Press.

———. 2017. "The Peplum Era." In *A Companion to Ancient Greece and Rome on Screen*, edited by Arthur John Pomeroy, 145–59. Hoboken, NJ: John Wiley & Sons.

Postrel, Virginia. 2013. *The Power of Glamor: Longing and the Art of Visual Persuasion*. New York: Simon & Schuster.

Potter, Amanda. 2010. "Who needs a Homeric Hero When We've Got Xena? The Confusion of Gendered Roles in *Xena Warrior Princess* Episodes 'Beware Greeks Bearing Gifts' and

'Ulysses.'" *Rosetta* 8, no. 5: 96–126. Accessed August 31, 2020. http://www.rosetta.bham.ac.uk/issue8supp/Potter_Xena.pdf.

Pounds, Micheal C. 1999. *Race in Space: The Representation of Ethnicity in Star Trek and Star Trek: The Next Generation*. Lanham, MD: Scarecrow Press.

Prasso, Sheridan. 2005. *The Asian Mystique: Dragon Ladies, Geisha Girls, and Our Fantasies of the Exotic Orient*. New York: Public Affairs.

Pratt, George C. 1973. *Spellbound in Darkness: A History of the Silent Film*. Greenwich, CT: New York Graphic Society.

Prettejohn, Elizabeth. 2006. "Reception and Ancient Art: The Case of the Venus de Milo." In *Classics and the Uses of Reception*, edited by Charles Martindale and Richard F. Thomas, 227–49. Oxford: Blackwell.

Prince, Stephen. 2009. *Firestorm: American Film in the Age of Terrorism*. New York: Columbia University Press.

Proch, Celina, and Michael Kleu. 2013. "Models of Masculinities in *Troy*: Achilles, Hector and Their Female Partners." In *Ancient Worlds in Film and Television: Gender and Politics*, edited by Almut-Barbara Renger and Jon Solomon, 175–93. Leiden, Netherlands: Brill.

Projansky, Sarah. 2001. *Watching Rape: Film and Television in Postfeminist Culture*. New York: New York University Press.

———. 2007. "Mass Magazine Cover Girls: Some Reflections on Postfeminist Girls and Postfeminism's Daughters." In *Interrogating Postfeminism: Gender and the Politics of Popular Culture*, edited by Yvonne Tasker and Diane Negra, 40–72. Durham, NC: Duke University Press.

Pulver, Andrew. 2018. "Film Critics Overwhelmingly White and Male, Says Study." *The Guardian*, June 11, 2018. https://www.theguardian.com/film/2018/jun/11/film-critics-white-and-male-study-rotten-tomatoes.

Purse, Lisa. 2005. "The New Spatial Dynamics of the Bullet-Time Effect." In *The Spectacle of the Real: From Hollywood to 'Reality' TV and Beyond*, edited by Geoff King, 151–60. Bristol, UK: Intellect.

Purves, Jeremy. 2014a. "Troy (Petersen, 2004)—10 Years Later: Part I." *Patheos*, May 24, 2014. http://www.patheos.com/blogs/1morefilmblog/troy-petersen-2004-10-years-later-part-i/.

———. 2014b. "Troy (Petersen, 2004)—10 Years Later: Part II." *Patheos*, June 1, 2014. http://www.patheos.com/blogs/1morefilmblog/troy-petersen-2004-10-years-later-part-ii/.

———. 2014c. "Troy (Petersen, 2004)—10 Years Later: Part III." *Patheos*, June 18, 2014. http://www.patheos.com/blogs/1morefilmblog/troy-petersen-2004-10-years-later-part-iii/.

Radway, Janice A. 1991. *Reading the Romance: Women, Patriarchy, and Popular Literature*. Chapel Hill: University of North Carolina Press.

Rampell, Ed. n.d. "The Unforgiven." *Goldsea*. Accessed August 26, 2020. http://www.goldsea.com/Personalities/Nuyenfrance/nuyenfrance.html.

Rapping, Elayne. 1992. *The Movie of the Week: Private Stories/Public Events*. Minneapolis: University of Minnesota Press.

Raucci, Stacie. 2013. "The Order of Orgies: Sex and the Cinematic Roman." In *Screening Love and Sex in the Ancient World*, edited by Monica Silveira Cyrino, 143–55. New York: Palgrave Macmillan.

Read, Jacinda. 2000. *The New Avengers: Feminism, Femininity, and the Rape-Revenge Cycle.* Manchester, UK: Manchester University Press.

Reagle, Joseph M. 2015. *Reading the Comments: Likers, Haters, and Manipulators at the Bottom of the Web.* Cambridge, MA: MIT Press.

Reed, Rex 2004. "Epic Pecs, Great Effects." *The Observer*, May 17, 2004.

Reid-Jeffery, Donna. 1982. "Star Trek: The Last Frontier in Modern American Myth." *Folklore and Mythology Studies* 6: 34–41.

Reilly, Rosa. 1929. "James Montgomery Flagg Looks the Stars Over." *Screenland*, June 1929.

Reynolds, Simon. 2008. "Diane Kruger: 'Troy' Kind of Sucked." Digital Spy, December 5, 2008. http://www.digitalspy.com/movies/news/a95760/diane-kruger-troy-kind-of-sucked/.

Ribeyrol, Charlotte. 2013. "The Lure of the Hermaphrodite in the Poetry and Painting of the English Aesthetes." In *Seduction and Power: Antiquity in the Visual and Performing Arts*, edited by Silke Knippschild and Marta García Morcillo, 295–309. London: Bloomsbury.

Ringgold, Gene. 1974. *The Films of Rita Hayworth: The Legend and Career of a Love Goddess.* Secaucus, NJ: Citadel Press.

Roberts, Adam. 2016. *The History of Science Fiction.* 2nd ed. London: Palgrave Macmillan.

Rodriguez, John "Bones." 2008. *Captain Kirk's Guide to Women.* New York: Pocket Books.

Rogers, Brett. 2011. "Heroes Unlimited: The Theory of the Hero's Journey and the Limitation of the Superhero Myth." In *Classics and Comics*, edited by George Kovacs and C. W. Marshall, 73–86. Oxford: Oxford University Press.

Rosen, Marjorie. 1973. *Popcorn Venus: Women, Movies and the American Dream.* New York: Coward, McCann & Geoghegan.

Rosenberg, Howard. 2003. "This 'Helen of Troy' Is So Tragically Bad It's Good." *Los Angeles Times*, April 18, 2003.

Rosenstone, Robert A. 2001 [1995]. "The Historical Film: Looking at the Past in a Postliterate Age." In *The Historical Film: History and Memory in Media*, edited by Marcia Landy, 50–66. New Brunswick, NJ: Rutgers University Press.

Ross, Wilma. 1927. The Picture Gallery." *Brooklyn Times Union*, December 18, 1927.

Rothstein, Edward. 2004. "To Homer, Iraq Would Be More of Same." *New York Times*, June 5, 2004. http://www.nytimes.com/2004/06/05/movies/connections-to-homer-iraq-would-be-more-of-same.html.

Rubin, Joan Shelley. 1992. *The Making of Middlebrow Culture.* Chapel Hill: University of North Carolina Press.

Rushing, Robert A. 2016. *Descended from Hercules: Biopolitics and the Muscled Male Body on Screen.* Bloomington: Indiana University Press.

Russell, Fred. 1954. "Italian Actresses Busy in Films." *Bridgeport Telegram*, October 25, 1954.

Russell, James. 2007. *The Historical Epic and Contemporary Hollywood: From Dances with Wolves to Gladiator.* New York: Continuum.

Russell, M. E. 2004. "Helmer of Troy." *In Focus*, May 2004. http://www.infocusmag.com/04may/petersenuncut.htm.

Ryan, Mary P. 1976. "The Projection of a New Womanhood: The Movie Moderns in the 1920's." In *Our American Sisters: Women in American Life and Thought*, edited by Jean E. Friedman and William G. Shade, 366–85. 2nd ed. Boston: Allyn and Bacon.

Ryan-Mosley, Tate. 2021. "I Asked an AI to Tell Me How Beautiful I Am." *MIT Technology Review*, March 5, 2021.

Salzman-Mitchell, P., and Jean Alvares. 2018. *Classical Myth and Film in the New Millennium*. New York: Oxford University Press.

Sanders, Julie. 2006. *Adaptation and Appropriation*. 2nd ed. London: Routledge.

Sands, Victoria. 2019. "'Baby One More Time' and the Pop Princesses Who Started a Moral Panic." *Bitch*, Winter 2019, 68–69.

Sargeant, Winthrop. 1947. "The Cult of the Love Goddess." *Life*, November 10, 1947.

Sayre, Nora. 1982. *Running Time: Films of the Cold War*. New York: Dial Press.

Schallert, Edwin. 1927. "'Helen of Troy' Novel in Results." *Los Angeles Times*, December 10, 1927.

———. 1952. "Deborah Kerr Takes Honors—for Others; Shows Profit in L.A." *Los Angeles Times*, March 9, 1952.

———. 1956. "'Helen' Triumphs in Pictorial Art." *Los Angeles Times*, January 27, 1956.

Schatz, Thomas. 1981. *Hollywood Genres: Formulas, Filmmaking, and the Studio System*. New York: Random House.

———. 1993. "The New Hollywood." In *Film Theory Goes to the Movies*, edited by Jim Collins, Hilary Radner, and Ava Preacher Collins, 8–36. New York: Routledge.

Schein, Seth L. 2007. "American Homer for the Twentieth Century." In *Homer in the Twentieth Century: Between World Literature and the Western Canon*, edited by Barbara Graziosi and Emily Greenwood, 268–85. New York: Oxford University Press.

———. 2008. "Our debt to Greece and Rome: Canons, Class and Ideology." In *A Companion to Classical Receptions*, edited by Lorna Hardwick and Christopher Stray, 75–85. Malden, MA: Blackwell.

Scherer, Margaret R. 1967. "Helen of Troy." *Metropolitan Museum of Art Bulletin* 25: 367–83.

Scheuer, Philip K. 1955. "A Thousand Ships Launched in Re-created 'Helen of Troy.'" *Los Angeles Times*, November 27, 1955.

Schruers, Fred. 2004a. "Troy Story." *Premiere*, May 2004.

———. 2004b. "She'll Always Have Paris." *Premiere*, May 2004.

Schulze, Laurie. 1990. "The-Made-for-TV movie: Industrial Practice, Cultural Form, Popular Reception." In *Hollywood in the Age of Television*, edited by Tino Balio, 351–76. Boston: Unwin Hyman.

Schumach, Murray. 1975. *The Face on the Cutting Room Floor: The Story of Movie and Television Censorship*. New York: Da Capo.

Scodel, Ruth, and Anja Bettenworth. 2009. *Whither Quo Vadis?* Malden, MA: Wiley Blackwell.

Scott, A. O. 2004. "Greeks Bearing Immortality." *New York Times*, May 14, 2004.

Scott, Vernon. 1956. "Little Known Italian Actress Picked as 'Helen of Troy.'" *Galveston Daily News*, January 4, 1956.

Sears, Steven L. 2018. "Afterword." In *The New Peplum: Essays on Sword and Sandal Films and Television Programs since the 1990s*, edited by Nicholas Diak, 219–22. Jefferson, NC: McFarland & Co.

Seldes, Gilbert. 1950. *The Great Audience*. New York: Viking.

Selley, April. 1986. "'I Have Been, and Ever Shall Be, Your Friend': Star Trek, The Deerslayer and the American Romance." *Journal of Popular Culture* 20: 89–104.

Sessions, Debbie. 2013. "1920s Hairstyles History: Long Hair to Bobbed Hair." Vintage Dancer, October 17, 2013. https://vintagedancer.com/1920s/1920s-long-hair-to-bobbed-hair/.

Shahabudin, Kim. 2007. "From Greek Myth to Hollywood Story: Explanatory Narrative in *Troy*." In *Troy: From Homer's Iliad to Hollywood Epic*, edited by Martin M. Winkler, 107–18. Malden, MA: Blackwell.

———. 2009. "Ancient Mythology and Modern Myths: Hercules Conquers Atlantis (1961)." In *Classics for All: Reworking Antiquity in Mass Culture*, edited by Dunstan Lowe and Kim Shahabudin, 196–216. Newcastle upon Tyne, UK: Cambridge Scholars.

Shales, Tom. 2003. "'Helen of Troy': A Long, Silly Iliad." *Washington Post*, April 19, 2003.

Shatner, William, and Chris Kreski. 1993. *Star Trek Memories*. New York: HarperCollins.

Shearer, Joe. 2004. "An Epic of Greek Proportions." *Indianapolis Star*, May 13, 2004.

Shearer, Stephen Michael. 2010. *Beautiful: The Life of Hedy Lamarr*. New York: St. Martin's Press.

Shepard, Alan, and Stephen D. Powell, eds. 2004. *Fantasies of Troy: Classical Tales and the Social Imaginary in Medieval and Early Modern Europe*. Toronto: Centre for Reformation and Renaissance Studies.

Shields, David S. 2013. *Still: American Silent Motion Picture Photography*. Chicago: University of Chicago Press.

Shillock, Larry T. 2011. "An Enduring Logic: Homer, Helen of Troy, and Narrative Mobility." In *Of Muscles and Men: Essays on the Sword and Sandal Film*, edited by Michael G. Cornelius, 124–43. Jefferson, NC: McFarland & Co.

Shirky, Clay. 2008. *Here Comes Everybody: The Power of Organizing without Organizations*. New York: Penguin.

Shohat, Ella. 1991. "Gender and Culture of Empire: Toward a Feminist Ethnography of the Cinema." *Quarterly Review of Film and Video* 13: 45–84.

Shone, Tom. 2004. *Blockbuster: How Hollywood Learned to Stop Worrying and Love the Summer*. New York: Free Press.

Silk, Michael, Ingo Gildenhard, and Rosemary Barrow. 2014. *The Classical Tradition: Art, Literature, Thought*. Malden, MA: Wiley-Blackwell.

Sims, Caeleigh. n.d. "A Brief History of Décolletage in Western Fashion." Miriam Baker (blog). Accessed August 26, 2020. https://miriam-baker.com/blogs/journal/a-brief-history-of-the-decolletage-in-western-fashion.

Skelton, Carolyn. 2010. "Xena: Warrior Princess." In *The Essential Cult TV Reader*, edited by David Lavery, 329–36. Lexington: University Press of Kentucky.

Slide, Anthony. 2010. *Inside the Hollywood Fan Magazine: A History of Star Makers, Fabricators, and Gossip Mongers*. Jackson: University Press of Mississippi.

Smith, Haydee. 2018. "Queering the Quest: Neo-Peplum and the Neo-Femme in *Xena: Warrior Princess*." In *The New Peplum: Essays on Sword and Sandal Films and Television Programs since the 1990s*, edited by Nicholas Diak, 208–18. Jefferson, NC: McFarland & Co.

Smith, Helena Huntington. 1927. "Professor's Progress." *The New Yorker*, December 10, 1927.

Smith, Liz. 2004. "Bana Holds His Own against Pitt." *Palm Beach Post*, May 12, 2004.

Smith, Murray. 1995. *Engaging Characters: Fiction, Emotion, and the Cinema*. Oxford: Oxford University Press.

Soares, Andre. 2013. "Rossana Podesta: *Helen of Troy* + Sex Comedy Actress." *Alt Film Guide*, December 10, 2013. http://www.altfg.com/blog/movie/rossana-podesta-helen-of-troy/.

Sobchack, Vivian. 1990. "The Virginity of Astronauts: Sex and the Science Fiction Film." In *Alien Zone: Cultural Theory and Contemporary Science Fiction Cinema*, edited by Annette Kuhn, 103–15. London: Verso.

———. 2003 [1990]. "Surge and Splendor: A Phenomenology of the Hollywood Historical Epic." In *Film Genre Reader III*, edited by Barry Keith Grant, 296–323. Austin: University of Texas Press.

Solomon, Jon. 2001. *The Ancient World in the Cinema*. New Haven, CT: Yale University Press.

———. 2007a. "The Vacillations of the Trojan Myth: Popularization & Classicization, Variation & Codification." *International Journal of the Classical Tradition* 14: 482–534.

———. 2007b. "Viewing *Troy*: Authenticity, Criticism, Interpretation." In *Troy: From Homer's Iliad to Hollywood Epic*, edited by Martin M. Winkler, 85–98. Malden, MA: Blackwell.

———. 2008. "Televising Antiquity: From *You Are There* to *Rome*." In *Rome, Season One: History Makes Television*, edited by Monica S. Cyrino, 11–28. Malden, MA: Blackwell.

———. 2015. "Homer's *Iliad* in Popular Culture: The Roads to *Troy*." In *Return to Troy: New Essays on the Hollywood Epic*, edited by Martin M. Winkler, 248–79. Leiden, Netherlands: Brill.

Solow, Herbert F., and Robert H. Justman. 1997. *Inside Star Trek: The Real Story*. New York: Pocket Books.

Sontag, Susan. 1982 [1963]. "From On Photography: The Image-World." In *A Susan Sontag Reader*, 349–67. New York: Farrar, Straus, Giroux.

Späth, Thomas, and Margrit Tröhler. 2013. "Muscles and Morals: Spartacus, Ancient Hero of Modern Times." In *Ancient Worlds in Film and Television: Gender and Politics*, edited by Almut-Barbara Renger and Jon Solomon, 41–63. Leiden, Netherlands: Brill.

Spear, Ivan. 1951. "'Quo Vadis' Is Hailed as MGM's Mightiest." *Box Office*, November 10, 1951.

Speier, Michael. 2003. "Review: 'Helen of Troy.'" *Variety*, April 15, 2003. https://variety.com/2003/tv/reviews/helen-of-troy-3-1200542190/.

Spelling, Ian. 2004. "War! What is it Good for?" *Film Review* 645: 72–74.

Spicciati, Scott. n.d. "Troy." Aggressive Voice. Accessed August 26, 2020. http://aggressive-voice.com/zzz166.html.

Spigel, Lynn, and Henry Jenkins. 1991. "Same Bat Channel, Different Bat Times: Mass Culture and Popular Memory." In *The Many Lives of the Batman: Critical Approaches to a Superhero and His Media*, edited by Roberta E. Pearson and William Uricchio, 117–48. New York and London: Routledge.

Squire, Michael. 2011. *The Art of the Body: Antiquity and Its Legacy*. Oxford: Oxford University Press.

Stacey, Jackie. 1991. "Feminine Fascinations: Forms of Identification in Star-Audience Relations." In *Stardom: Industry of Desire*, edited by Christine Gledhill, 141–63. London: Routledge.

———. 1994. *Star Gazing: Hollywood Cinema and Female Spectatorship*. London: Routledge.

Staiger, Janet. 1991. "Self-Regulation and the Classical Hollywood Cinema." *Journal of Dramatic Theory and Criticism* 6: 221–31.

———. 1992. *Interpreting Films: Studies in the Historical Reception of American Cinema*. Princeton, NJ: Princeton University Press.

———. 1995. *Bad Women: Regulating Sexuality in Early American Cinema*. Minneapolis: University of Minnesota Press.

———. 2000. *Perverse Spectators: The Practices of Film Reception*. New York: New York University Press.

Staley, Gregory. 2006. "'Beyond Glorious Ocean': Feminism, Myth, and America." In *Laughing with Medusa: Classical Myth and Feminist Thought*, edited by Vanda Zajko and Miriam Leonard, 209–30. Oxford: Oxford University Press.

Stam, Robert. 2000. "Beyond Fidelity: The Dialogics of Adaptation." In *Film Adaptation*, edited by James Naremore, 54–76. New Brunswick, NJ: Rutgers University Press.

———. 2004. *Literature through Film: Realism, Magic, and the Art of Adaptation*. Malden, MA: Blackwell.

Star Trek: The Original Series—The Complete Series. 2004. Paramount. DVD.

Stax. 2002. "Who is Helen of Troy?" *IGN*, November 8, 2002. http://www.ign.com/articles/2002/11/08/who-is-helen-of-troy.

Stead, Lisa Rose. 2011. "'So Oft to the Movies They've Been': British Fan Writing and Female Audiences in the Silent Cinema." *Transformative Works and Cultures* 6.

Steele, Valerie. 1985. *Fashion and Eroticism: Ideals of Feminine Beauty from the Victorian Era to the Jazz Age*. New York: Oxford University Press.

Steiner, Deborah Tarn. 2001. *Images in Mind: Statues in Archaic and Classical Greek Literature and Thought*. Princeton, NJ: Princeton University Press.

Stoddard, Samuel. n.d. "Helen of Troy (2003)." Rink Works. Accessed August 26, 2020. http://www.rinkworks.com/movies/m/helen.of.troy.2003.shtml.

Storey, John. 2003. *Inventing Popular Culture: From Folklore to Globalization*. Malden, MA: Blackwell.

———. 2006. *Cultural Theory and Popular Culture: An Introduction*. 4th ed. Harlow, UK: Pearson Prentice Hall.

Strinati, Dominic. 2004. *An Introduction to Theories of Popular Culture*. 2nd ed. New York: Routledge.

Strong, Anise K. 2018. "Xena: Warrior, Heroine, Tramp." In *Epic Heroes on Screen*, edited by Antony Augoustakis and Stacie Raucci, 141–55. Edinburgh: Edinburgh University Press.

Stubbs, Jonathan. 2013. *Historical Film: A Critical Introduction*. London: Bloomsbury.

Studlar, Gaylyn. 1996 [1991]. "The Perils of Pleasure? Fan Magazine Discourse as Women's Commodified Culture in the 1920s." In *Silent Film*, edited by Richard Abel, 263–97. New Brunswick, NJ: Rutgers University Press.

Stuttaford, Andrew. 2004. "The Fall of Troy." *Andrew Stuttaford* (blog). June 2, 2004. https://www.andrewstuttaford.com/archive/2004/06/02/the-fall-of-troy-wolfgang-shouldve-left-homer-alone.

Susman, Gary. 2003. "'Troy' Borrows Epic Luster from 'LOTR' Actors." *Entertainment Weekly*, February 25, 2003.

Sweet, Anne Currier. 2007. "Camp, Masquerade, and Subtext: The Subversion of Sexuality Norms and Gender Roles in Xena: Warrior Princess." *GRAAT*, June 2, 2007. http://www.graat.fr/queertv06.pdf.

Tashiro, C. S. 1998. *Pretty Pictures: Production Design and the History Film*. Austin: University of Texas Press.

Tasker, Yvonne. 1993. *Spectacular Bodies: Gender, Genre, and the Action Cinema*. New York: Routledge.

Tasker, Yvonne, and Diane Negra, eds. 2007a. *Interrogating Postfeminism: Gender and the Politics of Popular Culture*. Durham, NC: Duke University Press.

———. 2007b. "Introduction." In *Interrogating Postfeminism: Gender and the Politics of Popular Culture*, edited by Yvonne Tasker and Diane Negra, 1–25. Durham, NC: Duke University Press.

Taylor, Paul C. 2016. *Black Is Beautiful: A Philosophy of Black Aesthetics*. Hoboken, NJ: Wiley.

Theodorakopoulos, Elena. 2010. *Ancient Rome at the Cinema: Story and Spectacle in Hollywood and Rome*. Exeter, UK: Bristol Phoenix.

Thomas, Nick. 2019. "At 80, France Nuyen still counts her blessings." *Mansfield News Journal*, October 2, 2019. https://www.mansfieldnewsjournal.com/story/entertainment/2019/10/02/entertainment-france-nuyen-star-trek-actors/3818240002/.

Thompson, Frank T. 1995. *Robert Wise: A Bio-Bibliography*. Westport, CT: Greenwood.

Thompson, Kirsten Moana. 2011. "'Philip Never Saw Babylon': 360 Degree Vision and the Historical Epic in the Digital Era." In *The Epic Film in World Culture*, edited by Robert Burgoyne, 39–62. New York: Routledge.

Thumim, Janet. 1992. *Celluloid Sisters: Women and Popular Cinema*. New York: St. Martin's Press.

Tigges, Wim. 2017. "A Woman Like You? Emma Peel, Xena: Warrior Princess, and the Empowerment of Female Heroes of the Silver Screen." *Journal of Popular Culture* 50: 127–46.

Tomasso Vincent. 2015. "The Twilight of Olympus: Deicide and the End of the Greek Gods." In *Classical Myth on Screen*, edited by Monica Silveira Cyrino and Meredith Safran, 147–57. New York: Palgrave Macmillan.

Toner, Janet Amelia. n.d. "Sex Trek." GeoCities Archive. Accessed August 26, 2020. https://www.geocitiesarchive.org/mxd/~teepee47/relcolumn.html.

Travers, Peter. 2004. "Troy." *Rolling Stone*, May 5, 2004.

Tredy, Dennis. 2017. "Light Shadows: Loose Adaptations of Gothic Literature in American TV Series of the 1960s and early 1970." *TV/Series* 12 (February). http://journals.openedition.org/tvseries/2200.

Tulloch, John, and Henry Jenkins. 1995. *Science Fiction Audiences: Watching Doctor Who and Star Trek*. London: Routledge.

Turim, Maureen. 1990. "Designing Women: The Emergence of the New Sweetheart Line." In *Fabrications: Costume and the Female Body*, edited by Jane Gaines and Charlotte Herzog, 212–28. New York: Routledge.

Turner, Julia. 2004. "The Many Faces of Helen: How to Find an Actress Who Can Launch a Thousand Ships." *Slate*, May 13, 2004. http://www.slate.com/id/2100449/.

Tyler, Parker. 1947. *Magic and Myth of the Movies*. New York: Simon and Schuster.

Tyrell, William Blake. 2010 [1977]. "*Star Trek* as Myth and Television as Mythmaker." In *Star Trek as Myth: Essays on Symbol and Archetype at the Final Frontier*, edited by Matthew Kapell, 19–28. Jefferson, NC: McFarland & Co.

Upperco, Jackson. 2013. "Honorable Mentions: Eighteen More Excellent & Undervalued Episodes of Xena: Warrior Princess (Post 1 of 9)." *That's Entertainment* (blog). December 5, 2013. https://jacksonupperco.com/2013/12/05/honorable-mentions-eighteen-more-excellent-undervalued-episodes-of-xena-warrior-princess-post-1-of-9/#comments.

Uricchio, William, and Roberta E. Pearson 1996 [1990]. "Dante's Inferno and Caesar's Ghost: Intertextuality and Conditions of Reception in Early American Cinema." In *Silent Film*, edited by Richard Abel, 217–33. New Brunswick, NJ: Rutgers University Press.

van Beekus, Antonius. 2004. "Under Siege." *TotalDVD* 67, 18–25.

van Hise, John. 1998. *Hercules and Xena: The Unofficial Companion*. Los Angeles: Renaissance.

Vance, Carole S. 1992. "More Danger, More Pleasure: A Decade after the Barnard Sexuality Conference." In *Pleasure and Danger: Exploring Female Sexuality*, edited by Carole S. Vance, xvi–xxxix. 2nd ed. London: Pandora.

Villarreal, Phil. 2004. Review of *Troy*. *Arizona Daily Star*, May 13, 2004.

Vivante, Bella. 2013. "Gazing at Helen: Helen as Polysemous Icon in Robert Wise's *Helen of Troy* and Michael Cacoyannis' *The Trojan Women*." In *Ancient Greek Women in Film*, edited by Konstantinos P. Nikoloutsos, 19–50. Oxford: Oxford University Press.

Wagner, Jon, and Jan Lundeen. 1998. *Deep Space and Sacred Time: Star Trek in the American Mythos*. Westport, CT: Praeger.

Walker, Alexander. 1967. *The Celluloid Sacrifice: Aspects of Sex in the Movies*. New York: Hawthorn.

Warner, Marina. 1994. *From the Beast to the Blonde: On Fairy Tales and Their Tellers*. London: Chatto & Windus.

Warren, Paul. 2016. *Uptalk: The Phenomenon of Rising Intonation*. Cambridge: Cambridge University Press.

Wasserman, Robin. 2016. "What Does It Mean When We Call Women Girls?" *Literary Hub*, May 18, 2016. http://lithub.com/what-does-it-mean-when-we-call-women-girls/.

Waterbury, Ruth. 1928a. "Keeping in the Movies." *Des Moines Register*, January 29, 1928.

———. 1928b. "Olympus Moves to Hollywood." *Photoplay*, April 1928.

Watts, Diana. 1919a. "Finding Youth at Forty: Why Surrender to Old Age When Youthfulness Is Nature's Way?" *Muskogee Times-Democrat*, June 19, 1919.

———. 1919b. "Finding Youth at Forty: Keep Girlhood and You'll Have a Boy-Husband." *Muskogee Times-Democrat*, July 3, 1919.

Waxman, Sharon. 2004a. "At the Movies, at Least, Good Vanquishes Evil." *New York Times*, May 10, 2004.

———. 2004b "Hollywood's He-Men Are Bumped by Sensitive Guys; Six-Pack Abs Not Required for New Masculine Ideal." *New York Times*, July 1, 2004.

Wearing, Sadie. 2007. "Subjects of Rejuvenation: Aging in Postfeminist Culture." In *Interrogating Postfeminism: Gender and the Politics of Popular Culture*, edited by Yvonne Tasker and Diane Negra, 277–310. Durham, NC: Duke University Press.

Weinbaum, Alys Eve, and the Modern Girl Around the World Research Group. 2008. *The Modern Girl Around the World: Consumption, Modernity, and Globalization*. Durham, NC: Duke University Press.

Weinberg, Joanna. 2004. "Homer Erotic." *Tatler*, May 2004.

Weiner, Jesse, Benjamin Eldon Stevens, and Brett M. Rogers, eds. 2018. *Frankenstein and Its Classics: The Modern Prometheus from Antiquity to Science Fiction*. London: Bloomsbury.

Weinlich, Barbara P. 2015. "A New Briseis in *Troy*." In *Return to Troy: New Essays on the Hollywood Epic*, edited by Martin M. Winkler, 197–227. Leiden, Netherlands: Brill.

Weisbrot, Robert. 1998. *Xena: Warrior Princess: The Official Guide to the Xenaverse*. New York: Doubleday.

Weitz, Rose. 2004. *Rapunzel's Daughters: What Women's Hair Tells Us about Women's Lives*. New York: Farrar, Straus & Giroux.

Wells, Paul. 2007. "Classic Literature and Animation: All Adaptations Are Equal, but Some Are More Equal Than Others." In *The Cambridge Companion to Literature on Screen*, edited by Deborah Cartmell and Imelda Whelehan, 199–211. Cambridge: Cambridge University Press.

West, Thomas J. III. 2015. "Screening History: The Rise and Fall of the Biblical Epic Part One (1949–1955)." *Queerly Different* (blog). June 24, 2015. http://tjwest3.com/2015/06/24/screening-history-the-rise-and-fall-of-the-biblical-epic-part-one-1949-1955/.

Westfahl, Gary. 2003. "Space Opera." In *The Cambridge Companion to Science Fiction*, edited by Edward James and Farah Mendlesohn, 197–208. Cambridge: Cambridge University Press.

Wexman, Virginia Wright. 1993. *Creating the Couple: Love, Marriage, and Hollywood Performance*. Princeton, NJ: Princeton University Press.

Whelan, Anne. 1951. "Of People and Places." *Bridgeport Post*, April 8, 1951.

Whelehan, Imelda. 2000. *Overloaded: Popular Culture and the Future of Feminism*. London: Women's Press.

Whitaker, Alma. 1927. "Destiny Guides Maria." *Los Angeles Times*, December 4, 1927.

White, Mimi. 1992. *Tele-Advising: Therapeutic Discourse in American Television*. Chapel Hill: University of North Carolina Press.

Whitfield, Stephen E. 1968. *The Making of Star Trek*. New York: Ballantine.

Whitfield, Stephen J. 1996. *The Culture of the Cold War*. 2nd ed. Baltimore: Johns Hopkins University Press.

Wieber, Anja. 2002. "Hauptsache Helden? Zwischen Eskapismus und Identifikation—Zur Funktionalisierung der Antike im aktuellen Film." In *Pontes: Antike im Film*, edited by Martin Korenjak and Karlheinz Töchterle, 13–25. Vol. 2. Innsbruck, Austria: Studienverlag.

———. 2005. "Vor Troja nichts Neues?—Moderne Kinogeschichten zu Homers Ilias." In *Drehbuch Geschichte: Die antike Welt im Film*, edited by Martin Lindner, 137–62. Münster, Germany: LIT.

———. 2010. "Sicher Im Hafen Der Ehe?—Antike Paare Im Film." In *Ehe als Ernstfall der Geschlechterdifferenz: Herausforderungen für Frau und Mann in kulturellen Symbolsystemen*, edited by Bernd Heininger, 175–95. Berlin: LIT.

———. 2016. "Women and Religion in the Epic Films: The Fifties' Advocate for Conversion and Today's Pillar of Paganism?" In *Ancient Magic and the Supernatural in the Modern Visual and Performing Arts*, edited by Filippo Carlà and Irene Berti, 225–40. London: Bloomsbury.

Wieber-Scariot, Anja. 1998. "Herrscherin und doch ganz Frau. Zur Darstellung antiker Herrscherinnen im Film der 50er und 60er Jahre." *Metis* 7: 73–89.

Wiggins, Dubois K. 1926. "Made Helen a Real Person." *Brooklyn Daily Eagle*, October 31, 1926.

Williams, Christopher. 2000. "After the Classic, the Classical and Ideology: The Differences of Realism." In *Reinventing Film Studies*, edited by Christine Gledhill and Linda Williams, 206–20. London: Arnold.

Williams, Dick. 1956. "Battle Scenes Bolster 'Troy.'" *Mirror-News* [Los Angeles], January 27, 1956.

Williams, Linda. 1984. "When the Woman Looks." In *Re-vision: Essays in Feminist Film Criticism*, edited by Mary Ann Doane, Patricia Mellencamp, and Linda Williams, 83–99. Frederick, MD: University Publications of America.

———. 2001. *Playing the Race Card: Melodramas of Black and White from Uncle Tom to O. J. Simpson*. Princeton, NJ: Princeton University Press.

Williams, Michael. 2013a. *Film Stardom, Myth and Classicism: The Rise of Hollywood's Gods*. London: Palgrave Macmillan.

———. 2013b. "Gloria Swanson as Venus: Silent Stardom, Antiquity and the Classical Vernacular." In *The Ancient World in Silent Cinema*, edited by Pantelis Michelakis and Maria Wyke, 125–44. Cambridge: Cambridge University Press.

———. 2018. *Film Stardom and the Ancient Past: Idols, Artefacts and Epics*. London: Palgrave Macmillan.

Williamson, Judith. 1986. *Consuming Passions: The Dynamics of Popular Culture*. London: M. Boyars.

Willis, Ika. 2017. "Contemporary Mythography: In the Time of Ancient Gods, Warlords, and Kings." In *A Handbook to the Reception of Classical Mythology*, edited by Vanda Zajko and Helena Hoyle, 105–20. Malden, MA: Wiley-Blackwell.

Wilmington, Michael 2004. "Greece is the Word." *Chicago Tribune*, May 14, 2004.

Wilner, Isaiah. 2006. *The Man Time Forgot: A Tale of Genius, Betrayal, and the Creation of Time Magazine*. New York: HarperCollins.

Wingrove, David. 2016. "A Solo for Three Voices." *Shadowplay* (blog). March 15, 2016. https://dcairns.wordpress.com/2016/03/15/a-solo-for-three-voices/.

Winkler, Martin M., ed. 2007a. *Troy: From Homer's Iliad to Hollywood Epic*. Malden, MA: Blackwell.

———2007b. "The Trojan War on the Screen: An Annotated Filmography." In *Troy: From Homer's Iliad to Hollywood Epic*, edited by Martin M. Winkler, 202–15. Malden, MA: Blackwell.

Winkler, Martin M. 2007c. "Greek Myth on the Screen." In *The Cambridge Companion to Greek Mythology*, edited by Roger D. Woodard, 453–79. Cambridge: Cambridge University Press.

———. 2009. *Cinema and Classical Texts: Apollo's New Light*. Cambridge: Cambridge University Press.

———. 2015a. *Return to Troy: New Essays on the Hollywood Epic*. Leiden: Brill.

———. 2015b. "Introduction: *Troy* Revisited." In *Return to Troy: New Essays on the Hollywood Epic*, edited by Martin M. Winkler, 1–15. Leiden, Netherlands: Brill.

———. 2015c. "Wolfgang Petersen on Homer and *Troy*." In *Return to Troy: New Essays on the Hollywood Epic*, edited by Martin M. Winkler, 16–26. Leiden, Netherlands: Brill.

———. 2015d. "*Troy* and the Cinematic Afterlife of Homeric Gods." In *Return to Troy: New Essays on the Hollywood Epic*, edited by Martin M. Winkler, 108–64. Leiden, Netherlands: Brill.

———. 2016. "*Helenê kinêmatographikê*; or, Is This the Face That Launched a Thousand Films?" *Nuntius Antiquus* 12, no. 1: 215–57.

Winterer, Caroline. 2002. *The Culture of Classicism: Ancient Greece and Rome in American Intellectual Life, 1780–1910*. Baltimore: Johns Hopkins University Press.

Wise, Robert, dir. 2004 [1955]. *Helen of Troy*. Warner Brothers. DVD.

Wolf, Howard. 1927. "Press Agents Turn Helen into Flapper." *Akron Beacon Journal*, December 30, 1927.

Wolf, Naomi. 1991. *The Beauty Myth: How Images of Beauty Are Used against Women*. New York: W. Morrow.

Wood, Michael. 1989. *America in the Movies, or, "Santa Maria, It Had Slipped My Mind."* New York: Columbia University Press.

Woodward, Gary C. 2003. *The Idea of Identification*. Albany, NY: State University of New York Press.

Worland, Rick. 1988. "Captain Kirk: Cold Warrior." *Journal of Popular Film and Television* 16, no. 3: 109–17.

Wroblewski, Gregory. n.d. "Helen of Troy (2003) from Johnny Web (Uncle Scoopy; Greg Wroblewski)." *Uncle Scoopy's Movie House*. Accessed September 2, 2020. http://www.scoopy.com/helenoftroy.htm.

Wyke, Maria. 1997. *Projecting the Past: Ancient Rome, Cinema and History*. New York: Routledge.

———. 2002. *The Roman Mistress: Ancient and Modern Representations*. Oxford: Oxford University Press.

———. 2003. "Are You Not Entertained? Classicists and Cinema." *International Journal of the Classical Tradition* 9, no. 3 (Winter): 430–45.

Xena: Warrior Podcast. 2016. Episode six: 1x11–12, "The Black Wolf" and "Beware Greeks Bearing Gifts." December 26, 2016. Podcast. https://xenawarriorpodcast.libsyn.com/06-1x11-12-the-black-wolf-beware-of-greeks-bearing-gifts.

Xena: Warrior Podcasts. 2017. Episode twelve: "Beware Greeks Bearing Gifts." May 24, 2017. Podcast. http://mountolympuspod.libsyn.com/xena-warrior-podcasts-episode-12-beware-greeks-bearing-gifts.

Xena: Warrior Princess—The Complete Series. 2016. Universal Pictures Home Entertainment. DVD.

Young, Cathy. 2005. "What We Owe Xena." *Salon*, September 15, 2005. http://www.cathyyoung.net/features/whatweowexena.html.

Zacharek, Stephanie. 2004. "Troy." *Salon*, May 15, 2004. http://www.salon.com/2004/05/14/troy/.

Zeitlin, Froma I. 1996. *Playing the Other: Gender and Society in Classical Greek Literature*. Chicago: University of Chicago Press.

Ziolkowski, Theodore. 1977. *Disenchanted Images: A Literary Iconology*. Princeton, NJ: Princeton University Press.

IMAGE CREDITS

Fig. 1.1. *Photoplay*, April 1928. Media History Digital Library.

Fig. 1.2. *The Charleston Daily Mail*, December 11, 1921. www.newspapers.com.

Fig. 1.3. ABC News. SWNS.

Fig. 2.1. *Independent-Record* (Helena, MT) February 17, 1928 (left) (www.newspapers.com); unknown source (right). Public domain.

Fig. 2.2. Still for *The Private Life of Helen of Troy*, dir. Alexander Korda, First National Studios, 1927. Author's collection.

Fig. 2.3. *Photoplay*, November 1927. Media History Digital Library.

Fig. 2.4. *Winnipeg Tribune*, February 25, 1928. www.newspapers.com.

Fig. 2.5. *The Herald* (Australia), August 17, 1922. State Library of Victoria.

Fig. 2.6. Still for *Our Dancing Daughters*, dir. Harry Beaumont, MGM, 1928. Shutterstock.

Fig. 2.7. Still for *The Private Life of Helen of Troy*, dir. Alexander Korda, First National Studios, 1927. Author's collection.

Fig. 2.8. Still for *Our Dancing Daughters*, dir. Harry Beaumont, MGM, 1928. Author's collection.

Fig. 2.9. Stills for *The Private Life of Helen of Troy*, dir. Alexander Korda, First National Studios, 1927. Author's collection.

Fig. 2.10. Still for *The Private Life of Helen of Troy* dir. Alexander Korda, First National Studios, 1927. Courtesy George Eastman Museum.

Fig. 2.11. © RMN-Grand Palais / Art Resource, NY. Paris: Louvre 424.

Fig. 2.12. Still for *The Private Life of Helen of Troy* dir. Alexander Korda, First National Studios, 1927. Courtesy George Eastman Museum.

Fig. 2.13. Still for *The Private Life of Helen of Troy* (left); Greta Garbo publicity card (right). Author's collection.

Fig. 2.14. Still for *The Private Life of Helen of Troy,* dir. Alexander Korda, First National Studios, 1927 (left); still for Ben-Hur, dir. Fred Niblo, MGM, 1925 (right). Author's collection.

Fig. 2.15. Still for *The Private Life of Helen of Troy* dir. Alexander Korda, First National Studios, 1927. Courtesy George Eastman Museum.

Fig. 2.16. *The Atlanta Constitution,* August 8, 1920. www.newspapers.com.

Fig. 2.17. Still for *The Private Life of Helen of Troy,* dir. Alexander Korda, First National Studios, 1927. Author's collection.

Fig. 3.1. *The Private Life of Helen of Troy,* by John Erskine, Graphic Books, edition of 1956. Author's collection.

Fig. 3.2. Lobby card for *Helen of Troy,* dir. Robert Wise, Warner Bros., 1956. Author's collection.

Fig. 3.3. *Movie Pix* magazine. Author's collection.

Fig. 3.4. *Rushville Republican,* April 30, 1954. www.newspapers.com.

Fig. 3.5. Shot from *Helen of Troy,* dir. Robert Wise, Warner Bros., 1956.

Fig. 3.6. Still for *Helen of Troy,* dir. Robert Wise, Warner Bros., 1956. Author's collection.

Fig. 3.7. Still for *Quo Vadis,* dir. Mervyn Leroy, MGM, 1951. Author's collection.

Fig. 3.8. Ad for *Quo Vadis,* dir. Mervyn Leroy, MGM, 1951. Author's collection.

Fig. 3.9. Still for *Helen of Troy,* dir. Robert Wise, Warner Bros., 1956. Author's collection.

Fig. 3.10. *Helen of Troy,* dir. Robert Wise, Warner Bros., 1956.

Fig. 3.11. Still for *Salome,* dir. William Dieterle, Beckworth Corporation, 1953. Author's collection.

Fig. 4.1. *Troy,* dir. Wolfgang Petersen, Warner Bros., 2004.

Fig. 4.2. AF archive / Alamy Stock Photo.

Fig. 4.3. *Troy,* dir. Wolfgang Petersen, Warner Bros., 2004.

Fig. 5.1. Publicity still of France Nuyen. Author's collection.

Fig. 5.2. *Star Trek* episode "Elaan of Troyius" (1968).

Fig. 5.3. *Star Trek* episode "Mudd's Women" (1966).

Fig. 5.4. *Star Trek* episode "Elaan of Troyius" (1968).

Fig. 5.5. *Star Trek* episode "Plato's Stepchildren" (1968).

Fig. 5.6. *Star Trek* episode "Elaan of Troyius" (1968).

Fig. 5.7. *Xena: Warrior Princess* episode "Beware Greeks Bearing Gifts" (1996).

Fig. 5.8. *Xena: Warrior Princess* episode "Beware Greeks Bearing Gifts" (1996).

Fig. 5.9. *Xena: Warrior Princess* episode "Beware Greeks Bearing Gifts" (1966).

Fig. 5.10. *Xena: Warrior Princess* episode "Beware Greeks Bearing Gifts" (1996).

Fig. 5.11. *Xena: Warrior Princess* episode "Beware Greeks Bearing Gifts" (1996).

Fig. 5.12. *Xena: Warrior Princess* episode "Here She Comes . . . Miss Amphipolis" (1997).

Fig. 6.1. *Helen of Troy,* dir. John Kent Harrison, USA Network, 2003.

Fig. 6.2. *Helen of Troy,* dir. John Kent Harrison, USA Network, 2003.

Fig. 6.3. AF archive / Alamy Stock Photo.

Fig. 6.4. *Helen of Troy,* dir. John Kent Harrison, USA Network, 2003.

Plate 1. Lobby card for *Private Life of Helen of Troy,* dir. Alexander Korda, First National Studios, 1927. Author's collection.

Plate 2. *Helen of Troy,* dir. Robert Wise, Warner Bros., 1956.

Plate 3. Photograph by Ned Scott. Courtesy the Ned Scott Archive.

Plate 4. *Helen of Troy,* dir. Robert Wise, Warner Bros., 1956.

Plate 5. Still for *Quo Vadis,* dir. Mervyn Leroy, MGM, 1951.

Plate 6. Poster for Helen of Troy, dir. Robert Wise, Warner Bros., 1956. Author's collection.

Plate 7. Photo illustration by James Porto.

Plate 8. *Troy,* dir. Wolfgang Petersen, Warner Bros., 2004.

Plate 9. AF archive / Alamy Stock Photo.

Plate 10. *Star Trek* episode "Adonais" (1968).

Plate 11. *Star Trek* episode "Elaan of Troyius" (1968).

Plate 12. Photograph by Milton H. Greene © 2022 Joshua Greene. www.miltonhgreene.com.

Plate 13. Collage by Therese Bohn.

Plate 14. Publicity still for *Xena: Warrior Princess*. Author's collection.

Plate 15. *Helen of Troy*, dir. John Kent Harrison, USA Network, 2003.

INDEX